The Practice of Leadership

The Kravis-de Roulet Leadership Conference

The Kravis-de Roulet Leadership conference, which began in 1990, is an annual leadership conference funded jointly by an endowment from Henry R. Kravis and the de Roulet family. This perpetual funding, along with additional support from the Kravis Leadership Institute and Claremont McKenna College, enables us to attract the finest leadership scholars and practitioners as conference presenters and participants. The 15th annual Kravis-de Roulet Conference, *Best Practices in Leadership,* was held February 25–26, 2005.

The Kravis Leadership Institute

The Kravis Leadership Institute plays an active role in the development of young leaders via educational programs, research and scholarship, and the development of technologies for enhancing leadership potential.

KRAVIS
LEADERSHIP
INSTITUTE

Jay A. Conger

Ronald E. Riggio

Foreword by Bernard M. Bass

The Practice
of Leadership

Developing the Next Generation
of Leaders

JOSSEY-BASS
A Wiley Imprint
www.josseybass.com

John Wiley & Sons, Inc.

Substantial discounts on bulk quantities of Jossey-Bass books are available to
corporations, professional associations, and other organizations. For details and
discount information, contact the special sales department at Jossey-Bass Inc.,
Publishers (415) 433–1740; Fax (800) 605–2665.

For sales outside the United States, please contact your local Simon & Schuster
International Office.

Library of Congress Cataloging-in-Publication Data

Conger, Jay Alden.
  The practice of leadership : developing the next generation of leaders /
Jay A. Conger.—1st ed.
        p. cm.
  Includes bibliographical references and index.
  ISBN-13: 978-0-7879-8305-5 (alk. paper)
  ISBN-10: 0-7879-8305-5 (alk. paper)
  1. Leadership.   I. Riggio, Ronald E.   II. Title.
    HD57.7.C666 2006
    658.4'092—dc22

                                                        2006031371

FIRST EDITION
HB Printing   10 9 8 7 6 5 4 3 2 1

—ᴧᴧ— Contents

⟶ Foreword

In 1938, Kurt Lewin offered the widely quoted aphorism that there was nothing as good for research as a good theory. In 1974, I added that there was nothing as bad for research as a bad theory. It also needs to be said that along with good theory about leadership we need good practice, and we need to know the difference between good practices and bad practices—the practices that Marvin Dunnette labeled "management fads and folderol." Conger and Riggio have made a signal contribution with this discriminating collection of good leadership and management practices among the diverse areas of leadership study: at the individual level are represented essays on assessment, competence, innovation, ethics, and proactive influence tactics. At the organizational level are presentations on organizational transitions, strategy and social responsibility, corporate boardroom leadership, crisis management, diversity in organizations, cross-cultural perspectives, team leadership, and doing the right things in the right way. The authors are all well-published contributors to the field.

With an estimated six thousand management and leadership practice books published annually—some grounded in good leadership research, and unfortunately many others not so grounded—it is time to take stock of what we know and what we don't know about the good, better, and best practices available for selection, development, and organizational improvement.

This book is based on a conference held at the Kravis Leadership Institute at Claremont McKenna College on February 23–25, 2005. It is one of a series of books based on conferences on leadership held since 1999.

Binghamton University

BERNARD M. BASS
DISTINGUISHED PROFESSOR
OF MANAGEMENT

⎯⎯ᴡ⎯ About the Authors

C. Shawn Burke is a research scientist at the Institute for Simulation and Training of the University of Central Florida. Dr. Burke has published more than forty articles and chapters and presented at more than seventy peer-reviewed conferences. She is currently investigating team adaptability and its corresponding measurement, multicultural team performance, leadership, and training of such teams. Dr. Burke earned her doctorate in industrial/organizational psychology from George Mason University and serves as an ad hoc reviewer for *Human Factors, Leadership Quarterly, Human Resource Management,* and *Quality and Safety in Healthcare.* She has coedited a book on adaptability and is coediting a book on advances in team effectiveness research.

Jay A. Conger holds the Henry R. Kravis Research Chair in Leadership Studies at Claremont McKenna College. Author of many articles and book chapters and twelve books, he researches executive leadership, organizational change, boards of directors, executive derailment, and leadership development. Recent books include *Growing Your Company's Leaders: How Organizations Use Succession Management for Competitive Advantage, Shared Leadership: Reframing the Hows and Whys of Leading Others* (coauthored), *Charismatic Leadership in Organizations,* and *Corporate Boards: New Strategies for Adding Value at the Top* (coauthored). He earned an MBA from the University of Virginia, and DBA from Harvard Business School. He was selected by *Business Week* as the best professor to teach leadership to executives.

David V. Day is professor of organizational behavior in the Lee Kong Chian School of Business at the Singapore Management University. Day is also an adjunct research scientist with the Center for Creative Leadership and a senior research consortium fellow with the U.S. Army Research Institute. His research interests focus on the development of leaders and leadership in organizations. He recently completed a project sponsored by the Army Research Institute to develop an integrative theory of leader development for the U.S. Army.

Thomas Diamante is a consulting industrial psychologist at DOAR Litigation Consulting in New York. Formerly vice president for corporate strategy and development at Merrill Lynch's Global Securities Research and Economics Division, he has held senior management positions at KPMG and Altria (Philip Morris). He received his PhD in psychology with an industrial and organizational specialization from the Graduate Center, City University of New York, and completed postdoctoral training in clinical psychology. He is New York State licensed.

Dawn L. Eubanks is a doctoral candidate in the Industrial and Organizational Psychology Program at the University of Oklahoma. Prior to joining the doctoral program at the University of Oklahoma she worked as a business analyst at the Corporate Executive Board. After receiving her MS degree in I-O psychology from University of Baltimore, Dawn gained experience as a consultant at Watson Wyatt Worldwide, where she was involved with creation and analysis of employee satisfaction instruments.

George P. Hollenbeck is an organizational psychologist who writes and consults in the area of leadership development. His career includes positions at IBM, Merrill Lynch, Fidelity Investments, and the Harvard Business School (senior director, Executive Education). He earned a PhD from the University of Wisconsin in Madison, was a James McKeen Cattell Fund Fellow at the University of California, Berkeley, and, as a Merrill Lynch executive, he attended Harvard Business School's Advanced Management Program. George's writings include articles ("Behind Closed Doors: What Really Happens in Executive Coaching" appearing in the Winter 1999 issue of *Organization Dynamics*), book chapters ["Coaching Executives: Individual Leader Development" in *The 21st Century Executive* (Jossey-Bass, 2002)], and books (*Developing Global Executives: The Lessons of International Experience,* published in January 2002 by the Harvard Business School Press, coauthored with Morgan McCall). He was the recipient of the Distinguished Professional Contributions Award of the Society of Industrial/Organizational Psychology in 2003. He is a fellow of that society, a licensed psychologist in New York and Massachusetts, and a diplomate of the American Board of Professional Psychology. George lives in and works out of the Houston, Texas, area; he is an avid fisherman and a struggling golfer.

Ann Howard is chief scientist for Development Dimensions International. Her PhD in industrial-organizational psychology is from the University of Maryland, and she has an honorary doctor of science degree from Goucher College. She is the author or editor of more than ninety publications on topics such as assessment centers, management selection, managerial careers, leadership, and work and organizational change. Her book (with Douglas W. Bray) on the lives and careers of two cohorts of telephone company managers, *Managerial Lives in Transition: Advancing Age and Changing Times,* received the George R. Terry Award of Excellence from the Academy of Management. She is a past president of the Society for Industrial and Organizational Psychology and the Society of Psychologists in Management.

Craig E. Johnson is professor of leadership studies at George Fox University, Newberg, Oregon, where he directs the Doctor of Management Program. He teaches graduate and undergraduate courses in leadership, ethics, and communication. He is the author of *Meeting the Ethical Challenges of Leadership* and *Ethics in the Workplace,* and coauthor of *Leadership: A Communication Perspective.* His research findings have been published in the *Journal of Leadership Education, Selected Proceedings of the International Leadership Association, Journal of Leadership Studies, Communication Quarterly, Communication Education,* and *Communication Reports.*

Manuel London is Associate Dean of the College of Business, Director of the Center for Human Resource Management, and Professor of Management and Psychology at the State University of New York at Stony Brook. He received his PhD from the Ohio State University in industrial and organizational psychology. He taught at the University of Illinois at Champaign before moving to AT&T as a researcher and human resource manager. He joined Stony Brook 17 years ago. He has written extensively on the topics of 360-degree feedback, continuous learning, career dynamics, and management development. His books include *Leadership Development: Paths to Self-Insight and Professional Growth* (2002, Erlbaum) and *Continuous Learning: Individual, Group, and Organizational Perspectives* (with Valerie Sessa, 2006, Erlbaum).

Mitchell Lee Marks is on the faculty of the Department of Management at San Francisco State University and leads Joining Forces.org, a firm that advises on organizational change, team building, strategic direction, organizational effectiveness, corporate culture, human resources management, and the planning and implementation of major organizational transitions. He has advised in more than one hundred cases of mergers, acquisitions, restructurings, and other major transitions. Mitch is the author of five books—including *Charging Back Up the Hill: Workforce Recovery after Mergers, Acquisitions and Downsizing,* and with Philip Mirvis, *Joining Forces: Making One Plus One Equal Three in Mergers, Acquisitions, and Alliances*—and scores of articles in practitioner and scholarly journals. He earned his PhD in organizational psychology from the University of Michigan.

Kenneth Matos is a doctoral student in the Industrial/Organizational Psychology Program at the George Washington University. His research interests include mentoring, diversity, and survey techniques and response trends.

Morgan W. McCall Jr. is professor of management and organization, Marshall School of Business, University of Southern California (USC). A Cornell PhD, he was director of research and a senior behavioral scientist at the Center for Creative Leadership prior to joining USC. His research focuses on developing executive talent, and he is author or coauthor of *Developing Global Executives, High Flyers,* and *The Lessons of Experience.*

Ian I. Mitroff is adjunct professor of health policy at the School of Public Health, St. Louis University, St. Louis, Missouri, and professor emeritus at the University of Southern California (USC). He founded and directed the USC Center for Crisis Management at the Marshall School of Business. He has authored more than 350 papers, articles, op-eds, and twenty-six books on the topics of crisis management, business policy, corporate culture, contemporary media and current events, foreign affairs and nuclear deterrence, organizational change, organizational psychology and psychiatry, the philosophy and sociology of science, public policy, scientific method, spirituality in the workplace, and strategic planning. His recent books include *How to Emerge Better and Stronger from a Crisis* (2005), *Crisis Leadership* (2002), *Managing Crises before They Happen* (2000), and *A Spiritual Audit of Corporate America: A Hard Look at Spirituality, Religion, and Values in the Workplace* (1999).

Michael D. Mumford is a George Lynn Cross Distinguished Research Professor at the University of Oklahoma, where he is director of the

Center for Applied Social Research. Dr. Mumford received his PhD from the University of Georgia in 1983 and has held positions at the Georgia Institute of Technology and George Mason University. He has received more than $20 million in grant and contract funding and has published more than 160 articles on leadership, creativity, planning, and integrity. The most recent of his five books is *Pathways to Outstanding Leadership: A Comparative Analysis of Charismatic, Ideological, and Pragmatic Leaders.* He currently serves as senior editor of the *Leadership Quarterly,* and he sits on the editorial boards of the *Creativity Research Journal,* the *Journal of Creative Behavior,* and *IEEE Transactions on Organizational Management.* Dr. Mumford is a fellow of the American Psychological Association (Divisions 3, 5, and 14), the American Psychological Society, and the Society for Industrial and Organizational Psychology. He is a recipient of the Society for Industrial and Organizational Psychology's M. Scott Myers award for applied research in the workplace.

Stephen T. Murphy is a doctoral candidate in the Industrial and Organizational Psychology Program at the University of Oklahoma. Prior to joining the doctoral program at the University of Oklahoma he worked as a research analyst at Hogan Assessment Systems. Stephen also has experience as a personnel selection specialist for the State of Tennessee and the Personnel Board of Jefferson County after receiving his MA degree in I-O Psychology from Middle Tennessee State University.

Patricia M. G. O'Connor is research director of Emerging Leadership Practices at the Center for Creative Leadership (CCL), Singapore Campus. Her research and innovation work focuses on the identification and development of inter- and intra-organizational leadership practices required to address complex global challenges. She recently oversaw the design, delivery, and evaluation of a multiyear leadership development initiative with one of the United States' largest organizations. Engaging one hundred of their senior executives, the collaboration resulted in both developmental advancements and innovation outcomes of tangible benefit to the organization. Patricia's perspectives on leadership have developed through a combination of 12 years' experience as a senior-level manager and 6 years as a senior CCL faculty member. Previous to making the shift into an applied research faculty role, she served on CCL's management team as director of business development. Patricia holds a BS degree in human resources from the University of Illinois, Urbana-Champaign, an MBA in management and organizational behavior from Bernard M. Baruch College (CUNY), and is a member of the Academy of Management.

Lynn R. Offermann is professor of industrial/organizational psychology at the George Washington University. Her research on leadership and followership, teams, and diversity has appeared in such journals as the *Journal of Applied Psychology, Academy of Management Journal, Leadership Quarterly, American Psychologist,* and the *Harvard Business Review.* She is a member of the Academy of Management and a fellow of the Society for Industrial and Organizational Psychology, the American Psychological Association, and the Association for Psychological Science.

Ronald E. Riggio is the Henry R. Kravis Professor of Leadership and Organizational Psychology at Claremont McKenna College and director of the Kravis Leadership Institute. His research interests include prediction of leadership and managerial potential; charismatic leadership theory; nonverbal communication in social interaction; communication processes in organizational settings; assessment center methodology for personnel selection, employee development, and measurement of leadership potential; and learning strategies in higher education. His publications include numerous journal articles, book chapters, and edited books, including *Transformational Leadership* with Bernard M. Bass, *Improving Leadership in Nonprofit Organizations* with Sarah Smith Orr, and *Future of Leadership Development* and *Multiple Intelligences and Leadership* with Susan E. Murphy. He authored *Introduction to Industrial/Organizational Psychology.* He is an associate editor for the *Leadership Quarterly* and is on the editorial boards of *Leadership, Journal of Nonverbal Behavior,* and *Leadership Review.* Riggio earned his BS at Santa Clara University, and MA in psychology and PhD in social/personality psychology at the University of California, Riverside.

Eduardo Salas is Trustee Chair and Professor of Psychology at the University of Central Florida. He holds an appointment as program director for Human Systems Integration Research Department at the Institute for Simulation and Training and previously was senior research psychologist and head of the Training Technology Development Branch of NAVAIR-Orlando. Dr. Salas has coauthored more than three hundred journal articles and book chapters and has coedited fifteen books. He is or has been on the editorial boards of *Journal of Applied Psychology, Personnel Psychology, Military Psychology,*

Interamerican Journal of Psychology, Applied Psychology: An International Journal, International Journal of Aviation Psychology, Group Dynamics, and *Journal of Organizational Behavior,* and is past editor of *Human Factors* journal. In addition, he has edited two special issues (one on training and one on decision making in complex environments) for *Human Factors.* He has edited other special issues on team training and performance and training evaluation (*Military Psychology*), shared cognition (*Journal of Organizational Behavior*), and simulation and training (*International Journal of Aviation Psychology*). He currently edits an annual series, *Advances in Human Performance and Cognitive Engineering Research* (Elsevier). Dr. Salas has held numerous positions in the Human Factors and Ergonomics Society during the past fifteen years. He is the past chair of the Cognitive Engineering and Decision Making Technical Group and of the Training Technical Group, and served on the executive council. Dr. Salas is a fellow of the American Psychological Association (SIOP and Division 21), the Human Factors and Ergonomics Society. He received his PhD degree (1984) in industrial and organizational psychology from Old Dominion University.

James W. Smither is Lindback Professor of Human Resource Management at La Salle University, where he teaches courses in human resources management, training and development, and leadership skills. He has consulted with more than forty firms in human resources and leadership development. Previously, Jim was a senior manager/group leader in corporate human resources for AT&T, where he was responsible for developing and validating employee selection programs for management-level positions. He received his BA (in psychology) from La Salle and has an MA from Seton Hall University, an MA from Montclair State University, and a PhD in industrial/organizational psychology from Stevens Institute of Technology. Jim has published more than forty scholarly articles and chapters. He is a fellow of the Association for Psychological Science and the Society for Industrial and Organizational Psychology.

Kevin C. Stagl is a doctoral candidate in the Industrial and Organizational Psychology Program at the University of Central Florida (UCF). Kevin is currently employed at UCF's Institute for Simulation and Training, where his research centers on team leadership, team development, distributed team performance, and team adaptation. Prior to joining IST, Kevin spent 5 years as a member of an organizational consultancy that provides human capital management decision support.

Mary B. Teagarden is professor of global strategy at Thunderbird, the Garvin School of International Management, where she teaches global strategy and strategic human resource management. Her research interests focus on competitiveness, strategic alignment, and capability building with an emphasis on the management of technology-intensive firms, off-shore manufacturing, high technology transfer, and strategic human resource management in the People's Republic of China, India, and Mexico. Her current research focuses on the localization of leadership development for transformation and strategic alignment in the telecommunications and IT industries in India and China. She received her PhD in strategic management from the University of Southern California.

David A. Waldman received his PhD from Colorado State University in industrial/organizational psychology. He currently is a professor and chair of the Department of Management in the School of Global Management and Leadership at Arizona State University, and an affiliated faculty member of the Department of Management of the W. P. Carey School at Arizona State University. His research interests focus largely on leadership across levels of analyses, especially leadership at strategic levels and leadership in virtual contexts, and also include cross-cultural issues in leadership, as evidenced by his involvement as a country coinvestigator for the United States in the GLOBE project. Dr. Waldman's accomplishments include scholarly and practitioner articles or chapters in such journals/series as the *Journal of Applied Psychology,* the *Academy of Management Journal,* the *Academy of Management Review,* the *Academy of Management Executive, Personnel Psychology, Research in Personnel and Human Resources Management,* the *Journal of Vocational Behavior, Human Resource Management,* the *Journal of Organizational Behavior,* the *Journal of Management,* the *Leadership Quarterly, IEEE Transactions on Engineering Management, Research Policy,* and the *Journal of Engineering and Technology Management.* In addition, he has published a book on 360-degree feedback. He is currently on the editorial boards of the *Academy of Management Journal* and the *Leadership Quarterly,* and formerly on the editorial boards of the *Journal of Applied Psychology* and the *Journal of Organizational Behavior.* He is an associate editor of the *Academy of Management Learning and Education* and a fellow of the American Psychological Association, as well as the Society for Industrial and Organizational Psychology.

Gary Yukl received a PhD in industrial-organizational psychology from the University of California at Berkeley in 1967. He is currently a professor in the Management Department, University at Albany. Dr. Yukl's current research interests include leadership, power and influence, and management development. He has written many articles published in professional journals and has received four best paper or best article awards for his research. He is also the author or coauthor of several books, including *Leadership in Organizations* (6th edition, Prentice-Hall, 2006) and *Flexible Leadership* (Jossey-Bass, 2004). Dr. Yukl is a fellow of the American Psychological Association, the American Psychological Society, the Society for Industrial-Organizational Psychology, and the Academy of Management.

The Practice of Leadership

⟋⟍⟋ Introduction

Jay A. Conger
Ronald E. Riggio

Few topics in the field of management have flourished as dramatically as leadership. Each year, more than a hundred new books and thousands of articles are published on the topic. Google lists more than a billon "hits" when the term *leadership* is entered for a search. When it comes to insights on leadership, most of us are suffering from information overload. As editors of this book, we felt it was time to address this flood of information. We have a simple aim: a single, easy-to-read resource of the best and most current thinking on a broad yet essential range of leadership topics. We had several audiences in mind when we assembled this volume: (1) those of you who practice leadership as managers and executives and who desire to become more effective, (2) those of you who develop leaders and who want to improve the ways you help others learn to lead, and (3) those of you who study and research leadership and who want to become more informed on certain topics. We hope you will find this "one-stop" volume as informative, rich, and helpful as we intended it to be.

An underlying assumption of this book is that leadership can be developed. While there is an age-old debate about whether leaders are born or made, the authors in this book feel that both individuals and their organizations can proactively influence leadership capability long after birth. At a minimum, organizations can improve how they select and assess for leadership. But more important, the authors highlight how leaders can improve their own effectiveness across a wide range of situations, from those requiring change and innovation to those with diverse populations and differing cultures to those in crisis. Given

1

the book's emphasis on leadership practice, each of our authors frames his or her chapter's insights around the action steps and practical implications of the topic. While certain chapters discuss what can and cannot be developed, each chapter is designed to provide hands-on guidance to implementing its insights.

HOW THE BOOK IS ORGANIZED

The book is organized into four parts: leadership development and selection, the tasks and capabilities of leaders, the leadership of organizations, and leadership requirements of the unique demands of today's world. In Part One, on leadership development, we examine the critical issues of leadership assessment and selection. A great deal of research and investment has been made in both of these areas over the past decade. From there, we explore the use of action learning as a development methodology to promote new leadership forms and identities. We close Part One with a chapter that challenges the established paradigm of deploying behavioral competencies as the foundation for leadership development efforts.

In Chapter One, author Ann Howard explores the issue of how to select for leadership capability. Getting leader selection right can not only boost organizational performance, but also provide employees with an opportunity to excel in work they enjoy. "Best Practices in Leader Selection" describes how to get the selection process right. It reviews the objectives of selection, describes current selection techniques and evidence about their efficacy, and looks at how individual selection methods can be combined into an effective selection system.

In Chapter Two, authors Manuel London, James Smither, and Thomas Diamante examine leadership assessment—the process of determining the success or potential of individuals for leadership positions. They discuss how leadership assessment is used for predicting performance, evaluating performance, diagnosing performance gaps, and setting directions for improvement and career development. Leadership assessment involves measuring individual characteristics and evaluating behaviors as well as collecting indicators of group or organizational effectiveness that result from the leader's behavior. Assessments can and should occur on different levels—organization, team, and individual. They also should measure multiple dimensions—financial, personal, and interpersonal. The authors explore these many dimensions of assessment.

Authors Patricia O'Connor and David Day, in Chapter Three, "Shifting the Emphasis of Leadership Development: From 'Me' to 'All of Us,' " discuss the necessity of managers shifting their perceptions of leadership from seeing themselves as independent actors and leaders to seeing themselves as an interdependent "leadership collective" within their organizations. But developing such "collective leadership identities" goes against the grain of most people and organizations. The authors explore through two organizational case studies how one methodology—action learning—can promote collective leadership identities.

The last chapter in Part One challenges the conventional wisdom of the field—that a set of tangible leadership competencies should be the foundation of any developmental effort. Most contemporary leadership development initiatives begin with an elaborate (and expensive and time-consuming) process of identifying a small number of competencies that are believed to characterize effective leaders in an organization. In Chapter Four, authors Morgan McCall and George Hollenbeck challenge this competency-based approach. They argue that development initiatives need to focus on using experiences to develop *competence,* rather than on preconceived competencies. They lay out a blueprint for completely revamping our current approaches.

Part Two of the book—"The Tasks of the Leader"—focuses on certain fundamental or baseline capabilities and responsibilities of leaders. For example, leaders know when and where to deploy a particular tactic in their broad repertoire of influence approaches. They are particularly effective at directing and motivating teams and at fostering environments promoting innovation. Finally, the best are guided by a moral or ethical compass despite pressures to do otherwise.

Author Gary Yukl examines in Chapter Five the use of proactive influence tactics ranging from rational persuasion (using facts and logic) to inspirational appeals (linking a request to target values and ideals). He describes eleven types of proactive influence tactics, explains what we know about their relative effectiveness, explores the situations best suited to each, and provides guidelines on how to use them for leading people in organizations. He also describes how most of the proactive tactics can also be used to resist unwanted influence attempts by others.

Chapter Six—"Creating the Conditions for Success: Best Practices in Leading for Innovation" by Michael Mumford, Dawn Eubanks, and

Stephen Murphy—highlights the mix of the technical, organizational, and strategic skills required to lead the development of innovative new products and services. The authors identify each of the stages of the innovation process in which leaders must excel. Each stage is illustrated with the specific capabilities that leaders must demonstrate.

Craig Johnson, in his chapter entitled "Best Practices in Ethical Leadership," brings us to the critical responsibility of all leaders—to set a moral standard for their organizations. He begins by defining the tasks of ethical leadership and identifying key practices that enable leaders to carry out this responsibility. The first task is simply to behave morally as leaders carry out their roles. The second task is to shape the ethical contexts of their groups and organizations. The dual responsibilities of acting as a moral standard and shaping the ethical context for their organizations intertwine, but Johnson examines each one separately to provide a more complete picture of the task facing leadership practitioners. He then introduces a set of resources and tools that leaders can draw on when assuming ethical duties.

In Chapter Eight, "Best Practices in Team Leadership: What Team Leaders Do to Facilitate Team Effectiveness," authors Kevin Stagl, Eduardo Salas, and C. Shawn Burke explore one of the most critical capabilities of leaders: leveraging team performance. They provide an overview of the broad functions and behaviors that team leaders must enact to create the conditions required for team effectiveness. They discuss the need for leaders to create five conditions that serve as a set of mutually reinforcing resources that teams can draw upon when working toward outstanding performance. These five prerequisite conditions for team effectiveness include creating (1) a real team, (2) with a compelling direction, (3) an enabling structure, (4) a supportive organizational context, and (5) expert coaching. This chapter describes how leaders can successfully foster each condition.

In Part Three of the book, where we explore organizational leadership, we turn our attention to seniormost leaders and their roles in change and corporate governance. We examine critical questions such as, What are the actions and approaches that executive leaders must adopt as they lead change during difficult transitions for their organizations? What is the role of corporate social responsibility, and what are the corresponding actions required by executives to instill a culture of social responsibility? Finally, what kinds of leadership should corporate boards provide for the organizations they oversee and particularly in relation with the company's seniormost leader, the chief executive officer (CEO)?

Chapter Nine, by Mitchell Lee Marks, examines how leaders can help organizations and their members overcome the unintended consequences of major organizational transitions. Marks discusses the fact that senior leaders have two requirements to ensure workplace recovery. One is to weaken the forces that maintain the undesired status quo, and the second is to strengthen the forces for the desired new vision. They must intervene at both the emotional and business levels. Simultaneously, they engage employees by freeing up time and other resources to help them find ways to get their work done better. They must also generate energy by clarifying a vision of a new and better organization and creating a learning environment that creates incentives for people to experiment. Last, they enforce their desired posttransition organization by aligning systems and operating standards with new organizational realities. Marks explores how leaders can accomplish each of these outcomes.

Chapter Ten, by David Waldman, presents a view of executive leadership that centers on social responsibility values, the forms of leadership that emanate from such values, and the resulting effects on followers. The underlying premise of this chapter is that executive leaders can have a positive leadership effect on their followers over the long term only through a sense of social responsibility targeted toward multiple stakeholder groups. Waldman describes the behaviors and mindsets that are required if executive leaders are to successfully guide their corporations, deploying a moral compass and a set of performance standards that stretch way beyond today's narrow emphasis on profitability.

The last chapter in Part Three—"Best Practices in Corporate Boardroom Leadership"—examines the leadership roles that board members must embrace if they are to provide oversight from the boardroom. It explores a new generation of boardroom best practices in leadership. Specifically, alternative forms of leadership, such as nonexecutive chairpersons, lead directors, and stronger committee leadership, are described as a counterbalance to the CEO's authority. The pluses and minuses of each form of leadership are discussed. This chapter offers concrete guidance for boards wishing to implement these leadership alternatives.

In Part Four, the last part of the book, we take a look at leading in today's world. We address three specific topics highly relevant to the current times. Given the turmoil in the world, we feel it is particularly important to explore the demanding leadership requirements faced in times of crisis. We want readers to learn how to prepare their organizations in advance for crises. Our second topic—leading diverse organizations—is a reflection of the fact that diversity is the hallmark of today's workplace. It is imperative that we examine the leadership practices that recognize and leverage diversity at work. Finally, globalization is rapidly transforming how we work and lead. Understanding how to lead across cultures is a necessity for many managers and executives. There is a great deal of new research on the topic that has important practical implications for readers.

We begin Part Four with Ian Mitroff's chapter, "Best Practices in Leading under Crisis: Bottom-Up Leadership, or How to Be a Crisis Champion." Examples of crises abound, from the terrorist attacks on September 11, 2001, to the corporate scandals such as Enron/Andersen to natural disasters such as the tsunami in Southeast Asia and Hurricane Katrina in Louisiana. All of these cases represent failure of leadership. Mitroff argues that leaders must proactively and rigorously prepare their organizations for a broad range of potential crises. They begin the process by helping us to challenge the basic assumptions we hold about our lives and our organizations. These assumptions make us vulnerable and unprepared for crisis. Successful crisis leaders speed up the recognition and awareness of these assumptions across their organizations. They also implement the organizational strategies of anticipation and innovation to minimize the impact of a crisis. Mitroff explores how crisis leaders effectively accomplish these outcomes.

Chapter 13, by Lynn Offermann and Kenneth Matos, addresses the needs of leaders who wish to further develop their capabilities in working with diverse staff. The authors begin by examining the value that leaders gain from addressing organizational diversity and the costs of ignoring it. This is followed by a discussion of key concepts and approaches to understanding diversity in organizations as a foundation for understanding specific leadership practices. A summary of best practices for leaders of diverse organizations is then presented, along with a discussion of some of the most significant challenges in the implementing diversity leadership. The chapter concludes by offering a detailed example of how leaders can put these best practices to work by developing the capabilities of diverse staff through mentoring.

Mary Teagarden's chapter on cross-cultural leadership closes out this part of the book. She addresses five questions fundamental to understanding the topic. The first is, Does cross-cultural leadership really matter? A second issue is, How do we best understand and define the concept of cross-cultural leadership? Third, what are the behaviors, competencies, and skills that distinguish individuals who are adept at cross-cultural leadership? Fourth, is the cross-cultural leader's set of competencies innate, or can it be developed? The fifth question considers knowledge: What specifically does a cross-cultural leader need to know? What are the kinds of questions that these leaders must be asking themselves to ensure they possess insights needed to succeed in each situation? This chapter answers these questions with a set of leadership best practices.

Chapter Fifteen, our final chapter, summarizes the essential lessons on leadership practices from each of the book's contributors. It then identifies the common themes shared across the chapters. Specifically, we identify five major themes: (1) leaders need to engage and involve their followers; (2) effective leaders proactively monitor, measure, and adapt to their environments; (3) leaders need to model the way; (4) leaders must be proactive; and (5) there are no shortcuts to leadership—the developmental process is a long-term investment.

In preparing a volume such as this, we owe a tremendous thanks to our authors. They are all well-known experts in their respective topic areas. They also participated in a conference that we hosted in 2005 at the Kravis Leadership Institute at Claremont McKenna College on the topic of the practice of leadership. We also want to thank Sandy Counts, who helped us format and organize the book itself. She has been a godsend. We also thank Becky Reichard, who helped out in chapter editing. Finally, Kathe Sweeney, our editor at Jossey-Bass, and her team have been wonderfully supportive and helpful. Kathe saw the potential in the book and early on committed to making this volume a published reality.

Claremont, California   JAY A. CONGER
                                                                RONALD E. RIGGIO

PART ONE

Leadership Development and Selection

CHAPTER ONE

Best Practices in Leader Selection

Ann Howard

G etting the right leader in the top position stimulates organizations to prosper and grow. Chief executive officers (CEOs) account for 14 percent of the variance in organizational performance,[1] which means that there is a huge payoff if selection is done right. Moreover, it can cost millions of dollars if it's done wrong.

Unfortunately, there are a lot of CEO failures; estimates range from 30 percent to 50 percent.[2] A Booz Allen Hamilton study found that the rate of CEO dismissals in the world's 2,500 largest public companies increased by 170 percent from 1995 to 2003. Nearly one-third of the CEOs departing in 2003 (3 percent of a total of 9.5 percent) were fired for poor performance.[3] Given these failure rates, it is not surprising that confidence in leaders is often shaky. In one national survey of public opinion based on 1,300 interviews, the average level of overall confidence in business leaders was 2.78 on a 4-point scale.[4]

The problem of poorly selected leaders could worsen as the Baby Boom generation retires, the supply of quality candidates dwindles, and the competition for talent heats up. Surveys have found that human resource (HR) professionals anticipated greater difficulty filling leadership positions in the future. The higher the management level, the more difficulty expected: 66 percent of respondents expected more problems filling senior leadership positions compared to 52 percent for mid-level and 28 percent for first-level leader positions.[5]

There are multiple reasons why senior-level positions are so difficult to fill. The skill requirements for top-level jobs are high, as are the risks, evidenced by the excessive CEO failure rate. Detracting from the job are competitive pressures from a fast-moving global economy and elevated visibility and surveillance. CEOs and boards are now scrutinized intensely by shareholders, regulators, politicians, and the legal system, and their specific decisions are being second-guessed.[6] At the same time the pool of qualified, well-prepared candidates for top-level jobs has shrunk with the evaporation of many preparatory mid-level positions and organizations' neglect of thoughtful succession planning.

This chapter describes how to get leader selection right. It reviews the objectives of selection, describes current selection techniques and evidence about their efficacy, and looks at how individual selection methods can be combined into an effective selection system. The chapter draws from general selection research and provides specifics for leaders where available.

OBJECTIVES OF LEADER SELECTION
Purposes of Selection

Although selection is usually thought of as hiring from the outside, internal selection (hiring from within) is just as prevalent for leaders. In addition to promotions, candidates are selected into positions or programs for career development and succession planning. Figure 1.1 shows some of the points at which leader selection occurs.

Recruitment of candidates varies by purpose and by management level. Entry-level leaders are usually a mix of outside hires and internal promotions. Organizations often place recruits from college campuses in first-level positions as an introduction to management roles. A classic pitfall of internal promotions is the selection of the best producer or technical performer, who is not necessarily the best manager. Such an ill-considered promotion leaves the organization with a mediocre leader and without a top performer.

Figure 1.1. Sites for Leader Selection.

Middle managers are traditionally brought up from the lower-management ranks. Selection for career development can occur at any management level, but succession management programs are usually aimed at higher levels. External hiring is common for a CEO, particularly if the organization is in trouble or is moving in a new direction. Outsiders run more than a third (37 percent) of the Fortune 1,000 companies, according to public affairs firm Burson-Marsteller, while insiders preside over the other two-thirds.[7]

Criteria for Selection Systems

Some might believe that the ultimate measure of a selection system's value is organizational effectiveness. However, such a criterion confuses performance or behavior with results. Organizational effectiveness is determined by multiple factors that are beyond the control of an individual leader. These factors can be internal, such as production delays or a labor dispute, or external, such as competition and market conditions. As noted in the introduction to this chapter, a leader, particularly at high levels, can have substantial impact on organizational performance. However, organizational effectiveness is determined by more than a leader selection system.[8]

Criteria for measuring selection system success are of two types. The first concerns the output of the system, the most important of which is the individual performance of those selected. Organizations want the selection process to produce high-quality people who are well suited to their positions, will perform their required tasks well, and will remain motivated and committed. The system should also provide information about selected candidates that will prepare them and their managers for the growth and development that will inevitably be needed.

Additional criteria concern the nature of the selection system. It must be fair and appear fair to the candidates. It must work efficiently and remain viable over time. Each of these criteria warrants further exploration.

INDIVIDUAL PERFORMANCE. How well selected candidates perform in their new positions is the most important measure of selection system success. But there is more complexity in measuring the performance of leaders than that of individual contributors. A leader gets things accomplished through other people, so an important consideration is how leaders affect their work team and others in the organization. Thus satisfaction, retention, and performance of leaders' direct reports can add important data to the evaluation of leader quality.

There are three primary categories of things needed for success on a job.[9] These include declarative knowledge (knowledge about facts or things; knowing what to do), procedural knowledge and skill (knowing how to perform a task), and motivation (whether to expend effort, how much effort to expend, and persistence in that effort). The first two components are often called "can do" factors, while the latter is called the "will do" factor.

Traditional research has focused more on the "can do" than the "will do." Yet high-quality hires will have little impact on organizational effectiveness unless they are motivated to stay with the organization long enough to make a difference. On average, managers stay in one organization 9.9 years,[10] although this rate varies with economic conditions.

There is less research on the relationship between selection methods and attachment, whether measured as turnover, absences, or commitment. Factors other than the accuracy of selection come into play with these outcomes. Common causes of turnover are personal reasons, such as getting married or returning to school, and undesirable behavior by one's manager. In fact, satisfaction has been equated to satisfaction with one's supervisor.[11] Research is sparse on selection methods and leader satisfaction, although this is an important precursor to retention.[12]

INFORMING INDIVIDUAL DEVELOPMENT. A chosen leader will seldom be perfect, and a sound selection system should also identify individuals' relative strengths and development needs. For example, a leader might be strong in business management skills like operational decision making or financial acumen but need development in interpersonal skills such as building strategic relationships. For internal selection, information about what characteristics need strengthening are an essential part of the process, not only for those who are selected, but also for those not selected who want to try again. The shoring-up process, for knowledge as well as skill development, can come in the form of training, coaching, or a critical assignment.

Many organizations also want an external hire's on-boarding process to include a development plan to work on needed skills and abilities. This requires the selection method to provide fodder for development—specific information that the new leader and his or her manager can follow to establish development steps. Jump-starting development could be an important factor in retention. When asked to choose the one most important reason employees leave, respondents most often cited a lack of growth and development opportunities (chosen by 25.3 percent). Only 8.3 percent chose a poor relationship with the manager.[13] This suggests that employees endure a certain level of dissatisfaction with their managers as long as there are opportunities for growth.

LEGAL DEFENSIBILITY. Civil rights legislation and subsequent court cases have emphasized the importance of equal opportunity and the need for selection methods to be unbiased. Selection methods that produce adverse impact—defined as a selection rate for protected groups that is less than four-fifths (80 percent) of the rate for the highest group—must have clear evidence of job relevance and demonstrate that alternative methods are not feasible. This does not negate the use of methods with high adverse impact, but it makes them more subject to scrutiny.

CANDIDATE ACCEPTANCE. Selection is a two-way relationship, and there are consequences if a method affects candidates negatively. Candidates want to feel that their true skills, abilities, and potential are being evaluated and that they are being treated fairly relative to other candidates. Negative reactions are a particular concern to organizations because good candidates might withdraw from the competition and/or harbor negative feelings about the organization.

Unfortunately, research on candidate acceptance has seldom included leaders.[14] While those at lower levels expect and accept a more high-tech, high-volume selection approach like online screening and testing, C-level (chief or highest-level executives) candidates often feel that they are above standard methods of testing or assessment and that their prior performance should speak for itself.[15]

In the past few decades, boards of directors often employed executive search firms to locate and screen new CEOs. The exact methods for selection were secret and probably idiosyncratic, but search firms commonly use unstructured interviews along with reference checks. As will be shown, these methods, though acceptable to candidates, are not very accurate, despite the fact that the top job has the highest consequences of any in an organization.[16]

The benefits to organizations of this type of selection are ripe for challenge. Although outsiders are increasingly sought to fill CEO positions, insiders have better performance records. The Booz Allen Hamilton study mentioned earlier found that the median shareholder return in 2003 among companies run by insiders was 3 percent compared to −5 percent for companies run by outsiders. Among North American CEOs who left their jobs in 2003, their boards forced 55 percent of outside hires and only 34 percent of insiders to resign. In Europe, 70 percent of departing outsider CEOs were dismissed, compared with 55 percent of insiders.[17] This kind of evidence, combined with increased scrutiny of the practices of boards of directors, has laid the groundwork for acceptance of more sophisticated practices for selecting C-level leaders, including CEOs.

EFFICIENCY. Organizations should naturally favor selection methods that cost less and can be administered quickly and easily. However, HR professionals rarely track cost per hire.[18] The level of investment in a selection system needs to be weighed against its potential payoff.

For many organizations the cost of selection may have less of a bearing on evaluations of efficiency than speed, particularly for external hiring. It typically takes nearly 10 weeks to fill a management vacancy (compared to 6 weeks for nonmanagement staff), and 25 percent of the selection forecast HR professionals described hiring as slow or cumbersome.[19]

Leader selection in the future will likely be increasingly dependent on computer technology, which enhances not just efficiency but reach. Recruiting has already benefited from technological advances such as e-recruiting expanded pools of candidates, applicant tracking systems, online screening tools, and electronic job previews. Biographical data can also be collected with questionnaires or scored electronically from résumés. Tests and inventories are easily put in digital form and are increasingly delivered via the Internet.

Audio and video technology can deliver structured interviews with no apparent loss of reliability or additional adverse impact.[20] Assessment center simulations are also being automated. In-basket items can be delivered via e-mail, voice mail, or video on electronic desktops. These items can be supplemented by telephone or videoconference role plays. An advantage of online simulations is that communicating at a computer desktop better represents what modern leaders do.

Personnel Selection Paradigms

Selection works. Evidence accumulated through meta-analyses has shown that various selection methods have higher validity than might be expected.[21] That is, across studies—once researchers removed errors of small samples, restricted range, and unreliability—statistical relationships between scores on selection methods and performance were usually strongly significant. Because there is large variance in leader performance, utility ratios based on almost any selection technique with modest validity can be justified.

A problem with the traditional paradigm is that its lack of a theoretical basis made it difficult to map predictors to performance constructs across different measures, contexts, and samples. For example, determining that cognitive ability tests predict leaders' job performance better than personality tests does little to advance the understanding of leadership. A new personnel selection paradigm, which has emerged in the past two decades, focuses on the nature of constructs and their interrelationships in order to enhance understanding and build practical applications. That is, different dimensions of job performance are related to variations in the validity of selection methods across different contexts.[22] For example, the trait of consci-entiousness might be related to work standards in technically oriented leadership positions but not to the most important competencies for sales leadership.

The construct-oriented selection paradigm has led to various attempts to understand the multidimensionality of job performance. For example, John Campbell and his colleagues suggested eight general factors of performance across jobs (job-specific task proficiency, non-job-specific task proficiency, written and oral communication task proficiency, demonstrating effort, maintaining personal discipline, facilitating peer and team performance, supervision/leadership, and management/administration).[23]

Studies have shown that decision-making and problem-solving competencies relate to one's early managerial performance, whereas interpersonal skills come into play several years later in the career.[24] Executives reviewing this evidence suggested that it takes more time to impact human systems than physical resources. That is, general managers can quickly diagnose and address problems or opportunities where raw materials or capital assets could enhance organizational performance, but it takes much longer to manage relationships with people or implement a new vision that affects trust or corporate culture.[25] Another explanation for the later impact of interpersonal skills might be visibility. Lower-level managers' problem solving and decisions will show up in productivity figures, but their interpersonal skills might not be evident to anyone but their direct reports. As managers move into higher-level positions, they interact with many more people and reveal their interpersonal skills to a wider audience. The greater stress of higher-level positions also might bring out underlying personality factors (such as arrogance) that become derailers in visible interpersonal situations.

Criteria of Effective Leadership

Before selecting leaders, organizations need to define what they expect them to do. These expectations can be stated in terms of personal competencies, often grouped into performance domains. For example, operational decision making is a competency in the business management domain whereas developing strategic relationships is in the interpersonal domain. Leadership is not only multidimensional, but is also moderated by various situational factors, such as management level, cultural context, and specific types of business challenges.

DOMAINS OF LEADER PERFORMANCE. Broad domains should include interpersonal and communication skills, leadership of others, administrative or business skills, and motivation or effort. Beneath these broad rubrics, however, is a long list of more specific competencies.

Competencies. To define the behavioral requirements for jobs, organizational practice has shifted dramatically away from job analysis, which identifies task details or activities that differentiate jobs (such as inspecting or investigating), to competency modeling, which identifies individual-level competencies required for groups of jobs (for example, decision making or influence). Assessment centers always had competencies (often called *dimensions*), so these constructs are not new.[26]

One of the advantages of competency modeling is that it focuses on *how* work is accomplished (worker characteristics) whereas traditional job analysis concentrates on *what* is accomplished (job and task characteristics). Another advantage, particularly evident in recent years, is that competencies can provide a direct link to business goals and strategies. Competencies relate to behavioral repertoires—what people can perform and outcomes they can attain rather than tasks.[27] They are thus more appropriate for describing jobs that are changing.

Differences by Management Level. Leader requirements vary significantly by management level. There are pronounced differences among entry-level supervisors (leaders with one or possibly two direct reports), middle-level managers (leaders of leaders), operational leaders (those responsible for large business units), and strategic leaders (those who set organizational direction). The implication is that leader selection does not happen one time in a career. People are selected into the initial level of leadership, but even if they perform well there, there is no guarantee that they will be effective at a higher level of leadership. Thus, selection methods are usually reapplied at the major transition points shown in Figure 1.1.

Different abilities are needed for success at various levels.[28] For example, first-level leaders need skills in coaching, empowerment, and routine decision making. Mid-level leaders must make broader operational decisions and balance the needs of those above, beyond, and across from the subsystem they manage. Executives manage multiple units and have profit-and-loss responsibility. As leaders climb the management ladder, they are faced with challenges of increasing scope, complexity (scale), and ambiguity.

Cultural Differences. The extensive GLOBE (Global Leadership and Organizational Behavior Effectiveness) research found differences in the desirability of leader behaviors across cultures,[29] which complicates leader selection. However, multinational organizations often want a common model across geographical units. This is not out of the question, given that organizational cultures are often seen as having a stronger pull on behavioral styles than country cultures.

Another issue with cross-cultural applications is that there are country preferences for particular selection techniques. For example, assessment centers are popular in the United Kingdom, Germany, and the Netherlands but are seldom used in France.[30]

Business Challenges. Global competition and environmental changes have focused management's attention on strategy. Organizations often want to know whether a leader is able to tackle specific business challenges, such as a turnaround, start-up, rapid growth, or strategic change.

Some competencies are more critical than others for managing different business challenges and thus rise in importance as measures of effective leadership. For example, a business trying to cultivate innovation might emphasize competencies such as change leadership, selling a vision, and establishing strategic direction as key criteria for sizing up its executives. Specific market segments may also need to address common business challenges. For example, a recent survey of hospital CEOs identified the three most critical leadership skills for organizational success over the next three years as strategic thinking, team building, and internal and external communication.[31]

INDIVIDUAL SELECTION TECHNIQUES

Selection methods can be arrayed across a continuum that ranges from signs of behavior (predispositions to act in a certain way, as from a personality test scale of extraversion) to samples of behavior (demonstrations of complex behavioral responses, such as coaching a direct report). Figure 1.2 provides examples of leader selection methods that take three positions along that continuum.

1. *Inferences* are made about how people will behave in leadership situations from their answers to tests (which have correct and incorrect answers), inventories of their personal qualities or

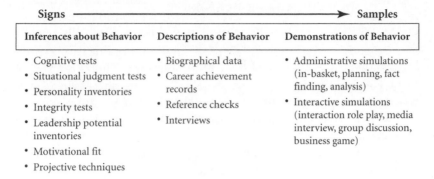

Figure 1.2.   Leader Selection Techniques.

beliefs, or other techniques. These methods answer the question "Who am I?" For example, a test might identify a leader as "conscientious" or "smart."

2. *Descriptions* of knowledge or experience are expressed in written or oral form. These include factual information about the candidates' backgrounds as well as their perspectives on past or future behavior. These methods answer the questions "What have I done?" and "What do I know?" For example, a biographical data form might describe a candidate as experienced in hospital administration.

3. *Demonstrations* of leader behaviors are elicited from work samples and simulations. These methods answer the question "What can I do?" For example, a candidate to head a hospital might demonstrate in a simulated interaction with a physician (a role player) that he or she can gain the physician's cooperation to save hospital costs.

Techniques that make inferences about behavior are usually closed-ended (multiple choice), while demonstrations of behavior are always open-ended (free response). Closed-ended tools lend themselves to computer scoring and are more efficient, while demonstrations of behavior provide the best information for individual development. Candidate acceptance is highest with job-relevant demonstrations of behavior and lowest with inference-making tools that are less well understood.

Inferences about Behavior

COGNITIVE TESTS. Tests of general mental ability (often called *g*) are very strong predictors of performance on jobs of all types, in large part by affecting the acquisition of job knowledge. Although *g* is derived from items measuring several specific abilities (such as verbal, numerical, or spatial), it represents a common factor that emerges regardless of specific content—a general property of the mind that reflects human differences in intellect.

Tests measuring *g* have their highest predictive validity for complex jobs. Positions of leadership, particularly high up in an organization, are unquestionably complex and are strongly predictive from cognitive tests. In practice, however, there is likely to be a restriction of range in *g* as leaders move up the management hierarchy.

While arguably industrial/organizational (I/O) psychology's most powerful tool, cognitive tests incur the largest adverse impact against minorities. Candidates do not react as favorably toward these tests as to interviews or work samples[32] and may be particularly uneasy if they anticipate adverse impact. A practical problem with using cognitive tests for selection is that they measure capabilities that are not readily amenable to change.

SITUATIONAL JUDGMENT TESTS. These tests of decision making and judgment in work settings are primarily used at lower levels of management. Items typically describe a scenario and respondents identify the most appropriate response from a list of alternatives. Other versions of these tools do not present a situation but ask respondents to indicate their level of agreement with statements about the appropriateness of various work behaviors. These tests may not have incremental validity beyond cognitive ability tests.[33]

PERSONALITY INVENTORIES. Personality inventories measure candidates' attitudes, motivations, and psychological character. They get at the "will do" aspect of individual performance. They also predict style of leadership: "Who we are determines how we lead."[34]

There is extensive research on the clusters of personal traits known as the "Big 5": extraversion, emotional stability, agreeableness, conscientiousness, and openness to experience. Yet these measures have shown low validity for management jobs. Large personality domains are better at predicting global performance criteria than particular performance areas.[35] Researchers have recently focused on mapping more specific personality traits to aspects of a job.

Personality inventories can also be used to forecast potential derailment of leaders. An old saw in executive search is "Hired on experience, fired on personality."[36] The problem is that the dark side of personality can coexist with well-developed social skills, and potential derailers may lurk undetected. Stated more starkly, the bright side is the person you meet in an interview while the dark side is the one who comes to work.[37]

Some have questioned whether personality traits should be linked to outcomes in a linear fashion.[38] For example, you can be too conscientious, conventional, and rule bound. Or take impulse expression: if you're too high, you blurt things out; if too low, you're fearful and rigid.[39] Research on leader derailment has shown that strengths taken to extremes can become weaknesses.[40]

Another complexity in scoring personality tests is consideration of score profiles, which can be difficult to work with.[41] In line with the new selection paradigm, combinations of personality test constructs need to be mapped to relevant aspects of performance. The more traditional approach has been to use an inventory that covers the major dimensions of personality and then determine empirically which dimensions are relevant.[42]

Personality inventories are limited in that there is no direct translation into performance outcomes. Rather, you must translate personality into behavior and then into outcomes.[43] Personality doesn't create business results; behavior does.

Another problem with personality questionnaires is that applicant acceptance is lower than that for interviews, work samples, or even cognitive tests.[44] Some personality tests reject high scorers as fakers, raising potential legal issues. Sex differences can also bring charges of adverse impact. Added to this brew is the understanding that personality can't readily be changed: it has been speculated that traits like emotional stability and extraversion might have neuropsychological roots.[45] However, people who understand the nature of their personality can take steps to mitigate the biggest problems it might cause them.[46]

Faking is another potential problem with personality tests. Although some studies show that this effect is overblown,[47] there is still a concern that it is easy to distort these instruments if you are motivated to do so.

INTEGRITY TESTS. One type of personality instrument that has come into vogue, particularly in light of the many recent corporate scandals, is the integrity test. Integrity tests use facets of conscientiousness and emotional stability in their construction. Parallel surveys over time showed more than double the use of integrity tests between 1999 (7.9 percent of respondents) and 2004 (16.4 percent of respondents).[48]

LEADERSHIP POTENTIAL INVENTORIES. Some inventories directly measure leader characteristics and potential. Older tests based on the global factors of consideration and initiating structure included the Leadership Opinion Questionnaire, Leader Behavior Description Questionnaire, and Supervisory Behavior Description Questionnaire. However, these tests have no established validity.[49] There is considerably more evidence to support transformational and transactional leadership theory, particularly from the Bass Multifactor Leadership Questionnaire, or MLQ. Transformational leadership appears to be more related to follower satisfaction than performance of the leader or group.[50] Although some relationships with performance have been shown, it is not yet clear whether transformational leadership measures can aid top-level selection.[51]

MOTIVATIONAL FIT. Motivational fit measures get at the "will do" factor by addressing whether the candidate will be personally satisfied with the work (job fit), the company culture (organization fit), or the company's location (location fit). Inventories allow candidates to compare their preferences and values with the nature of the job and organization. Although this approach is seldom used to reject candidates, it can help them to screen themselves out.

Motivational fit can also be evaluated with interview questions. The interviewer asks the interviewee how he or she would react to certain job characteristics. For example, if a leadership position required working with diverse groups of people, an interviewer might ask a candidate, "Tell me about a time when you worked with people with a wide range of backgrounds or perspectives. How satisfied were you with that and why?"

PROJECTIVE TECHNIQUES. Projective techniques present ambiguous stimuli and ask people to fill in what's missing. The theory behind projectives is that personality structure influences the way individuals interpret their environment.

A fundamental problem with all projective measures is that the level of inference is so great that they require a trained scorer. This constraint poses a challenge for selection system efficiency.

Descriptions of Behavior

Descriptions of behavior can be oriented toward the past (what you did) or the future (what you would do). The premise behind describing what you have done is behavior consistency: past behavior is the best predictor of future behavior. The premise behind describing what you would do in the future is that behavioral intentions predict future behavior.

BIODATA. Biographical information, or biodata, quantifies descriptions of past activities and accomplishments, such as degrees earned or specific work experiences. It can be collected in various ways, such as checklists of skills and experiences, forms requesting background information, and computerized résumé screening.

Several types of research suggest that these measures relate to leader effectiveness. For example, a review of seven studies found that personal history correlated .38 with success in management.[52] Other studies have explored how personal experiences relate to leader effectiveness. For example, in AT&T's Management Progress Study, college major and extracurricular activities predicted interpersonal skills in an assessment center.[53] Biographical data lends itself to automated screening, as when applicants fill in forms on the Internet that are then scored against the organization's criteria.

CAREER ACHIEVEMENT RECORDS. Career achievement records capture key experiences that demonstrate effective performance of competencies. They are usually completed by applicants and reviewed for accuracy by their managers. They require descriptions of actual behavior, organized by important competencies.

Career achievement records have several advantages, particularly in restructuring (and often downsizing) situations when internal candidates are applying for positions in an organization pointing in a new strategic direction. Candidates are given a voice in the selection process, which helps them perceive it as fair. These measures often replace poorly constructed performance data for experienced candidates who are being screened for transfer or promotion. Their meta-analytic predictive validity with overall job performance is .45.[54]

On the downside, career achievement records can be time consuming and costly to construct and score. Because the process seldom includes follow-up questions, the documented behaviors can be difficult to verify.

REFERENCE CHECKS. Despite their small but statistically significant correlation with job performance, problems with lawsuits in the United States have made many organizations reluctant to give out very meaningful data. The popularity of reference checks also varies in other countries. For example, the British use them a lot (74 percent of companies surveyed), but the French seldom do (11 percent).[55]

INTERVIEWS. One clear research result is that unstructured interviews don't work nearly as well as structured. One estimate, based on reliability analyses, of the upper limits of validity was .67 for highly structured interviews and .34 for unstructured.[56]

Perhaps because of their prevalence, interviews are the focus of the majority of legal court challenges to selection.[57] Another disadvantage of interviews is that they are time consuming and thus not very efficient compared to other selection methods. Moreover, interviewers need training in conducting and evaluating interviews, particularly those that are structured around competencies. Video or audio delivery of structured interviews offers hope for enhancing interview efficiency.[58]

One controversy concerns the relative effectiveness of interviews structured around past experiences (behavior description interviews, or BDI) or hypothetical situations (situational interviews, or SI). Both types are usually competency based. However, BDI ask about what you did ("Describe a time when you weren't sure what a customer wanted. How did you handle the situation?"), and SI ask about what you would do (A situation is described where it's unclear what a customer wanted. "What would you do?").

There is sufficient empirical data to support both SI and BDI as predictors of job performance, although three studies found the BDI more valid for higher-level jobs.[59] It was speculated that the addition of descriptively anchored rating scales to the BDI significantly enhanced its validity. Not only do such scales enhance reliability, but they also improve construct validity by more clearly specifying the performance domain.[60]

Situational interviews have an advantage when organizations want to directly compare the responses of candidates for future jobs. But they are measures of maximal performance, whereas BDI are measures of typical performance.[61]

Another controversy is whether interviews lose validity if conducted by telephone rather than face to face. Some data showed lower relationships to later job performance for phone-based interviews. Regardless of delivery mode, interviews have been criticized for measuring social skills, experience, and job knowledge rather than the constructs or competencies they are purported to measure.[62]

Demonstrations of Behavior

Candidates being evaluated for jobs as individual contributors are sometimes asked to provide work samples that show what they can do. The validity of work samples should be enhanced to the extent that there is point-to-point correspondence between predictor elements and criterion elements. Their predictive validity with overall job performance is quite high (.54),[63] and they add significantly to prediction from cognitive ability tests.

For complex leadership roles, candidates are usually asked to demonstrate their capabilities in several diverse simulations of key managerial roles. Managerial simulations range in complexity from brief mini-simulations conducted with interviews to lengthy and involved analyses used for executive assessments. Factors that determine the complexity of a simulation include the length of preparation time needed, richness of detail provided, difficulty level of the issues, and number of competencies covered. Leader simulations are of many types but usually fall into two broad categories, administrative and interactive.

ADMINISTRATIVE SIMULATIONS. These simulations involve individual problem solving.

In-Basket. These exercises have participants review information similar to that found in a manager's in-basket. Participants respond to correspondence or voice mail messages involving, for example, productivity, morale, public relations, and training needs.

Planning. In a planning or scheduling exercise, participants are given resources with which to accomplish specific tasks. Leader candidates might be asked to schedule others' activities or schedule people to jobs.

Fact-Finding Exercise. The participant is given a brief description of a hypothetical situation. The task is to seek information from a resource person and make a decision about that situation within a limited time period.

Analysis. In these exercises participants analyze quantitative and narrative data and make short- and/or long-term recommendations to improve matters such as productivity, quality, profitability, organizational structure, and morale.

INTERACTIVE SIMULATIONS. In these simulations candidates interact with role players or participate in groups.

Interaction Role Plays. Participants review background information on a peer, internal or external customer, direct report, or prospective client. They then meet with a trained role player to resolve a problem or gain commitment to a course of action. Role plays are often structured to bring out a primary competency such as coaching, influencing others, or managing conflict.

Media Interview. Typically confined to executive assessments, these exercises provide participants with background information about a situation that has attracted media attention. Candidates then meet with a media representative (a trained role player) to answer probing questions and defend their organization's actions.

Presentation or Visionary Address. Participants make formal presentations or an inspirational talk on some selected problem or topic to one or more role players or external observers.

Group Discussion. A group of candidates reviews background material on a situation or set of issues, and then meets to discuss the issues and decide how to resolve them. Group discussions vary in that they may or may not assign roles, appoint leaders, or inject competition into the discussion.

Business Game. In a business game, a group is assigned a problem and members must work together to solve it. Business games usually have a competitive element and require some organization of effort and division of labor among team members.

VALUE OF SIMULATIONS. Simulations are traditionally associated with assessment centers, and the majority of evidence about their validity comes from this context. The assessment center itself has a long track record of predictive validity,[64] although research evidence for individual types of exercises is sparse. Significant relationships with performance criteria, including advancement into higher levels of management, have been found for such simulations as leaderless group discussions, in-basket exercises, and business games.[65]

Simulations offer organizations several advantages. Because participants demonstrate live behavior, there is little opportunity to fake and no need to speculate about what behavior would be like. Simulations can be directed at future jobs or challenges, which gives them an advantage over current descriptions of performance. Applicants usually react positively, believing the technique to be fair and job related. Adverse impact is less for administrative simulations than for cognitive tests and negligible for exercises measuring interpersonal skills.[66]

A significant advantage of simulations over other selection methods is their usefulness for development. They are mostly aimed at skills and abilities that can be learned, and demonstrations of live behavior in simulations provide excellent material for credible feedback.

But simulations are labor intensive, adding to time and costs. In recent years Web delivery has cut down considerably on administrative burdens, but simulations don't lend themselves to automatic scoring such as that for tests and inventories. Moreover, interrater reliability must be continually checked and reinforced, as assessors apply holistic judgment to scoring. Simulations don't readily measure all leadership competencies, in particular those that require actions that extend over long periods of time, such as customer networking.

Questionable Methods

Two popular but questionable methods should also be mentioned. For very different reasons, these techniques are *not* recommended for leader selection.

MULTIRATER SURVEYS. Multirater surveys (also known as *multisource* or *360-degree surveys*) attempt to capture the behavioral observations of those close to leaders. Respondents typically include direct reports, peers, and supervisors, although customers or suppliers can also be tapped for their opinions. These surveys can be very useful for development. Leaders can learn from others about their reputations and consider how to optimize their favorable qualities and change undesirable aspects.

If used for selection, however, multirater surveys can become vulnerable to gaming the system or sources of work stress. Raters might have different motives for responding and undermine trust in a work group.[67]

GRAPHOLOGY. Analyses of handwriting have no established validity. Data supporting the method came from essays, where content was evaluated and presumably influenced ratings. Graphology also incurs very negative applicant reactions. Nevertheless, the method is widely used in France and Israel.[68]

SELECTION SYSTEMS

Although proponents of different selection techniques make various claims about their superiority, a single method is usually inadequate to meet organizational objectives. Thus, the best practice is to capitalize on the advantages and mitigate the disadvantages of any one method by combining it with others into a selection system.

The type of job affects how comprehensive the system can reasonably be. Practitioners can put together a more complete system for leaders, where the candidates are fewer and the stakes higher, than for lower-level positions, where the volume of candidates is high and the stakes lower.

Is Combining Selection Techniques Worthwhile?

Combining selection techniques is considered worthwhile if it can reduce the adverse impact associated with a single method. Multiple tools are also valuable if they raise the level of accuracy over one tool alone.

REDUCING ADVERSE IMPACT. The strong adverse impact of cognitive tests has led practitioners toward using them with personality tests, hoping to enhance the overall proportion of acceptable minority candidates. Generally this has not worked as well as hoped.[69] Combinations that include cognitive ability almost never meet the four-fifths standard for selection rates described earlier.[70]

Even noncognitive composites—groups of tests that emphasize personality traits, values, attitudes, or other human characteristics that don't depend on intellectual ability—can show adverse impact, especially if the selection ratio (proportion of candidates selected) is low (50 percent or fewer are chosen). A better approach to reducing adverse impact might be to vary forms of administration. Video-based tests can remove unnecessary variance due to reading comprehension.[71] For example, a video-based situational judgment test showed less adverse impact than a written version.[72]

INCREMENTAL VALIDITY. Even if adverse impact is not substantially reduced, it is clear that leadership requires more than *g*. Whereas cognitive ability affects thinking and knowledge, personality factors relate to interpersonal behavior and communication.[73] Using both methods together should produce incremental validity, or a stronger relationship with leader performance than using one method alone.

Cognitive and personality measures are fairly distinct, but if two selection methods are highly correlated, there is no advantage to adding the second. Where the lines between methods are murky, incremental validity research can be useful. For example, there is some evidence that personality inventories add incremental validity to assessment centers in the prediction of performance.[74] On the other hand, biodata can be oriented toward personality or *g* factors and may not add value beyond what is measured elsewhere. More complete studies of incremental validity are needed to sort out the relative contribution of different measures in order to construct a powerful yet efficient selection system.

The correlation of cognitive ability with employment interview evaluations (.40 in a meta-analysis) suggested that the interview might not add much to a selection system in which *g* was being measured by a test.[75] However, the correlation was less pronounced for high-complexity jobs, such as manager, perhaps because of a narrower range of test scores or better impression management skills. The correlation between cognitive ability and interview ratings was also smaller with more interview structure, perhaps because structured interviews are better at assessing other constructs that also relate to job performance.

Techniques for Combining Selection Methods

There are several common techniques for combining information from various selection methods into a decision about a candidate.

MECHANICAL OR JUDGMENTAL COMBINATION. Although previous research showed that statistical formulas were better for combining scores on various measures than clinical judgment,[76] these "mechanical" methods are seldom used in practice. One problem is the need to regularly cross-validate weighted formulas. Most often, practitioners take measures that are scored both clinically and statistically and combine them judgmentally.[77] This holistic method is based on the premise that the whole is greater than sum of the parts, that human judgment can discern patterns of behavior that should influence final decisions.

MULTIPLE HURDLES. Multiple hurdles are common in practice but receive little research attention. The idea behind multiple hurdles is to first screen out candidates with more efficient tools. In other words, use an inexpensive inventory to wash out those clearly unsuited to the position and reduce the number of candidates eligible for more expensive, labor-intensive methods, such as interviews or assessment centers. Figure 1.3 gives an example of what a selection funnel with multiple hurdles might look like.

After the important criteria have been established, a computer can screen candidates for relevant background and experience with a scorable biodata instrument. Tests and inventories can yield more information about fit to the position. Some or all of these results might be revealed to the candidate (for example, motivational fit results) to permit both a realistic preview of the job and self-selection. Remaining candidates can be put through simulations of the target job, and those that survive this process can be interviewed by hiring managers. An on-boarding process, including development plans, is launched as the candidate is hired.

An important consideration with multiple hurdles is where to set cutoff scores at each stage. A high bar might leave too few candidates. Moreover, quality candidates might be lost if a less valid predictor is used as an initial hurdle. A hurdle too low won't offer much gain in efficiency.

Another issue is the utility of later tools. To the extent that initial and later tools are correlated, there may be a restriction of range in

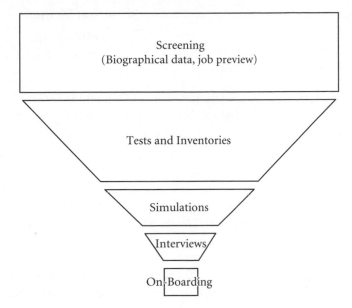

Figure 1.3.   Multiple Hurdles.

the later methods that constrains their validity. Another concern is that information from an earlier screen might not be brought forward and integrated into the final evaluation of the candidate.

INDIVIDUAL ASSESSMENT. In individual assessment, one evaluator, usually a clinical psychologist, interprets results of an array of selection tools and makes a recommendation about a candidate's suitability. The method is frequently used for higher management, often in connection with succession planning.

Common selection tools include personal history information, ability tests, personality and interest inventories, and interviews.[78] Direct observations of behavior, as through simulations, are seldom used and have been one source of criticism of the practice.[79] Clinical psychologists are often unfamiliar with simulations and lack access to them. The approach to combining information from different tools is clinical and holistic.

One problem with individual assessment is that there are no standards or training to guide the practice, not even a systematic job analysis. Like simulations, job analysis is part of the standard repertoire of industrial-organizational psychologists but not clinical psychologists. There is little research to support the efficacy of individual assessment, but small samples and other factors make such research difficult.[80]

ASSESSMENT CENTERS. Assessment centers use information from a variety of selection tools to rate competencies and form an overall judgment about leadership potential. Best practices for assessment centers have been documented in the *Guidelines and Ethical Considerations for Assessment Center Operations*.[81] The hallmarks of assessment centers are simulations, which are required for the process to be called an assessment center. Assessment centers require multiple assessors and an integration of data in order to avoid the biases of individual raters.

An assessment center can be a stage in a multiple hurdle. A decision-making committee brings together competency ratings from the assessment center and information from the other hurdles and makes a go/no-go decision. Alternatively, the entire selection system could be implemented as an assessment center. That is, the decision-making body uses information from all selection tools, including the assessment center simulations, and makes final ratings of competencies before deciding whether to accept the candidate. This model positions an assessment center within an assessment center.[82]

Assessment centers originally included all sorts of selection methods, including projective tests, personality inventories, cognitive tests, and so forth.[83] However, when put into operational use with managers as assessors, the more psychological measures were dropped and the method became primarily dependent on simulations. Now that there is a return to professional assessors, personality tests are sometimes brought in to help interpret the behavior observed in the simulations in terms of personal traits.

A great deal of research has demonstrated the criterion-related validity of overall assessment ratings (OAR) with career progress, potential ratings, training, and performance. Estimates of the relationship between assessment center ratings and success in management range from .31 to .43,[84] with an upper bound of .63 under optimal conditions.[85]

Assessment centers share the advantages reviewed about simulations, but as a system have other benefits as well. Particularly when presented as an integrated "Day in the Life" format, assessment centers form a realistic job preview for candidates, which can guide those who are not a good fit to opt out of the process. This is especially important at the first level of leadership, where candidates might not realize what leadership entails. It can also be a revelation to senior-level candidates who don't appreciate the difference between operational and strategic leadership.

Assessment center simulations are fundamentally plastic; that is, they can be designed to represent various organizational challenges. This is problematic for research, as wide variations in exercises make generalization more difficult. The method allows for personal treatment as administrators and role players interact with candidates—an appealing characteristic for aspiring senior managers. Adverse impact is minimal, and most candidates accept assessment centers as job relevant and fair.

MAKING LEADER SELECTION SUCCESSFUL

The next time you are asked to recommend the best system for selecting leaders, you won't go wrong with one or both of the following answers: "It depends," and "It's complicated." The variety of selection techniques, each with its advantages and disadvantages, is complicated enough. Add to that the myriad of circumstances that can influence leader effectiveness—organizational and company cultures, management level, purposes of selection, nature of candidate pools, market and competitive conditions of organizations, and so forth—and it's clear that there is no one best system for leader selection. Practitioners need to be well informed and strategic to develop the best system for their organization's particular circumstances.

Best Practices and Common Practices

Despite the accumulation of solid research support for the accuracy of various selection tools, it is dismaying to find that organizations still prefer unstructured interviews.[86] Even larger and more sophisticated organizations often fail to capitalize on the best techniques available. This suggests that the benefits of sound selection methods—and potential pitfalls of using poor ones—have not been adequately communicated. In Development Dimensions International's selection forecast, 40 percent or more of HR professionals never used testing or assessment methods.[87] A survey of British organizations showed similar a similar pattern: between 30 percent and 41 percent never used tests or assessment. However, French organizations were considerably less scientific than the British, shunning cognitive tests, biodata, and assessment centers for more intuitive and interpretative approaches like graphology and personality measures.[88]

Various psychologist researchers have lamented the gap between research and practice in personnel selection. Cropanzano pointed to the "justice dilemma," whereby practices that raise validity lower perceptions of fairness, while practices that raise perceptions of fairness may lower validity.[89] Employers are sensitive to the acceptability of selection instruments and thus gravitate away from cognitive tests and toward unstructured interviews. Anderson and colleagues argued that professionals should aim for methods with both high practical relevance (useful to organizations) and high methodological rigor (well grounded in research), an ideal they call "Pragmatic Science." In reality, there is much work in the academic literature that is rigorous but not very useful (Pedantic Science) and too many methods that organizations use that are not grounded in rigorous research (Popularist Science).[90]

Automation and Web delivery have inadvertently aided Popularist Science. Though enabling rich enhancements to selection systems, the Web has also provided access to a seemingly endless supply of poorly developed selection devices. The Internet is flooded with snake oil. Personality inventories are particularly vulnerable to homemade nonsense. Never has it been more important for organizations to look for well-designed and researched tools from reputable practitioners.

Clearly there is much room for improvement in hiring practices. But there are signs of progress. Between 1984 and 1989, British organizations tripled or more the usage (in at least half of their selection processes) of cognitive tests, personality inventories, biodata, and assessment centers.[91] Between 1999 and 2004, across an international sample, there was an increase of 40 percent or more in the proportion sometimes or extensively using integrity tests, computer-assisted interviews, and biodata.[92] Another positive sign is the growing use of assessment centers for succession planning and their emergence for CEO selection.

Realizing Selection System Objectives

Fulfilling the promise of best practices in leader selection must go beyond popularizing more valid selection tools in organizations. Attention must be paid to meeting *all* the criteria for selection systems laid out at the beginning of this chapter. As Cropanzano suggested, there are "win-win" integrative solutions, such as work samples and assessment centers, that are both seen as fair and have high validity.[93]

Where feasible, connections should be made between sound selection practices and important organizational outcomes like profits or turnover.[94] But there is need for caution in how these are presented. Utility formulas can estimate dollar returns from hiring better leaders, but when these are delivered as a "hard sell," they can actually decrease management's intentions to use a selection system.[95]

Even a well-constructed selection system can still fail to accomplish its objectives unless attention is paid to how it is introduced to and embedded within the organization. To realize the selection system's objectives, practitioners should attend to five components of execution.[96]

1. *Communication.* Make a business case for investing in a selection system that will meet your criteria. The organization must be willing to commit the necessary resources, from time and money to manpower, including the attention of senior leaders.

2. *Accountability.* Complex selection systems require the commitment of many people across the organization. A senior executive should champion the initiative and hold others accountable for performing the roles that will lead to its successful execution.

3. *Skill Development.* Stakeholders using new tools and interviewing methods must be equipped with the knowledge and skills to use them. And leaders must have the skills to manage the operational changes that the new system will bring.

4. *Alignment.* The new selection system can't realize its potential if other organizational systems dilute or undermine what it needs to be successful. It is particularly important to align selection with related systems and processes like performance management, leader development, succession management, and retention initiatives.

5. *Measurement.* To demonstrate the effectiveness of the system, it's important to measure what's happening. Measures pertaining to both individual performance and the nature of the selection system should be collected at the time of selection (lead measures) and after enough passage of time that the outcome of selection can become evident (lag measures).

EXECUTIVE SUMMARY

Selection of leaders is too important to leave to serendipity or chance. Ineffective leaders, particularly at the top, can be extremely costly to an organization, and unfortunately leaders fail all too often. Getting leader selection right can not only be a boon to organizational performance, but also give people an opportunity to excel in work they enjoy. The following six steps will help your organization realize the advantages of a leader selection system.

1. *Clarify your purpose.* Is the goal of your selection system external hiring, promotion, career development, succession planning, or some combination? What levels of leadership are you trying to fill? Your overarching purpose should guide expectations for your selection system and how they can best be met.

2. *Set selection system criteria.* Some of the criteria by which to judge the success of your selection system should focus on the outputs of the system. Most important will be the individual performance of selected candidates in their new positions. While organizational performance should also be affected, this is a less-than-perfect criterion because an individual leader controls only some of the factors that go into organizational effectiveness. Another important system output might be information that a leader can use to continue to grow and develop.

Other selection system criteria concern the nature of the system itself. These include (a) legal defensibility: if the selection system selects out a disproportionate number of members of protected groups (as cognitive tests do), you must be able to justify the practice; (b) candidate acceptance: if candidates don't believe their true skills and ability are being evaluated fairly (as often happens with graphology), their negative feelings might generalize to the organization; and (c) efficiency: if it takes too long to fill vacancies, particularly with external candidates, organizations won't look favorably on the selection system.

3. *Define leader success.* The characteristics of effective leaders must be defined in advance. Typically, these are competencies related to different aspects of interpersonal skills, leadership, and business management with additional attention to motivation. The particular configuration of competencies a leader needs depends on the key business challenges the leader must confront, the criteria management level of the position, and the culture in which the leader is embedded.

4. *Choose selection techniques.* A single selection technique is unlikely to accomplish all of your goals or provide all the information you want, so be prepared to include multiple methods in your system. There will be many valid selection techniques at your disposal, each of which will have advantages and drawbacks that need to be balanced.

Selection methods vary along a continuum from signs to samples of behavior. At the "signs" end of the continuum are tools like cognitive tests and personality inventories from which one can make *inferences about behavior* in leadership situations. These measures most easily meet the efficiency criterion, but they often lack candidate acceptance and have limited usefulness for guiding development. While cognitive tests are especially strong in terms of predicting individual performance, they incur the most adverse impact among selection measures.

A second type of selection method draws out *descriptions of behavior,* knowledge, and experience. These methods include biographical data, career achievement records, and interviews. Structure improves the validity of these methods for predicting job performance. While they can provide important information about work experience, the extent to which these methods are independent measures of key leadership constructs is still unclear.

The third category of selection methods, on the "samples" end of the continuum, represents *demonstrations of behavior.* These methods include diverse work samples and simulations, most often used in assessment centers, whose predictive validity is well established. Simulations have the added advantages of being able to address future jobs, provide information on trainable behaviors that are useful for developmental feedback, and engender positive reactions from candidates. However, simulations are labor intensive and inappropriate for competencies that roll out over extended periods of time, such as networking.

5. *Combine tools into a selection system.* The next step is deciding how to put your preferred individual techniques into a selection

system. How comprehensive you need to be will depend on the volume of candidates you expect, the potential impact of the leader on your organization's effectiveness, and available resources, including the time to fill positions, budget, and executives' and hiring managers' time and commitment. However, comprehensiveness needs to be weighed against incremental validity and usefulness. More tools are not necessarily better if you can forecast leader performance just as well with a smaller set.

Selection system efficiency can be enhanced with multiple hurdles. In other words, use efficient, computer-scored tools to eliminate lower-end candidates and reserve labor-intensive, expensive methods like interviews and assessment centers to differentiate among a smaller pool of more promising candidates.

6. *Execute your plan.* Last but not least, consider how you will introduce the system into your organization and assure its continued success. Important activities include communicating the business case for the system, assigning accountability for its execution, developing the skills of those who will carry it out, aligning other systems, and measuring the lead and lag indicators that will tell you if the system is meeting its objectives.

In case this all looks too complicated or tiresome, remember that effective leader selection can mean millions of dollars for your organization. Selection system failure has the same financial implications; they just go in the opposite direction.

Selection matters. Leader selection matters much more.

CHAPTER TWO

Best Practices In Leadership Assessment

Manuel London
James W. Smither
Thomas Diamante

In this chapter, we examine best practices in leadership assessment, with a focus on chief executive officers (CEOs) and senior executives. These executives include heads of multinational corporations, business units, or large divisions in business, government, or not-for-profit organizations; entrepreneurs who started and grew their own businesses; and executives of large or medium-sized organizations who were promoted from within or hired from outside. Our goal is to understand methods for assessing executives' performance and potential to perform well at a more senior level of an organization.

Executive turnover poses major challenges for corporations. During the first 10 months of 2004, 516 major companies changed CEOs.[1] In the airline industry alone, all seven of the major airlines in the United States changed CEOs since September 11, 2001.[2] Surveys of management performance often find that as many as half or more leaders are not performing up to par in critical areas.[3]

As a prelude, we emphasize that leadership assessment entails measuring process and outcomes. That is, measurements should capture not only the results of a leader's behavior and decisions but also how the leader accomplished those outcomes. Also, leadership assessment itself is a process. It can be used to track performance improvement and ongoing development. It is part of an ongoing, cyclical process of organizational needs assessment, goal setting, development, appraisal, feedback, further development, and tracking change. Responsibility for assessment is led or directed by top executives, guided by human resource executives, and administered by managers and leaders throughout the organization.

To organize our review of best practices in leadership assessment, we follow a framework that addresses (1) the purpose of the assessment (for instance, whether to measure past performance, determine readiness for promotion, predict performance for selection or placement, and/or use the data for development); (2) what is assessed (competencies for today and the future); (3) challenges relative to context (pressures faced by the executive; degree of current or anticipated change in responsibilities or expectations); (4) assessment methods that focus on what was accomplished (outcomes) and how (process); and (5) assessing assessments—determining their accuracy, validity, and financial value so that assessment results are not misused and organizations have reasonable expectations of their ability to predict leadership behavior. Figure 2.1 outlines the topics we cover.

USES FOR LEADERSHIP ASSESSMENT

There are three basic purposes for leadership assessment: (1) prediction, (2) performance review, and (3) development. Regarding prediction, assessment may be used to select executives from within or outside the organization, place executives in key positions, determine whom to promote, or determine whom to lay off. Outsiders, such as venture capitalists, may assess members of the executive team of a company to help potential investors determine whether the firm is a sound investment. Assessment may also be used to make administrative decisions, such as how much bonus pay a person deserves. Assessment may evaluate readiness to advance, such as determining the individual's ability to function effectively in different situations and handle challenges. As such, assessments may evaluate potential and leadership emergence.

Regarding performance review, the dimensions of performance that are used for assessment send a message to the individuals assessed about what is important in the organization—what gets measured and

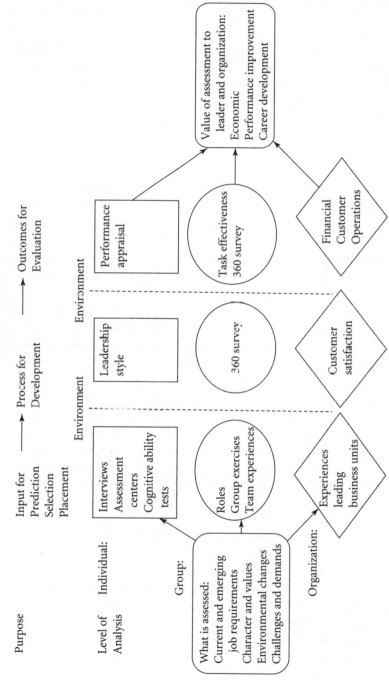

Figure 2.1. Leadership Assessment Model.

rewarded. Goal setting and assessments can be a way to align organizational, team, and individual goals in the form of competency models and balanced scorecards.

Another use of assessment as appraisal is to enhance performance. That is, the goal is to achieve organizational excellence through performance management, which includes appraisal and feedback. In addition, assessment is a vehicle for holding executives accountable to different stakeholders (executives in the parent company, the company's board and stockholders), each of whom may have different criteria and expectations for performance.

Regarding development, assessment provides executives with feedback that points out strengths and areas for improvement. Executives often have a blind spot when it comes to recognizing their own performance. Higher-level executives tend to have an inflated view of their emotional intelligence and less congruence with how coworkers view them.[4] While high performers tend to match the perceptions and ratings of others, leaders often do not receive the feedback they need to understand how they are perceived by others. Upward feedback from subordinates is limited, since employees may see risks to their careers if they share feedback about problematic behavior of their superiors. At the executive level, many of one's peers are in reality competitors, and therefore there is little incentive to share feedback that might improve a competitor's effectiveness. So executives are likely to inflate their self-evaluations, and raters provide middle-of-the-road ratings. Research and practice needs to address how to incorporate performance feedback as a routine part of daily practice, rather than a once-a-year main event with potentially threatening consequences.

WHAT IS MEASURED

There are three basic steps to developing an assessment:

1. Gain a solid understanding of the job requirements (the actual position) and the needs of the organization. This can be accomplished through interviews with key staff, including those who are in similar positions, or using any of the well-established approaches to job analysis.[5]
2. Relate these requirements to personal characteristics (elements of character, values, motivation, or personality) or behaviors

(for example, strategic vision, charisma, stress resilience, coalition building, communication, people development).

3. Develop methods for measuring these qualities. Developing a *competency model* entails identifying, defining, and measuring characteristics that are associated with successful job performance.[6] Competency models have the advantage of clarifying what skills and abilities are important in the organization. However, they have some disadvantages. They may emphasize some characteristics and give short shrift to others (that is, not including them in assessments and appraisals) because they are not part of the company's model. Competency models may not reflect the wide range of individual difference variables that may be important to leadership success. In addition, the competencies need to be revised periodically, since they reflect the competencies that are valued today, and other competencies may be needed in the future.

Next we describe specific leadership dimensions for assessment. We examine leadership potential, character, values, and motivation.

Leadership Potential and Emergence

A range of characteristics may be relevant to a given executive position. Sometimes the demands of the position are not known or are likely to change, and the challenge of assessment is to identify potential. In this case, potential is "the ability to take advantage of developmental experiences that will be offered."[7] Assessment for prediction of potential, however, cannot rely solely on measurements of past behaviors and experiences. The skills of an executive are developed over time, and as such, "end state" characteristics may not be present early in a manager's career and would be hard to observe and use to predict later success.[8]

The ability to learn from experience may be seen by assessing such characteristics as curiosity about how people and things work, sense of adventure, hardiness (not threatened by criticism), bias toward action, accepting responsibility for learning and change, respecting differences, seeking and using feedback, and consistent growth. Leadership emergence is especially difficult to predict. Research has identified signs of leadership potential and emergence. For instance, elected group leaders speak more than other members and rate themselves higher on extraversion, and more skilled communicators are perceived by group members as more effective leaders.[9] Individuals evaluated more highly in selection interviews tend to be more nonverbally expressive and possess impression management skills.[10]

Leadership Character and Values

Assessments for selection determine whether specific candidates for executive positions will be a good fit with the organization, have consistent work performance over time, and demonstrate sound judgment when threatened or tempted or when doing the right thing may not be in their best interest.[11] Having superior knowledge, technical abilities, and skills does not mean that executives will live up to their promise. Character may be an important predictor of future success. Dimensions of character include self-determination, acceptance of responsibility, cooperativeness, self-transcendence (respect, caring, good citizenship—the polar opposite of self-interest), and good judgment (analysis, reflection, and enactment).[12] Values include characteristics such as loyalty, duty, respect, selfless service, honesty, integrity, personal courage.[13] The most important personal characteristics organizations seek are honesty, integrity, conscientiousness, interest in the job, and the "right general personality."[14] Employers perceive the interview as the best way to assess these attributes, although there is a growing use of personality tests, measures of "emotional intelligence," and "honesty and integrity" testing.[15]

Character may be assessed by modifying the standard executive assessment method of psychological inventories, interview protocols, and simulation activities.[16] Simulations are likely to be a useful method for assessing executive character. While well-crafted simulations and role playing can reflect the intensity of real-life pressures, behavioral indicators of an individual's capacity to contain disruptive emotions are harder to come by. This is because nonverbal, contextual, and historical factors must be taken into account to recognize the ability to manage emotions and apply good reasoning while solving tough problems. Clearly, these are areas for the development and research of new simulations and measures. Character is one aspect of personality and does not replace the need for broader personality assessment in the executive selection process. Rather, it complements and broadens individual assessment methods.[17] We discuss methods of assessment in more detail next.

Leadership Motivation

Another key characteristic for executive assessment is motivation to lead. Leadership motivation may be a function of the desire to achieve such extrinsic outcomes as wealth, status, and power as well as influence others to accomplish larger goals, such as the development and marketing of a product or helping others. The leader motive pattern (LMP) is high need for power, lower than average need for affiliation, and a moderate degree of activity inhibition—using power only for social or organization goals, not for personal needs. This pattern has been shown to be related to managerial advancement ($r = .33$).[18]

Another aspect of leadership motivation is entrepreneurship. Entrepreneurial leaders have ambition to start a new organization. They place emphasis on business growth, culture development, establishing credibility, and concern with the survival of the organization.[19] Having long-term goals and being high in self-efficacy have been found to be positively related to venture growth, such as sales revenue and employees, and these factors mediate the effects of passion, tenacity, and new resource skill on subsequent growth.[20]

To conclude this section on what is measured, overall, measures for leadership assessment stem from the process of studying the job itself (behaviors and outcomes expected), linking these job characteristics to individual characteristics and behaviors necessary to carry them out, and then developing measures of the individual characteristics and past behaviors. Competency models specify the abilities leaders need to be successful in the particular organization. To the extent that future-oriented competencies can be predicted now, they can be used to assess an individual's leadership potential. Assessments of leadership potential can be used to identify people who should be in a development program that will prepare them for more responsible leadership positions.

CONTEXTUAL CHALLENGES FOR LEADERSHIP ASSESSMENT

As suggested previously, leadership assessment forces the organization to determine the dimensions of leadership that are important in the particular organizational context. Moreover, for assessment to be useful, it needs to recognize the changing nature of executive work (for example, the growing importance of knowledge management, the need for innovation and adaptation to technology, and stakeholders' high expectations). Information about changes in competency requirements comes from leaders of the organization and industry who understand the context for leadership and what's happening in the organization.

In general, the context presents requirements and challenges that need to be reflected in behaviors and characteristics for leadership assessment. Contextual factors may deal with market or economic forces driving the business, suggesting the need for leaders to have extensive financial knowledge and ability. Technological factors may be critical, which requires leaders who understand technology, not necessarily in the depth that an engineer would, but conceptually, in being able to comprehend and envision capabilities and how technologies tie together and generate market potential. Organizational and national culture and values will affect characteristics to be assessed—for instance, whether the organization has a long-term perspective that puts a premium on sustainability or a short-term profit motive. Selecting executives for international assignment requires assessing executives' cultural awareness, cultural sensitivity, and ability to adapt to foreign situations.

Context influences leadership assessment by creating requirements and expectations for leadership characteristics and behaviors. Context needs to be incorporated in assessment methods, whether they are simulations, interviews, or performance reviews. For example, a business game used in an assessment can be designed to mirror the nature of the industry. A performance review that asks for ratings on what a leader could be expected to do can ask about expected behaviors under conditions and situations that are important to the company (for instance, developing new uses for existing products). Context also needs to be incorporated into uses for assessment data, for example, using assessment of general leadership characteristics to advise an individual about career prospects in a specific company or industry. For instance, information about an individual's skills in organizing and planning can be compared to what type of organization and planning is needed in the current organization—maintain daily transactions or effect major transformations. Assessment that ignores context is likely to be irrelevant or of little use to making decisions or guiding individuals.

ASSESSMENT METHODS

Measures and methods for leadership assessment include assessment for predicting leadership ability (that is, for selection, placement, and venture capital investment decisions), assessment for performance appraisal and review, including financial measures and balanced scorecards, and assessment for executive development. A review of all existing instruments and measurement techniques is beyond the scope of this chapter. Here we describe examples of frequently used measures that fit contemporary organizational needs.

Assessment for Executive Selection, Placement, and Investment Decisions

A variety of assessment approaches are used, often in combination, for selecting executives. Psychologists are often called on by companies to conduct individual assessments of candidates. Such individual assessments are used for executive selection, promotion, development, and career counseling. The psychologist examines the job requirements and compiles a series of assessment methods that address the extent to which the candidates have the characteristics needed to meet expectations. However, the method suffers from a lack of reliability (agreement) among independent clinical assessments.[21]

INTERVIEWS. The interview is the most commonly used method for executive assessment.[22] A structured interview process that asks the same core questions of all candidates will have higher validity than unstructured approaches. Structured interviews tend to have higher validity than unstructured interviews because structured interviews focus more on constructs that have a stronger relationship with job performance, such as applied mental skills (problem solving, judgment, decision making, critical thinking, planning, organizing) and social skills (for example, ability to function effectively in social situations).[23] Informal interviews will be more susceptible to legal challenges than structured approaches if only because two candidates may experience different interviews for the same position.[24] Structured interviews may ask about experiences and/or about what the candidate would do in different hypothetical situations.

ASSESSMENT CENTERS. Assessment center ratings can be used to identify people with senior management potential. An assessment center combines a number of exercises that might ask the assessed to write memos, prepare and give a presentation, or prioritize tasks and make decisions. Trained observers evaluate participants' behaviors and products. While costly in time and money, they are popular tools due to their strong record of criterion-related validity, long-term predictive validity, and face validity. In other words, they tend to be related to actual job performance, predict future performance, and appear to be realistic to those assessed. However, their construct validity, that is, the extent to which they measure different elements of performance, has been called into question because ratings tend to be influenced more by specific exercises than by underlying performance dimensions. Guidelines for developing assessment centers provide ways to enhance their content, construct, and predictive validity.[25] These include adequate training to be sure that the assessors (observers and raters) understand differences in the elements of performance and how the same element of performance can be reflected in different situations (that is, exercises).

COGNITIVE ABILITY TESTS. Cognitive tests measure the capacity to learn new skills. The Wechsler Adult Intelligence Scale and Watson-Glaser Critical Thinking Appraisal are frequently used tests. General mental ability measured by cognitive assessment is often the best single predictor of job performance across a range of leadership positions, with predictive validity higher on jobs of increasing job complexity.[27] However, cognitive ability does not always predict performance better than other measures, and it raises the potential for adverse impact against ethnic minority groups.[28] Therefore, cognitive ability tests should be used as a component of a larger assessment battery, not a standalone assessment method.

PERSONALITY INVENTORIES. Measures of personality assess attitudes, motivation, and psychological character. *Projective tests* present ambiguous stimuli, such as pictures of people interacting, and then ask assessees to describe what is happening, under the assumption that personality structure affects how people perceive, organize, and interpret their experiences. Projective techniques, such as the Miner Sentence Completion Scale, have strong track records of validly predicting managerial and entrepreneurial motivation.[29] Assessees are asked to complete sentences such as "My primary goal is. . . ." The items are scored as positive, neutral, or negative based on guidelines and examples provided in the scoring guide. Different forms of the instrument measure different dimensions, such as professional commitment, acquiring knowledge, achievement motivation, attitude toward supervisors, and planning for the future.

Objective personality measures ask assessees questions about their preferences, attitudes, or values. Measures of the "Big 5" personality constructs assess conscientiousness, extraversion, agreeableness, emotional stability, and openness. All Big 5 personality dimensions have been found to be useful in predicting a range of specific performance criteria.[30] Conscientiousness, in particular, has been found to be valid for many jobs.[31] The validity of personality is generally modest, although it is larger when personality scales are selected based on a job analysis.

Assessing Leader Performance with Financial Measures

Financial performance and other objective indicators, such as sales and units produced at the organization and business unit level, are indirect measures of executives' performance. Popular techniques recognize the multidimensional nature of executive performance and the importance of linking individual performance goals and measures to organization and business unit objectives—that is, alignment.

Financial metrics have historically played a very large role in assessing the performance of senior leaders. The role of financial measures in assessing leader performance is heightened because such measures are often closely linked to leader compensation. Although financial metrics have the appeal of appearing, at first glance, to be objective (at least when compared to assessing leader behaviors and competencies), a number of intractable dilemmas arise when using financial metrics to assess leader performance. Here we explore the issue of which financial measures might serve as appropriate indicators of leader performance.

Ideally, it would be desirable to identify measures that reflect the leader's contribution and that make adjustments for factors that are beyond the leader's control. Unfortunately, there is no single measure that accomplishes this goal. Several questions arise. One is whether measures should focus on individual or team (for example, corporate) performance. A second question concerns the relative emphasis on current or short-term performance versus longer-term measures. A third issue is the challenge of identifying a short-term financial measure that reflects the interests of shareholders and is aligned with long-term shareholder value. The core problem is that performance measures need to be selected so that when leaders pursue those measures, the firm's objectives are advanced. What goes unmeasured will likely be ignored by senior leaders.

INDIVIDUAL OR TEAM PERFORMANCE? One measure of individual performance is the leader's performance against a budget, profit plan, or other agreed-upon goals. But budgets, profit plans, and goals can be distorted when created by senior leaders (for example, in an attempt to make it easier to achieve the plan's goals). At first glance, financial measures at the business unit or division level would seem to be useful measures of a senior leader's performance. But focusing on business unit or division measures can create several problems. First, financial measures at the business unit level are of little use when several business units are highly interrelated (for example, thereby raising questions about how to allocate joint revenues and joint costs). Second, as Alfred Sloan noted more than 80 years ago at General Motors, leaders are too often inclined to focus narrowly on the performance (for example, profitability) of their own business unit or division and ignore how their efforts affect the performance of the firm as a whole. This question is especially important when tying compensation to leader performance. But linking rewards to team (for example, corporate) performance often creates a "line of sight" problem; leaders often fail to see a direct link between their behavior and corporate performance, and this lowers the motivational effect of team (corporate) rewards. In addition, leaders are often concerned with the possibility of social loafing or the "free rider" problem, when someone is rewarded because the leadership team as a whole performed well despite the poor performance of the individual. In sum, assessment of leader performance usually requires a mix of measures—some that assess individual performance and some that reflect team or corporate performance. Business unit or division performance measures are most appropriate in very decentralized firms where there is little interaction among business units or divisions. Corporate performance measures appear to be more appropriate in vertically integrated firms, where success depends on a high level of coordination among divisions.[32]

SHORT-TERM OR LONG-TERM PERFORMANCE? The management and popular business literature is filled with examples of leaders who have sacrificed a firm's long-term value to maximize short-term profits (and thereby receive a bonus linked to short-term financial metrics). Stock options are often suggested as a solution to this dilemma because they are thought to align the interest of shareholders (the principals) with those of senior leaders (the agents). That is, stock price presumably reflects the extent to which investors value leaders' actions. To the extent that stock markets assess the future consequences of leaders' current actions, the firm's stock price is a useful indicator of leader performance. However, stock prices are affected by many factors other than leader performance (for example, business conditions that affect an industry as a whole, a "bull" or "bear" market). One way to address this issue is to develop indices by which the performance of senior leaders is measured relative to the performance of comparable organizations in the same industry (thereby eliminating the effect of general market movements). Also, it appears that stock options sometimes influence leaders to avoid risky investments and decisions, whereas an ideal mix or set of performance measures will influence leaders (agents) to have the same risk preferences as owners or shareholders (principals).[33]

Short-term measures can be used to supplement stock price. Examples include earnings per share, pre-tax income, sales and backlog, or return on shareholders' investment (equity). Short-term measures are often more directly affected by leaders' actions than stock price. However, there is an imperfect association between accounting income and the long-term economic wealth of the firm. Moreover, senior leaders can take actions that increase reported income in the short-term but that decrease the firm's long-term value (for example, failing to make investments in research and development (R&D), employee development, and maintenance that might increase the firm's long-term value at the expense of short-term earnings; selling off assets whose market value is far in excess of book value).[34] In sum, the problem with accounting measures is the opposite of the problem with stock; accounting measures may be too easily affected (or manipulated) by the actions of senior leaders. One possible solution is for the corporate board (or its compensation committee), when assessing leader performance, to define earnings to exclude expenditures on long-term intangibles (such as R&D, employee development, and so on), thereby encouraging leaders to invest in such areas. But such practices are uncommon, perhaps because boards are not comfortable rewarding leaders based on one income figure while reporting a different figure to shareholders and creditors.

An alternative to focusing only on short-term accounting measures of performance is to assess leader performance by examining trends in accounting measures over several years (for example, growth in earnings per share (EPS) over a 3- to 5-year period). For example, firms sometimes award company stock to leaders who achieve a specified target in growth of EPS over a 5-year period.[35] Leader performance can also be assessed by examining the business unit's operating results over a 3- to 5-year period. But when longer-term measures of a business unit's performance are linked to leaders' compensation, it can make it difficult to rotate leaders across business units.

In sum, when assessing leader performance using financial measures, it is generally advisable to include appropriate measures of current or short-term performance as well as measures that reflect long-term value. The most desirable measures are those that can be influenced by effective leadership actions and, at the same time, are not too easily manipulated by leaders willing to sacrifice long-term value for short-term profits (or by mere accounting manipulations).

Assessing Leader Performance with a Balanced Scorecard

An important trend in assessing leader performance is the increasing use of balanced scorecards. The balanced scorecard is based on the premise that focusing *only* on financial measures in performance management is insufficient because such measures are lag indicators (that is, they describe merely the outcomes of leaders' past actions) and, as noted previously, can promote behavior that sacrifices long-term value for short-term performance.[36] Previous performance measurement systems that included nonfinancial measures generally used ad hoc collections of such measures rather than a comprehensive system of linked measurements. In contrast, the balanced scorecard selects a small number of measures that are directly linked to the firm's strategy. In developing a balanced scorecard, firms must articulate a vision and ask, If the vision succeeds, how will we be different to our shareholders and customers and with respect to internal business processes and innovation and learning?

Balanced scorecards are also based on the premise that firms with different strategies require different measures. For example, senior investment bankers in a firm such as Goldman Sachs are valuable because of their knowledge about complex financial products and their ability to develop trust with sophisticated customers. But people with the same knowledge, experience, and capabilities would be of little value to a financial services company that emphasizes operational efficiency, low cost, and technology-based trading. That is, the value of an intangible asset depends on the firm's strategy.

The mere use of financial and nonfinancial measures does not constitute a balanced scorecard. Instead, effective balanced scorecards are closely linked to the organization's strategy so that people can understand the strategy by looking only at the scorecard and its strategy map. Balanced scorecards select a limited number of critical measures within each of four perspectives (financial, customer, internal processes, learning and innovation). Across all four perspectives there are usually only fifteen to twenty measures. Examples of financial measures include economic value added, return on capital employed, operating profit, cash flow, return on assets, project profitability, sales backlog, return on equity, and earnings per share. Examples of customer measures include customer retention, customer satisfaction (for example, from surveys), on-time delivery, share of key accounts' purchases, market share, brand image, and the firm's share in the most profitable segments. Examples of measures of internal business processes include quality, speed to market, rework, safety indices, complaint resolution time, cycle time, yield, and unit cost. Examples of learning and innovation measures include employee skill development, rate of improvement in key operational measures, number and quality of employee suggestions, development time for the next generation of products, percentage of sales from new products, employee turnover, and employee satisfaction (from surveys). The balanced scorecard communicates priorities to managers, employees, investors, and customers. It also helps facilitate change by forcing leaders to reach consensus on high-priority areas, increasing market orientation, creating a shared understanding throughout the firm concerning goals and what it takes to achieve them, linking compensation of senior leaders to the scorecard, and focusing improvement efforts in local units on key measures.

In general, several characteristics should be considered when selecting performance measures. Specifically, performance measures should be aligned with strategy, objective (for example, independently measured and verified), complete (capturing all relevant aspects of performance), responsive (leaders need to believe they can influence the measure), and linked to creating long-term value.[37] Also, the number of measures should be limited so that leaders can focus on a small number of variables that are critical to success. A properly implemented balanced scorecard satisfies these criteria.

Assessment for Executive Development

DEVELOPMENTAL ASSESSMENT CENTERS. Developmental assessment centers are similar in content and process to the assessment centers described earlier that have long been used for selection. Executive leadership requires a full spectrum of competencies needed in a constantly changing and increasingly competitive marketplace. Assessment exercises may represent a wide range of strategic, organizational, and interpersonal challenges. Behavior on these exercises coupled with results of the various tests may be used to predict versatility competencies, such as visionary thinking, shaping strategy, empowering others, influencing and negotiating, fostering open dialogue, and cross-functional capability measured by coworker ratings.[38]

MEASURES OF LEADERSHIP STYLE. There are a variety of measures of different approaches to leadership style and behavior. Often these are used in research on leadership, but they may also be used to assess the character and quality of leadership in an organization, give feedback to executives, and identify developmental needs. For instance, the Leader Behavior Description Questionnaire assesses leaders on dimensions of task and relationship orientation (initiating structure and showing consideration, respectively).[39] The Multifactor Leadership Questionnaire measures five factors: two facets of transactional leadership (Contingent Reward and Management-by-Exception) and three facets of transformational leadership (Charismatic Leadership, Individualized Consideration, and Intellectual Stimulation).[40]

MULTISOURCE (360-DEGREE) FEEDBACK. Multisource (also called *360-degree*) feedback surveys collect anonymous performance ratings from supervisors, subordinates, peers, and sometimes customers for comparison to self-ratings.[41] Sometimes data are collected only from subordinates, called *upward feedback*. The survey is often delivered electronically, distributed by e-mail that points the respondent to a

Web site with the survey. Feedback reports usually contain item-by-item results with ratings averaged across respondents within groups, assuring anonymity of respondents by requiring a minimum number of respondents within the group of subordinates, peers, or customers. Recipients can tell, for example, how their subordinates or peers on average rated them on each item. Results may be averaged across items to reflect key performance dimensions and reduce the amount of feedback. Some reports also contain an index of the variation, or disagreement, among raters on the item or dimensions. Normative results—how other managers in the organization were seen by their raters on average—may also be presented to help the recipient interpret the results. Companies may administer the survey on a regular basis, perhaps annually or semi-annually, and provide recipients with data on change in performance ratings. A 360-degree survey may be administered for executives just prior to their attending a leadership development workshop and the results fed back to participants in order to pave the way for other assessment, coaching, and developmental goal setting. Another procedure, taking advantage of electronic media, allows executives to formulate their own survey whenever they want to assess how they are doing. Called *just-in-time feedback,* executives can select from a set of prewritten items or write their own and determine who receives the survey.

The popularity of 360 feedback has led some organizations to implement it haphazardly without adequate development, explanation of its purpose, or involvement of raters and ratees in writing items and formulating the administration and feedback process. Numerous guidelines have been offered about ways to make 360 feedback more effective.[42] Human resource experts argue that multisource feedback should be used for development alone, not for administrative decisions, such as compensation or promotion. However, companies that are not performing well sometimes turn to multisource feedback results to make difficult decisions about people or simply because the organization invested in the data.[43] The problem is that raters are likely to be biased (for instance, inflate their ratings) when they know the results will be used to make decisions about the people they are rating.

Multisource feedback should be viewed as part of a long-term performance management process, not a one-time event. The results should be used to set goals for performance improvement and development, perhaps in consultation with an executive coach or discussions with one's supervisor or other coworkers. Also, changes in behavior and performance should be tracked over time, with change evident in subsequent multisource surveys and other objective and subjective indicators of performance.

ASSESSING DEVELOPMENTAL JOB COMPONENTS. As we stated earlier, assessment for selection requires periodic analysis of performance requirements. The same applies for assessment of executive development. Individual characteristics can be matched to developmental job components. The Developmental Challenge Profile (DCP) is one instrument used to assess the developmental components of managerial jobs.[44] The scale measures job transitions, task-related characteristics (creating change, high level of responsibility, and influencing others without authority), and obstacles faced on the job.

SUMMARY. Assessment for development needs to incorporate job and organization evaluation as well as the measurement of individuals. We need frequent organizational assessment to determine changes in performance dimensions, which in turn will change what is assessed for evaluation and prediction. New methods for measuring individual performance and leadership style will be developed to counter biases and improve rating accuracy. The Internet poses opportunities for online measurement, tracking performance, and delivering assessment instruments to respondents. Information technology also allows customized questionnaires that probe more deeply when key questions raise issues. Executives can form and administer their own multisource feedback surveys when they feel they want others' opinions about their performance. It doesn't have to wait for the company's formal survey that may only happen annually.

ASSESSMENT OF ASSESSMENT

The value of leadership assessment can be viewed in terms of its economic value and issues of whether standards were followed in the development of the assessment method and whether the measurement methods have construct validity.

Economic Value

The financial impact of the assessment process can be evaluated. This is the fiscal return on the dollars expended as an organization's investment in identifying, selecting, and developing leaders. Selection can be evaluated in terms of fit and performance. Measures of success may be intrinsic (career satisfaction, personality fit) or extrinsic (compensation level, rate of promotion, and perceptions of authority). Profits and cash flow are as much as 20 percent higher in companies with strategic HR practices. Assessments that help organizations hire the right executives for their organization, market, and goals will result in an increase in productivity.[45] Hiring a high-performing individual can generate gains of 120 percent in sales positions and 88 times their salaries.[46]

The financial value of assessment can be determined in large and small samples.[47] For large samples, say when a national organization uses an assessment center to hire entry-level managers in offices throughout the country, the payoff in dollars is a function of the product of quantity and quality minus costs. Quantity is the product of the average tenure of the executive in the position and the number of applicants selected. Quality is the product of the average score on the predictor (for instance, an assessment center overall score), the validity of the predictor (determined in a study of the correlation between the assessment center score and a performance measure), and the standard deviation of the performance measure. Cost is the expense of recruiting candidates and administering the assessment center. In small companies hiring few individuals, these key parameters can be estimated. Cumulative data across many studies can be collected to estimate validity. The standard deviation of performance can be estimated as 40 percent of mean salary.[48]

The value of assessment can be demonstrated by presenting evidence of construct validity. For individual executive assessments (for instance, a psychologist hired to evaluate candidates for a single executive position), a qualitative approach is needed to determine utility of the assessment method. Three steps are involved: (1) linking job tasks and individual characteristics, (2) linking individual characteristics to instruments of prediction, and (3) linking instruments of prediction to job tasks.[49] The first step is to generate information about the tasks to be done by the incumbent and the personal characteristics (knowledge, skills, abilities, and other characteristics—KSAOs) required to do these tasks. The idea is to identify the common constructs that underlie the job and the individual. The next step is to link the KSAOs to prediction instruments, such as work samples, attitude and ability tests, and interviews to show that the KSAOs needed are measured. Then individual components of these predictors (for example, test items or structured situations posed during an interview) should be linked to job tasks in order to show that the constructs needed for effective job performance are actually measured by the assessment methods. Several subject matter experts may be asked to do this to ensure reliability of the judgment.

A CASE EXAMPLE

Leadership assessment occurs within the context of specific conditions, requirements, and issues. The following case illustrates how leader assessment center and 360-degree survey feedback are used along with consultation to select and improve an executive's performance.

Melinda was promoted to head the sales department of a large manufacturer of consumer products. She was selected after an intensive search and selection process that included putting candidates through a specially designed assessment center involving case exercises, structured interviews, and personality tests. At the end of Melinda's first month, her sales figures were not impressive. She met individually with the sales directors who reported to her to review their goals, operational plans, and metrics. She inserted some new sales strategies and methods of gaining product visibility. However, the first month turned into the first quarter with negligible improvement in sales. Realizing that her suggestions were not working, Melinda set concrete demands and ever-higher expectations on her management team. Some of the sales directors contacted the CEO to complain. Unaware of the discontent among her staff, Melinda focused on making the numbers. She made progress, too. Not incredible progress, but she gained 2 percentage points in the second quarter. Still, morale in Melinda's unit was suffering. Her sales directors alleged she used intimidation and verbal abuse to drive their performance.

The CEO consulted with the vice president (VP) of human resources, who met with Melinda to review the situation. The VP suggested that they collect some additional information. "Maybe" he said, "it's just a style thing." Melinda acquiesced, and the VP arranged for a 360-degree process. The CEO, her direct reports (the regional sales directors), and her peers (the other VPs) provided ratings. At first glance, the findings seemed conclusive. Melinda thought well of herself, but her subordinates rated her low on many performance dimensions, for instance, low ratings in providing resources, serving as a coach, offering encouragement, listening, being open to new ideas, and setting reasonable goals (ratings were made on 5-point scales, and dimension means from the subordinate ratings ranged between 1.0 and 2.5). On the other hand, the CEO and her peers found her to be a cooperative colleague who understood the changing needs of the business. An executive coach delivered the results. Melinda listened, perused the data, focused on her subordinates' ratings, and with cunning insight concluded,

"So they hate me. Is this supposed to be a revelation?" The coach pressed Melinda for a finer-grained analysis of the data. After several hours of discussion, Melinda recognized that the sales directors viewed her as stronger in diagnosing market conditions, refining strategy, setting goals, and tracking performance and weaker in listening, involving them in decision making, and being open to new ideas. She talked to the coach about why she felt the difficult market conditions meant she had to maintain tight control over sales strategy, and they discussed ways she could be more participative and take advantage of her directors' vast experience and detailed knowledge of their own territories.

Melinda made a concerted effort to change by holding brainstorming and strategy sessions with the sales directors, asking them to set goals and timelines, and then holding meetings to examine their degree of success, determine ways they could improve, and revise their goals. This wasn't always easy for Melinda. She had to force herself to be less controlling and more trusting. Sometimes she caught herself "telling" rather than "asking," but she was more attentive to what she was saying and how others were reacting to her. Also, when she became directive, her sales managers would point this out, and they would laugh about it. Still, Melinda and her sales managers realized there were times when she had to make a decision, and that she was ultimately accountable and it was her prerogative to call the shots even if they disagreed, and this happened occasionally. When it did, the sales managers were more accepting than they were initially because Melinda had taken their views into account.

Melinda's promotion and coaching coincided with the company's implementation of a balanced scorecard to help department heads set and track goals in line with corporate interests. She was able to use this process with her sales managers as a basis for discussion and ongoing evaluation. The process was also a tool for assessing Melinda's and other department heads' success at developing their people, involving them in formulating and implementing strategy at the local level, and seeing how their success contributed to performance metrics at the department, division, and ultimately the corporate level.

This case shows how assessment center results, 360-degree feedback data, coaching, and ongoing monitoring of objective performance were all components of leadership assessment and development. An effort that began with individual assessment was supported by a companywide balanced scorecard process for leadership goal setting and performance evaluation.

EXECUTIVE SUMMARY

We began this chapter by emphasizing that leadership assessment entails measuring process and outcomes and that assessment in itself is a process. Assessment occurs on different levels—organization, team, and individual. Also, it measures multiple dimensions—financial, personal, and interpersonal. Measures alone have little meaning unless they are compared to goals, standards, or norms over time.

Leadership assessment is used for predicting performance (selection and placement), evaluating performance (holding executives accountable and compensating them), and diagnosing performance gaps and setting directions for improvement and career development. The assessment process forces attention to what is measured and raises the question, Is this important? The assessment process and results reflect the culture of the organization and also can be an intervention to alter the organization's culture.

Assessment requires determining important components of job behaviors, performance, and outcomes, linking these to organizational and individual characteristics, and identifying measures of these characteristics. Methods of assessment for selection, placement, and investment decisions include interviews, assessment centers, cognitive tests, and personality inventories. Methods of assessment for appraisal entail measuring multiple dimensions of performance, including indicators of financial conditions, customer interactions and outcomes, internal work processes, and participation in learning and creation of innovations. A balanced scorecard of these measures aligns organization, team, and individual goals with associated performance indicators. Assessment methods for executive development include assessment centers, measures of leadership style, and multisource (360-degree) feedback surveys. Assessment methods themselves should be assessed to determine that they were developed using professional guidelines, have construct validity, and create economic value. The case demonstrated assessment for leader selection, performance improvement, and development.

We conclude with ten recommendations for leadership assessment:

1. Determine the purpose of assessment. Is it selection, performance evaluation, and/or development?

2. Given the purpose, what do you want to measure? Alternatives include measures of current performance, potential for future performance, capabilities, knowledge, motivation, and character (values).

3. Examine how situational conditions determine what elements of leadership are important. Consider how to incorporate context

into the assessments, for instance, observing performance in simulated environments that are similar to actual work settings.

4. Determine organizational goals, current conditions, and anticipated shifts in your organization and environment that influence leadership behaviors to be assessed.

5. Consider how to measure both performance *processes* (how leaders go about doing their jobs) and *outcomes* (results).

6. Determine whether your focus is on the individual, team, and/or organizational level. Characteristics assessed may be personal (abilities, skills, knowledge, motivation, and values), interpersonal (group performance, cross-enterprise partnerships), or financial (for example, business unit profitability).

7. Identify or develop methods of assessment, including assessment centers, personality measures, interviews, and 360-degree feedback surveys.

8. Use goals, standards, and norms to provide a basis for interpreting results. That is, interpret assessment results in terms of what is important in the organization or industry.

9. Use balanced scorecards to align organization, team, and individual goals with a range of performance measures.

10. Show the value of your assessment process and results—both the economic value to the organization (for example, how assessment is used to affect the bottom line of the organization) and evidence that the constructs measured are valid (that is, the discrete elements of performance that are relevant to the organization and leadership in general).

CHAPTER THREE

Shifting the Emphasis of Leadership Development

From "Me" to "All of Us"

Patricia M. G. O'Connor
David V. Day

> **A clear sense of identity serves as a rudder for navigating difficult waters.**[1]

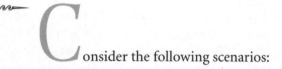

onsider the following scenarios:

- An industry innovation leader attempts to recoup slipping market share after the introduction of a new business model involving the outsourcing of the customer service function to overseas contractors.

- A multinational organization struggles with honoring a local practice for doing business (in this case, bribery) while simultaneously upholding a strong company value of fair, above-board negotiations.

- A rising star executive suddenly finds her previously successful stakeholder strategy obsolete, when a national security breach shuts down her operation, leaving her to respond to unexpected demands from the media, federal and local authorities, and community groups.

Given the complexity of challenges facing organizations, it is critical that all employees shift how they think about leadership and their role within it. They must move from seeing themselves as independent actors ("me") to seeing themselves as an interdependent collective ("all of us") whose purpose is to produce leadership when and where the organization requires it. Only in this way will organizations be able to adapt to a highly complex world. But developing what we refer to as "collective leadership identities" goes against the grain of most people and organizations.

Attempting to understand and practice leadership solely as something that individuals in position of authority do ignores the broader context within which leadership occurs. It ignores the interaction effects of all who participate in leadership, and the shared beliefs that drive those interactions. For these reasons, there has been increased attention given to "postheroic" forms of leadership that attempt to understand how leadership capacity develops among a collective and to design ways to help develop it more deeply in organizations.[2]

In this chapter, we explore how one methodology—action learning—supported two organizations' efforts to address complex challenges, in part by developing collective leadership identities. We begin by defining what we mean by *leadership identities,* explore why identity development is important, and address how this approach goes against the grain of established leadership practices and beliefs. We then provide illustrations from two case organizations that enhanced their collective leadership identities as well as produced outcomes of tangible benefit, in the form of competitive and innovative strategies, work processes, and tools.

WHAT ARE LEADERSHIP IDENTITIES?

Identity, simply put, is how one thinks about oneself and answers the question "Who am I?" Identities (like organizations) are dynamic and multilevel phenomena that are created and recreated over time through social processes. For example, an identity that is tightly held at one point in time, such as high school basketball team member, may no longer be important in middle age (representing the dynamic component). In terms of the multilevel nature of identity, someone might identify with being a member of a company (collective level) and also with being a scientist (individual level).

Regarding the specific question, "Who am I in relation to leadership?", both individual-level (that is, leader identities) and collective-level (that is, leadership identities) understanding are thought to develop. Leader identities are informed through a variety of adult development processes, including ongoing self-development, changing views of self in relation to others, and group influences. These identities are molded through both direct and vicarious personal experiences in leadership contexts. The rising star executive in our opening example has found herself in a situation that has significantly challenged her understanding of what effective leadership will require of her going forward.

Collective leadership identities are thought to develop through purposeful efforts to create or change organizations, communities, and societies. These identities are shaped through shared practices that require interaction among various systems, engaging in paradoxes, and inquiry into the collective's purpose. As noted by the example at the beginning of the chapter, employees of multinational corporations often find themselves in the position of having to surface and make sense of conflicting practices across countries within which they operate. Attempts to resolve these contradictory perspectives—in this case, on the use of bribes—challenges assumptions about who we are as an organization and what values we hold to be important.

Research and theory on identity is consistent in arguing that it is a multidimensional construct. We do not have *an* identity, but rather a composite of subidentities. Some people hold more subidentities than others or have them more highly integrated. An example of this can be seen by looking at the various roles that people hold. Someone might consider herself a mother, a civil engineer, a gardener, and perhaps a leader. These different facets of identity may be differentially salient depending on the situation. When these roles conflict, as they sometimes do (for example, sick child sent home from school on the day of a major project deadline), they can lead to an experience of role stress. To the degree that these various roles are internalized as facets of identity, these kinds of conflicts can lead to more chronic identity crises. Another example involves a vice president of business development who also participates in a lobbyist group that aggressively targets the cigarette industry. One Monday morning he is given responsibility for landing a sizable contract with a tobacco conglomerate. In this situation, both identities—rainmaker and activist—are salient and thus in considerable conflict.

There are two aspects of identity that are central to the action learning initiatives we discuss. The first regards the extent to which an identity as a leader is internalized. One of the goals of leader development initiatives is to raise this facet of identity to awareness so that it can be reflected on and enhanced. Put another way, if someone does not consider himself a leader, then it is unlikely that he will undertake self-initiated challenges to further develop his leadership skills. Furthermore, there is less of a chance that he will contribute to the major leadership tasks of the organization. Understanding oneself as a leader is an organizing and motivating force for cognition and behavior (that is, thinking and acting like a leader).

A second identity-related aspect central to the initiatives is that one's self-concept is organized around three fundamental components: individual self (me), relational self (you and me), and collective self (all of us).[3] From this hierarchical organization of self, people seek to construct their identities in terms of their unique individual traits (me), through interpersonal relationships with others (you and me), and by means of their group membership (all of us).

Take the previously mentioned aspect of identity as a leader. At the individual level, a person would tend to think in terms of specific traits or other personal characteristics that distinguish them as an effective leader (for example, "I am a leader because I persevere in reaching my goals"). At the relational level, the self as leader would be defined mainly in terms of the significant relationships one had formed with others (for example, "The relationships I build and maintain with significant others in this organization define my leadership"). At the collective level, the self as leader would be viewed mainly through identification with a broader collective such as an organization (for example, "Working together, we are industry leaders in this field").

An interesting aspect of identity is that individuals hold all three levels of self-concept. However, only one of these self-concepts can be active at any point in time, and these self-concepts tend to differ in strength or development. So if I am thinking about myself as an individual leader, it is impossible for me to think simultaneously as a relational or collective leader. In terms of differential strength of self-concepts, it should come as no surprise that there is a prevailing tendency among managers to think about leadership as an individual-level phenomenon. Due to cultural and socialization influences, an individual leader identity may be overly (perhaps chronically) accessed in workplace situations, which suppresses other, more inclusive, forms

Identity Level	Primary Concern	Source of Leadership
Individual	Me	Personal attributes
Relational	You and me	Dyadic relationships
Collective	All of us	Shared practices and beliefs

Table 3.1.   Identity and Leadership.

of leader identity. As a result of this highly developed "me = leadership" identity, the kinds of collective effort needed to address the complex challenges faced by organizations today are often restricted. Thus, one of the overarching goals of the initiatives discussed in our cases is to prime the relational and collective aspects of leader identity. The ultimate objective is to get individual leaders to work together relationally and collectively in accomplishing the major leadership tasks needed by the organization.

The research from this emerging field of leadership and identity has demonstrated that leaders not only can develop their own self-concepts but can also support this development in their followers. This is of great importance because, as Lord and Brown note in a review of this area of research, "After all, subordinates produce the desirable organizational effects that are generally attributed to their leaders."[4] The implication is that if followers construct themselves entirely around an individual self-concept, there will be little cooperative effort toward trying to attain more collective goals. Especially in terms of moving beyond transactional approaches to leadership ("You do this and I will reward you with that"), leaders need to access more inclusive levels of self-concept in followers. Extending this logic to a broader level, the question driving the initiatives we describe is whether the organization can serve as a proxy for "leader" and through supporting action learning initiatives build more inclusive and collective leader identities in its "followers" (who happen to be the senior leaders in the organization). Table 3.1 summarizes the fundamental leadership identity elements just discussed.

WHY DEVELOP COLLECTIVE LEADERSHIP IDENTITIES—AND WHY IS IT SO DIFFICULT?

As evidenced by the scenarios at the opening of the chapter, organizations and their leaders are facing increasing episodes of "*vu jade*" or the opposite of *déjà vu*—"I have never experienced anything like this before. . . . I have no idea what is happening. . . . I have no idea who can help me."[5] Or . . . "I can't identify!" *Vu jade* is essentially the state of being rudderless. There is little argument that the challenges faced by organizations and societies today are far too complex and unpredictable for any single individual or team to effectively address. And yet we persist in recognizing and developing leadership as an individual phenomenon.

There are some very powerful examples of why more collective forms of leadership are needed. One memorable case pertained to helping the South African government and the African National Congress opposition to implement a peaceful transition from authoritarian apartheid to a racially egalitarian democracy.[6] The exact details of how the team of facilitators assisted with this remarkable transition are beyond the scope of the chapter. But suffice it to say that it was not accomplished by any single leader setting the course of action to take and then building the commitment to make it happen. Instead, the team worked with members of various constituent stakeholders who were simultaneously engaged in scenario-planning exercises built on the fundamental assumption that there was more than one possible future and that the actions they and others took would determine which future would unfold. Through collectively envisioning a shared future and mapping out how to go about realizing it, writing about apartheid Kahane came to recognize that across many contexts there is a widespread "apartheid syndrome." As he explains:

> By this I mean trying to solve a highly complex problem using a piece-meal, backward-looking, and authoritarian process that is suitable only for solving simple problems. In this syndrome, people at the top of a complex system try to manage its development through a divide-and-conquer strategy: through compartmentalization—the Afrikaans word *apartheid* means "apartness"—and command and control. Because people at the bottom resist these commands, the system either becomes stuck, or ends up becoming unstuck by force. This apartheid syndrome occurs in all kinds of social systems, all over the world: in families, organizations, communities, and countries [italics in original].[7]

It is clear from this example that we live in a world that is increasing in both the diversity of its people and the interdependence of its processes. One of these dynamics alone can challenge organizations beyond their present leadership capacity. When taken together, these challenges can escalate exponentially in ways that can leave organizations struggling to make sense and adapt effectively. As information flows more easily through traditional hierarchical and geographic boundaries, more and more individuals become connected. As individuals connect, the diversity of expertise, worldview, and demography brought to bear on any given situation, task, challenge, or opportunity increases. In a world of inter-dependent diversity, we need to more fully understand the interplay among leader identities, the relationship between individual and orga-nizational identity, and perhaps most important, the influence of both of these on an organization's capacity to address complex challenges.

One reason why developing collective leadership identities is so difficult is the persistent and historical influence of heroic leadership figures in religious, political, corporate, parental, and community contexts. For example, leadership (and leader) profiles and typologies of *individuals* abound: strategic, servant, visionary, charismatic, trans-formational, authentic, and on it goes. The public's appetite appears virtually insatiable for leader biographies, prescriptions, pearls of wis-dom, and so-called nuggets of truth. But these forms of individual-based leadership are limited because they require that the hero-leader make sense of a leadership challenge, come up with a viable solution, and then convince "followers" to, well, follow. The kinds of complex challenges faced by organizations today render heroic leadership mod-els extremely limited if not obsolete. It is unrealistic to expect that any one individual (hero or otherwise) can make sense of these types of ill-structured, complex challenges, let alone devise a correct strategy or solution.

It is thus clear that identities inform both how leadership is under-stood and how it is accomplished. In this way, leadership identities exert an important influence over the beliefs and practices that are experienced by employees as "the organization." Development prac-tices that target the evolution of leadership identities at both levels enable organizational capacity to address complex challenges in ways that other investments in executive and organizational learning do not. The practical aspect of identity is that it is a developable resource for organizations that can serve as a sustainable competitive advan-tage. Specifically, it can help organizations accomplish leadership in the forms of more innovative direction, more flexible alignment, and more sustainable levels of commitment.

Thus, the goal of leadership development is not merely a matter of having smarter, more passionate, and more self-aware individual leaders. It is a matter of recognizing the limits of individualism. The development of strong, independent selves—informed by our experiences, philosophies, mental models, values, assumptions, and worldviews—can limit our effectiveness in accomplishing leadership in an interdependent and diverse world. The ultimate—and challenging—goal is to develop identities that simultaneously support both independent and interdependent leadership practices. We now turn to case illustrations from two organizations working to realize this goal.

PRACTICAL ISSUES OF COLLECTIVE LEADERSHIP IDENTITY DEVELOPMENT

In this next section of the chapter, we describe the practical application of the ideas that have been put forth thus far. Specifically, we provide a detailed description of the action learning methodology, and illustrations of best practices from two case organizations with which we have collaborated.

Leadership Development Frame

One of the major challenges associated with developmental efforts in organizations is how to link individual leader development with more collective leadership development.[8] Or, put another way, how can organizations develop an *individual's capacity* to participate in more collective forms of leadership in order to build the overall *organizational capacity* for setting direction, creating alignment, and building commitment?[9] The factors associated with the development of identity and self-concept just discussed offer a promising lens for building links across levels. To the extent that action learning engages participants emotionally, cognitively, and behaviorally in the actual leadership context of their organization, it is a methodology well-suited for supporting multilevel identity development.

As an organizing frame for the initiatives we are about to discuss, we define *leadership* as the social structures and processes that yield direction, alignment, and commitment.[10] This perspective on "what" leadership is leads us to make certain assumptions about "how" leadership is developed. The focus on the *social aspects of leadership* helps overcome the limitation of treating individuals and the organizations they work within as distinct from each other. The emphasis on structures and processes advances an argument that leadership can be enhanced by *directly developing the work that is actually done* in an organizational context by people participating in leadership, as opposed to focusing entirely on individual leader attributes. Finally, a focus on direction, alignment, and commitment defines leadership as real work that *accomplishes important outcomes for the organization* that lends a pragmatic frame for output-driven managers.

Action Learning Methodology

In each of the two cases presented, the primary developmental methodology used was action learning. Action learning is a systematic way by which individuals, groups, and organizations learn in the context of real (not simulated) work. It attempts to balance the role of action and reflection for the purpose of learning from experience and developing more complex ways of knowing, doing, and being.

Action learning creates an environment that promotes just-in-time learning without the need to transfer from a classroom experience back into a workplace. Furthermore, action learning primes the development of shared practices, which are required for a group to navigate the relationship between individual and collective leadership identities. In our practice, *action learning* refers to (1) the achievement of both the performance and learning objectives of an organization's leadership development agenda; (2) through real work on strategically important complex challenges; (3) engaged by senior-level, peer-based, nonexpert teams; and (4) supported by coaches, sponsors, and a steering committee.

There are various schools of thought concerning action learning, but we draw primarily from the approach that emphasizes purposeful reflection and questioning inquiry into personal and organizational belief systems. As with most action learning applications, these initiatives incorporated (1) projects that addressed highly complex challenges, (2) off-site programs, (3) team coaches, and (4) project sponsors. Due to the organization-level change targets, these initiatives also incorporated much rarer elements, such as a thorough upfront "discovery" process (that is, needs assessment), the establishment and ongoing advisory function of a steering committee, the crafting of an explicit learning agenda, and the deployment of a multidimensional evaluation strategy. Three other core elements of these two cases that differentiate them from typical action learning initiatives are summarized in Table 3.2.

Element	Cases	Typical
Target Population	Teams of *senior* managers addressing issues of strategic importance	High-potential middle managers, as either individuals or teams
Task Structure	Teams spend time in the early phases of the initiatives *sense making* and clarifying their project charter/complex challenge	Teams are assigned an already clearly defined project charter
Developmental Purpose	To understand and experiment with more interdependent *leadership practices* for achieving the organization's mission	To develop individual leader competencies

Table 3.2.   Elements of Case versus Typical Action Learning Initiatives.

As the developmental purpose of both initiatives was to create more interdependent leadership practices, it might be useful to provide an illustration. An example of what we consider to be an important leadership practice is that of *engaging across boundaries,* which can be understood as a manifestation of the relative amount of development at all three levels:

1. Individuals must develop awareness and knowledge related to the organizational boundaries most relevant to a given project, including why engagement has been difficult or nonexistent to date.

2. Teams must develop efficacy with tools that support more inclusive and effective ways for groups—typically separated by these boundaries—to engage with one another (for example, the use of large-group dialogue).

3. Organizations must develop structures and strategies that not only support but also encourage and reward the practice of engaging across boundaries (for example, institutionalizing a process to support groups to more interdependently craft joint strategic goals).

It was hypothesized that as leadership practices are the integration of all three levels of development, directly working to enhance the practice would increase the likelihood of change in leadership identities.

Although evaluation processes are still ongoing in the two case organizations, preliminary reports have indicated (1) a broadening of leadership identity (that is, a shift in primary concern from "me" to "all of us") and (2) increased efficacy in engaging in more interdependent leadership practices.

It should be noted that classroom-based methodologies (that is, programs) have been shown to be effective in developing cognitive aspects of leadership (for example, increased self-awareness, deepened understanding of key concepts), and to some extent the emotional aspects of leadership (for example, strengthened connection to the organizational purpose). Programs also provide an opportunity for participants to stop and reflect on key leadership issues in a safe, confidential environment. The primary limitation of programs as compared to action learning is that little behavioral development can be practiced, demonstrated, and sustained as a result of a multi-day off-site experience. Even when cognitive, emotional, or behavioral change is experienced through programs, it is almost exclusively at the individual level, that is, the development of the "self as leader" identity. We consider programs as an important but insufficient methodology for multilevel identity development. Action learning provides the opportunity and tools to develop the "leadership through relationships" and "leadership through collectives" identities. The cases incorporated programmatic elements into the overall action learning initiative, garnering the benefits from both methodologies.

Action learning was expressly designed to address multiple levels of identity development. At an individual level of identity (that is, me producing leadership), through working with a project team, individual leaders reflect on what kinds of unique skills and leadership strengths they as individuals bring to the team. As with most "classic" leader development initiatives, individuals are provided feedback about their individual personalities based on their responses to self-assessment inventories. In essence, participants have the opportunity to work on their individual knowledge, skills, and capabilities as leaders.

At the relational level of identity (that is, my relationships producing leadership), action learning includes the opportunity to gain an understanding and enhanced self-awareness of one's impact on others through the use of 360-degree feedback assessments. This encourages adopting an interpersonal, relational perspective in terms of how relationships can profoundly shape and define leadership.

At the collective level of identity (that is, all of us collectively producing leadership), action learning emphasizes gaining an understanding of "who we are" as an organization and visioning who we want or need to be—that is, what is our desired organizational image. Thus, it could be said that the highest-level objectives of these action learning projects are to build explicit links between individual self-concepts and organizational identity and image.

Best Practice Case Organizations

In illustrating examples of what we consider to be best practices, we draw examples from two leadership development initiatives. The first initiative is ongoing in a faith-based health care system with a strong service-focused culture. In April 2006, it launched its third cohort of executives into a 14-month leadership development process, involving a total of seventy-six senior managers to date. The overarching objective of its leadership development initiative is to *advance the understanding and practice of the mission in enhanced and useful ways.* In that mission is regarded as this organization's core strategic attribute, it is believed to have a significant influence on the outcomes of leadership (that is, direction, alignment, and commitment). To underscore the criticality of this relationship, the initiative referred to "mission leadership" as the central developmental target. This fit well with at least two levels of identity, as individuals learned to more fully lead from a mission perspective and the organization sought to develop collective, cross-boundary leadership practices guided by the mission imperative.

The second initiative took place in a quasi-governmental service agency with a strong operations-focused culture. In September 2005, it completed the pilot phase of a 6-month leadership development process involving a total of 100 executives. The overarching objective of this leadership development initiative is to *build capacity in the organization to address complex challenges relevant to its transformation.* "Transformation" refers both to an actual Transformation Plan for keeping the organization viable as well as to the transformational organization change required to achieve the plan. For example, the organization was challenged to shift from a primary focus on internal operation excellence to developing greater capacity in scanning and engaging the external environment. Engaging in a shift in core capability holds clear implications for changes in identity, at both the individual and organizational levels.

Health Care System	Service Agency
Practicing and developing a greater sense of "systemness"* resulting in:	Practicing and developing the leadership capabilities on a systemwide basis:
1. Achieving operational excellence 2. Strengthening individual and organizational identity 3. Recruiting, retaining, and developing talent	1. Engaging across boundaries 2. Leading from an integrated understanding of the organization 3. Demonstrating a shift from internal environment to external environment 4. Bringing best of self to the organization

Table 3.3.   Targeted Leadership Practices.

*Systemness refers to greater leveraging of the benefits of the whole system, while continuing to enjoy the specialized contributions of the individual hospitals, clinics, and regional entities that comprise the system.

"Build capacity in the organization" refers to leadership capacity, which the organization recognized as developed through individuals (skills, perspectives, knowledge), groups (norms and tools), and systemic practices (strategies, processes). Each case organization participated in an initial discovery process that surfaced three or four specific collective leadership practices (see Table 3.3) that once developed would likely move each organization toward its respective overall objective.

Although representing seemingly very different leadership contexts, the two organizations have four commonalities that led them to experiment with new development practices. Readers may recognize these same factors in their organizations:

1. Each is experiencing *threats to their sustainability.*
   • For the health care system, the specific threat is the dwindling number of religious founders that originally gave rise to the organization, requiring greater numbers of secular members to take up the vision and drive of its early founders.
   • For the service agency, the specific threat is sweeping changes in the business model of the 200-year-old organization.
2. Each organization recognized the *limits to building only individual leader capacity.* Each sought an approach to leadership

development that not only developed individuals, but also developed the practices and culture of the organization to equip them to more effectively address the threats to their sustainability.

• Each organization recognizes *mission orientation as providing key competitive advantage,* in terms of providing a rich and storied history in which to ground the organization, attracting and retaining highly committed employees, and yielding superior "above and beyond the call of duty" performance at all levels. As one organizational member observed, "We may not agree on everything, but we all believe in the importance of our mission. And that is what helps us overcome our differences and ultimately pull in the same direction."

3. Each organization is *looking to a critical mass of senior managers* (that is, two- to three-down from the CEO) to collectively leverage the mission and help develop the organization forward. These populations are considered to have a significant role in shaping the future of the organization.

4. Each organization is also beginning to understand and experience *identity's role in translating mission from statement to strategic action.* That is, the way in which senior managers primarily understand the source of leadership (that is, me, my relationships, or all of us) influences how they attempt to put the mission into action. For example, does a manager rely on her own abilities, draw insight and support from key relationships, or engage collectively with others to accomplish leadership? There is a strong argument that the individual— and increasingly the relational—approaches to leadership may be insufficient to address the complexity involved in translating missions from statement to strategic action. Table 3.4 outlines for each of these two initiatives the overall objective, the specific developmental targets and implications for identity.

Best Practices for Building Collective Leadership Identities

Although a variety of best practices aimed at individual-, team-, and organizational-level development were incorporated into these

Organization	Overall Objective of Initiative (Why?)	Developmental Targets (What?)	Implications for Identity (So what?)
Health Care System	To advance the understanding and practice of the mission in enhanced and useful ways	Practicing and developing a greater sense of "systemness" resulting in: 1. Achieving operational excellence 2. Strengthening individual and organizational identity 3. Recruiting, retaining, and developing talent	Understanding and practicing "systemness" requires a clearer sense of the individual identities within organizational units as well as the collective; the ways in which the mission is interpreted and applied in day-to-day decisions is shaped by the relative integration of individual identities with the larger, collective identity
Service Agency	To build capacity in the organization to address complex challenges relevant to its transformation*	Practicing and developing the leadership capabilities on a systemwide basis: 1. Engaging across boundaries 2. Leading from an integrated understanding of the organization 3. Demonstrating a shift from internal environment to external environment 4. Bringing best of self to the organization	Transforming how organizations fulfill mission-critical objectives requires employees to understand the organization's desired collective identity, the implications of the shift from actual to aspired, and the relationship between their self-identify and that of the developing collective

Table 3.4. Initiative Objective, Developmental Targets, and Implications for Identity.

Transformation refers both to an actual Transformation Plan for keeping the organization viable and to the transformational organization change required to achieve the plan. The plan was devised in order to equip the organization to continue to fulfill its mission.

initiatives, the focus here will be on those practices that supported the development of collective leadership identities. Specifically:

1. *Creating alignment* with organizational identity
2. Building *collective self-concepts,* and
3. Developing *systemic social networks*

CREATING ALIGNMENT WITH ORGANIZATIONAL IDENTITY. This dimension concerns clarifying and developing the relationship between individuals participating in leadership ("me") and the broader organization ("all of us"). For example, what is the interplay between an individual's efforts to advance his leadership career and the organization's imperative to advance the collective corporate reputation? This relationship is a dynamic one that is constantly under construction and influencing not only an employee's commitment levels but also the broader practices that occur within organizations. Creating alignment with organizational identity does not suggest the desire for a direct fit between an individual's self-concept and that espoused and enacted by the broader collective. Pushing this alignment too far, individuals can risk losing an overall sense of self if their identity is overly prescribed by job or career issues. Alignment in this sense is not only developing an ability to understand the relationship between individual's sense of self-concept and the identity expressed through organizational policy and practice. It also requires learning how to preserve alignment in those situations where an employee does not recognize in the self the attributes demonstrated in the collective. Given the earlier observation about the increasing number of issues associated with workforce diversity, we imagine such situations will become more and more frequent.

The action learning initiatives were designed to give participants an experience that would explicitly call out the practical implications of identity alignment. Because the teams were composed of diverse members and were tasked to address a complex challenge facing the organization, the teams were required by the nature of the work to wrestle with alignments and misalignments. The teams' initial insights addressed what can be described as "surface" identities, such as those classically bestowed on headquarters and field operations, functional specialties, line (revenue center) and staff (cost center), and on geographic regions.

These insights were drawn out by the action learning leadership coach, through periodic debriefings and just-in-time interventions. This was the primary role of the coaches who facilitated the team's use of structured reflection and dialogue to ensure collective learning and the integration of insights into their project work. At times, the reflection and dialogue was welcomed. Other times it surfaced defensiveness, indicating a lack of readiness on the part of individuals or the team to address identity issues. In these instances, the coach recognized the lack of readiness, encouraged the team to consider identity differences as important (and not necessarily negative) input to collective work. The coach then brought the team back to the task at hand.

It is to be noted that coaches conduct explicit contracting with their teams at the beginning of the initiative to negotiate roles and clarify expectations for the coach's participation. If this was not first accomplished, intervening on topics as delicate as identity may have been perceived as inappropriate and could have resulted in hampering rather than helping the team's development.

As teams worked the project, they began to use less differentiated "us versus them" language and began to better appreciate ways in which alignment was both desirable and possible. Of course, this was not always accomplished with ease. As teams dug deeper in the projects and the organization, and through numerous opportunities for reflective thinking, they identified the "deeper" identities that gave rise to competing commitments between groups within the organization. Some of these deeper identity issues included diversity in values, change orientation, learning and risk-taking preferences, use of authority and, ultimately, ingrained beliefs about how leadership is most effectively accomplished. The result of these insights was greater self-awareness on the part of the team members as to how their identity shaped their actions and, in some cases, attempted to shape the actions of others. It also resulted in significant awareness of a team and organizational identity. From this individual and team learning, the teams developed a deeper appreciation of the sources of conflict and misalignment within organizations.

Shared identification with the organization's mission (that is, "all of us") served as a powerful reintegrating mechanism when team members and organizational stakeholders found themselves divided by different assumptions about roles they each should play in the project (that is, "me"). For example, several teams encountered resistance from groups in the organization who identified themselves as "owning" the issue that the action learning teams were addressing. These groups adopted a defensive stance, possibly confused and threatened by this novice team "mucking around in our work." Beyond the learning benefits of overcoming that defensiveness, those teams that were able to effectively collaborate with the formal organizational groups produced project recommendations that have a higher likelihood of organizational adoption.

Another example of the balancing act between preserving individual identities and aligning with the broader, collective identity of the organization is captured in this quote from a hospital administrator in the health care case organization, who was a member of an action learning team tasked with examining the issue of enhancing physician relations:

> Physician relations is a challenge for us, in terms of really engaging them in the organization's mission. We know from experience—and in interviewing docs—that their primary focus is their practice. If you ask them about what they are professionally committed to, they are more likely to talk about their specialty or their patients, rather than our system. They simply don't identify with us and our goals. Or if they do, they identify with it in a less than positive way. Given they are not technically our employees and have challenges of their own to deal with, I can't say that I blame them for not taking a bigger role as, how you would say, a "corporate citizen." And yet, they hold a very central role in the eyes of our patients and their families. And, thus, our mission.

BUILDING COLLECTIVE SELF-CONCEPTS. This identity development dimension addresses the need for individuals to build collective self-concepts in addition to developing a clear and grounded self-identity. There were three nested collectives that managers potentially identified with: (1) the action learning leadership team to which they belonged, (2) the program cohort comprised of multiple teams, and (3) the broader network of program alumnae. From a leadership development perspective, the purpose of building collective self-concepts is to move highly effective individual managers from focusing solely on developing their personal leader identities to focusing on the broader identity dynamics that connect (or divide) collectives in their attempts to achieve direction, alignment, and commitment in complex contexts.

Developing from self as leader to self as a participant in a collective leadership community resulted in a shift in developmental complexity of the leadership practice. The assumption here is that in order

Purpose	Method
Support shift from mindful individuals to a mindful collective	Adoption of tools and norms that encourage more focused and shared participation in leadership tasks
Recognize relationship between collective self-concept and effectiveness with addressing the complex challenge	Use of collective, reflective processes such as fishbowls, open space, and lessons-learned debriefs
Test organizational readiness for collectives other than the senior executive team to provide direction on what in the organization must change and what must remain the same	Conducting small experiments, regularly checking assumptions with key stakeholders, and noting organizational response to changes proposed by action learning teams

Table 3.5.   Methods for Building Collective Self-Concepts.

to effectively address complex challenges, organizations need to develop and deploy more developmentally complex leadership practices. Teams that were capable of moving from "us" to "all of us" also reported higher satisfaction with the developmental experience and generally were more successful in producing project outcomes of tangible benefit to the organization.

Three different methods were employed to assist the teams in building collective self-concepts (see Table 3.5). The first was the introduction of norms, tools, and practices designed to move a group of individuals into a mindful collective. For example, a norm of stopping, reflecting, and silently writing down ideas (that is, structured self-reflection) was employed to initiate and regulate team discussions. (While initially introduced and reinforced by the action learning leadership coach, the intention was for the team to eventually adopt and initiate this practice on their own, when they recognized a need for it.) This allowed for more focused and shared participation, and avoided one or more "loud voices" from dominating the discussion and possibly overinfluencing the direction of the thinking. This helped to enhance team learning. When individuals are given a chance to capture their ideas in a thoughtful way and to share those ideas aloud with a team, it allows them to focus more attentively on others when it is no longer their turn to share. It can also help individuals begin to pay attention to and address the nonverbal dynamics and other processes developing in the room, which often provide more powerful data than the specific contributions of any one member.

A second method used was reflective processes focused on getting the team and the broader cohort to recognize the relationship between collective self-concepts and effectiveness at addressing complex challenges. The reflective processes varied from fishbowls to the use of open space and lessons-learned focused debriefing sessions. A couple of examples of the relationship between collective self-concepts and effectiveness might help to illustrate this connection:

> I experience us as a very driven team. That excites me! But on the other hand, we say we're going to follow a certain group process, and then 5 minutes later we're all off doing our own thing. We'll never get anywhere on this project if we're constantly dividing and conquering. It'll be lots of individual action and potentially no collective results. (Vice president, Finance, making an observation during a team work session debriefing)

> If we each continue to think only of ourselves as individual executives—and not as a collective force in this organization—our challenges will continue to seem insurmountable. What will it take for us to recognize that we, as a group of executives, have the ability and opportunity to help the organization do a better job of challenging assumptions that limit our ability to think outside the box? (Attorney, contributing to a fishbowl dialogue)

A third method for developing collective self-concepts was testing the organizational readiness for collectives of managers other than the top executive team to provide direction on what in the organization must change and what must remain the same. This is a particularly delicate issue that arises through action learning initiatives, insomuch as it calls into question the relationship between hierarchical authority (that is, looking up for the direction on change) and peer-based leadership (that is, working across organizational boundaries to determine the needed change and then producing it). The action learning projects are designed to produce outcomes of tangible benefit to the organization and to provide a practice field for developing more complex leadership practices intended to serve the organization well beyond the life of the project. Both of these objectives require, and generally achieve, individual and organizational change.

DEVELOPING SYSTEMIC SOCIAL NETWORKS. The third dimension of building collective leadership identities involved the development of systemic social networks. Systemic social networks are the web of inter- and intra-organizational relationships that facilitate the creation of meaning, strategic action, and forward progress on shared goals. These are distinct from a particular individual's social networks, which are generally created to support individual needs, such as information, advice, or career advancement.

There were two sets of systemic social networks developed as a result of the initiative:

1. The networks accessed and/or developed by each team in order to accomplish the action learning leadership project work, and

2. Postprogram alumnae networks accessed in order to continue developing more effective leadership practices for addressing complex challenges

Social networks are developmental insomuch as they give shape to the overall organizational identity. They are also instrumental in that they provide the vehicle for getting things done in the organization. Social networks can be launched or altered through leadership development initiatives in ways that support the program's objectives. For example, one of the targeted leadership capabilities of the service agency was to more effectively engage across boundaries. This capability is easy for those with broad and deep networks. Unfortunately, historical organizational practices kept executives within their silos, limiting the relationships with other units and geographic regions. Thus, boundary crossing was both difficult and not completely welcomed. Recognizing the power of and need for the executives to be working more laterally, social network development was designed into the initiative.

Systemic social network development was accomplished through five tactics:

1. *Up-front composition of program cohort and action learning leadership teams.* As stated earlier, teams and cohorts were composed of diverse members. They were considered diverse not just from the standpoint of demographics, but diverse in terms of who they were typically connected to and worked with.

2. *Project work that required the sharing of individual networks and development of collective networks.* As the teams were given projects in areas for which none of them had deep experience or expertise, the work required them to access those outside of the

team, introduced team members to their contacts, and gave members greater exposure to a greater diversity of organizational colleagues.

3. *Guidance and support from executive sponsors.* Each action learning leadership team had a project sponsor who was not expert in the content area of the project and thus was not a project customer or stakeholder. This was done intentionally to help the sponsors resist steering the project and instead focus on the team learnings and processes as they navigated through the organizational system. Sponsors brought deep experience with the organization's dynamics—particularly how to effect change in the organization—as well as political and other systemic perspectives due to their respective positions. Sponsors helped the teams develop social networks through introductions to key people in the system, helping the team gain access to otherwise inaccessible people, and gave advice to the team regarding who they should be involving in the course of the project.

4. *Standing invitation to access networks.* At the conclusion of each cohort's experience, participants repeatedly reported that, going forward, they would make themselves available to anyone in the cohort who needed them. Several reported that if they had a list of calls to return, and any alumnae of this initiative was among them, they would get priority. The trust created as a result of working together on a challenging project forged the network, and all were invited to access the network any time, for any reason.

5. *Promotions and transfers to extend the network.* As alumnae of the initiative received promotions, transfers, and other new job assignments, the social networks became extended further into the organization. For example, an alumnus of one cohort was promoted to hospital CEO and became a project sponsor for a team in the following cohort. Needless to say, this CEO extended his new network to this team, which enabled the team to navigate their project challenge with greater confidence.

EXECUTIVE SUMMARY

This chapter advanced a perspective grounded in both theory and practice that highlights the importance of developing collective leadership identities as a strategy for helping organizations more effectively address complex challenges. The case study organizations discussed in this chapter used action learning to integrate in real time both the developmental and the performance requirements of navigating increasingly complex business environments. The shift in emphasis from "me" to "all of us" is, of course, an ongoing process in these organizations. Nevertheless, the profound insights and innovative project outcomes produced by the participating cohorts provided compelling cases of what is possible for the rest of the organization.

When learning is intentionally situated in the context of real work, the potential for developmental growth increases, but so do the factors that can inhibit learning. Many action learning interventions fall short of their targets due to lack of organizational readiness to engage in a practice that holds learning and experimentation as critical an outcome as the more traditional performance metrics. It should be noted that while action learning can deliver significant outcomes, like any other developmental methodology, it requires expert and ongoing facilitation. We strongly encourage practitioners who are less familiar with the methodology to seek assistance from experienced professionals, and to speak with other organizations that have used the methodology, before embarking on initiatives such as those described within this chapter. It should also be recognized that action learning is not a panacea for an organization's leadership development needs. It is an expensive, time-consuming, and challenging intervention that requires unequivocal support from the top to be successful. And even then, of course, there are no guarantees of universal effectiveness.

Despite these caveats and potential boundary conditions, action learning has been demonstrated to be one means for developing broader leadership capacity in an organization. We believe that the underlying psychological mechanism on which much of the success hinges is the development of collective leadership identities. It is very difficult to imagine how collective identities could develop without people working together in meaningful and purposeful ways to enhance the leadership of their respective organizations.

CHAPTER FOUR

Getting Leader Development Right

Competence Not Competencies

Morgan W. McCall Jr.
George P. Hollenbeck

L eader development is not working. Witness the "corporate crises *du jour*," for example, at Disney, AOL Time Warner, Morgan Stanley. Beneath the surface of each is a failure of leadership. Despite 30-plus years of "best practice" and "best efforts" at developing leaders, daily proclamations that leader development is a science, and an unending flow of books, videotapes, and leadership gurus, despite leadership development that costs millions of dollars each year, our situation is no different than that described by Citicorp legend Walter Wriston in the 1970s: it's easier to find millions of dollars of capital than a competent executive.

Surveys of the leader gap find that most companies (85 percent in one survey) don't have enough leaders to carry out their strategies. Twenty years ago, John Kotter made the same point: leadership is a scarce commodity.[1] The search for new chief executive officers (CEOs) leads outside the organization more frequently today than it did then, and there is little evidence that outsiders succeed at a higher rate. The "war for talent" is popular because nobody is producing enough leaders to fill the available jobs. Even conceding that leadership is harder today than it used to be, leader development efforts haven't kept pace with leader demand.

How can we avoid a similar litany of failure 5 or 10 or 30 years from today? The key lies in following a few well-established principles that, like most words of wisdom, may be more easily said than done. We can find examples, however, of companies that *are* doing some of the right things, even if the whole set may still elude them.

A typical contemporary leadership development approach begins with an elaborate (expensive and time-consuming) process of identifying competencies believed to characterize effective leaders. These competencies provide a basis for developing human resource (HR) programs, especially training programs, intended to develop the competencies. When used for selection, the competencies are used to identify people believed to have the ability to fill key positions. Once in those positions, they are on their own.

As appealing and logical as the competency approach may be, the emphasis is misplaced. The focus instead should be on using experiences to develop *competence*, rather than on preconceived competencies that may not have anything to do with effective leadership. We believe a more effective approach would:

1. Identify strategically relevant leadership challenges, not a list of individual competencies

2. Use the strategic challenges to identify critical developmental experiences, not as the rationale for competency models that drive training and HR programs

3. Identify people who can make the most of the experiences offered, not those who already can do what the experiences could teach

4. Find ways to get people into the experiences they need, rather than just selecting people for jobs or sending them to training programs

5. Help people learn from their experiences rather than let them sink or swim

WHY LEADER DEVELOPMENT ISN'T WORKING

The common lament from the HR community is that leader development is not working because senior management doesn't support it: "Why can't we get the CEO to support leadership development?" But have HR people missed the point?

The real reason leader development is not working is that it has the wrong focus. It has focused on competencies rather than on results. Executive culture and language is about business results and financials—leader development is instead tied to a short list of knowledge, skills, attitudes, abilities that are theoretically necessary to be an effective leader. Sold as "a common language" and as the first step in "developing and validating a company-tailored leadership model," the competency lists look remarkably similar from organization to organization.

But senior executives know intuitively that lists of competencies do not leaders make. Leaders, those executives know, are forged by the fires of experience: the assignments, people, challenges, and screw-ups that, over the course of a lifetime, push us beyond what we are.[2] What matters is not their competencies but their *competence . . .* how effective they are at doing the work and getting the results the organization needs.

The "common language" of the competency movement turns out to be the *lingua franca* only of those who design development programs around the competency models. The CEO's signature endorsing the model is mistakenly taken for conviction. Those actually making the day-to-day people decisions make little or no use of the "common language" of the company's competency model and, when asked, have difficulty coming up with the list of competencies. When we sat in on the developmental staffing discussions of the CEO and his team in a large high-tech company, we found exactly that—the language of the executive suite was competence, demonstrated by experience, results, and capabilities, not competencies. Here is the language of a real-life top team:

- "The customers bring up his name to me."
- "It's a tough job dealing with [a major customer] day in and day out, and she's done a fabulous job."
- "He is relentless in cutting cost out and he will deliver."
- "He's a general business guy but he has the engineers' respect."
- "He's technically excellent and builds a team beyond belief."

In contrast, a competency model might describe the same people with such ambiguous terms as *customer focused, persuasive, action oriented, team player.* These are nice words describing competencies, but they are disconnected from any tangible outcome.

Leader developers have assumed that if they can produce the right leader development program, the competencies will produce the right leader behaviors that will then result in leader and organizational success. Truly an engineering model, the assumption is that we can develop it, fix it, and/or make it work with the right development program.

When the programs fail to develop the leaders needed, in frustration executives observe, "You can't do it," and retreat to the old saw, "Leaders are born and not made." Frustrated, HR vainly tries to provide a "leader development return on investment," which nobody takes seriously, and leader development is outsourced either literally as a cost reduction move, or figuratively by pushing responsibility for development onto the budding leaders themselves.

Indeed, "you can't do it" if doing it means manufacturing leaders. But neither are leaders born and not made—our studies of the backgrounds of leaders unfailingly find that the executives studied are able to identify key events that shaped them as leaders. Those experiences, however, are seldom leader development programs, but are instead the key job experiences that taught them the lessons of leadership.

WHAT COMPANIES COULD BE DOING

Although experience is clearly the principal school for leadership, the bad marriage to the competency approach is perversely strong. Its logical appeal and usefulness in creating the *appearance* of integrated processes and systems apparently compensates, in the minds of many, for its ineffectiveness in actually developing leadership talent. Simply paying attention to development by creating competency lists and doing something by offering programs and processes masks the fundamental fallacy of the approach.

Identify Challenges, Not Competencies

The key is having the leadership talent to carry out the organization's strategy. Most commonly, senior executives are asked to identify the qualities needed by individuals given the future direction of the company. The executive "common language" is translated into competencies that bear little resemblance to the actual language of executives.

Imagine that part of your business is in trouble. Who would you choose to fix it? A person who had demonstrated competence by successfully turning around troubled operations in the past, or one rated highly on a competency inventory? If you are like the vast majority of executives we have talked to, demonstrated competence trumps competency ratings every time. High scores on competencies don't necessarily translate into the ability to accomplish specific tasks. So it's no surprise that executives base placement decisions primarily on their assessment of whether a person can do the job, as demonstrated by past performance in challenges similar to the ones that lie ahead.

Where do executives learn how to deal with these kinds of challenges? Through experience. What experiences? Step 1 in leader development should be identifying the leadership challenges that the strategy will create. It is then possible to talk about the kinds of experiences that a talented person might need to prepare him or her for those challenges. From a business perspective, there is a clear preference for those who have done it before over those who might benefit from learning how to do it. How people use their abilities to handle situations is more important than the list of abilities they are seen to have. If people can learn how to handle various situations, then development can be driven by giving them the experiences that allow them to put existing abilities to use and to develop the new ones needed. In other words, the opportunity for talented people to grow lies in the challenges they face (or the "stretch" required), so the focus of development must be on giving people the challenges (embedded in their assignments) that over time will enhance their ability to accomplish the goals of the organization. This means that the challenges talented people are given need to be those most directly relevant to the business strategy and objectives of the organization.

There is no better example of this philosophy in operation than Carlos Ghosn, chief executive officer of Nissan and Renault. In his recent book he commented:

> It's imperative for a company to prepare its future leaders. You can't prepare them by leaving them at company headquarters to work in administrative functions. You prepare them by sending them to the most difficult places. A certain number of them will fail, but the ones who emerge will provide the breeding ground for tomorrow's leaders. Tomorrow's leaders get their training by dealing with today's challenges. You have to take the ones with the most potential and send

them where the action is. . . . Leaders are formed in the fire of experience. It's up to the head of the company to prepare a new generation and to send them to hot spots as part of their training.[3]

Using the business strategy to identify the important developmental opportunities is the crucial link. Trying to identify a list of competencies that top executives should have is a distraction from the true task, which is developing competence through experience. While many organizations engage in the theoretical exercise of identifying "nice to have" attributes given the strategic aims, relatively few HR organizations tackle the bottom-line question of what experiences are important to developing competent executives. It is ironic that the intuitively powerful and well-accepted practice of putting talented people into challenging assignments would be so difficult to apply systematically, yet that appears to be the case. Instead of a well-defined process, such placements are usually made on an ad hoc basis by line managers responding to serendipitous opportunities. It is rare to see the business strategy translated into leadership challenges, much less to see systematic identification of the important developmental experiences (assignments, projects, roles models, and so on) related to them. Even more unusual is to see deliberate developmental moves coupled with specific strategies to help the person learn what the experience was chosen to teach. In contrast, consider how well developed the HR processes are for such traditions as performance management or management training.

One organization that has linked leadership development to strategy is Canada's largest financial institution, RBC. With a history of commercial banking, RBC carefully articulated strategic priorities that their five business platforms must be able to deliver against. These strategic priorities served as the foundation for leadership development processes that included identification of ten key experiences that define an RBC leader, as well as the cross-unit talent management processes required to provide high potentials with the experiences. At the most general level, RBC's strategy dictated that cross-business leadership would be necessary in the new enterprise, that it would need both generalist and specialist leaders. Assessment of their current executive population showed a wide gap between current capability and future needs; so began a systematic process of determining both potential and ambition for cross-business roles, and talent management to assure that cross-business development opportunities were targeted at those executives most likely to profit from them.

Identify Experiences, Not Programs

A substantial amount of research has identified what lessons different kinds of experiences offer that executives need to learn. Certain kinds of assignments (start-ups, turnarounds, increases in scope and scale, various projects, and the like), exposure to exceptional people (usually superiors, both good and bad), overcoming hardships and difficult times, and even some training and educational programs, are what drive development. On-the-job experience, supplemented by strategic interventions, is where the greatest leverage is.

The good news is that experience is available every day to everyone. The bad news is that using experience effectively to develop executive talent is not as straightforward as offering training programs. It is not the first priority of a business to develop people, so critical business needs may dictate giving jobs to proven players rather than to the people who might develop the most from having them. Furthermore, there is no science to dictate how to use specific experiences to develop specific skills in specific people at the right time. For all these reasons, using experience rather than programs to drive the development process is itself a challenging proposition.

One organization that has made a concerted effort to shift the focus of development from programs to on-line experience is Procter & Gamble (P&G). This 100-plus-year old company with sales in 145 countries and 28,000 managers (10 percent of them expatriates) places a premium on building talent via experience. They began by studying the kinds of experiences their most successful company presidents had been through and by identifying the kinds of experiences critical to strategic success (for example, brand management, working in a global business unit, and being a general manager of a country operation). It was made clear what experiences are required to move toward a destination job, and a process was introduced in which employees keep track of the types of experience they have had. Building blocks to an executive career have been identified and a host of ancillary processes (including open job posting, a talent development process, and a general management college) put in place to make it work. P&G is able to ensure that executives are placed in positions that can provide new learning and development, rather than "wasting an assignment" (from the corporate viewpoint) and "wasting time" (from the executive's view).

Boeing has offered one of the most impressive examples we have seen of a company that puts experience at the core of development.[4] Their goal was to develop leaders while they were running the business by being intentional about the experiences that talented people were given. Called the "Waypoint Project" (from the electronic signals pilots use to navigate), Boeing researchers are 4 years into a 10-year longitudinal study aimed at using experience effectively for development. Since the year 2000, 120 executives and managers have been taking part in the 10-year study of their careers and the key experiences in their development. This research has already produced types of experiences and the strategically relevant lessons that can be learned from each of the experiences. A variety of tools (many of them Web-based) have been developed (using the language and metaphors of the executives) to facilitate access to experience and the learning that takes place in it.

Identify People Who Can Make the Most of the Experiences Offered

We are suggesting that an effective development approach begins by identifying the kinds of experiences talented people need, given the business strategy. This does not avoid the question of personal attributes, but it does change the focus of it. Instead of looking for some specific and uniform set of attributes, we assume instead that many of the required abilities are learned, that successful job performance can be achieved in different ways, and that successful people do not necessarily have—or need to have—all of the same attributes. People with very different personalities and different skill sets can bring their existing abilities, along with what they learn along the way, to bear on accomplishing the task at hand. How else can we explain the success of so many different kinds of leaders?

If the goal is to use experience to develop competent executives rather than to develop executive competencies, then the challenge is to identify those people who will learn the most from the experiences they are offered. Adult learning is seldom very predictable, and it takes time. If it takes 10 years to become a master chess player, then leadership mastery would require at least as much investment in learning. It is interesting to note that years ago John Kotter suggested that it takes at least 10 years or more to become a general manager. Perhaps if we could better understand the patterns, connections, and content that constitute the "language" relevant to executive behavior, we could come closer than simple competency models to realistically assessing developmental progress.

That complexity aside, several attempts have been made to identify and measure the capacity to learn from experience. The most common high-potential assessment practice (often unsystematic and fraught with error) is supervisor's judgment. Organizations take a number of approaches to improve on the quality of information used to judge the "high potential." General Electric (GE) has historically used an Accomplishment Analysis Process that uses trained interviewers to capture a candidate's experience, achievements, successes, and failures and then to verify those with prior bosses and peers before summarizing them in an assessment report.[5] Sorcher describes the Group Evaluation Technique that uses the behavioral observations of next-level executives who know the potential executive, capturing the wealth of information that is already available in the organization.[6] Ram Charan, Stephen Drotter, and James Noel in the *Leadership Pipeline* emphasize well-defined common standards of potential and frequent reviews of executives.[7] All of these efforts focus on capturing in a more systematic and defined way the information that is needed, and then making timely (and frequent) decisions based on it.

Other efforts to identify people most likely to learn from experience have resulted in tools that attempt to assess the characteristics associated with learning. One study of more than 800 international managers and executives provided a profile of people who learn from experience based on four general factors: willingness to "pay the price of admission" by their commitment to results and willingness to take risks, showing a "sense of adventure" by taking or making opportunities to learn, doing things that help themselves learn, and learning from their mistakes and changing as a result of their experiences.[8]

Create Mechanisms for Getting People into the Experiences They Need

After the learners and the experiences have been identified, getting these right people into the right experiences is critical. Many forces operate to prevent developmental interventions. Executives often are reluctant to give up their talented people; they may be reluctant to fill a key position, which also may be a developmental one, with an "unknown quantity." And both of these dynamics are exacerbated if the culture of the organization is one that breeds distrust, defensiveness, and protection of turf.

If we assume a base of sufficient mutual respect, trust, and commitment to development, then how does one go about matching developmental need to developmental opportunity? Much development can take place absent a promotion or lateral move, such as setting specific goals, designing the work to optimize development, providing coaching and feedback, exposure to significant people and projects, use of temporary assignments, access to information and resources, attending training and educational programs.

But many powerful developmental opportunities require that a boundary be crossed in order to get the person needing the experience into it—several managers must cooperate. It is no small challenge to pull this off, and the most common process used to determine who gets what job is succession planning.

A typical succession planning process involves identifying key positions, developing lists of candidates, and evaluating those candidates in terms of readiness to fill positions. For those who are seen as having potential but are not yet ready to be promoted, there may be some discussion about what further development or seasoning is needed. The resulting succession or replacement tables are really assessments of current bench strength relative to existing positions. Identification of development needs is incidental to the process, and specific development plans for individuals are usually the product of a separate process if they are created at all.

Using succession planning to drive development requires a different approach. At one company we worked with, succession planning was broken into two phases. The first step was having senior executives assess the talent pool and replacements for key positions likely to come open within a year. The second step, however, aimed directly at making developmental moves. With the help of their HR business partners, executives identify specific positions in their organizations that would come open in the near future and that were potentially quite developmental. "Developmental" was determined by analyzing the jobs against criteria based on research into what makes experiences potentially developmental. They also identified from among their most talented subordinate managers those who needed and were ready for a developmental opportunity. In a half-day meeting, the

developmental jobs were presented by the executive (or business partner) responsible for them. The ensuing conversations then identified
those high-potential candidates who might profit from the experiences, and a list was created for each open position. In follow-up meetings decisions were made on who got which jobs. As a result of this
process, eleven executives were given developmental assignments. A
few weeks later these eleven were brought together to assess their experiences so far and to gather suggestions for improvement. One of the
most important (and in retrospect obvious) suggestions was to pass
on to the developing executive the essence of the conversation in
the executive review that led to the placement. In other words, why
was this experience chosen and what was he or she expected to learn
from it?

Help People Learn from the Experiences They Have

Experience may be the best teacher, but our understanding of how it
teaches leaves much to be desired. The fickle nature of experience has
spawned aphorisms, such as "Some people have 20 years of experience
while others have one year of experience 20 times." Unlike formal
courses with specific teaching objectives and examinations to test
acquisition of knowledge, experience has no textbook or instructor's
guide. Each experience is at some level unique, and the interaction of
a specific person with a specific experience in a specific context makes
predicting a learning outcome problematic. True, research has established probabilities—certain lessons are clearly associated with certain kinds of experiences. But what a person will learn, if anything,
from a particular experience is difficult to predict.

There are, of course, a wide variety of interventions sometimes used
to aid learning from experience. Some training programs are timed to
coincide with important transitions, such as entry into management, and
provide a framework for learning from a particular event. Three-
hundred-sixty-degree feedback can provide multiple perspectives on an
individual's behavior on the job. Some organizations make extensive use
of coaches and mentors to work with individuals as they go about their
daily tasks. Boeing, as mentioned earlier, provides a number of easy-to-
use Web-based tools to help its managers learn from experience. But
overall, our experience is that most organizations do very little to help
people mine the lessons of their experience.

We have been studying the forces that help and hinder learning from experience by asking executives to retrospectively describe learning from challenging assignments and by following leaders on a weekly or bi-weekly basis as they move into new assignments. The results have opened our eyes to the complexity of on-the-job learning. First of all, people have very different styles of learning, or at least of figuring out if they have learned. For some it is the traditional action-reflection-learning-action cycle. But some don't realize they've learned anything until they face a similar situation again and respond to it differently. Others find themselves making the same mistakes again, perhaps learning something the second or third time around. In short, there often is a gap between realization and implementation, and different individuals at different times may learn in different ways—even from similar experiences. The implication is that development is highly individual and must be treated that way. We've long known that "one size" rarely fits all except in socks, but the desire for a universal model and efficient systems presents a formidable challenge.

What is learned seems to vary significantly as well. Many learn almost exclusively those things necessary for the immediate accomplishment of the task—what works, what this boss values, why quality is down. Whether or not any of these very specific insights, as necessary as they may be for performance, will generalize to the next assignment is problematic. For others, the learning is more generic, such as how the organization works or what its values are. Still others learn powerfully about themselves—what they love, where their hot buttons are.

What makes the difference between an epiphany and a relatively mundane technical lesson? Timing clearly matters. Job transitions are powerful learning opportunities, but at the same time can be loaded, even overloaded, with the need to master immediate, performance-relevant details. This might be the worst possible time for an intervention, as even welcomed help may get lost in the immediacy. As John Gabarro observed in his classic study of new general managers taking charge, the "taking hold" stage can be all consuming.[9] Indeed, much of action in the early stage is based on what a person already knows and on immediate needs, so it is only later that the opening for new learning—at least learning above the task requirements of the moment—appears. One executive, for example, recently had joined the company in a job that was the equivalent of a skip-level promotion. Although he was from the same industry, he was not familiar with the culture, people, or processes of the new company, much less with the leadership demands of the new level. To make matters even more interesting, this piece of the business was in deep trouble, almost in crisis mode.

To "help" with the transition, the company assigned a quality black belt to the new executive. Instead of making things easier, the new resource quickly became an additional burden as the executive, with little time to devote to developing new quality initiatives or to engage in extensive statistical analysis, found himself spending time trying to come up with things to keep the black belt busy. This same executive, asked if having a coach would help, responded that the amount of time required to bring a coach up to speed with the problems and context would make it impossible. One solution is to incorporate "after action reviews" (AARs) designed to capture available learnings from the transitions. A good example of these AARs is provided in an article appearing in the *Wall Street Journal* on May 23, 1997, "Lessons Learned: Army Devises System to Decide What Does, Does Not, Work."

THE ESSENTIAL ROLE OF THE DEVELOPMENTAL LEADER

The most important external factor in a manager's learning from job experience is the immediate boss. Our research has demonstrated that the boss is across the board the most important factor in developing executives. There is more, however, to being a developmental boss than modeling best practices, mentoring, and coaching. We identify two things, one intentional and one that takes place as a by-product of effective leadership.

The developmental leader continues the developmental conversation long after the talent review, keeping attention on "What are the challenges we can offer this person? What opportunities can we provide for learning?" Jack Welch is legendary for maintaining a continuing dialogue at GE about talent and how it can be developed. As he puts it in *Jack,* "There weren't enough hours in the day or year to spend on people. This meant everything to me. I'd always try to remind managers at every level that they had to share my passion."[10] In addition to keeping developmental discussions alive, the developmental leader builds a developmental organization as a part of the performing organization, not as a distraction from it.

Our research with development-wise executives, however, is showing that production and development—rather than being at opposite ends of a continuum—often are opposite sides of the same coin. Effective leaders are able to make leader development a side effect of execution rather than an end in itself. They engage people along the way in examining ongoing work: What happened last week? What did you learn? How are you applying your learnings? By asking "dumb" or straightforward questions in a disciplined manner, it is possible to shift perspective and actually get busy managers to reflect on what they are learning. The result is that people grow and learn while in pursuit of the execution goals of the organization.

How do they do it? What is happening in these high-development organizations so that people develop while they work? Our interviews with executives who have made it happen suggest that the solution, while perhaps not simple, is in many ways natural. With a little tweaking and an added focus, it all comes together.

What do we know about "what, when, where, how, and why" leaders develop?

- *The work is challenging.* It stretches our limits, it may be a sprint or a marathon, but it is no "walk in the park." There is lots of ambiguity; we feel we are operating in uncharted waters, on the edge.

- *There are clear goals and direction.* People know what is expected of them. The expectations may be broad (solve the problem, open a plant) or narrow (ship 40 percent more boxes with no errors), but people know what has to get done.

- *People are held accountable.* Sometimes the accountability is implicit, such as the self-imposed pressure to succeed in the eyes of one's peers; sometimes it is more explicit, when performance, both good and bad, has consequences, and everybody knows what they are.

- *There is emotion in the organization.* People learn and remember when ideas and feelings happen together. There may be ups and downs, high points and low, but engaged organizations are seldom boring. As one executive said, "It is very exciting; it scares you to death and opens you to learning." Fast-paced, uncertain, changing contexts with high external demands and high stakes create emotion in the organization. A classic example of such a context is described in Tracy Kidder's 1974 book, *The Soul of a New Machine.*[11]

• *Learning and understanding are seen as a part of the management process.* Executive expertise—the very thing required to lead execution—grows from the day-to-day, focused process of learning what to look for and what the connections are among the events. As one of our executives said, "At first everything was new, but after a while I began to see patterns, and how they fit together, and what was happening at a system level." Often, the required analysis was stimulated by the skillful questioning of a leader who got people to think, analyze, and question themselves.

• *Mistakes are analyzed.* Our executives, while not prescribing failure, pointed out that mistakes and failures are rich learning opportunities that need to be taken advantage of . . . both for the sake of execution and of development. As mentioned earlier, this is a variation of the "after action review" used by the military to analyze what went right, what went wrong, and what can be done differently next time. The goal is not a witch hunt or a blame-placing investigation, but rather an objective review focused on learning that assumes that all concerned share responsibility for continual improvement. The key here is creating a culture that is supportive of learning. The AAR process helps prevent repetition of mistakes, and encourages use of things that work. While those who make the mistakes may be identified and criticized, the need to translate and transmit the lessons learned overrides the blame. In a sense, it becomes "heroic" to err!

As we looked over our list, it occurred to us that it reads like a textbook description of good leadership. It also occurred to us that every executive we know can look at each of these and think of things they could do—ways they can make slight changes in focus that will encourage more development (and execution) in their own organizations.

So what is the lesson here? What is the bottom line? Just this: the essential role of the leader in developing executives is to lead. Adding *development* to the leader's focus, however, will suggest fine-tuning that pays dividends to the leader, to the organization, and to the executive we hope to develop. And . . . get better results.

Whatever efforts are made, the essential point is that the effectiveness of development efforts can be magnified when organizations provide help with the learning. Too often, in a sink-or-swim performance situation, the learning executive must learn incidentally rather than intentionally.

THE ROLE OF EXECUTIVE COACHING

The range of leadership development interventions continues to expand, limited only by the imagination of HR people. Examples include 360 feedback, action learning problems, outdoor exercises. Executive coaching, however, may well be the fastest growing and now most common practice designed specifically to help people learn on the job. Sometimes described as the "Wild West of HR," executive coaching burst onto the scene in the past 10 years and has rapidly become the method of choice for leadership development. And for good reason—it can be tailored to the individual executive and his or her needs, in terms of time, costs, delivery, and content. Organizations have found that the "manager as coach" model described by Tom Peters in *A Passion for Excellence* is a tough sell to 24/7 executives.[12] A ready supply of external executive coaches has made it easy for the "developmental leader" to outsource individual development. But executive coaching comes with its own set of problems: it can be expensive and tends to be unending; coaches vary widely in their qualifications, and they may be difficult to control and expensive; coaching can be effective, most would agree, but there is little hard evidence that on a broad scale it "works." The jury is still out on whether executive coaching will be the "feel good" fad of the turn of the century, or a targeted, efficient, and effective addition to the development cabinet.

That said, what makes coaching work? There is a growing consensus on the essentials for an effective executive coaching program:

1. *Qualified coaches.* Choosing an executive coach is surprisingly similar to selecting other consultants—good coaches have credibility based on expertise in helping executives, an understanding of business; they know what they are doing; they are trustworthy—skilled at handling confidentiality and juggling the sometimes competing demands of the organization and the business. Businesses that would screen information technology consultants for detailed knowledge can be surprisingly lax in hiring executive coaches even

though individuals with little expertise offer themselves as executive coaches. Best practice organizations like JPMorganChase and Microsoft and Prudential have carefully developed screening processes to assure that the executive coaches they hire know what they are doing.[13]

2. *Targeted development.* Executive coaching goes off track when there is no clear focus for the engagement. Coaching-experienced organizations find that coaching gets the best results for both the organization and the executive when the focus is on improving performance (for example, giving better feedback to direct reports) rather than changing the executive (helping the executive to be happier!). Such performance targets may be as simple as giving feedback to employees or as complex as learning to think strategically. Experienced executive coaches sometimes find that the most important gains may well be in areas that were not immediately apparent at the beginning of the engagement, but starting with the end in mind avoids the drift away from business results to personal counseling.

3. *A partnership of effort.* The individual executive, the coach, and the organization are partners in the effort to improve performance. The effort is not a "go it alone" project for any of the three partners. If the partners fail to combine their efforts, or worse yet, are pitted against each other, none of them is likely to be satisfied with the outcome. Stories abound of executives and their coaches operating independently of the executive's boss or HR or anyone else in the organization.

4. *Time-limited applications.* Executive coaching works when there is a sunset clause, a defined period (often 6 months or a year) for the engagement. When coaching is working, there is a tendency to extend the engagement indefinitely. But with coaching, like other consulting, there are diminishing returns at the same time that there is a natural tendency to continue the relationship. Best practice organizations set a limit. A survey of the unbridled use of executive coaching in one organization found that some of their executives had been in executive coaching for 5 years!

Whatever efforts are made to increase the probability that a talented person will learn from experience, the best intervention might be coaching with the person's boss rather than with the person.

EXECUTIVE SUMMARY

We have presented in this chapter a critique of leadership development today and offered a framework for what we believe can be a more productive endeavor. Although we are short on examples of companies that have applied our framework in every detail, this is not simply theory, but a practical approach that fits into the course of business.

KEY TAKEAWAY 1. Leader development took a wrong turn, we argue, when it began focusing on a laundry list of competencies and on programs to measure and train them rather than on the competence to handle leadership challenges and on the experiences that build it. Difficult though it may be to break the enchantment, it's time to kiss the frog. Avoiding the pitfalls of the past requires a redirection.

Neither as concrete nor apparently certain as the focus on competencies, a competence focus also is not as elegant or integrated. As messy as life is, however, there is little doubt that effective leaders are not all alike, that there is no one personality or style that marks them, and that none of them have all the perfect qualities, no matter how much we would like them to. Instead of a holy grail of competencies, we should be using the language of paradox, equifinality, tapestry— whatever is necessary to realistically acknowledge that leadership is about bringing one's talents, whatever they may be, to bear on the challenges that face an organization.

KEY TAKEAWAY 2. Organizations should focus on competence, not competencies, and should aim their efforts at producing leaders who will be able to meet the strategic challenges ahead. The strategic challenges of the organization in turn dictate the development challenges for future leaders. A powerful example exists at Bristol Myers Squibb—under tremendous pressures in 2001 to survive as an organization, the strategic imperative was that it must bring new products to market while at the same time carefully controlling costs. The leadership development function, faced with a staff cut from thirty to four, realized that it must focus its efforts on making a difference in the critical new product function. Rather than focus on a competency model, the leadership development function targeted its efforts to helping select and develop specifically those executives on the new product teams.

With different assumptions about people, leader development can move ahead, or at least in a different direction. It is almost trite to suggest, as all previous generations have, that leadership development must be driven by the business strategy. Even the competencies in competency models are at least superficially connected to strategic direction. However, when developing competence through experience is the focus, development must not only flow from the strategy it must be a fundamental part of it.

James Burke, CEO of Johnson & Johnson (J&J) during the Tylenol crisis, spoke to a class in the Harvard Business School in 1984 about the credo. J&J is highly respected for its credo and the intensity with which it has inculcated it into the fabric of the company. During the question and answer period, Burke was asked which was more important to J&J's success, the much-heralded credo or the equally well-known strategy of decentralization. After a brief pause, Burke answered that he really couldn't say which was more important because they are so completely intertwined.

That is the kind of answer we would hope to see for leadership development and strategy. The only reason to invest in developing leaders is to have the wherewithal to achieve the business objectives. Therefore, the leadership challenges presented by the business strategy determine what experiences talented people need if they are to develop competence. Further, the only viable way to assure that talented people get the experiences they need is to build access to those experiences into the strategy itself.

KEY TAKEAWAY 3. The key experiences that develop leaders are controlled by line executives, not by human resources staff, and line executives are responsible for results first. It follows then the mechanisms developed to get talented people into the experiences they need must be consistent with line objectives, which means they must take into account the potential costs of developmental moves. The only way to do that is to make development an integral strategic aim that balances short- and long-term costs, and adjust the performance criteria accordingly.

KEY TAKEAWAY 4. The leader development process does not end with getting people into the experiences they need. Because it is a business decision to risk developmental moves, it is simply good business to do whatever can be done to make the moves successful. And success is defined not simply by performance, but also by achieving the learning goals that prompted the move in the first place. Just sitting back and seeing how it comes out is not acceptable.

KEY TAKEAWAY 5. The definition of "high potential" must include a person's ability to and desire to learn from the experiences they have, not just their "ability to move ahead two levels." Selection for jobs that contain the prime developmental challenges must include an element of how much the person will learn, rather than just how much they will produce in the short run.

KEY TAKEAWAY 6. Developmental leaders are themselves the most frequent ingredient, and sometimes the most important, in the learning process that results in a high potential's learning the lessons of challenging jobs. The developmental leader has a role to play directly with potential leaders, but also indirectly in providing developmental organizations that build development into the course of business.

Shifting the focus of development from competencies to experience will not be easy. Accumulating experience takes time, so it must start early. Moving people into assignments for which they are not fully qualified has costs to the business in lost efficiency and risks of failure for the person and the business. Line executives must have both the commitment and the skills to take responsibility for making it happen. But it is clear that the popular emphasis on competency models is not sufficient. While we need a common language to describe desired leader behavior, putting such theoretical constructs at the heart of development has caused us to misdirect our efforts. The most likely source for developing executive talent is experience, and that, not competencies, should be the driving force.

PART TWO

The Tasks of the Leader

CHAPTER FIVE

Best Practices in the Use of Proactive Influence Tactics by Leaders

Gary Yukl

To be effective, a leader must influence people to carry out requests, support proposals, and implement decisions. In large organizations it is necessary to exert influence on superiors and peers as well as on subordinates. Influence in one direction tends to enhance influence in other directions.

The type of behavior used by one person (the "agent") in an attempt to influence another person (the "target") is called an *influence tactic*. Proactive tactics have an immediate task objective, such as influencing the target person to carry out a new task, provide assistance on a project, provide necessary resources, or approve a proposed change. Examples include rational persuasion (using facts and logic) and inspirational appeals (linking a request to target values and ideals). Proactive tactics can be distinguished from impression management tactics, which are used to influence someone to like you more or to evaluate your skills and performance more favorably.

This chapter describes eleven types of proactive influence tactics, explains what has been learned about their relative effectiveness, and provides guidelines on how to use them for leading people in organizations. The chapter also includes a brief description of how the proactive tactics can be used to resist unwanted influence attempts by others.

INFLUENCE OUTCOMES

The effectiveness of a proactive tactic can be evaluated in terms of the immediate outcome of the influence attempt for which it is used. Three qualitatively distinct outcomes can be differentiated: commitment, compliance, and resistance. *Commitment* occurs when the person you are attempting to influence internally agrees with a request and makes a great effort to carry it out effectively. This is usually the most successful outcome for a complex, difficult task that requires enthusiasm and initiative from the individual being influenced. Influencing commitment is especially important when it is necessary for a leader to implement major change.

Compliance occurs when someone is willing to carry out a request but is apathetic rather than enthusiastic about it and will make only a minimal effort. The person is not convinced the decision or action is the best thing to do or even that it will be effective for accomplishing its purpose. Compliance is a less successful outcome, but for a simple, routine task it may be all that is necessary to accomplish the influence objective. For example, getting subordinates to wear safety glasses and follow standard procedures for avoiding accidents requires compliance but not commitment.

Resistance occurs when the target person is opposed to a request and tries to avoid doing it. The person may refuse to carry out the request, try to persuade the leader to withdraw or change the request, delay acting in the hope that the leader will forget about the request, ask higher authorities to overrule the request, or pretend to comply but try to sabotage the task. Resistance is usually regarded as an unsuccessful outcome, but it can be a favorable outcome if the net effect is to avoid making a serious mistake. For example, you develop a detailed plan for a new project, but subordinates will not implement it until you correct some serious flaws that you had overlooked.

The success of an influence attempt can also be evaluated in terms of how it affects the way people subsequently view the leader (for example, ethical, supportive, competent, trustworthy), and these perceptions will affect the success of subsequent influence attempts. For example, after making an innovative change that is highly successful, a leader's reputation is enhanced and people are more willing to accept additional changes.

DESCRIPTION OF THE PROACTIVE TACTICS

Research programs conducted during the 1980s and 1990s identified eleven distinct types of proactive influence tactics, and they are shown in Table 5.1.[1] This section of the chapter briefly explains each type of proactive tactic and clarifies differences among the tactics. Later in the chapter the most effective tactics are described in more detail and guidelines for their effective use are provided.

Rational Persuasion	The agent uses logical arguments and factual evidence to show that a request or proposal is feasible and relevant for important task objectives.
Inspirational Appeals	The agent appeals to the target's values and ideals or seeks to arouse the target person's emotions to gain commitment for a request or proposal.
Consultation	The agent asks the target person to suggest improvements or help plan a proposed activity or change for which the target person's support is desired.
Exchange	The agent offers something the target person wants, or offers to reciprocate at a later time, if the target will do what the agent requests.
Collaboration	The agent offers to provide assistance or necessary resources if the target will carry out a request or approve a proposed change.
Apprising	The agent explains how carrying out a request or supporting a proposal will benefit the target personally or help to advance the target's career.
Ingratiation	The agent uses praise and flattery before or during an attempt to influence the target person to carry out a request or support a proposal.
Personal Appeals	The agent asks the target to carry out a request or support a proposal out of friendship, or asks for a personal favor before saying what it is.
Legitimating Tactics	The agent seeks to establish the legitimacy of a request or to verify that he/she has the authority to make it.
Pressure	The agent uses demands, threats, frequent checking, or persistent reminders to influence the target to do something.
Coalition Tactics	The agent enlists the aid of others, or uses the support of others, as a way to influence the target to do something.

Table 5.1.   Definitions of the Proactive Influence Tactics.

Copyright © 2001 by Gary Yukl.

Rational Persuasion

Rational persuasion involves the use of explanations, logical arguments, and factual evidence to explain why a request or proposal will benefit the organization or help to achieve an important task objective. This tactic may also involve presentation of factual evidence that a project or change is likely to be successful. Rational persuasion is a flexible tactic that can be used in many situations. It is most appropriate when the target person shares the leader's task objectives but does not recognize that the proposal is the best way to attain them. A strong form of rational persuasion, such as a detailed proposal with concrete evidence, is much more effective than a weak form of rational persuasion, such as a brief explanation or an assertion without supporting evidence. For example, in a presentation to superiors to get approval for a proposed change in work procedures, the leader explains how the change will reduce costs and provides evidence from a trial run that the change can be implemented without any problems.

Inspirational Appeals

This tactic involves an emotional or value-based appeal, in contrast to the logical arguments used in rational persuasion. An inspirational appeal is an attempt to develop enthusiasm and commitment by arousing strong emotions and linking a request or proposal to a person's needs, values, hopes, and ideals. Some bases for appealing to most people include the desire to be important, to feel useful, to accomplish something worthwhile, to perform an exceptional feat, to be a member of the best team, or to participate in an exciting effort to make things better. Charismatic and transformational leaders use inspirational appeals to gain follower commitment to innovative changes and motivate them to accomplish things that initially may have seemed impossible.[2]

Consultation

With consultation the leader invites an individual (or the members of a team) to participate in planning how to carry out a request or implement a proposed change. Consultation can take a variety of forms. One common form is for a leader to present a detailed proposal or plan and ask people if they have any doubts or concerns. After hearing these concerns, the leader can explain why the concerns are unwarranted or modify the proposal to reflect the person's concerns. Another form of consultation is to present a general objective rather than a detailed proposal and ask people to suggest specific action steps for implementing it. Active involvement in planning can result in commitment if people begin to take ownership for the strategy or plans they helped to develop (it is "their plan" rather than "the leader's plan"). The successful use of consultation requires at least moderate agreement that the objective is worthwhile; otherwise there will be no interest in developing an effective strategy or plan for attaining the objective.

Exchange

Exchange involves the explicit or implicit offer to reward someone for carrying out a request. Use of this tactic is especially appropriate when the person is indifferent or reluctant about complying with a request because it offers no important benefits and would involve considerable effort and inconvenience. An exchange tactic makes compliance with a request more acceptable, because the person will receive something desirable, such as tangible rewards, scarce resources needed for another task, or help in attaining another objective that is important to the person. For example, the leader wants a peer to do a new task, and in exchange the leader offers to show the peer how to use some new software that is unrelated to the task. Sometimes the promise involved in an exchange tactic may be implicit rather than explicit. That is, the leader may suggest returning the favor in some unspecified way at a future time.

Collaboration

Collaboration involves an offer to provide necessary resources and assistance if someone will agree to carry out a request or approve a proposal. This influence tactic is useful when an individual or team initially believes that a proposed activity or change is too risky or difficult to justify their enthusiastic support. Collaboration may seem similar to exchange in that both tactics involve a conditional offer to do something for the target person. However, there are important differences in the underlying motivational processes and facilitating conditions. Exchange involves increasing the benefits to be obtained by carrying out a request, whereas collaboration involves reducing the difficulty and costs of carrying out a request. Exchange usually involves an impersonal trade of unrelated benefits, whereas collaboration usually involves a joint effort to accomplish the same task. In the example described earlier for exchange, collaboration might involve an offer to have one of the leader's subordinates show the peer how to do the new task or to help in doing the extra work that would be required to complete the task.

Apprising

Apprising involves an explanation of how a request or proposal is likely to benefit the target person as an individual. The benefits may involve the person's career advancement, job satisfaction, or compensation. Apprising may involve the use of facts and logic, but unlike rational persuasion, the benefits described are for the individual, not for the organization. Unlike exchange tactics, the benefits are a by-product of carrying out the request, not something the leader will directly provide. For example, when asking a subordinate to carry out a task that is different from previous responsibilities, the leader explains how it will help increase skills the subordinate needs for promotion to a higher-level position.

Ingratiation

Ingratiation can take many forms, and common examples include providing praise, acting deferential, and acting friendly before making a request. For example, when asking a subordinate to do a new task, the leader says that the subordinate is the most qualified person to do it. When ingratiation is perceived to be sincere, it tends to strengthen positive regard and make a target person more willing to consider a request. Ingratiation is more likely to be viewed as insincere when used just prior to a request, especially if it is not directly relevant to the request. For example, saying you like someone's new hair style just before asking for a favor is not likely to be effective.

Personal Appeals

A personal appeal involves asking someone to do a favor based on friendship or loyalty. The stronger the friendship, the more one can ask of the target person. However, there is little need for a personal appeal if the relationship between an agent and target person is very strong. A personal appeal is most likely to be used for requesting assistance with a task or for obtaining a personal favor unrelated to the work. Leaders use personal appeals more often with peers than with bosses or subordinates.

Legitimating Tactics

Compliance with a request or command is more likely when it is viewed as legitimate and proper. Legitimating tactics involve an attempt to establish one's authority or right to make a particular type of request. Legitimacy is more likely to be questioned when a request is unusual, when it clearly exceeds the agent's authority, or when it is made by someone whose authority is not known to the target person. There are several different types of legitimating tactics, and most of them are mutually compatible. Examples include providing evidence that a request is consistent with a contract, formal agreement, legal precedent, organization bylaws, formal policies, rules and standard procedures, or written job descriptions that specify each person's duties and authority.

Pressure

Pressure tactics include threats, warnings, and assertive behavior such as repeated demands or frequent checking to see if the target person has complied with a request. Pressure is sometimes successful in inducing compliance, particularly if the target person is just lazy or apathetic rather than strongly opposed to the request. However, pressure is unlikely to result in commitment and may have serious side effects such as resentment and hostility. Hard forms of pressure such as threats, warnings, and demands are more likely to undermine working relationships than are softer forms of pressure, such as persistent requests or frequent checking.

Coalition Tactics

Coalition tactics involve getting help from other people to influence the target person. This type of proactive tactic is useful to gain approval for an organizational change initiative. The coalition partners may be peers, subordinates, superiors, or outsiders. Common examples include mentioning the endorsement of other people, and bringing an ally to the meeting in which the leader will make the proposal. Another coalition tactic (which is sometimes called an *upward appeal*) is to seek assistance from a superior who has authority over the target person.

EFFECTIVENESS OF INDIVIDUAL TACTICS

The effectiveness of each type of tactic depends in part on the context in which it is used.[3] A tactic is more likely to be effective if it is compatible with the leader's power and authority in relation to the target person. For example, exchange is more effective when a leader has substantial control over rewards that are valued by the target person. Finally, a tactic is more likely to be effective if appropriate for the type of interpersonal relationship that exists between the agent and target. Rational persuasion, consultation, and collaboration are more effective when the agent and target have shared objectives and mutual trust. A personal appeal requires a moderate degree of friendship. Finally, a tactic is more likely to be effective if it is consistent with strong social values in the national culture and the organizational culture.[4] For example, consultation is more effective in a country with strong democratic traditions than in a country in which obedience to leaders is a strong cultural value.

Despite these situational factors, some proactive tactics are usually more effective than others for eliciting commitment to a request or proposal. Studies on the relative effectiveness of different proactive tactics found that the tactics most likely to elicit commitment were rational persuasion, inspirational appeals, consultation, and collaboration.[5] These "core tactics" can be effective for influencing subordinates, peers, and bosses, although a particular tactic may be easier to use with one type of target than with another. Cross-cultural research has found that the core tactics are highly effective in many countries, despite some differences in how often each tactic is used and what form of the tactic is used.

Exchange and apprising are moderately effective but are more likely to result in compliance than in commitment. These tactics are more useful for influencing a subordinate or peer than for influencing a superior. Subordinates usually have little reward power in relation to their boss, and they are not likely to have more knowledge than the boss about opportunities for career advancement in the organization unless the boss was just recently hired from a different organization.

Ingratiation is moderately effective as a supplementary tactic for influencing a subordinate or peer. Ingratiation is less useful for an immediate influence attempt with a boss, because it is more likely to appear insincere in this context. However, when used over a period of time as an impression management tactic, ingratiation can help to build a good relationship with the boss.

A personal appeal is more likely to elicit compliance than commitment. The underlying basis for influence is the target person's desire to maintain at least a minimal level of cooperation with the agent, but the target person will not be willing to invest much effort in carrying out the request. Leaders who want to make a request or proposal that is important for the organization or potentially beneficial to the target person should use other tactics, such as rational persuasion, exchange, or apprising, instead of a personal appeal.

Pressure and legitimating tactics are unlikely to result in commitment, because they do not improve the target person's attitudes about the intrinsic merit of a request or proposal. However, the use of either tactic can result in target compliance, and as noted earlier, it is sometimes a sufficient outcome. For example, the leader may remind people who are reluctant to do a task that it is consistent with legal requirements or company policies, and failure to comply will result in disciplinary action.

A coalition can be effective for influencing a peer or superior to support a change or innovation, especially if coalition partners use the core tactics. However, asking others to help influence a target person only after encountering initial resistance is less effective, because in that situation it is likely to be seen as a pressure tactic.

GUIDELINES FOR USING THE CORE TACTICS

This section of the chapter provides guidelines for using the four core tactics, which include rational persuasion, inspirational appeals, consultation, and collaboration. The guidelines are suggestions rather than prescriptions, because it is always necessary to evaluate the situation and determine the appropriate way to use each tactic.

Rational Persuasion

Rational appeals involve logical arguments and factual evidence about the importance and feasibility of a request or proposal. This flexible tactic can be used to influence a group of people as well as an individual.

- Explain the reason that a request or proposal is important.

    People are more likely to comply with a request if they understand the reason why it is necessary and important. When asked to do something unusual, people may wonder whether it is really necessary or just an impulsive whim. Explain how a proposed initiative or change would help to achieve an important objective such as improved quality, productivity, profits, or customer service. Explain why a request is essential for the success of an important project or activity, or how it will help to solve a serious problem for the team or organization.

- Provide evidence that a request or proposal is feasible.

    It is not enough for a request or proposal to be relevant; it must also be seen as practical and realistic to gain someone's enthusiastic support and cooperation. If you expect the target person to have doubts about the feasibility of a request or proposal, provide supporting evidence for it. Explain the underlying theoretical rationale for assuming that a proposed plan of action will lead to the desired objective. Describe a specific sequence of action steps that could be used to overcome obstacles and accomplish the objective. Provide detailed information about costs and benefits for a proposed initiative or change. Cite supporting evidence from empirical research, such as a pilot study or survey showing a favorable response to a proposed new product or service. Describe how a similar approach was successful when used in the past by yourself or someone else. If appropriate, provide an actual demonstration for the person to observe ("Seeing is believing").

- Explain why a proposal is better than competing ones.

    If a proposal is competing with others for the person's support, explain why your proposal is better than any of the alternatives. Point out the advantages of your proposal. Possible advantages are that it is less costly, it is easier to implement, it is more likely to accomplish the objective, it is more likely to be approved, or it has less risk of undesirable side effects. Point out the weaknesses and problems with each competing proposal. If feasible, cite evidence from a test of the competing proposals to show that yours is better. Note that your comparison will be more credible if you also acknowledge some positive features of the competing proposals rather than ignoring them altogether, especially if the person is already aware of these features.

Inspirational Appeals

Inspirational appeals seek to develop enthusiasm and commitment by linking a request to the person's values and arousing strong emotions. Like rational persuasion, this tactic can be used to influence a team as well as an individual.

- Appeal to the ideals, values, and self-image of the target persons.

  Values and ideals that may provide the basis for an inspirational appeal include patriotism, loyalty, liberty, freedom, justice, fairness, equality, tolerance, excellence, humanitarianism, and progress. A proposed activity or assignment may be linked to values that are central to the target person's self image. For example, most scientists have strong values about the discovery of new knowledge and its application to improve humanity. Most physicians and other health care professionals have strong values about healing people and keeping them healthy. A proposed change or activity may be described as something that will make a revolutionary breakthrough, set a new standard for excellence, or enable the team to perform an exceptional feat. For example, the task of developing a new type of software may be likened to the role of a missionary who is going to revolutionize the way computers are used.

- Link the request to a clear and appealing vision.

  Efforts to introduce major changes or innovations are more likely to be successful when they involve an appealing vision of what could be accomplished or how the future could look if the proposed activity or change is implemented successfully. The vision may be an existing one the target person is known to embrace, or one you created to help gain commitment to a new project or activity. The vision should emphasize ideological values rather than tangible economic benefits to the organization or the target person.

- Use a dramatic, expressive style of speaking.

  A dramatic, expressive style of speaking often increases the effectiveness of an emotional appeal. Conviction and intensity of feeling are communicated by one's voice (including tone, inflection, and pauses), by facial expressions, by gestures, and by body movement. Use a strong, clear tone of voice, but vary the pace and intensity. Use pauses at appropriate times to emphasize key words, maintain interest, and arouse excitement. Maintain strong eye contact, use strong gestures, and move around to display energy and intensity of feeling.

- Use positive, optimistic language.

  Confidence and optimism about a project or change can be contagious. It is especially important to foster optimism when the task is very difficult and people lack self-confidence. State your personal belief in the project and your strong commitment to see it through to a successful conclusion. Use positive language to communicate confidence that a proposed project or change will be successful. For example, talk about the wonderful things that "will" happen after a change is made, rather than what "may" happen.

Consultation

Consultation increases the target person's motivation to carry out a request by allowing the person to participate in determining how it will be done.

- State your objective and ask what the person or team can do to help attain it.

  If you know that the person shares your task objective, state it clearly and ask what the person can do to help you attain it. The target person is likely to suggest some ways to be of assistance. In the process of discussing what is needed, other things the target person can do are likely to be identified.

- Ask for suggestions on how to improve a tentative proposal.

  More participation is likely if you present a proposal as tentative and ask for suggestions on how to improve it, rather than asking the target person to react to an elaborate plan that appears complete. People will be less inhibited about expressing concerns or suggestions for a proposal that is still in the developmental stage. Show appreciation for any suggestions. Jointly explore ways to incorporate promising suggestions, and make sure the target person understands the reasons why an impractical suggestion cannot be used.

• Involve the person or team in planning action steps to attain an objective.

Present a general strategy or objective and ask the person or team to help develop specific action steps for implementing it. If the action plan will be detailed, it is best to schedule a meeting at a later time to review the plan and reach a mutual agreement about it. This consultation tactic is especially useful for assigning responsibilities to a subordinate or asking a peer to carry out supporting activities on a project. To be feasible, the target person should have at least moderate agreement with the strategy or objective.

• Respond in a positive way to target person concerns.

Consultation is most effective when used as an initial influence tactic, but it can be a useful follow-up tactic if the target person expresses concerns about a request, either openly or in a less explicit way. Acknowledge these concerns and mutually discuss ways to deal with them. Explain how problems will be avoided or minimized. Ask the person for additional suggestions on how to deal with the concerns.

Collaboration

Collaboration involves an offer to reduce the difficulty and costs of carrying out a request. This tactic can be used in many situations, and it sends a message that you are supportive and willing to facilitate the person's efforts to carry out a request.

• Offer to provide necessary assistance or resources.

Sometimes the target person is reluctant to do a requested task because it is difficult or unpleasant. If the person lacks experience in doing the task, offer to provide advice and guidance. If the task is unpleasant, offer to help the person do it.

Sometimes a tedious task can be more enjoyable if performed by two people working together than by one person working alone. If the task requires additional resources, offer to provide them or to help the person get them.

• Offer to help solve problems caused by a request.

A request is more likely to be resisted if it will cause new problems for the target person. For example, the request to do a new task may interfere with the target person's other job responsibilities. The request to change the contents of a monthly report may make it necessary for the target person to get information from other people who are reluctant to provide it. The leader should try to anticipate such problems and be prepared to offer ways to avoid them or help deal with them. When the problems caused by a request are not obvious to the leader, some probing questions may be necessary to learn about them. One option is to ask what problems could delay completion of the task.

• Offer to help implement a proposed change.

A major source of resistance to change to a proposed change is the extra work that would be required for the target person to implement it. To gain the person's support and approval for a proposed change, offer to help implement it. A requirement for the use of this form of collaboration is the capability to actually provide assistance in implementing the proposed change.

OTHER DETERMINANTS OF INFLUENCE SUCCESS

Up to now each proactive tactic was considered singly, but most influence attempts involve the use of more than one of the tactics. The effectiveness of an influence attempt is partially dependent on which tactics are combined and how they are sequenced. The interpersonal relationship and the target's perception of the agent's motives also affect the success of an influence attempt.

Combining Tactics

Some studies have found that an influence attempt is more likely to be successful if two or more different tactics are combined. However, the outcome may depend on the potency of the component tactics and the extent to which they are compatible with each other. Compatible tactics are easy to use together and enhance each other's effectiveness. The research on tactic combinations is very limited, but it suggests that some tactics are more easily combined than others.[6]

Rational persuasion is a very flexible tactic, and it is usually compatible with any of the other proactive tactics. The effectiveness of consultation can be enhanced by combining it with rational persuasion. For example, rational persuasion is used to clarify why a proposed change is important, and consultation is used to involve the target person in finding an acceptable way to implement the change. Rational persuasion can be combined with inspirational appeals when proposing a new initiative or major change. For example, in a speech to gain commitment from the members of a product development team, the leader emphasizes how success in developing a proposed new medical device can save many lives as well as increase company profits. Another useful combination is rational persuasion and apprising. For example, after explaining why a proposed change in marketing procedures will improve sales, the leader points out how much the target person's annual bonus is likely to increase as a result of higher sales.

The effectiveness of consultation can be increased by combining it with collaboration. For example, when a discussion of how to achieve a shared task objective reveals concerns about obstacles, the leader can offer to help the target person deal with these obstacles. When a coalition partner helps a leader influence the target person, the process will automatically involve combining a coalition tactic with other tactics. For example, the agent and coalition partner may both use rational persuasion to influence the target person.

Some tactics are less compatible. A hard form of pressure is usually incompatible with personal appeals or ingratiation because it undermines the feelings of friendship and loyalty that are the basis for these tactics. Pressure can also undermine the trust necessary for the effectiveness of a tactic such as consultation. Nevertheless, when assistance is needed from a person who does not agree with the leader's task objectives, substantial pressure may be necessary before consultation will be feasible. Threats or the use of an upward appeal to authority figures may help to convince the target person that cooperation with the leader is more beneficial than noncooperation. However, the benefits of using pressure in this way must be weighed against potential adverse side effects, such as lingering resentment and hostility. Combining pressure with consultation should be avoided except when absolutely necessary.

Sequencing of Influence Tactics

An influence attempt often involves a series of separate influence episodes that span a period of days or weeks. The limited research on this subject indicates that some tactics are used more in initial influence attempts and other tactics are used more in follow-up influence attempts.[7] It is prudent for a leader to initially select tactics that are likely to gain the desired outcome (compliance or commitment) with the least effort and cost. Initial influence attempts with subordinates or peers often involve either a simple request or a relatively weak form of rational persuasion, because these tactics are easy to use and entail little in the way of costs. If some resistance is anticipated, then the leader is likely to use a stronger form of rational persuasion, and "soft" tactics such as personal appeals, consultation, collaboration, apprising, and inspirational appeals. In the face of continued resistance by a target, the leader will either escalate to "harder" tactics or abandon the effort if the request does not justify the risks of escalation.

The sequencing of tactics can affect the target person's perception of the agent's motives. Ingratiation (for example, praising the person's ability) is more credible when used early as part of the rationale for a request. Consultation may be viewed as more sincere if used initially rather than saving it until an influence attempt has already faltered.

Legitimating may be used either early or late, but it should be used early if the target person is expected to have doubts about the legitimacy of a request. Exchange can be costly when used to gain compliance with a request that would otherwise be resisted, because it usually requires expending a valuable resource. Thus, exchange should not be used early in an influence attempt unless it is clearly necessary. Pressure involves the risk of undesirable side effects such as target resentment, and hard forms of pressure should be used only as a last resort after other tactics have failed.

Coalitions are commonly used as a follow-up tactic but can be effective as an early tactic to help gain endorsements and supporters for a change that is likely to be costly and risky. To avoid eliciting initial target resistance that may be difficult to overcome, it is useful to show that a proposed change or new initiative has widespread support by people whom the target respects. Another form of coalition that can be used as an initial tactic is popular in countries such as China where people are very concerned about avoiding the loss of face. Instead of directly confronting the target person and risking a rejection that would be embarrassing to both parties, the agent asks a mutual friend to talk to the target person and determine if a favorable response is likely.[8]

Trust and Credibility

As noted earlier, the effectiveness of an influence attempt depends in part on the interpersonal relationship between the agent and target. The tactics are usually more effective when the agent is trusted by the target and perceived to be ethical and competent. Moreover, in a cooperative, trusting relationship, there is less need to use the proactive tactics. Thus, it is beneficial for the agent to develop a good relationship with the target and to preserve a reputation for integrity and competence. Many of the behaviors described by theories of effective leadership are relevant for developing a favorable relationship and reputation.[9]

The credibility and integrity of leaders is very much affected by how they use their power and influence. Any tactic can be used in a way that is unethical. For example, rational persuasion and apprising may involve lies and distortion. Inspirational appeals based on emotions such as fear or envy may be used to influence people in destructive ways. Collaboration and exchange may be empty promises. Ingratiation may be insincere. The proactive tactics should be used in ethical ways to accomplish shared objectives, not to exploit others for the leader's personal gain. Leaders should be careful to avoid using tactics in a way that is deceptive or manipulative. Some leaders believe that deception may be justified in the short term to achieve worthwhile objectives, but the long-term effects are usually negative for both the leader and the organization.

RESISTING UNWANTED INFLUENCE ATTEMPTS

In proactive influence attempts, the agent initiates the interaction, but effective leaders must also be able to respond in appropriate ways to an unwanted influence attempt initiated by someone else, including a boss, peer, or client. Leaders must be able to deal effectively with a request that is irrelevant, impractical, or unethical. The choice of resistance tactics has important consequences not only for immediate outcome, but also for the future relationship with the person making the request.

Only a few studies have investigated how people resist influence attempts.[10] The initial findings suggest that most of the tactics used for proactive influence attempts can also be used for resistance, although the tactics may take a somewhat different form. Little is known about the best tactics for resisting unwanted influence, but it is likely that they include the core tactics. When used as a resistance tactic, rational persuasion may involve explaining why the agent's proposed plan is unlikely to be successful. Consultation may be used to gain more insight about the agent's reasons or underlying assumptions for a request or proposal. Collaboration may involve an offer to help accomplish the agent's objective in a different way. Inspirational appeals may involve efforts to construe a request or proposal as contrary to core values and ideals in the organizational culture.

Legitimating can be an effective resistance tactic when the agent's request is inconsistent with company rules or a formal contract. Apprising can be useful for resisting a request or proposal that could have serious unanticipated consequences for the agent, such as derailing the agent's career. Pressure may be necessary when the target person is asked to do something unethical. An example is a subordinate who threatens to resign if the boss insists on making changes that are unethical or inconsistent with core values in the organization.

EXECUTIVE SUMMARY

Research using several different methods has identified eleven distinct types of proactive tactics that can be used by leaders to influence subordinates, peers, and bosses. Some tactics are more difficult to use than others, and some are likely to be more effective than others. However, the best tactics do not always result in task commitment, and the worst tactics do not always result in resistance. The outcome of any particular influence attempt is strongly dependent on other factors in addition to the type of tactics that are used, including the power and authority of the agent, the influence objective, the agent-target relationship, and cultural norms about the use of the tactics. Any tactic can result in resistance if it is not used in a skilful manner, or if it is used for a request that is improper or unethical.

Success in influencing people requires skill in diagnosing the situation and determining what influence strategy is relevant. Effective leaders are flexible and adaptive as the situation changes.[11] The following general principles should be remembered when deciding how to influence others to gain their cooperation and support:

1. *Understand the attitudes, values, and emotions of the persons you need to influence.* This knowledge is important for understanding how difficult it will be to influence the target person and which tactics are most relevant for a request or proposal.

2. *Select influence tactics that are appropriate for your relationship with the target person.* For example, it is easier to use exchange and apprising with a subordinate or peer than with a boss. These two tactics are also very useful for influencing a target person who may not share your task objectives (for example, a customer or supplier).

3. *Select influence tactics that are compatible with the nature of the requested task.* For example, apprising is not appropriate for a task that does not involve the possibility of personal benefits for the target. An inspirational appeal is not appropriate for tasks that do not involve strong values.

4. *Acquire the information and expertise needed to support the use of tactics that are likely to be relevant.* For example, rational persuasion is more likely to be effective when the leader has extensive knowledge and information about the task. Apprising is more likely to be effective if the leader has more knowledge than the target person does about reward contingencies and career issues.

5. *Maintain a good relationship with people on whom you are dependent for cooperation and assistance,* especially when you have little or no authority over them. It is easier to gain cooperation and commitment from people when there is a high level of mutual trust and respect.

6. *Determine if the core tactics are relevant for an important influence attempt.* Rational persuasion is usually relevant, but consider carefully whether one or more of the other core tactics is also relevant. Leaders in business organizations often fail to use consultation, collaboration, and inspirational appeals in situations where they are relevant.

7. *Combine tactics that are compatible and complementary.* For a very difficult influence attempt, multiple tactics increase the likelihood of success, but the potential benefits will not be achieved unless the tactics are compatible.

8. *Sequence tactics in a way that will maximize the positive effects.* Some tactics are equally effective when used early or late in an influence attempt, but the effectiveness of other tactics depends on when they are used. A tactic may appear insincere or manipulative if used with inappropriate timing.

9. *Always maintain credibility and personal integrity.* Lack of credibility will reduce the utility of the proactive tactics and is likely to derail the leader's career. Effective leaders use their power in a subtle, nonthreatening way to achieve worthwhile objectives, and they do not attempt to deceive or manipulate people.

Leaders who understand how and when to use each proactive tactic are likely to be more effective in their efforts to influence subordinates, peers, and bosses. Knowing how to successfully combine different tactics requires considerable insight and skill. At least some of the relevant skills can be enhanced with feedback and training. For example, a recent study showed that a short feedback workshop was able to improve the use of core tactics by middle managers in regional savings banks.[12] Research on the use of influence tactics by leaders in business organizations is still in its infancy. As we continue to learn more about this important subject, it will be possible to develop additional guidelines on how to influence people whose cooperation is needed for success in leadership positions.

CHAPTER SIX

Creating the Conditions for Success

Best Practices in Leading for Innovation

Michael D. Mumford

Dawn L. Eubanks

Stephen T. Murphy

Few phenomena have as much impact on our lives, and our world, as innovation—the translation of new ideas into useful products—and creativity—the basis for initial generation of these new ideas.[1] Innovation in its many varied forms is responsible for the drugs that have extended human life, the information technology systems that allow us to do our work, and the entertainment we pursue in our leisure hours.[2] Not only is innovation a profound influence on our lives, as we move into the twenty-first century; it has become clear that innovation will be the major engine of economic growth.[3] Recognizing the fundamental importance of innovation, organizations (businesses, nonprofit, and governmental organizations) have begun to adapt new forms— forms expressly intended to encourage innovation.[4]

These changes—changes involved in moving from a manufacturing to an idea production economy—pose a fundamental question for students of leadership. What is required of leaders in an idea production enterprise? At this juncture, many answers to this question have been proposed—yet none really seems to satisfy. The confusion that surrounds this question is aptly illustrated in the various training interventions that have been used to prepare leaders to manage innovative product development efforts. In a review of this literature, one finds programs that teach creative thought, systems thinking, market analysis, project management, climate creation, humor, painting, and extrasensory perception. The implication of this laundry list of developmental programs is obvious: although we have lots of ideas, we really do not know what leaders must do to promote innovation. With this point in mind, our intent in this chapter is twofold. First, we present a model of the core processes that provide a basis for the leadership of innovative efforts. Second, we use this model to identify some of the strategies that might be used to enhance performance in the leadership of innovative efforts.

A MODEL FOR LEADING INNOVATION
Background

Models of the creative process underlying innovation have traditionally been based on a romantic worldview.[5] In this romantic framework, idea generation, a potential in all people, is seen as a mystical event. Recent research, however, has painted a rather different picture of creative thought. Creative thought is commonly held to occur selectively in response to complex, novel, ill-defined problems in which the individual has discretion concerning the approach, or approaches, to be taken in problem solving.[6] Typically, generation of solutions to these kinds of problems requires a high level of expertise and a substantial investment of cognitive resources.[7] To solve these problems, people must define the problem, gather relevant information, identify appropriate concepts, combine and reorganize concepts, generate ideas based on this new conceptual structure, evaluate and revise these ideas, plan and execute implementation of the idea, and monitor idea implementation.[8] Effective execution of these processing operations requires appropriate application of strategies for working with information relevant to the domain at hand.[9] Even given expertise, effort, and effective execution of requisite processing strategies, most creative efforts fail.[10]

The high failure rate of new ideas frames the problem confronting organizations in an idea-driven economy.[11] It is not always clear if a new idea is needed. And, even when new ideas are needed, substantial time and effort must be invested in idea development,[12] and the likelihood of rejection by the market is substantial—remember the Edsel.

To complicate matters further, organizational routines and economies of scale cannot be readily used to offset this risk.[13] Further, multiple parties, with conflicting and competing agendas, will be involved in the generation, development, and fielding of new ideas, resulting in conflict that can bring idea generation and development to a halt[14]—a point nicely illustrated in Detroit's late development of front-wheel drive cars.[15] Even if organizations somehow manage to shepherd an idea through all these gates, they are left with a problem. Someone else may come along and steal the idea without incurring the costs entailed in the initial idea development.[16]

The Model

This thumbnail sketch of the challenges involved in idea generation, and the development of innovative new products, is important because it frames the problem confronting leaders who seek innovation. Ultimately, the leaders of innovative ventures must (1) identify and define problems worth pursuing—those problems where the potential payoffs of the solution justify the risk; (2) create a context that allows multiple parties to work together in generating viable ideas—ideas that have a chance of successful implementation; and (3) manage the context of idea development and fielding—to ensure that viable ideas are likely to be adopted in the market place.

Figure 6.1 illustrates the nature of the model implied by this definition, generation, and implementation framework. Within this framework, environmental analysis, recognition of opportunities or potentialities, along with the significance of failures or deficiencies, vis-à-vis the environment, is held to trigger strategic analysis of the problem by a leadership team. This leadership team, based on its analysis of the problem, or potentiality, defines a mission focused on certain broad objectives. Mission definition, in turn, allows formation of the teams to be tasked with the creative problem solving and establishment of the climate and context in which the team will operate. Team products and processes are then evaluated by leaders and other members of the organization, with relevant criteria and broader organizational considerations shaping evaluation and revision of the idea. Evaluation and revision provide a basis for planning idea development and subsequent fielding of the product, or products, developed on the basis of this idea—activities that require adequate support and resources as well as process management.

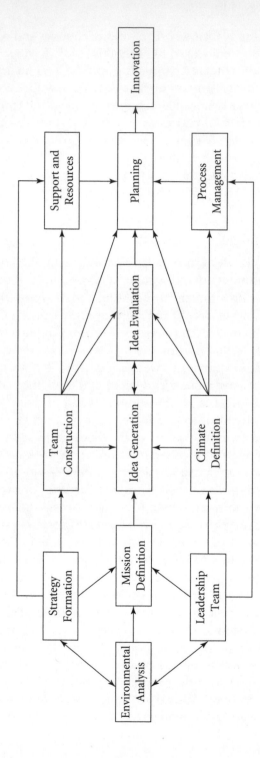

Figure 6.1. Core Functional Requirements for Leaders of Creative Efforts.

In the context of the present discussion, this model is noteworthy because it indicates the key considerations that must be taken into account as leaders define problems, shape idea generation, and shepherd people through the process of idea development and fielding. An understanding of what leaders must do suggests the kind of actions that might be taken to enhance performance in leading for innovation.

DEFINING PROBLEMS
Environmental Analysis

The missions that provide a basis for innovation in organizations do not arise spontaneously. Instead, they appear closely linked to the demands made by, and potentialities evident in, the environment in which the organization is operating. In fact, internal and external turbulence seems to stimulate innovation by energizing a search for adaptive solutions.[17] Souitaris's findings indicated that use of external information sources such as customer feedback, supplier feedback, market research, competition monitoring, technology monitoring, joint ventures, and international contacts all contributed to innovation.[18] External information, including events (for example, product failures) that have adaptive implications, is especially likely to induce innovation when problems are revealed.[19] However, at least at times, identification of potentialities (for example, new technological capabilities) can also induce innovation.[20]

The importance of environmental adaptation in determining the need for, and feasibility of, innovation has a rather straightforward implication with regard to the leadership. Leadership requires active monitoring of the internal and external environment. Some support for this conclusion has been provided by Koberg, Uhlenbruck, and Sarason, who found that innovation was positively related to environmental scanning and analysis by senior leaders.[21] Although it appears that information seeking is critical to innovation, it is of little value unless leaders can identify the portents of this information. For example, failure to recognize the importance of personal computers led IBM to enter the market late, after surrendering substantial market share to competitors. In research along this theme, Kickul and Gundry found that leader creative abilities moderate the impact of scanning on innovation.[22] Similarly, O'Connor found that the ability of leaders to forecast future trends was critical to innovation.[23] These findings point to the value of attempts to develop creative thinking and forecasting skills.[24]

The available evidence also indicates that the diversity of the information sought in scanning contributes to innovation. As a result, senior leaders who initiate innovation possess a diverse network of atypical contacts[25]—for example, a plastics manufacturer who has contacts in the building industry. However, Bonnardel and Marméche found that diverse external information contributes to innovation only when people have substantial expertise.[26] Apparently, without appropriate expertise, people have difficulty integrating information from different sources and extrapolating the implications of this information. Thus, to lead for innovation, people need expertise in the domain where the innovation is taking place.[27]

Leadership Team

What should be recognized in this regard, however, is that organizations are complex, multifunctional entities that must respond to a complex, multifaceted, internal and external environment. Given the time required to develop expertise and its specificity to a particular content area or domain, these characteristics of organizations suggest that effective leadership of major innovative efforts will require leadership *teams*—teams containing diverse expertise—rather than an individual leader.[28] The advantage of diverse leadership teams in contributing to innovation is that they increase the amount of different external information available.[29] Another way diverse teams contribute to innovation is that they provide the multiple perspectives needed for integrative thought and comprehensive evaluation.[30] Still another way they contribute to innovation is by providing leaders who can fulfill different roles in different phases of the idea generation and development process.[31] Thus Hauschildt and Kirchmann found that the technical and financial success of innovative projects increased when multiple leaders filling multiple different roles were involved.[32]

From a practical perspective, these findings indicate that leadership for innovation will require shared leadership.[33] Shared leadership, which entails both power sharing and collaborative decision making, is only likely to prove effective if attempts are made to enhance team performance. Thus, interventions intended to clarify goals and objectives, build trust, define shared mental models, and encourage open, lateral, communication may prove useful.[34] Finally, to ensure collaboration, joint accountability—evaluations based on project success rather than individual achievement—will be required.

Strategy Formation

Identification of a potential opportunity or a problem requiring attention, however, does not imply that leaders should automatically seek innovation. Instead, a decision should be made as to whether or not innovation represents a viable, adaptive response. In making these strategic decisions, the leaders must take into account a number of considerations, including (1) the readiness of the market; (2) the strategic envelope, or conditions of the market, in which pursuing the idea will prove valuable; (3) the cost of idea development; (4) the feasibility of protecting the advantages accruing to initial development of the idea; (5) the available skills and resources for idea development; (6) likely synergies with other efforts; and (7) long-term strategic positioning.[35] The problem that arises here, however, is that by virtue of their novelty and ambiguity, strategic decisions with regard to innovation are difficult and will be undermined by the application of short-term financial criteria.[36] Thus leaders must apply a long time frame, in which risk is accepted.

When appraising problems and potentialities, leaders are most likely to define and pursue efforts that "fit" with the organization's current culture, markets, core competencies, and technologies. Of course, these high-fit, or incremental, innovations have a greater chance of success and can be developed at lower cost over a shorter time frame.[37] Moreover, sustained chains of incremental innovation can be used to build truly high performance organizations—consider DuPont's work in polymers. The difficulty that arises when fit is used to frame strategy with regard to innovation, however, is that the problems and opportunities identified, and the solutions pursued, will be similar to those considered in past efforts—consider General Motors' failure to pursue hybrid engines. As a result, application-of-fit standards in framing innovation strategy may lead to missed opportunities and an inability to cope with radical environmental and technological change.

One implication of these observations is that leaders must create a perception of fit that articulates how ideas fit in the context of other ongoing organizational activities.[38] Thus, leaders seeking innovation must engage in political tactics, not only acquiring top management support but also building acceptance for the legitimacy of the effort based on competitor threats, linkage to other initiatives, and competency building.[39] Leaders, moreover, in strategy formulation must determine how to structure and manage the effort to buffer and maintain the work.[40] In other words, the leaders of creative efforts must shape the context in which the work will be conducted—they cannot simply order innovation.

Mission Definition

Strategy, of course, establishes the parameters around which a mission is formulated. In contrast to a vision, which articulates an idealized future, a mission is product- or solution-oriented, to be executed within certain defined parameters. Missions (for example, DuPont's attempt to develop synthetic fibers that mimicked the properties of wool), specifically challenging technical missions that produce valued outcomes, have been found to be powerful motivators for creative people.[41] In fact, studies by Rickards, Chen, and Moger, at an individual level, and Pinto and Prescott, at a group level, have shown that a sense of mission is critical to innovation in organizational settings.[42]

A sense of mission contributes to innovation in four ways. First, clear objectives to which team members are committed maintain motivation in the face of failure or resistance.[43] Second, missions provide a structure around which collaborative relationships can be established and conflicts resolved on a task rather than a personalized basis.[44] Third, missions provide a framework for structured idea development that does not unduly restrict the autonomy and potential unique contributions of team members.[45] Finally, missions provide a framework for sense making, and sense making is critical to performance wherever people must work on the kind of novel, ill-defined tasks that call for creative thought.[46]

These varied, and powerful, effects of mission indicate that leadership will involve defining, and engaging people in, the mission at hand. In defining missions, leaders must take into account a number of considerations. To begin, missions must be defined that prove challenging to people with respect to the development and application of their professional expertise. And missions must be defined in such a way that they are neither too narrow, thereby restricting creativity, nor too broad, thereby providing insufficient guidance.

Not only must leaders carefully define missions; they must engage, and reengage, people in the mission. One way leaders engage people in a mission is by creating a sense of crisis, or urgency, surrounding the mission.[47] Another way leaders engage people in a mission is by articulating its significance for others and the organization as a whole.[48] Still another way leaders engage others in a mission is by energizing people emotionally.[49] A case in point may be found in Oppenheimer's development of the first atomic bomb, where war, patriotism, and the excitement of breaking new technical ground made multiple innovations possible.

STRUCTURING CREATIVE PROBLEM SOLVING
Idea Generation

In organizations, creative problem solutions are developed and built around missions. Traditionally, leaders have not been viewed as integral to creative problem-solving efforts. Having defined the mission, their job is to stand back and let the creative people do their work. Although this view seems plausible, it is simply not borne out by the facts of the matter. In one study along these lines, Andrews and Farris obtained measures of leader attributes that might be related to innovation, including technical evaluation, motivating others, and autonomy granted and found that leader technical skills was the best predictor of team creative performance.[50] In another study along these lines, Barnowe examined the productivity of research and development teams with respect to five leader attributes: (1) support, (2) participation, (3) closeness of supervision, (4) task emphasis, and (5) technical skill.[51] He found that the leader's technical skill was the best predictor of creativity and innovation.

The importance of leader technical skills to team performance indicates that leaders make a real tangible contribution to problem solving and idea generation. Leaders perform a critical function by obtaining, and calling the group's attention to, external information that must be considered in problem solving.[52] Leaders, moreover, serve to stimulate the elaboration and exploration of idea implications, which has been found to be critical to the generation of creative problem solutions.[53] Finally, leaders define viable and nonviable solution paths within the broader context of the effort at hand—an important determinant of the nature and success of creative problem-solving efforts in technical fields.[54] It is, of course, difficult to see how any of these functions can be executed if leaders lack requisite technical skills and good creative problem-solving skills.

Not only must leaders shape solutions; they must also shape the interactional context in which creative problem-solutions are generated. Thus, leaders must stimulate active intellectual engagement—to spur the development of new ideas and approaches.[55] They must not only encourage participation but know whose participation is likely to prove crucial.[56] And they must manage debate surrounding technical issues in such a way that the integration of different technical perspectives becomes possible. Thus, technical and creative problem-solving skills (for example, problem definition, conceptual combination) allow leaders to orchestrate the context for the integrative efforts that provide a basis for idea generation. The need for leaders to orchestrate the idea generation context, however, suggests that wisdom and interpersonal skills may also be at a premium in leading for innovation.[57]

Idea Evaluation

Leaders, of course, must do something more than shape the context for idea generation; ultimately, leaders must evaluate the problem solutions proposed by others.[58] Traditionally, solution evaluation has been viewed as a reactive, nongenerative activity in which the merits of a proposed idea are evaluated with respect to fixed standards such as cost effectiveness, market share, and risk. In contrast to this traditional view of the idea evaluation process, more recent research suggests that idea evaluation may be an inherently generative activity in which initial ideas are reshaped and reformed to enhance their chances of success.[59]

This point is nicely illustrated in a recent study by Lonergan, Scott, and Mumford, who asked undergraduates to assume the role of marketing managers reviewing advertising campaigns being developed for a new product.[60] The campaigns presented to these "managers" were selected to reflect varying levels of quality and originality. It was found that the most original and highest-quality campaigns were obtained when the standards for initial evaluation and revision of ideas applied led to revisions intended to enhance the workability of highly original ideas and when the standards applied led to revisions intended to enhance the originality of higher-quality ideas.

Thus, leaders' evaluations, vis-à-vis subsequent revisions, contributed to the generation of more creative products.

One implication of these findings is that leaders should try to provide compensatory feedback in appraising new ideas. An example may be found in the kind of feedback Lee Iacocca provided to the designers during his turnaround of the Chrysler Corporation—encouraging the design of practical cars, not just technology development. Another, perhaps somewhat more subtle, implication of these findings is that leaders should apply different standards when appraising different ideas—varying evaluation criteria over time as initial ideas are elaborated and extended. Hence, a key contribution made by leaders is defining the kind of standards that should be applied in evaluating and revising ideas at a given point in time and in certain settings.[61]

With regard to idea evaluation, however, another point should be borne in mind. In evaluating ideas, leaders, like people in general, are subject to a number of potential biasing factors.[62] Leaders, for example, may be too quick to reject risky ideas, especially when the short-term benefits of these ideas are not immediately apparent.[63] They may also underestimate the originality of truly novel ideas.[64] And they may underestimate the demands imposed by idea implementation due to the operation of optimistic biases.[65] All of these phenomena will undermine the value of feedback with regard to idea revision, suggesting that interventions intended to minimize these errors—both structural interventions (for example, requiring active analysis of idea implications) and training interventions (for example, looking for the truly original features of ideas)—may well prove useful in enhancing leader performance.

Climate Definition

Beyond their contributions to idea generation and evaluation, the actions taken by leaders in defining the environment in which the work takes place will influence creativity and innovation. Leaders play a key role in defining climate—people's beliefs about expectations in their work environment.[66] The role of leaders in defining climate is noteworthy because climate perceptions have been found to have a marked impact on innovation, producing multiple correlations in the .40 to .50 range with measures of idea generation and innovation.[67] In fact, evidence indicates that creative people may be unusually sensitive to environmental requirements and contingencies.[68]

A variety of climate dimensions have been identified that might influence innovation. In a review of this literature, Mumford and his colleagues identified twelve dimensions that are commonly considered core aspects of a creative climate: (1) autonomy, (2) risk taking, (3) intellectual stimulation, (4) participation, (5) rewards for innovation, (6) positive peer group relationships, (7) cohesiveness, (8) positive supervisory relationships, (9) rewards for innovation, (10) organizational integration, (11) mission clarity, and (12) appropriate challenge.[69] Broadly speaking, it appears that an environment where people can safely pursue and develop new ideas in collaboration with others, where idea development is supported by the organization, contributes to innovation.

Although it is not surprising that these perceptions would contribute to people's willingness to pursue creative work, one is left with a question. How should leaders go about engineering this kind of climate? One answer to this question may be found in Jaussi and Dionne, who found that leader role modeling of relevant behaviors was integral in shaping climate perceptions and encouraging innovation.[70] Clearly, leaders may create feelings of autonomy and participation by avoiding overly close supervision and involving people in decision making. Perceptions concerning the value of risk taking and rewards will be influenced by how leaders react to and evaluate new ideas, as well as their willingness to support idea development efforts. In this regard, however, it is important to bear in mind the observations of Taggar, who indicated that interventions of this sort are best structured around missions and people's intellectual contributions to these missions.[71] Thus, climate interventions, if they are to prove successful, must encourage open exchange within the context of the work being done.

It should be recognized that however important leader behavior may be in shaping climate, climate perceptions are not fully under the control of leaders. The broader culture of the organization, particularly in organizations that evidence strong cultures, will influence the kind of climate likely to emerge in teams working on creative tasks.[72] This point is of some importance for two reasons. First, leaders must manage climate interventions within a group vis-à-vis the broader culture of the organization. Second, leaders must seek to understand the culture, structure, and strategy of the organization and how these variables operate to shape the approaches that can be used in developing a creative climate.

Team Construction

Climate, of course, is also a function of the people who have been brought together to work on a project. As a result, the actions taken by leaders in team construction may have a marked impact on initial idea generation and subsequent innovation. There appear to be two major ways leaders' actions in team formation influence idea generation and innovation: (1) structural interventions and (2) process interventions.

With regard to structure, research indicates that innovation increases with team size up to a size of about five to seven individuals. After this maximum size is exceeded, group process demands result in diminished innovation, with this process loss being particularly marked when the group contains a relatively large number of highly creative individuals.[73] The problem confronting leaders of creative ventures, however, is that many, perhaps most, real-world innovative work projects will involve a far larger number of people. Leaders, as a result, must often manage innovative work by creating multiple subteams with distinct missions where the activities of these subteams are integrated by a steering committee.[74] The problem here is that leaders must engage in integrative sense-making activities intended to articulate how the efforts and missions of various subteams make uniquely valuable contributions to the broader mission at hand.[75]

With regard to process, evidence indicates that cohesive teams possessing shared, albeit moderately diverse, mental models tend to evidence higher levels of innovation, in part because these conditions permit the collaborations needed for innovation.[76] The problem that arises in this regard, however, is that highly cohesive teams with well-established normative structures may become isolated and fall prey to a "not invented here" syndrome in which people reject information and ideas that originate outside the group.[77] Thus, the leaders must ensure effective cross-team exchange, with these exchanges becoming more important as the group becomes more cohesive and ideas move from initial generation to development, thereby involving a wider range of functions and stakeholders.[78]

MANAGING IDEA DEVELOPMENT
Planning

Once an idea has been generated, development of the idea and the eventual fielding of an innovative new product will, it is hoped, occur. The translation of ideas into viable new products or processes is a difficult, demanding activity in most organizations, requiring the involvement and support of multiple units. Complexity and the need for coordination[79] implies that planning idea development and fielding will be a critical activity in any creative venture. In keeping with this observation, Maidique and Zirger found that senior managers' investment of time and effort in planning the development and fielding of new ideas was critical to the success of the product development effort.[80]

In one sense, the influence of planning on idea development and fielding is straightforward. Typically, multiple parties (for example, manufacturing, marketing, sales, and purchasing) will, at some stage, be involved in the development and fielding of new ideas. Unless leaders have developed viable plans, it is unlikely that the multifunctional coordination needed for idea development and fielding will occur. In another sense, however, planning has a somewhat more subtle, and perhaps more pervasive, influence. Plans ultimately represent a mental simulation of future actions, in which these simulations are used to identify key actions, causal factors that must be leveraged, requisite resources, contingencies on actions, and applicable restrictions.[81] The availability of this framework not only allows leaders to identify and manage the variables (for example, resources and restrictions) that determine the success of idea development; it provides the basis for recognition of emergent opportunities and construction of the backup plans that permit rapid adaptation of activities to respond to problems encountered in the idea development effort.[82]

These observations are noteworthy, in part, because they indicate that a critical function of leadership teams will be construction and revision of the plan for development and fielding of new ideas. In leadership teams, planning tends to be case based, where past experience, practical experience, is used to forecast the implications of different approaches or actions.[83] One implication of this finding is that relevant and diverse practical experience may be necessary for effective planning in new product development efforts. Planning, however, also depends on the analysis of experience. This point is of some importance because of the various errors that occur in planning, including overreliance on salient past cases, failure to consider multiple, complex, interactive outcomes, and errors of optimism with regard to support and contingencies.[84] As a result, leaders must apply critical analytic thought to cherished new ideas, but cannot undermine the enthusiasm that surrounds creative efforts. Thus, leaders—like Steve Jobs—who create conditions where sustained innovation is possible must be both critics and cheerleaders.

Although people will invest cognitive resources in idea analysis as implementation plans are being formulated, once plan execution begins people appear to adopt an implementation mindset in which the plan is simply implemented.[85] In innovation, however, multiple issues will arise that must be addressed if successful development and fielding is to occur. Leaders, as a result, must actively monitor the progress made with respect to implementation plans, challenging people to find ways to adjust and adapt these plans to current conditions and information. Thus, leaders must not only create structures that allow them to stay on top of things; they must establish a climate that encourages ongoing, adaptive revision of ideas and idea development strategies. Illustrations of this point may be found in such diverse companies as Intel and 3M.

Process Management

Idea development and fielding will typically involve a broader range of people and perspectives than initial idea generation to ensure that different forms of expertise are actively engaged. The use of multifunctional teams contributes both to the speed with which new products are developed and to the ultimate success of new product development efforts.[86] Although multifunctional teams contribute to innovation by encouraging external communication, enhancing coordination, and ensuring the ready availability of relevant expertise, their use presents the leaders with three challenges.

First, by virtue of differences in background, multifunctional teams evidence lower cohesion and greater conflict.[87] Second, diversity and lack of a shared history inhibits coordination and makes communication of team members' activities more difficult.[88] Third, conflict, coordination difficulties, and lower cohesion, along with the implied loss of social support, induce stress.[89] And stress may inhibit the adaptive refinements needed for idea development.

These characteristics of multifunctional teams imply that the management of these teams represents a critical problem confronting leaders. For multifunctional teams to prove successful, leaders must be found who are capable of building credibility, evidence personal commitment to the mission, ensure that all voices get a fair hearing to build shared commitment, and use this commitment as a basis for building cohesion. Finally, because leaders cannot rely on established social processes, they must create formal structures that act to promote effective exchange among diverse people with different agendas and limited familiarity. Thus, the leaders of creative efforts must be capable of rapidly identifying and establishing the formal structures needed when diverse groups of people must work together.[90]

Support and Resources

The development and fielding of new ideas is a demanding, inherently costly effort. As a result, idea development and fielding efforts are likely to flounder if adequate time and adequate resources have not been provided.[91] Thus, as Dougherty and Hardy found, sustained support was critical to the success of new product development efforts.[92] In organizations, however, where time is short and resources are limited, it is not an easy task to ensure that requisite time and resources are available. Accordingly, a key role of the leadership team is ensuring that requisite time and resources are available to see the project through. One important implication of this observation is that the leaders must sell senior management on the value of the effort and ensure the ongoing commitment of senior management to the project. Early involvement of senior management in the project, of course, is one strategy that might be used to acquire support.[93] What should be recognized here, however, is that early involvement is likely to prove of little value if this involvement is not sustained over time.

In selling projects, however, leaders must recognize that ideas and products are not, from an organizational perspective, something of value in their own right. Thus, in acquiring support, leaders must be able to link ideas, and the products flowing from these ideas, to broader organizational strategy.[94] Consider for example, the relationship between Fox Television News and the Murdoch newspaper chain, which are under common ownership. Thus, the leadership of innovative efforts requires strategic awareness—an awareness that may well be rare among the technically oriented people who drive the development of new ideas. In selling projects, moreover, it is important to bear in mind the point that the pursuit of new ideas is an inherently ambiguous and risky undertaking. As a result, politics will be embroiled in the evaluation of ideas and the willingness of senior managers to pursue ideas. Accordingly, leaders must not only have an understanding of the politics operating in an organization; they must have the ability to build the kind of stable political alliances that will ensure long-term support.

To complicate matters further, ideas are not an easy thing to sell in organizations. One cannot always make a rational economic case for new ideas because their significance may be hard to understand. As a result, the leaders of creative efforts must become "actors"—actors who are capable of constantly engaging people in the promise of an idea even as they try to manage the many problems and pitfalls involved in the development of new ideas.[95] Thus, Henry Chauncey, in founding the American standardized testing industry, articulated the bright future of standardized tests even as he grappled with the many challenges continually facing the educational testing service in its early years.[96]

Discussion

Before turning to the broader conclusions of our observations, certain limitations should be noted. To begin, we have examined the requirements for the leadership of creative ventures from a general cross-field perspective rather than focusing on a particular occupation. This point is of some importance, because some cross-field differences in the requirements for the leadership of creative efforts will exist as a result of field demands.[97] Along related lines, in the present effort we have focused on critical functions that must be executed by leaders or leadership teams. Thus, relatively little attention has been given to followers' perceptions of and reactions to leaders. Moreover, little has been said about potential multilevel influences—senior executive team, board, stockholders, competitors, and employees, for example—even though there is reason to suspect that multilevel interactions represent a complex set of influences shaping innovation requirements and thus the demands imposed on the leaders of innovative projects.[98]

Even bearing these caveats in mind, we believe that the present effort has some noteworthy implications for understanding both the requirements for the leadership of innovative ventures and the kind of actions that may be taken to enhance leader performance. Perhaps the most clear-cut conclusion that may be drawn is that the requirements imposed on those who must lead innovative projects are far more complex than we typically assume. It is not enough for leaders simply to encourage idea generation by others. Instead, leaders must scan the internal and external environment, using this scanning and analysis of strategic potentials to define the missions that provide the structure guiding idea generation and innovation. Thus, leaders, typically leadership teams, define the context in which innovation will occur.

Nor is it enough for leaders simply to define the context in which innovation will occur. Instead, leaders play an active role in setting the parameters for idea generation, exerting a profound influence on the nature of the ideas generated vis-à-vis the evaluations and feedback they provide. While the leaders of creative efforts make real, tangible contributions to idea generation, especially in terms of the integration of broader systems considerations, leaders must also create and maintain a viable climate for idea generation. After idea generation, leaders take on a new role, planning idea development and fielding, acquiring requisite support and resources, and managing the idea development and fielding process. Thus, to direct innovative projects, leaders must be able to think both generatively and practically—managing people just as they manage ideas.

These observations about the nature of creative leadership have some important implications for best practices of leader performance. Far and away, the strategy most commonly used to prepare leaders to direct innovative projects is creativity training—typically training that seeks to enhance creative problem-solving skills and reshape common assumptions about the nature of creative work.[99] Given the need for leaders to recognize and respond to original ideas, and establish a direction for creating problem-solving activities, there would seem to be value in attempts to develop creative thinking skills. It is, however, an open a question whether other forms of creativity training (for example, imagery, story writing) will have much value in preparing people to lead projects calling for innovation.

Despite the wide range of training used to prepare leaders to direct these projects, the model presented in this chapter suggests that there are some noteworthy deficiencies evident in the kind of training currently available. For example, training in scanning and innovation strategy formation would seem to have real promise given the role of scanning and strategy in mission definition, yet it is not common to provide this training to those who will lead projects calling for creative work. Moreover, there would seem to be value in training that helps leaders define and articulate mission.[100] Unfortunately, few training programs exist to help leaders engage in planning for innovation.

Not only does this model suggest some new types of training that might be used to prepare leaders to direct innovative projects; it suggests that creativity training taken unto itself may not prove sufficient. However important creative thought may be for leaders,[101] the leaders of projects involving innovation will need a number of other types of training. Given the importance of planning to successful product development and fielding, training intended to provide leaders with forecasting and project management skills would seem useful. Along similar lines, leaders might find training beneficial that describes potential climate intervention strategies. Thus, a broader, more comprehensive, approach to training appears to be required given the multiple, complex functions involved in leading for innovation.

In addition to extending current training interventions, and tailoring these interventions to the needs of the people leading innovative ventures, the model we have presented in this chapter indicates that training is neither the sole nor necessarily the most effective way of enhancing leader performance with regard to innovation. For example, leaders might be given guidelines and procedures for the appraisal of creative ideas. Alternatively, experts in high-potential areas might be explicitly involved in strategy sessions to provide the background information needed to link strategy to scanning and help establish the connections needed to acquire relevant political support. Although other examples of this sort might be cited, the foregoing examples seem sufficient to make our point. The key work functions underlying successful leadership for innovation suggest that a far wider variety of interventions might be designed that would contribute to performance.

Indeed, given the nature of leadership on innovative projects, one might argue that a far wider range of interventions should be applied. For example, the role of experience in planning and team management suggests that there might be value in the design of systematic career development programs, especially programs that provide exposure to understudy roles.[102] Along similar lines, given the requirements imposed on leaders, it would be valuable to have assessments available that expressly target critical competencies such as planning, climate management skills, and innovation strategy formation.[103] Given the fact that innovation ultimately involves change—often a rather significant change—and the marshalling and management of teams, there may also be value in interventions intended to provide the leaders of creative efforts with change management and team management skills.[104]

These observations about the kind of interventions likely to enhance leader performance point to a broader conclusion. Traditionally, the leadership of creative people and innovative product development efforts has been seen as a narrow activity of limited general interest. In contrast to this traditional, stereotypic view, leadership for innovation is an unusually complex and demanding activity involving multiple functions unfolding over time as missions are identified, ideas generated and evaluated, and plans constructed for idea development and fielding. When this observation is considered in light of the critical role creativity and innovation play in the success and survival of organizations in our knowledge-based twenty-first-century economy, it would seem that the leadership for innovation might provide an ideal test bed for "best practice" models developed to address a number of different types of leader performance interventions.

EXECUTIVE SUMMARY

In a competitive global economy, organizational success and survival depends on ideas—creative new ideas that result in new products and services. The need for innovation—sustained innovation—requires people who can lead the creative people who are the ultimate source of these ideas and manage the development of these ideas into viable new products and services. In the present chapter we have argued that to lead the development of innovative new products and services leaders must be able to accomplish three things: (1) define viable problems, (2) stimulate creative problem solving, and (3) manage the development of these ideas into viable new products or services.

In organizations, the definition of viable problems requires ongoing scanning and monitoring of the organization's operations and the broader environment in which the organization must operate by leadership teams. These teams must use this information to formulate a strategy for innovation that capitalizes on the organization's core competencies. This strategy must be used to define missions that will organize and engage people in creative work.

Leaders, however, cannot just define the missions to be pursued by creative people; they must be actively involved in the creative work. One key role leaders play in directing creative work is providing feedback that improves ideas and brings ideas into line with organizational capabilities. Another key role leaders play in directing creative work is creating a climate, or environment, where people are willing to propose and pursue new ideas in collaboration with others.

Not only must leaders stimulate the development of new ideas, they must drive the development of these ideas into viable new products and services. The translation of ideas into viable new products and services requires leaders who have project management and planning skills, who can create and lead multifunctional teams, and who can build and maintain support for the initiative.

The mix of technical, organizational, and strategic skills required to lead projects invoking the development of innovative new products and services indicate that organizations cannot just "sit back" and wait for leaders to emerge. Instead, organizations must initiate systematic programs intended to prepare talented, creative people to lead the projects that will produce the new products and services that are the basis for the sustained innovation that will allow organizations to survive and prosper in the twenty-first-century economy.

CHAPTER SEVEN

Best Practices in Ethical Leadership

Craig E. Johnson

━◦◦◦━ T he arrival of the new millennium brought with it a tsunami of corporate scandals. Just as the publicity from one wave of discredited companies (Enron, WorldCom, Tyco, Adelphia) subsided, another wave rose to take its place (Health South, Strong Mutual Funds), only to be followed by yet another (Fannie Mae, AIG Insurance). All of these cases of moral failure serve as vivid reminders of the importance of ethical leadership. In every instance, leaders engaged in immoral behavior and encouraged their followers to do the same.

Despite its significance, scholars, educators, and practitioners frequently overlook the ethical dimension of leadership. Social scientific research into leadership ethics is "a relatively new topic."[1] Management school instructors often limit discussion of the subject to a single period scheduled near the end of the quarter or semester, which may be dropped if time runs short. Many organizational leaders pay grudging attention to ethics largely in response to outside pressures like media scrutiny, federal sentencing guidelines, and congressional investigations.[2] They institute ethics programs (ethics hotlines, written codes, complaint procedures) but then give them minimal support. As a result, these procedures have little influence on day-to-day operations.[3]

This chapter brings ethics to the forefront of leadership practice, based on the premise that exerting moral influence is critical to organizational performance. The first section defines the task of ethical leadership and identifies key practices that enable leaders to carry out this responsibility. The second section introduces resources or tools that leaders can draw on when assuming ethical duties. The final portion of the chapter describes the positive outcomes produced by ethical leadership.

THE TWOFOLD TASK OF ETHICAL LEADERSHIP

There are two components to ethical leadership. First, leaders behave morally as they carry out their roles. Second, they shape the ethical contexts of their groups and organizations. These dual responsibilities intertwine (the leader's behavior acts as a model for the rest of the organization, for example), but examining each one separately provides a more complete picture of the task facing leadership practitioners.

Ethical Demands of the Leadership Role

The nature of the leadership role imposes a particular set of ethical responsibilities.[4] As compared to followers, leaders (1) are more powerful, (2) enjoy greater privileges, (3) are privy to more information, (4) have wider spans of authority or responsibility, (5) deal with a broader range of constituencies who demand consistent treatment, and (6) balance a wider variety of loyalties when making decisions.[5] Because leaders exert widespread influence, how they respond to the ethical demands of their roles has an immediate impact on followers, for good or ill. Educator Parker Palmer argues that the difference between moral and immoral leadership can be as dramatic as the contrast between light and darkness. He describes a leader as "a person who has an unusual degree of power to create the conditions under which other people must live and move and have their being, conditions that can either be as illuminating as heaven or as shadowy as hell." [6]

Table 7.1 summarizes issues raised by each of the ethical demands of leadership. The last column highlights some of the ways that leaders cast shadows by failing to meet these moral challenges. Name a fallen leader, and the chances are good that he or she failed to

Responsibility	Issues	Abuses
Greater Power	What forms of power to use	Exclusive reliance on positional power (legitimate, coercive, reward)
	What goals to pursue	Serving selfish interests
	How much power to keep	Hoarding power/reducing the power of followers
	How to avoid the corruptive influence of having too much power	Refusing to be influenced
		Petty tyranny/brutality
Greater Privilege	How many additional privileges leaders should have	Excessive compensation and severance packages
	Determining the relative difference in privileges between leaders and followers	Extreme pay gaps between leaders and followers
	How to close the gap between the haves and have-nots	Self-absorption/ignoring the less fortunate
Greater Information	When to release information and to whom	Withholding needed information
	Whether to reveal possession of information	Releasing information to the wrong people
	Whether to lie or to tell the truth	Lying, deception
	What information to collect	Using information solely for personal benefit
	How to collect information	Violation of privacy rights
Multiple Constituencies	Whether to treat all followers equally	Playing favorites/creating "out groups"
	When to bend the rules and for whom	Acting arbitrarily
	How to treat outsiders	Privileging some outside groups at the expense of others
Broader Responsibility	How far the leader's responsibility extends	Failing to prevent follower misdeeds
	Whether leaders are responsible for the unethical behavior of followers	Ignoring ethical problems
	What leaders "owe" followers	Failing to take responsibility for the consequences of directives
		Denying duties to followers
		Holding followers to higher standards
Multiple Loyalties	How to balance loyalties or duties to many different groups	Serving selfish interests
	Where to place loyalties	Ignoring the larger community
	Whether to keep or to break trust	Breaking promises
		Taking advantage of vulnerable followers

Table 7.1. Ethical Demands of the Leadership Role.

adequately address one or more of the issues posed by power, privilege, information, responsibility, consistency, and loyalty. Enron's chairman Kenneth Lay and chief executive officer (CEO) Jeffrey Skilling cast a great many shadows by threatening their enemies, spending lavishly, manipulating information, failing to take responsibility for their actions, bending the rules for star performers, and violating the trust of employees.

Other experts have joined Palmer in pointing out the "shadow" side of leadership. Lipman-Blumen[7] uses the term "toxic" to describe leaders who engage in a range of destructive behaviors and exhibit dysfunctional personal characteristics. Toxic behaviors include damaging followers and violating their rights, encouraging dependence, lying, accumulating power, scapegoating, and playing favorites. Toxic personal characteristics include a lack of integrity, insatiable ambition, avarice, ethical insensitivity, and cowardice. Kellerman classifies "bad" leaders as both ineffective and unethical.[8] Ineffective leaders fail to produce the required results; unethical leaders violate "common codes of decency and good conduct." Unethical leaders put personal needs first, fail to display private virtues like courage and temperance, and put their group's narrow interests ahead of the larger good. The actions of unethical leaders stem in large part from unhealthy motivations, including:

1. *Fear.* Leaders are particularly afraid of chaos and failure. To combat disorder, they impose structures, rules, and regulations that can stifle creativity and dissent.[9] Such petty rules and regulations (for example, making employees rewrite their resignation letters, chaining laptop computers to desktops) provide plenty of material for *Dilbert* cartoonist Scott Adams to poke fun at. To stave off failure, leaders take few risks, extend the life of outdated projects and programs, and punish those who take initiative but fall short. Too few have the attitude of the founder of the Johnson & Johnson company, who declared, "If I wasn't making mistakes, I wasn't making decisions."[10] Two realizations can calm fears of chaos and disorder. First, the creative process is naturally "messy" and chaotic. Second, many successful leaders have experienced significant failure at some point during their careers.[11]

2. *Greed.* Greed encourages dishonesty, blinds leaders to the needs of others, and focuses attention on selfish interests rather than

the greater good. There are plenty of examples of leader excess. Former Adelphia CEO John Rigas looted the cable company to build a golf course in his backyard, buy a hockey team, and enrich his family members. Tyco CEO Dennis Kozlowski paid for expensive artwork with money from a program designed to help employees buy company stock. He then tried to avoid paying New York state sales tax on his purchases.[12] Greed can be dampened with a change in perspective. Leaders who adopt a stewardship orientation are much less likely to take advantage of others.[13] They believe that they are entrusted with their roles and use their authority to serve the needs of followers.

3. *Ego.* Ego distorts decision-making processes, which can lead to a number of immoral choices. Those in positions of high authority, like former House majority leader Tom DeLay, Martha Stewart, and WorldCom founder Bernie Ebbers, are most in danger of suffering from inflated egos that lead to foolish choices.[14] Their access to many sources of information convinces them that they are all-knowing (the sense of omniscience). Possessing great power, they mistakenly believe that they can do anything they want in or outside their organizations (the sense of omnipotence). Subservient employees and staff seduce powerful individuals into believing that they are well protected from the consequences of lying, stealing, manipulating earnings, accepting gifts from congressional lobbyists, and other misbehaviors (the sense of invulnerability). One way to keep ego in check is by asking a series of questions, such as "Have I invited and tolerated dissent?" "What have I omitted from my analysis?" "Are my decisions or behavior having a negative impact on the relationships involved?" "Am I rewarding ego-dominant, relationship-destroying attitudes in others?"[15]

Shaping the Ethical Context

Moral leaders practice self-reflection, looking inward to identify and then to combat unhealthy motivations that lead to ethical failures. In addition to behaving morally, ethical leaders have to convince others to do likewise. Moral leadership actively influences the ethical context. Fulfilling this second component of the ethical leadership task calls for both defensive and proactive measures. Defensive strategies seek to prevent unethical, destructive behaviors; proactive tactics intentionally foster a positive ethical climate. Johnson & Johnson tries to prevent uncivil behavior by including the following statement in its credo: "We are responsible to our employees. . . . We must respect their dignity." Former Waste Management CEO Maurice (Marty) Myers led a successful effort to reform the ethical culture of his corporation after previous executives were accused of overstating a billion dollars in earnings between 1992 and 1997. Myers created a positive ethical climate by meeting with employees to regain their trust, creating an anonymous hotline to receive reports of unethical behavior, honestly reporting financial results, and reinstituting the position of ethics officer.[16]

PREVENTING DESTRUCTIVE BEHAVIORS. There is a shadow side to organizations just as there is to individual leaders. "Dark side" organizational behaviors are deliberate attempts to harm others or the organization.[17] Categories of misbehaviors include:

- *Incivility.* Rude or discourteous actions, intentional or unintentional, that disregard others and violate norms for respect (for example, failing to acknowledge a coworker, claiming credit for someone else's work, and making a sarcastic comment about a peer).[18]

- *Aggression.* Consciously trying to hurt or injure others or the organization itself. Can be physical-verbal (destructive words or deeds); active-passive (doing harm by acting or by failing to act); or direct-indirect (doing harm directly to the individual or indirectly through an intermediary and by attacking something the target values).[19]

- *Sexual Harassment.* A form of aggression largely directed at women. *Quid pro quo* harassment consists of forcing someone to provide sexual favors in return for keeping a job or getting a promotion. Hostile work environment harassment occurs when job conditions (sexist behavior, threats, and demeaning comments) interfere with job performance.[20]

- *Discrimination.* Putting members of selected groups at a disadvantage based on prejudice and stereotypes. Often expressed subtly through such behaviors as avoiding members of low status groups and dismissing the achievements of women and people of color.[21]

How leaders respond to these unethical behaviors has a significant impact on the ethical context. Unfortunately, leaders set a negative tone in far too many cases. Their positions of power and influence make it more likely that they will act uncivilly, bully others, and offer favors in return for sex. Even if they refrain from misbehaving, leaders signal that destructive activities are sanctioned or tolerated if they take no action against offenders. The ethical climate deteriorates as a result. Unchecked incivility escalates into more aggressive behavior. An organizational culture of aggression emerges when abusive individuals are allowed to act as role models.[22] Incidents of sexual harassment go unreported when organizational leaders fail to investigate charges or to punish offenders.[23] Discriminatory behavior continues unless leaders intervene to challenge these patterns.[24]

Ethical leadership means taking steps to prevent and control dark side behaviors, starting at the top of the organization. Executives create zero-tolerance policies that outlaw antisocial behaviors and follow these guidelines themselves. They use their power constructively, confronting and punishing offenders at the first sign of trouble.[25] Moral leaders also address contextual triggers of destructive actions such as oppressive supervision, job stress, unpleasant working conditions, perceived injustice, threats to group identity, and extreme competitiveness.[26]

Financier Warren Buffett demonstrated his commitment to rooting out misbehavior when he took over Salomon Inc in the early 1990s after a government bond-trading scandal erupted in the firm's highly competitive, reckless culture. Buffett appointed himself as the company's chief compliance officer. He then ordered all Salomon officers to report every legal and moral violation, with the exception of parking tickets, directly to him. Much of Buffett's time was devoted to cooperating with federal investigators and answering questions from the press. His commitment to restoring the firm's ethical image saved it from collapse.[27]

CREATING A POSITIVE ETHICAL CLIMATE. Leaders engaged in combating destructive behaviors often behave like firefighters, trying to prevent misbehavior from flaring up and putting out unethical blazes when they break out. However, to adequately shape the ethical context, leaders also need to act as architects, designing sound moral climates. An ethical climate describes the perceptions members share of the organization's moral atmosphere.[28] Climate improves when leaders ensure that the following elements are in place:

Formal Ethics Policies and Procedures. As noted earlier, reporting mechanisms, disciplinary procedures, and ethics officers do not create a positive ethical climate on their own. They are an important first step, however, to reaching this end.[29] Formal ethics statements and procedures focus attention on ethical issues and signal that leaders are committed to moral behavior. Such documents also address misbehaviors by identifying them, outlining penalties, and providing investigation procedures. The Boeing Company instituted a strict code of ethics after employees of the firm were caught stealing secrets from competitor Lockheed Martin and offering an Air Force procurement official a job in return for federal contracts. Workers had to sign a pledge stating, "Employees will not engage in conduct or activity that may raise questions as to the company's honesty, impartiality, reputation or otherwise cause embarrassment to the company." Based on this pledge, Boeing's board decided to fire CEO Harry Stonecipher (married at the time) for carrying on a consensual affair with a corporate vice president that threatened the company's efforts to restore its reputation.[30]

Core Ideology. Core ideology is the central identity or character of an organization, which remains constant even as the group changes to meet shifting environmental conditions.[31] Ideology, in turn, consists of core values and core purpose. Worthy moral values (for example, quality, excellence, concern for the less fortunate, innovation) rally people to common causes, empower leaders and followers to act, gain the support of larger audiences outside the organization, and broaden the moral perspective of members. Values also serve as criteria for making decisions and for judging the behavior of individuals and departments.

Purpose is the group's reason for being and reflects the ideals of its members. Formal mission statements must not only be clear; they should be motivating as well. Making a profit is not sufficient motivation for many followers. They want to pursue more inspiring goals, such as providing valuable products and services and improving the community.

Starbucks is one large corporation with a clear ideology. The company's guiding principles include (1) respect and dignity for partners (employees), (2) embracing diversity, (3) applying the highest standards of excellence to the coffee business, (4) developing "enthusiastically satisfied customers;" (5) contributing positively to communities and the environment, and (6) maintaining profitability. Its stated mission is to "establish Starbucks as the premier purveyor of the finest coffee in the world while maintaining our uncompromising principles as we grow."[32]

Integrity. Integrity refers to ethical soundness, wholeness, and consistency, which come from (1) incorporating core ideology throughout every organizational unit and level and (2) living out ethical commitments and codes. Leaders who act with integrity treat ethics as "a driving force of an enterprise."[33] They recognize that values serve as the organization's core and draw upon these principles when making every type of decision—planning, budgeting, hiring, marketing. Further, they equip constituents to govern their own behavior following these same values.

Structural Reinforcement. In positive moral climates, elements of an organization's structure encourage higher ethical performance.[34] Employee orientation and training reinforce important values and ethical guidelines. Performance evaluation systems use anonymous feedback to detect dark side behaviors, which are often hidden because lower- and middle-level leaders may abuse their followers at the same time they present a positive image to superiors.[35] Reward systems promote honesty, fair treatment of customers, courtesy, excellent service, and other moral behaviors. At AES, the world's largest independent energy producer, executives are evaluated based on their adherence to corporate principles as well as on their financial performance. Board members assign bonuses based on whether top managers promote AES values (integrity, fairness, fun, social responsibility), safety, a cleaner environment, and community relations.[36]

Process Focus. Concern for how a group achieves its goals is a marker of a healthy ethical climate. High rates of unethical behavior occur when leaders set demanding goals without specifying how these objectives are to be reached. Followers experience anomie, a feeling of powerlessness and alienation because the rules have lost their force.[37] This estrangement reduces their motivation to act morally as well as their resistance to authority figures who want them to break the law.

Leaders address the problem of anomie by ensuring that goals are achieved through ethical means. All debts must be fully disclosed to investors, for example, profits must not be overstated, and false promises cannot be used to land accounts. The U.S. Army's chief recruiting officer recognized the importance of ethical process when a number of recruiters were caught helping unqualified applicants cheat so that they could enlist. He instituted a "values stand down," a daylong session focused on the importance of adhering to military values during the recruiting process. During that day recruiters reviewed their oaths of office and proper procedures, viewed a video on Army values, and engaged in small-group discussions of current recruiting conditions.[38]

TOOLS FOR THE TASK

Carrying out the task of ethical leadership requires the proper tools. Fortunately, practitioners can draw upon a variety of resources as they tackle their moral responsibilities. Two sets of tools are particularly useful to leaders—character building and mastering the components of moral action.

Character Building

Character deficiencies are a major contributing factor to the shadow side of leadership. Palmer[39] believes that leaders project darkness onto their external worlds because they do not master the inner fears and insecurities described earlier. Lipman-Blumen[40] and Kellerman's[41] "toxic" and "bad" leaders fail to demonstrate such traits as integrity, courage, moderation, and compassion for the needs of others.

Ethicists refer to positive personal qualities as *virtues*. Proponents of virtue ethics focus on the actor, believing that individuals of high moral character will make positive ethical choices.[42] Virtues emerge over time and are woven into the leader's unique core identity.[43] As a result, there is no universal blueprint for character development. However, several approaches have found to be effective: locating role models, telling and living out collective stories, fostering virtuous habits, and learning from leadership passages.

ROLE MODELS. Observation and imitation play a critical role in the development of virtues. Role models demonstrate what it means to act with compassion, courage, persistence, and consistency. These moral exemplars can be drawn from friends and associates, contemporary political, business, and military leaders, and historical figures.

Malden Mills CEO Aaron Feuerstein acted as a role model when he continued to pay the salaries of his workers after the company's plant burned down, for example. He also decided to rebuild in Lawrence, Massachusetts, rather than moving operations overseas. Southwest Airlines founder Herb Kelleher demonstrated that a highly successful business could be built around the principles of equality, strong relationships, and doing business in a loving manner.[44]

STORIES. Families, schools, businesses, governments, religious bodies, and other organizations provide the context for character development.[45] These collectives impart values and encourage self-discipline and integrity through narratives.[46] Shared stories provide a framework for interpreting events and promote desired behavior. For example, the tale of a new employee who successfully challenges a vice president's dishonesty encourages other workers to speak up about ethical misdeeds.

Collective stories are lived as well as told. Leaders are actors in the group's ongoing narrative.[47] They need to ensure that they align themselves with worthy organizational stories marked by significant purpose and values. Leaders experience character growth as they live up to their roles in these narratives. As virtue ethicist Alasdair MacIntyre explains, "I can only answer the question 'What am I to do?' if I can answer the prior questions, 'Of what story or stories do I find myself a part?'"[48]

HABITS. Habits are regular routines or practices designed to foster virtuous behavior—treating every person courteously, carrying through on every promise (no matter how small), and never hiding bad news from followers or supervisors. These practices take significant time and effort to develop but become easier to maintain once in place. Some leaders also turn to such spiritual disciplines as meditation, study, simplicity, solitude, and service to enhance their character development.

PASSAGES. Intense experiences that challenge leaders help to mold their characters. These significant events, which often involve hardship, serve as passages in leadership development. Leadership passages fall into four categories:[49] (1) diversity of work experiences (joining an organization, accepting a major new assignment); (2) work adversity (significant failure, coping with a bad boss, losing a job); (3) diversity of life experiences (living abroad, blending work and family into a meaningful whole); (4) life adversity (death or divorce, illness). These passages offer the opportunity to develop empathy, become more resilient, open up to others, let go of ambitions, and so forth.[50] However, benefiting from these experiences takes "adaptive capacity."[51] Effective leaders of all ages learn important principles and skills from their struggles that they then apply to upcoming challenges. They see passages, particularly the most difficult ones, as learning opportunities that serve as opportunities for growth. Václav Havel prepared for his role as Czech president while imprisoned during the Communist regime. Instead of falling into despair, he developed a deeper understanding of the importance of the ethical and spiritual dimension of leadership.

Components of Moral Action

Knowing how moral decisions are made and implemented can greatly improve a leader's personal ethical performance and that of the organization as a whole. According to psychologist James Rest,[52] moral behavior is the product of four psychological subprocesses: (1) moral sensitivity (recognition); (2) moral judgment or reasoning; (3) moral motivation; and (4) moral character.

MORAL SENSITIVITY (RECOGNITION). The term *moral sensitivity* refers to the identification of ethical problems. To recognize the presence of a moral dilemma, leaders must be aware of how their behavior impacts others, identify possible courses of action, and then determine the likely consequences of each option. Moral sensitivity is critical because it is impossible to solve a dilemma without first recognizing that a problem exists. Also, a great many ethical miscues are the result of moral insensitivity. Executives at the Nestlé Company saw no moral problem with marketing baby formula to poor African women in the 1980s, for instance.[53] They failed to recognize that (1) poor women were better off breast feeding and saving their money for other basic needs, and (2) mixing formula with polluted water caused thousands of infants to sicken and die.

Moral muteness and moral blind spots make it difficult to recognize ethical issues. Leaders often follow an ethical code of silence, rarely talking about problems in ethical terms.[54] They may want to avoid controversy or believe that keeping silent will make them appear powerful and self-sufficient. However, their silence keeps followers from framing events as ethical scenarios and engaging in moral reasoning. In addition, managers can also fail to recognize the ethical implications of their decisions.[55] Their typical ways of thinking or mental models don't include important ethical considerations, so they are blind to important moral dilemmas. For example, officials at Nike gave little thought to working conditions at their overseas manufacturing facilities during the company's formative years, arguing that treatment of foreign workers was not their responsibility since the work was done by subcontractors.[56] Public criticism later forced the company to recognize that low pay and poor working conditions were significant moral dilemmas. In response, the firm has taken steps to curb abuses and became the first athletic clothing manufacturer to reveal the locations of all its foreign facilities.[57]

There are two steps that leaders can take to enhance their and their followers' ethical sensitivity. First, employ moral terminology to highlight the moral dimension of decisions. Use such terms as *justice, values, immoral, right,* and *wrong* to encourage followers to frame an event as an ethical problem and to engage in moral reasoning. Second, incorporate ethical considerations into every important decision. Harvard ethics professor Lynn Paine offers a "moral compass" for doing so.[58] Paine believes that leaders can focus their attention (and that of the rest of the group) on the moral dimension of choices by engaging in four frames of analysis. Taken together, these lenses increase moral sensitivity, making it easier for organizational members to recognize and discuss moral issues.

Lens 1: Purpose. Will this action serve a worthwhile purpose? Proposed courses of action need to serve worthy goals.

Lens 2: Principle. Is this action consistent with relevant principles of our organization? This mode of analysis applies ethical standards to the problem at hand. These guidelines can be general ethical principles, norms of good business practice, codes of conduct, legal requirements, and personal ideals.

Lens 3: People. *Does this action respect the legitimate claims of the people likely to be affected?* Identifying possible harm to stakeholder groups can prevent damage. Such analysis requires understanding the perspectives of others as well as careful reasoning.

Lens 4: Power. Do we have the power to take this action? Answers to the first three sets of questions mean little unless leaders have the legitimate authority to act and the ability to do so.

MORAL JUDGMENT. The second step of moral action is to choose among the courses of action identified in component 1 (moral sensitivity), determining what is the right or wrong thing to do in this specific situation. Understanding cognitive moral development is key to this stage. Kohlberg[59] argued that individuals progress through a series of moral stages just as they do physical ones. Each stage is more advanced than the one before. Reasoning becomes more sophisticated as decision makers become less self-centered and develop a broader understanding of what it means to act morally. The most advanced moral thinkers (postconventional) use universal moral principles when making choices. Kohlberg found that most adults are conventional rather than principled. They want to live up to the expectations of family members and other significant people. At the same time, conventional thinkers recognize the importance of fulfilling job responsibilities and going along with the laws of society.

Based on the conventional level of moral reasoning of most adults, it should come as no surprise that organizational members rarely challenge unethical organizational practices. They look to others for guidance and believe that they are acting morally by faithfully carrying out their work responsibilities. Nevertheless, decision makers of all ages can improve their moral reasoning through training and education.[60] Leaders can develop the decision-making abilities of followers (and themselves) by encouraging continuing education and by providing ethics workshops. They can also improve the moral climate of the organization through becoming postconventional thinkers. By engaging in principled reasoning themselves, they encourage those around them to do the same.[61]

MORAL MOTIVATION. After reaching a conclusion about the best course of action, decision makers must be motivated to follow through on their choices. Moral behavior will only result if ethical considerations take priority over competing priorities such as job security and social acceptance. As noted earlier, ethical values are more likely to take precedence when reinforced by reward systems.[62] Be careful not to encourage unethical behavior by rewarding it, as in the case of the software company that paid programmers $20 to correct each software bug they found. Soon programmers were deliberately creating bugs to fix.[63] Instead, honor those who act with integrity. Eligibility for the incentive compensation plan at Lockheed Martin is based on promoting moral conduct. Business and personal goals must be reached in keeping with the company's ethics policy. Regular performance reviews include criteria that measure ethical conduct and support for the firm's ethics program.[64]

Emotional states also impact moral motivation. Positive affect (joy, happiness, contentment) makes members more optimistic and therefore more inclined to follow through on ethical choices. Those in positive moods are also more likely to help coworkers and others. In contrast, negative affect (jealousy, rage, envy) is linked to antisocial behaviors.[65] Those who regulate their moods (replacing negative thoughts with calmer ones) enhance their moral motivation.[66] These findings suggest that leaders need to honor and reward moral behavior, create working environments that foster positive emotions, and carefully monitor and manage their emotions when facing ethical choices.

MORAL CHARACTER (IMPLEMENTATION). The fourth and final stage of moral action—executing the plan—draws upon the virtues described earlier. Leaders have to overcome a number of obstacles, such as fatigue, opponents, and distractions, to carry out their choices. To succeed, they have to have a strong will, self-confidence, and a belief that the individual can actively influence events.[67] Leaders must complement their resolve with the necessary skills required to take action. Take the case of a regional sales manager who wants to convince her organization to change an unethical marketing practice. In order to reach this goal, she must utilize political, interpersonal, persuasive, organizational, and communication skills in order to recruit allies, build working relationships, construct arguments, develop a strategy, and speak and write effectively.

MEASURING PROGRESS: OUTCOMES OF ETHICAL LEADERSHIP

Engaging in ethical leadership greatly reduces the risk of falling victim to the same types of large-scale corporate scandals that marked the arrival of the new millennium. These scandals demonstrate that the price of moral failure is steep. Tens of thousands lost their jobs and retirement savings; stock values shrank; top executives were ousted and, in some cases, faced lawsuits, criminal charges, and jail time; individual and organizational reputations were tarnished.

Avoiding such negative consequences would be justification enough for taking the task of ethical leadership seriously. The advantages of ethical leadership extend well beyond reduced exposure to risk, however, to include a number of important individual and organizational benefits. These positive outcomes serve as markers of ethical progress, signaling that practitioners are successfully carrying out their moral responsibilities. Tools for measuring each outcome are listed in Table 7.2.

Individual Outcomes	Measures
Greater Personal Integrity	Credibility ratings Self-reports of ethical/unethical behavior Loss data (theft, lawsuits, discrimination cases) Employee turnover
Mental, Physical, and Career Health	Absenteeism records Safety data Job and career satisfaction scores Stress inventories Employee turnover
Expanded Ethical Capacity	Ethics performance evaluations 360-degree feedback Moral judgment and sensitivity scales
Organizational Outcomes	**Measures**
Greater Collaboration	Trust scales Job satisfaction scores Organizational commitment instruments Performance data (sales, productivity, quality)
Improved Social Standing and Market Share	Public opinion surveys Consumer feedback Sales and market data Stock price
Collective Moral Development	Ethics audits Ethics climate inventories Annual social responsibility reports

Table 7.2. Ethical Leadership: Outcome Measures.

Individual Outcomes

GREATER PERSONAL INTEGRITY. Organizational integrity encourages personal integrity. Those who work for organizations with codes of ethics judge themselves and others as more ethical than those employed by organizations without codes.[68] Organizations that take steps to combat destructive behavior see a drop in employee theft[69] as well as lower levels of violence and harassment.[70] Operating in a positive moral climate reduces the tension that frequently arises when members abandon their personal moral codes in order to succeed at work. Most leaders and followers want to the right thing. They can do so in ethical organizations and, as a result, are more committed to collective goals and are less likely to seek employment elsewhere.[71]

MENTAL, PHYSICAL, AND CAREER HEALTH. All destructive behaviors have something in common. They do significant damage to individual well-being, producing mental anguish, emotional disturbances, physical ailments, injuries, derailed careers, and other negative outcomes. Preventing antisocial behaviors greatly reduces these human costs. Building an ethical climate promotes wellness by generating positive emotions, safer environments, higher job satisfaction, and greater commitment to the organization.

EXPANDED ETHICAL CAPACITY. Leaders develop their ethical competence in the same way that they develop other leadership capacities, such as heightened self-confidence, greater creativity, and strategic thinking.[72] Ethical skills, attitudes, and motivations developed in one leadership role can increase effectiveness in other leadership positions. Moral sensitivity and principled moral reasoning, as noted earlier, are two particularly important ethical abilities. Those who successfully carry out the task of ethical leadership are more sensitive to the possible ethical implications of their choices and base their reasoning on sound moral principles.

Organizational Outcomes

GREATER COLLABORATION. Collaboration is essential to the success of any collective effort, as individuals, small group members, departments, and organizations must coordinate their actions in order to achieve their goals. Trust is the key element underlying collaborative efforts. Those who trust believe that other parties will carry through on their commitments and promises.[73] High levels of trust have been linked to greater satisfaction, commitment, and performance levels.[74] Interpersonal trust is one of the first causalities of shadowy leader and organizational behavior. Abuse of power and privilege, incivility, aggression, and other immoral acts poison the atmosphere, making it less likely that followers will put themselves in vulnerable positions. Ethical behavior has just the opposite effects. Moral leaders set the stage for greater collaboration as parties learn that they can rely on others.

IMPROVED SOCIAL STANDING AND EXPANDED MARKET SHARE. Corporations and other groups are expected to act as responsible citizens contributing to the well-being of the environment and the community. Ethical leaders enable organizations to meet and exceed these expectations, building their social standing. Consumers, investors, and donors are increasingly attracted to both business and nonprofit organizations with ethical reputations. They want to shop, invest, and give to such groups. Eighty-four percent of Americans surveyed said that, if price and quality were similar, they would switch brands to companies associated with worthy causes. Social investing is surging in popularity as well. Over $2 trillion is now invested in mutual funds that screen investments based on firms' commitment to the environment, ethics, and social responsibility.[75] Ethical businesses often outperform other companies making up the S&P 500.[76]

COLLECTIVE MORAL DEVELOPMENT. The ethical capacity of the organization, like that of the individual, expands in a positive moral environment. Reidenbach and Robin[77] offer one typology that can be used to benchmark the progress of organizational ethical development.

> *Stage I amoral organizations* are the least developed. Such companies (telemarketers, spammers) focus solely on the bottom line while largely ignoring ethical considerations.

> *Stage II legalistic organizations* (tobacco manufacturers) equate ethics with following government regulations. Their primary focus is on protecting their groups from adverse publicity, fines, and lawsuits.

> *Stage III responsive organizations* like Proctor & Gamble respond to ethical problems when they arise.

Stage IV emergent ethical organizations (Starbucks) actively manage their cultures to improve ethical climate.

Stage V ethical organizations (independent power producer AES, Johnson & Johnson) demonstrate the highest level of ethical development. They integrate values into all decisions and try to anticipate ethical issues before they arise.

EXECUTIVE SUMMARY

Ethics has always been at "the heart of leadership."[78] Unfortunately, a great many contemporary scholars, educators, and practitioners have downplayed that fact, contributing to wave after wave of organizational scandal. Providing ethical leadership may well be a leader's most important task. Managers can prepare themselves for this responsibility by meeting the ethical challenges of leadership, shaping the ethical setting or context, acquiring the tools of ethical leadership, and monitoring moral progress.

Meet the Ethical Challenges of Leadership

The first component of ethical leadership is behaving morally when entrusted with a leadership position. Carrying out this task requires that leaders:

- *Accept the ethical burdens of leadership.* As compared to followers, leaders (1) are more powerful, (2) enjoy greater privileges, (3) are privy to more information, (4) have wider spans of authority or responsibility, (5) deal with a broader range of constituencies who demand consistent treatment, and (6) balance a wider variety of loyalties. Leaders have a moral responsibility to take these challenges seriously. How they respond to the ethical demands of the leadership role will determine whether they exert positive or negative influence over the lives of followers.

- *Avoid casting shadows.* Immoral leaders cast shadows by abusing their power and privilege, misusing information, acting irresponsibly and inconsistently, and breaking loyalties. Avoiding the shadow side of leadership starts with acknowledging its existence and confronting unhealthy motivations—fear, greed, and ego. Recognize that leaders and followers have intrinsic value no matter what their job description. It is critical for leaders to learn from failures, seek to serve followers, and keep their egos in check.

Shape the Ethical Context

The second component of ethical leadership is creating a moral environment in the group or organization. This requires both defensive tactics that prevent unethical behaviors and proactive measures that intentionally foster a positive moral climate.

- *Adopt defensive strategies to prevent unethical, destructive behaviors.* Organizations have shadow sides just like leaders. "Dark side" organizational behaviors are deliberate attempts to harm others or the organization. They include such misbehaviors as incivility (rude, discourteous actions), aggression, sexual harassment, and discrimination. The ethical climate deteriorates if leaders engage in such activities or fail to take action against offenders. Leaders need to create (and follow) zero-tolerance policies that outlaw antisocial behaviors and punish violators at the first sign of trouble. Further, they can eliminate contextual triggers that provoke destructive actions, like oppressive supervision, unpleasant working conditions, perceived injustice, job stress, threats to group identity, and extreme competitiveness.

- *Take proactive steps to create a positive ethical climate.* Ethical leaders act as architects who design sound moral climates. Ethical climate—the perceptions that members share of the organization's moral atmosphere—improves when leaders ensure that the following elements are in place:

   Formal ethics statements and procedures. These include codes of ethics, reporting mechanisms, ethics offices, and disciplinary procedures.

   Core ideology. Core ideology reflects the central identity or character of an organization revealed through clearly identified values and purpose.

   Integrity. Integrity refers to ethical soundness, wholeness, and consistency that comes from linking values and mission to every decision and operation.

Structural reinforcement. In positive moral climates, every element of an organization's structure—employee orientation,
training, and performance evaluation systems—promotes and
rewards ethical behavior.

Process focus. Concern for how a group achieves its goals is a
marker of a healthy ethical climate. Objectives are achieved
through ethical means. Customers are treated honestly and
fairly, losses are fully disclosed to investors, and so on.

Acquire the Tools of Ethical Leadership

Carrying out the task of ethical leadership requires the proper tools.
Two sets of tools are particularly important to leaders: character building and mastering the components of moral action.

- *Build personal character (develop personal virtues).* Character
  deficiencies are a major contributing factor to the shadow side of
  leadership. Leaders are more likely to make positive ethical
  choices if they develop high character based on personal virtues.
  Approaches to character building include (1) observing and imi-
  tating moral role models; (2) becoming part of worthy organizational stories that encourage virtue development; (3) building
  habits (routines or practices) that foster virtuous behavior; and
  (4) learning principles and skills from intense life experiences
  called passages.

- *Master the components of moral action.* Learning how moral
  decisions are made and implemented can greatly improve a
  leader's personal ethical performance as well as that of the organization as a whole. Moral behavior is the product of four
  processes: moral sensitivity (recognition), moral judgment or
  reasoning, moral motivation, and moral character. Moral sensitivity is the ability to identify ethical problems. Sensitivity is
  heightened when managers use moral terms (*justice, values,
  right,* and *wrong*) to describe situations and when they consider
  the ethical aspects of every important decision. Moral judgment
  improves when decision makers incorporate widely used ethical
  theories and principles into the problem-solving process. Such
  thinking can be encouraged through ethics training and education. Motivation to follow through on ethical choices is highest

when leaders honor and reward moral behavior, create working environments that foster positive emotions, and regulate their moods to eliminate destructive thoughts. Executing the plan requires personal character and developing the necessary communication and political skills to take action.

Monitor Ethical Progress

Engaging in ethical leadership greatly reduces the risk of costly scandal and generates a number of important individual and organizational benefits. These positive outcomes mark moral progress, signaling that practitioners are successfully carrying out their moral responsibilities.

- *Positive individual outcomes.* Organizational integrity encourages personal integrity, reducing the frequency of destructive behavior. Serving an important purpose and upholding worthy values helps create a sense of personal fulfillment or meaning. Building an ethical climate promotes wellness by generating positive emotions, safer environments, higher job satisfaction, and greater commitment to the organization. Managers who master the task of ethical leadership are more sensitive to the possible moral implications of their choices and base their reasoning on sound ethical principles.

- *Positive organizational outcomes.* Ethical leadership builds a foundation of trust that encourages collaboration. Collaboration, in turn, is linked to higher satisfaction, commitment, and performance levels. Organizations perceived as ethical gain higher standing in the community and a greater market share. Finally, ethical leaders promote organization-wide moral development, helping their groups better anticipate and respond to ethical dilemmas.

CHAPTER EIGHT

Best Practices in Team Leadership
What Team Leaders Do to Facilitate Team Effectiveness

Kevin C. Stagl
Eduardo Salas
C. Shawn Burke

T eam leadership is exalted as one of the most important factors driving the performance and ultimately the success of teams in organizations.[1] Not surprisingly, the totality of research evidence supports this assertion; team leadership is critical to achieving both affective[2] and behaviorally based[3] team outcomes. Team leadership is also a valued outcome of team performance, as witnessed by the additional leadership capacity generated as a team learns from navigating its internal and external challenges.[4]

This chapter provides a snapshot of the broad functions and specific behaviors team leaders must enact to create the conditions required for team effectiveness. The perspective advanced here suggests that team leaders influence the attainment of important team outcomes by creating five conditions that serve as a set of mutually reinforcing resources that teams draw upon when working toward efficacious performance.[5] According to Richard Hackman, a social and organizational psychology professor at Harvard University, team leaders can set the stage for team effectiveness by establishing (1) a real team that has (2) a compelling direction, (3) an enabling structure, (4) a supportive context, and (5) access to expert coaching.

Best practice leadership functions and behaviors are advanced as exemplars of what team leaders do to create these five conditions. In order to identity these best practices, frequently researched theories of leadership are leveraged, including functional leadership, transactional and transformational leadership, initiating structure and consideration, empowerment leadership, leader-member exchange, and boundary-spanning leadership. Moreover, the insights illuminated by initiatives undertaken to examine specific aspects of team leadership and or team performance are also provided to bolster the guidance this chapter offers practitioners charged with fostering team leadership and team effectiveness in the wild.

THE NATURE OF TEAM LEADERSHIP, TEAMWORK, AND TEAM PERFORMANCE

Team leadership is an ongoing process of influence.[6] Sometimes team leaders sway team members and teams directly via the use of a sequenced combination of proactive influence tactics (see Chapter 5). For example, transformational leaders often use inspirational appeals to energize team members' higher-level needs, values, and ideals. The value of this approach is well documented, as research results suggest transformational behaviors account for 11 percent of the variance in team effectiveness and 6 percent of the variance in team productivity.[7] In contrast, transactional leaders exert their influence by relying upon apprising tactics to make rewards contingent upon effective performance. This approach is also valuable, as meta-analytic results suggest transactional behaviors account for 6 percent of the variance in team effectiveness.[8] Given the myriad of factors that contribute to and impinge upon team effectiveness and productivity, team leadership is a potent facilitator of these valued outcomes. Moreover, effective team leaders do not rigidly display a single type of leadership behavior, but rely upon a sequenced combination of monetary rewards and idealistic appeals to simultaneously extrinsically and intrinsically energize team member and team performance.

The evidence presented earlier supports the traditional view of team leadership, which conceptualizes team leaders as agents who influence team effectiveness by directly intervening in teamwork.

While useful, this chapter extends this traditional perspective by adopting a more complex and a more encompassing view of how team leaders influence team effectiveness. The tenets of this approach suggest that while effective team leaders can directly intervene in teamwork, they are more likely to spend a majority of their time and effort influencing team effectiveness by putting in place a set of mutually reinforcing conditions.[9] These conditions, in turn, shape the tasks, performance strategies, team member and team actions, interventions undertaken by key stakeholders, and cultures that emanate within an organization before, during, and after performance episodes.

Team leaders fulfill functions and enact actions in order to establish a real team, with a compelling direction, an enabling structure, a supportive context, and access to expert coaching.[10] In turn, these conditions influence how team members perceive the relationships between themselves and their teammates, between themselves and their team, between their team and its broader organizational context, and between their team and the environment external to the organization. For example, team leaders contribute to an enabling structure (combining tasks to promote teamwork) by engaging in empowering behaviors (allowing team members input into process control) to design work in a manner such that team members are encouraged to engage in self-management. Moreover, the conditions team leaders establish to influence team effectiveness interact, as was the case at Xerox Corporation, where well-designed teams reaped greater benefits from expert coaching and were undermined less by ineffective coaching.[11]

The impact of the five conditions team leaders establish is manifested in the effectiveness with which teams execute teamwork and team performance to produce team performance outcomes. These constructs, while tightly linked, are distinct phenomena.[12] Teams are complex entities, comprised of two or more individuals who interact socially, dynamically, episodically, and adaptively. Teams engage in teamwork, which is a set of adaptively enacted processes displayed by both team members (for example, communication) and teams (for example, coordination). Several initiatives have been undertaken to map the processes comprising teamwork.[13] Most have identified similar processes.

Teamwork is a necessary but insufficient condition for effective team performance. Team performance emerges as team members draw from their individual and collective resources to enact taskwork processes (for example, writing software code), team member processes (providing backup behavior to fellow programmers on a software development project team), and integrated team-level processes (such as the dynamic reallocation of capital during project team performance). For example, two members of a basketball team might draw from their shared situational awareness to execute a no-look pass. This example typifies a small slice of team performance because the team members call upon their shared reservoir of cognition to coordinate for a score. As team performance unfolds, higher-level contextual forces simultaneously shape and constrain interdependent interaction. In keeping with the basketball example, it is highly unlikely a no-look pass would be attempted during the last play of the game. This new scenario illustrates how situational factors in the team's context impinge upon the types of cognitive and behavioral actions that ultimately comprise team performance. Thus, team performance is an emergent multilevel phenomenon resulting in performance outcomes and stakeholder judgments of team effectiveness.[14] The nature of team effectiveness is addressed in greater detail in the next section of the chapter.

THE CONDITIONS FOR TEAM EFFECTIVENESS

As team performance unfolds, team members, team leaders, organizational stakeholders, strategic partners, and clientele develop and refine impressions about a team's effectiveness. These parties continuously evaluate a team's performance processes and outcomes against objective and subjective standards. Using these standards, they gauge the desirability of the actions undertaken and results produced by the team. When judgments are made about a team's effectiveness, several criteria are often considered by concerned parties, including (1) whether a team's product or service meets or exceeds the standards of the team's clientele, (2) whether the social dynamic arising from team performance strengthened the capability of members to work together in the future, and (3) whether team members learned and had their own needs fulfilled.[15]

Given these assertions, team effectiveness is contingent upon both who is asked and the aspect of effectiveness in question. Despite this apparent complexity, effectiveness is often largely contingent upon whether a team meets its targeted production or service goals. This is no doubt a high standard, as contextual factors (for example, an economic recession, competitor innovation, supply shortages) outside a team's control often impinge on team performance and sometimes serve to curtail team outputs. Furthermore, there are trade-offs between these standards. The single-minded pursuit of high levels of performance can be detrimental to the efficacy of newly formed teams and even derail the long-term viability of expert teams. Fortunately, stakeholders who judge the effectiveness of a team also typically consider whether a team grows as a result of its performance. Growth signals a team is more prepared to, and capable of, performing at a higher level during future performance episodes. The third criterion considered by parties making effectiveness judgments is whether team members learned and derived satisfaction from their interactions. When members' needs are met by team performance, they are more likely to be intrinsically motivated by their work and persist in their efforts in the long run.[16]

TEAM LEADERSHIP AND THE CONDITIONS FOR TEAM EFFECTIVENESS

The discussion of team leadership, teamwork, team performance, and team effectiveness, as presented thus far in this chapter, provides the conceptual foundation for illuminating what team leaders must do to facilitate these phenomena. The primary responsibility of team leaders seeking to foster team effectiveness is to establish and maintain a set of mutually reinforcing conditions that create, guide, and support teams.[17] Once instituted, teams draw upon these conditions before, during, and after task performance episodes. Thus, they serve to influence teams and their members and to increase the probability a team will ultimately be deemed effective on the standards discussed in the previous section.

Hackman suggests team leaders must establish five conditions to increase the likelihood teams will be judged effective on the three criteria noted above. These five prerequisite conditions for team effectiveness include creating (1) a real team, with (2) a compelling direction, (3) an enabling structure, (4) a supportive organizational context, and (5) expert coaching. The first three of these conditions contribute to the basic design of the team, whereas the latter two capitalize on this core. Each of these conditions is reviewed here in light of the assertions of several prominent theories of leadership.

These theories of leadership are used to extract general functions and specific behaviors team leaders should enact to influence team effectiveness.

A Real Team

A team is not a mere collection of collocated experts who perform similar work and occasionally interact during goal accomplishment or afterward at the water cooler. In fact, real teams are quite different from this characterization: they perform team tasks, are bounded, and have delimited authority and stable membership.[18] Long before effectiveness can be achieved, team leaders must ensure these features are in place, functioning properly, and that team members clearly understand their implications for performance. Each of these features of a real team is discussed in the following pages and suggestions for establishing them are provided.

Team Task

BEST PRACTICE #1. *Define and create interdependencies.*

Interdependence is one the primary reasons teams are formed, so it is not surprising that real teams with congruent task, goal, and feedback interdependencies are more effective.[19] Accumulating research evidence supports the importance of within-team interdependencies. For example, in information technology teams employed across thirteen Fortune 500 organizations in six industries, interdependence was found to be related to both team performance and member satisfaction.[20] A second example comes from multiple samples of teams in the financial services sector, where task, goal, and feedback interdependencies were found to be related to indices of team productivity, team effectiveness, and team member satisfaction.[21] A third example of the importance of fostering interdependence can be found in research conducted with customer service technician teams, where team independence moderated the influence of a customer driven quality system.[22] The results of this research suggested the intervention was greatly beneficial to interdependent customer service technician teams and actually detrimental to the performance of teams with low levels of interdependencies.

Hackman suggests that in order to leverage the benefits of teamwork, a team must actually do the work. However, intrateam links mandate higher levels of communication, cooperation, collaboration, and coordination among team members to meet stated objectives.[23] When a team's interdependencies are undefined, ambiguous, or implicit, team leaders initiate structure[24] by organizing and coordinating collective activities in a manner that creates new, or capitalizes on existing, codependencies. Team leaders can initiate structure by creating complementary roles, superordinate goals, and shared outcomes. For example, senior stakeholders, team leaders, and management consultants can come together to institute a staffing solution that includes the individual assessment of potential team members for the purpose of diagnosing which roles within the team an applicant is predisposed to fill most effectively. By actively staffing the team, team leaders can help ensure complementary roles are filled.

BEST PRACTICE #2. *Reinforce task interdependencies with congruent goals and feedback.*

Once the coordination demands of a team's task are identified, team leaders can reinforce these interdependencies by synchronizing team goals and performance feedback. Goals and goal-related feedback guide the allocation of resources during performance.[25] Feedback directs attention toward work efforts and provides the information required so that one can be accountable for one's efforts.[26] Therefore, feedback should be aligned with both the tasks and the goals of a team. Team leaders who institute specific, difficult team goals rather than ambiguous team goals or individual goals should produce greater coordination and more effective performance.[27] For example, feedback should be delivered about how well the team is executing its performance strategies rather than directing members' attention toward their own performance.

Bounded Team

BEST PRACTICE #3. *Identify who is responsible and accountable for outcomes.*

The second feature of a real team is its boundaries. Easily identifiable boundaries clarify team members' perceptions about who is ultimately accountable for team performance outcomes.[28] Explicit boundaries are particularly useful in organizations in which support staff temporarily step in to provide expertise about problems encountered by the team and thereby contribute to team performance. For example, the standard operating procedure of an organization may specify that research and development (R&D) teams should draw upon the joint resources of engineering, production, and sales when formulating innovative ideas. The continuous flow of engineers and sales representatives in and out of the R&D team may serve to create the illusion that someone other than the actual members of the R&D team will be held responsible for team outputs.

In order to avoid the scenario described, a team leader initiates structure[29] to keep a team informed of who is actually on the team and thereby responsible for team outcomes. There are a number of specific actions a team leader can enact to keep a team aware of who is responsible for achieving team effectiveness. For example, team leaders can demarcate boundaries by holding preliminary meetings to instill a shared understanding of a team's purposes and membership. Team leaders can also create membership rosters that differentiate core members from the supporting cast.[30] Leaders can also establish norms that reinforce who will participate in team performance and at what times. Finally, clear channels of communication help ensure that members are kept up to date about incoming and exiting coworkers. A team Web page can provide a central location for members to receive and exchange this information via message postings, chat rooms, and digital avatars.

Delimited Authority

BEST PRACTICE #4. *Designate the team's decision making authority.*

The third characteristic of real teams is they have limited authority for the core functions they fulfill, such as direction setting, designing, executing, monitoring, and managing performance processes. For example, an executive team of a small privately held corporation typically has free reign to set, execute, and manage the accomplishment of its strategic priorities. In contrast, the executive team of a publicly held firm typically answers to its board of directors and shareholders, so it has less discretion when it comes to changing agreed upon objectives.

Allocating authority is a balancing act for team leaders, because most teams in work settings are empowered to some degree to provide input into, and maintain control over, their operations. If the boundaries of a team's authority are not clearly demarcated, however, team members may incorrectly intuit their power and either fail to seize opportunities or act inappropriately when actions are taken. In order to help ensure the proper balance is struck, team leaders initiate structure[31] to define which of the team's core functions fall under its jurisdiction. Team leaders also initiate structure by informing teams about which of the team's functions are under its domain of control. For example, team leaders can communicate the standards that must be achieved by the team in order to be empowered with additional responsibilities for various functions, such as managing its processes.

To help determine the extent of authority a team should have, it is first necessary to consider who is best suited to handle the functions a team fulfills.[32] One way to accomplish this is to assess a team's capability to handle various aspects of its work. When teams are intact and have a history of working together, archival data from performance reviews can be collected or new observations can be made of the team in context.[33] In a newly formed team, the level of expertise and other competencies that team members bring to the table help determine the type of responsibilities they are prepared to handle going forward. In either case, team leaders should be prepared to relinquish at least some degree of control over various functions as the team matures and demonstrates its capabilities in context.

Membership Stability

BEST PRACTICE #5. *Strive to keep teams intact.*

The final feature of real teams is that they are characterized by relatively stable membership.[34] In fact, research shows that longer tenures in management teams are associated with greater sales growth.[35] The implications of unstable team membership are grave, as witnessed by the fact that 73 percent of all aviation accidents occurred during the first flight an aviation crew had taken together.[36] Similarly, research suggests that position and personnel turbulence in tank crews results in lower levels of performance.[37] The positive effects of stability and negative implications of instability may be one of the reasons the National Football League (NFL) keeps its officiating crews intact for the entire regular season. A caveat does apply to this advice: in R&D teams and other settings in which creativity is highly desirable, research suggests there is a point of diminishing returns for team tenure at approximately the 5-year mark.[38]

Stable teams are better positioned for success because as they perform over time they develop shared cognitive, affective, and behavioral resources that are drawn upon when engaging in subsequent performance episodes. For example, as a ballet troupe's performance unfolds across levels and time, its members develop shared mental models of the tasks they are performing and the capabilities of the team to engage in these tasks. Troupe members develop a shared understanding of each other's specific strengths and weaknesses. This knowledge becomes ingrained so that when a particular sequence of maneuvers is best suited to the assets of a particular performer, that member is seamlessly called upon to practice. These cognitive models are not only essential to facilitating routine performance, they also guide the processes teams select and execute when adapting to change.[39]

In order to reap the benefits of stability, team leaders demonstrate consideration[40] so team members develop the shared commitment it takes to persist over the long run. Team leaders who show consideration by actively listening to team members' suggestions and using elicited advice in making decisions foster more trust and commitment to the team. For example, when the management team of a Fortune 500 technology firm showed more consideration to member input during an executive program on strategic management, members were more committed to their team, trusted their leaders more, and made better quality decisions.[41] Similarly, leader-member exchange theory postulates that leaders can build a sense of obligation to the team by building dyadic relationships characterized by mutual trust and respect.[42]

Compelling Direction

The second condition team leaders establish to facilitate team effectiveness is a compelling direction.[43] According to Hackman, direction is compelling when it is challenging, clear, and consequential. Each of these three elements is apparent in the vision articulated by the National Human Genome Research Institute (NHGRI). In 2004, the NHGRI funded and charged seven research teams with the long-term challenge of developing revolutionary technologies that facilitate the sequencing of a human genome for $1,000 or less. Such dramatic cost reductions would enable the sequencing of individual genomes as part of medical care and ultimately help physicians tailor therapies to an individual's genetic profile.

When direction is challenging, such as the kind provided by the NHGRI, it energizes a team and thereby enhances its motivation to perform. Clear direction orients a team because it meshes the team's performance strategy with its purposes. Direction that is consequential serves to engage teams and thereby helps ensure available human capital is fully employed during performance. Thus, a compelling direction serves three functions: it energizes, orients, and engages a team.[44] The activities team leaders undertake to provide direction that fulfills these functions are discussed next.

Energizes

BEST PRACTICE #6. *Exercise authority to establish a compelling direction.*

Direction defines, communicates, and operationalizes a vision for teams, their members, their leaders, and stakeholders in the wider organization.[45] The direction articulated by team leaders must be challenging, clear, and consequential, not because it is framed or delivered in an exhilarating fashion but because a team's purposes really are inspiring to its members. If a team's purposes are by nature compelling, then direction that is challenging serves to energize members by stirring their motivational juices.

Team leaders fulfill the function of motivating personnel[46] by exercising authority to set direction for their teams. This type of direction precisely specifies desired end states but not the means of task accomplishment.[47] For example, with 75 percent of the 2005 NFL regular season complete, the Pittsburgh Steelers were faced with the real possibility of missing the playoffs. With the season on the line, head coach Bill Cowher went to the team's whiteboard, on which the team's objectives had been stated since the preseason, and wiped it clean. Cowher exercised his authority to set a new vision for the Steelers, a "one week at a time" philosophy. This approach revitalized the team's spirit, led to eight straight victories, and guided the team to becoming the first number six playoff seed in history to win the Superbowl. The direction provided by Cowher precisely specified the desired end state for the team—a victory this week—but left plenty of room for him, his staff, and his team to craft and execute a flexible game plan for each opponent faced.

BEST PRACTICE #7. *Stimulate and inspire by challenging the status quo.*

Effective direction, like an effective mission statement, balances the possible and impossible.[48] The specific content of the direction a team receives must be dictated by the contingencies of the team under consideration. Direction given to stir a team to action must be neither too challenging nor too easy to fulfill. This kind of direction is most often associated with the charismatic/transformational genre of leadership.[49] For example, transformational senior leaders at 3M asked their action teams to do nothing short of increasing the technology at 3M by a quantum leap while concurrently slashing production development time by 50 percent.[50]

Transcendent aspirations have also been articulated by team leaders whose organizations faced a crisis. Wayne Hale, chairman of the National Aeronautics and Space Administration's Space Shuttle Mission Management Team during space shuttle *Discovery*'s Return to Flight mission STS-114, once stated, "Do we have the judgment to weigh it all in the balance? Do we have the character to dare great deeds? History is watching."[51] Under Hale's watch, *Discovery*'s crew returned to flight, executed innovative in-orbit maneuvers, conducted unprecedented in-flight repairs, and rekindled the imagination of the inhabitants across our small blue planet.

Orients

BEST PRACTICE #8. *Instill collective aspirations via a common mission.*

A compelling direction does much more than stir the passions of a team's members; it also serves to guide their ongoing activities. This is because effective direction orients team members by aligning a team's performance strategy with its purposes.[52] A compelling direction makes salient the consistencies between a team member's self-concept and the actions engaged in on behalf of the team.[53] For example, when members of U.S. Army infantry teams discuss their actions in postmission debriefings they often use the word *we* instead of *I*. Socialization processes, experience, and leader actions serve to ensure the self-concepts of these soldiers are thoroughly intertwined with the shared core values underlying the mission of their team, squad, platoon, and company. Defining themselves in terms of the larger collective becomes as implicit as always having one's weapon within reach.

In order for direction to instill a collective identity and thereby orient a team, team leaders define a common mission so that team members understand that subordinating their own self-interests can help facilitate the achievement of overriding objectives. One way team leaders do this is by engaging in transformational leadership[54] to define team member roles in terms of ideological values. For example, when the leaders of the previously noted infantry teams define member responsibilities in terms of exemplifying collective values (for example, treat prisoners of war with respect), each member has a standard for interpreting his or her own contemplated actions. Thus, overarching values serve as precepts when a team develops or selects task performance strategies. In this manner, direction provides a common criterion that can be used to evaluate alternative ways of proceeding, which can be useful when several paths seem equally appealing.[55]

Engages

BEST PRACTICE #9. *Provide consequential direction to fully engage talent.*

The third function good direction serves is to engage team members. When direction is consequential for a team, the team is more likely to draw upon the full repertoire of its members' experiences, expertise, and competencies during task performance.[56] Moreover, by providing direction that has important consequences for the team, team leaders create the impetus for senior team members to monitor the actions of more junior team members. In turn, mutual performance monitoring is critical to providing timely backup behavior when less experienced members are overloaded or are making errors during task performance.

Team leaders provide engaging direction by enacting functional leadership behaviors that help ensure the maximum utilization of team member talent.[57] One means of ensuring that a team's capabilities are fully engaged is to develop task cohesion by proactively discussing a team's goals, objectives, and performance standards.[58] By linking the tasks at hand to agreed-upon performance standards and goals, team members can more readily perceive the connections between their actions and the consequences of those actions for collective success.

Enabling Structure

The third condition that team leaders create to foster team effectiveness is an enabling structure.[59] An enabling structure simultaneously provides the broad framework in which teams operate while providing the flexibility for teams to decide the specific manner in which operations will be conducted. According to Hackman, there are three structural features that team leaders shape to create an enabling structure: (1) the design of a team's work, (2) the establishment and enforcement of norms of conduct, and (3) the manner in which teams are staffed or composed. Each of these three aspects of an enabling structure is discussed next.

Designing Work

BEST PRACTICE #10. *Promote self-goal setting, self-observation, and self-reward.*

The first feature of an enabling structure is the design of the work that teams are charged to perform. According to the tenets of job characteristics theory,[60] sociotechnical systems theory,[61] and cognitive evaluation theory,[62] the tasks teams perform should be designed so workers have some measure of authority or discretion over their work. For example, Volvo empowered teams at its Kalmar (Sweden) plant to be responsible for an entire portion of the automobile manufacturing process. By eschewing the traditional scientific management approach, whereby employees only work on a very small piece of an automobile, in favor of a process where teams craft a larger product from start to finish, Volvo provided the team with skill variety and a sense of task ownership. This approach served to both motivate and satisfy Volvo's incumbents, who eventually came to produce some of the finest driving machines on the road.

Team leaders can create this sense of ownership by engaging in empowering behaviors aimed at increasing the self-management of the team and its members.[63] Leaders should design the work that teams perform to include several core characteristics in order to promote within-team goal setting, observation, and reward. These job dimensions include skill variety, task identity, task significance, autonomy, and feedback. The first of these dimensions, skill variety, can be created by combining tasks as illustrated in the Volvo example given and by establishing relationships with clients.[64] The second dimension, task identity, is engendered by forming natural work units and combining tasks. Leaders can create task significance by forming natural units of work. Autonomy is created when teams are charged with managing client relations and via vertical loading, a process whereby teams are empowered to handle additional management responsibilities. The final dimension, feedback, is generated via team-client interactions and by the leader's efforts to open communication channels throughout the organization.[65]

Norms of Conduct

BEST PRACTICE #11. *Establish norms for how the team scans its environment for opportunities and what teams must and cannot do to seize opportunities.*

The second feature of an enabling structure is norms of conduct. Norms are structural characteristics of a team that regulate and regularize its behavior.[66] Team leaders establish norms of conduct to reinforce desired behaviors and sanction inappropriate actions. For example, managers at Xerox who participated in focus groups suggested that one of the core drivers of customer service team effectiveness is norms.[67] In this setting, norms were defined as common expectations for the behavior of work group members, and particularly those with special responsibilities. Not surprisingly, subsequent research supported the managers' views: norms were related to objective indices of performance, customer satisfaction, and manager ratings of team effectiveness.[68] Norms can also arise informally, as witnessed by the production norms discovered at the Hawthorne Works of the Western Electric Company nearly a century ago.[69]

In order to establish basic norms of conduct, team leaders initiate structure[70] for the team by specifying in detail what is deemed (un)acceptable conduct during task performance. Hackman[71] suggests that team leaders must specify outward-looking norms that address how teams monitor and interact with their operational context and specify what must be done and not done in relation to opportunities arising in this environment. For example, the provision of timely upward feedback delivered from regionally dispersed teams to a central location may be mandated in one organization (for example, the Federal Bureau of Investigation) and disregarded or even antithetical to operations in another organization (for example, LDDS World-Com). External norms of conduct are complemented by secondary norms addressing within-team behavior. These norms address social interactions, acceptable member behavior, and applications of rules and regulations.[72] Once crystallized, the mere visualization of one's fellow teammates' disapproval can be a powerful deterrent.[73]

Team Composition

BEST PRACTICE #12. *Allocate the optimal number and mix of personnel.*

The third aspect of an enabling structure is team composition. In regard to this feature, leaders engage in functional behaviors to allocate personnel[74] to ensure a team has an appropriate size and composition. Team leaders allocate personnel to teams in a manner that actively manages a team's size, diversity of talent, balance of knowledge, skills, abilities, and other characteristics because research suggests each of these aspects has important implications for team functioning and effectiveness.[75]

Team leaders manage the composition of a team in part by ensuring that it has the optimal number of team members to execute its functions. In this regard, leaders of effective teams lean toward assigning too few team members to accomplish a team's tasks rather than assigning too many, because while organizations can have slack resources, teams cannot.[76] The rationale behind this assertion suggests that as team size increases, so too do the coordination demands, motivational decrements, and other process losses associated with teamwork.[77] Not surprisingly, accumulated research results support this line of thinking.[78] It seems a negatively accelerated function exists between team size and performance such that there are diminishing returns for extra members. Research suggests the optimal number of team members is between four and seven.[79]

Team leaders also actively balance the mixture of knowledge, skills, abilities, and other characteristics on a team in order to produce an optimal blend.[80] Team leaders produce an appropriate balance of characteristics within a team by leveraging their organization's human capital systems to hire or fire team members, develop existing members, or secure the services of ad hoc members.[81] Traditionally, team leaders have used these systems to staff their teams with the highest mean levels of the targeted characteristic in question. However, the results of a new wave of research have begun to challenge this philosophy. For example, the results of one initiative suggest the proportion of extraverted members on a team is curvilinearly related to performance.[82] This suggests that too many extraverted members on a team can be detrimental to team performance and thereby team effectiveness.

Supportive Organizational Context

Thus far in this chapter, three conditions have been discussed that team leaders put in place to increase the probability a team and its products and/or services will be deemed effective. These three conditions—a real team, a compelling direction, and an enabling structure—contribute to the basic design of a team.[83] The remainder of the chapter discusses two additional conditions—a supportive organizational context and expert coaching—that reinforce this basic design. This subsection addresses the actions team leaders take to provide a supportive organizational context, which includes establishing a reward system, an information system, and an educational system. The final condition, expert coaching, deals with the activities team leaders engage in to develop teams and team members before, during, and after performance.

Reward System

BEST PRACTICE #13. *Implement team-based performance-contingent rewards.*

Once a team leader has organized a team's work into team tasks, it is important not to undermine established interdependencies by holding particularly (un)successful individual team members largely accountable for team performance outcomes.[84] In practice, this is often difficult to do, because in most organizations exceptional individual performance is exalted at the expense of collective achievements. This is unfortunate, because leaders who reward individual performance and expect team performance send mixed signals about what is really valued both by the leader and in the wider organization. In fact, research suggests teams perform at higher levels when their reward system and tasks are consistent.[85]

Team leaders are charged with fostering team motivation and coordination, and thereby effective team outcomes, so a new mindset is required. Rather than rewarding one thing and expecting another, effective team leaders engage in transactional behaviors[86] to strengthen the linkages between team processes and team rewards. Team leaders must establish and communicate the transactional linkages between valued team rewards, such as pay, promotion, management recognition, desirable work assignments and schedules, and time off, and the coordinated exchanges teams enact.[87] For example, one director at a large telecommunications firm showed pictures of the exotic vacation locations team members could visit if they achieved targeted collective outcomes.[88] This type of transactional leadership serves to bolster team interdependencies by creating the expectancy that collective effort will result in adaptive coordinated exchanges that are, in turn, instrumental to securing valued team rewards.[89]

BEST PRACTICE #14. *Institutionalize multitiered reward systems.*

While the contingencies between team-level performance and team-level rewards must be clear and meaningful, team leaders must also reinforce the developmental efforts of team members in order to promote the third criterion of team effectiveness. Hackman suggests the third criterion of team effectiveness is whether or not team members learned and grew as a result of their interactions and experiences during team performance. This creates a conundrum for team leaders, who must reward individual growth while not overemphasizing individual achievement and thereby undermining team performance.

The solution, Hackman suggests, is for team leaders to institutionalize multitiered reward systems. Essentially, team leaders fulfill the function of motivating personnel[90] by linking mutually reinforcing rewards that promote individual growth, team effectiveness, and overall organizational performance. One way to accomplish this is to phase in team performance as a distinct facet of each team member's performance evaluation.[91] For example, General Foods' Topeka, Kansas, plant used reward systems that compensated employees for mastering both individual and team competencies.[92] This type of system places the onus on members to self-develop.

Information System

BEST PRACTICE #15. *Ensure provided information is performance targeted.*

Information systems provide teams with mission-critical data needed to plan, execute, and monitor their work activities. The information provided by these systems is particularly important as teams navigate the permanent whitewater created by the rapid pace of change in a global village.[93] For example, research with customer service work teams in a Fortune 500 firm suggested work group support, in terms of providing necessary information and helping teams to utilize information for continuous improvement, was related to indices of response time and manager ratings of performance effectiveness.[94] Moreover, in teams of knowledge workers at multiple organizations, information transmission was related to team performance, team commitment, and team satisfaction.[95]

Although teams often have difficulties setting up an information management system,[96] with the increasing power and affordability of information technologies it is increasingly feasible to provide teams with real-time data about their performance and performance context.

What is needed is for team leaders to manage the kinds and flow of information a team receives so that collectives have access to actionable information rather than mountains of unusable data. This requires team leaders to engage in boundary spanning behaviors[97] whereby they work closely with parties in their organization or outside vendors who design the information systems a team will rely upon. Team leaders should engage in networking communication with information system designers and programmers to help ensure teams get information about their current performance as well as insight into ongoing changes in production and service that could alter the timing or pace of future performance episodes. For example, Mitsubishi uses a "House of Quality" approach to translate customer-expressed needs into the language of engineers.[98] Team leaders at Mitsubishi manage this interface to help ensure their teams have targeted information to design better products and thereby more fully satisfy their clientele.

BEST PRACTICE #16. *Negotiate access to sensitive information if it facilitates planning and selection of performance strategies.*
    It might be trite to say information is power, but nevertheless it is true. Senior stakeholders know all too well that their competitors want to know what they know so they can leverage it to their competitive advantage. This is why the really good stuff is kept under lock and key or is floating through cyberspace encrypted. Unfortunately, this veil of secrecy often prevents the very teams who need specific information to set and adjust their task performance strategies from getting it in a timely manner, if at all.[99]
    In order to foster a supportive context, team leaders must engage in boundary spanning behaviors[100] to proactively search the team, organization, and environment to procure resources. For example, team leaders engage in ambassadorial activities by presenting a compelling case to information gatekeepers why the risk of not giving teams access to important information is greater than the risk of giving it to them and having it leaked to competitors. Ambassadorial activities aimed at securing resources have been found to be related to budget and schedule compliance, team processes, and innovation. Other boundary spanning behaviors, such as providing access to the workflow structure, creating tighter couplings with other teams, and adding expertise to the team, were also found to be related to indices of team effectiveness.[101]

Educational System

BEST PRACTICE #17. *Provide and secure developmental opportunities.*

The function of an educational system is to provide whatever knowledge, skills, attitudes, and other characteristics a team needs to fulfill its purposes. Often, the largest component of an educational system is formally administered training programs. Leaders schedule training as a planned intervention to enhance the direct determinants of team performance, including job-relevant knowledge, skill, and volitional choice behavior.[102] In turn, differences in direct determinants are a function of indirect determinants such as training, socialization, cognitive and psychomotor abilities, personality characteristics, experience, and organizational initiatives.[103]

Team leaders must conduct or arrange for formal training because teams are not always prepared to handle the challenges they are asked to navigate. One example of the successful use of formal training can be found in the aviation industry, which relies upon crew resource management (CRM) training as a strategy to reduce the 60 percent to 80 percent of accidents attributed to human error.[104] There is voluminous evidence that suggests CRM interventions are effective and well received in the aviation community.[105]

Expert Coaching

Expert coaching is the final condition team leaders put in place to facilitate team effectiveness.[106] This condition interacts with the previous four conditions, as was found by research conducted at Xerox, where well-designed teams benefited more from team coaching than their poorly designed counterparts.[107] Team coaching is defined herein as a "direct interaction with a team intended to help members make coordinated and task-appropriate use of their collective resources in accomplishing the team's work."[108] This definition makes clear that the purpose of coaching is to help teams perform the taskwork and teamwork processes at the heart of team performance rather than to address the quality of members' interpersonal relationships. This emphasis is different than most existing approaches to coaching (for example, process consultation, team building), which voluminous evidence suggests may be useful for affecting attitudes and clarifying roles, but have little impact on improving team performance.[109]

More broadly, this perspective reflects a shift in the conceptualization of the nature of what leaders do and when they do it to facilitate team effectiveness. Traditionally, team leaders have been viewed as domineering figures whose purpose it was to provide explicit directions, closely monitor progress, and make important decisions on behalf of the team. In the past decade, however, team leadership has been reframed in terms of predominantly consisting of coaching and facilitating team performance, rather than directing and controlling performance.[110]

In order to offset process losses and produce process gains, coaching interventions are most needed at the beginning, midpoint, and ending of team performance, although they are delivered at other times as well.[111] Coaching delivered by team leaders at the beginning of team performance is motivational in nature and is utilized to target a team's effort. In contrast, coaching delivered at the midpoint of team performance is consultative in nature and is used to help a team select appropriate performance strategies. Coaching delivered at the end of team performance is educational in nature and is delivered to develop team competence. At all three time periods, the team reflects upon its prior performance to distill lessons learned that can guide subsequent performance episodes.

Intervention in the form of team coaching is a matter of timing; leaders must seek out natural opportunities to create learning experiences. Team leaders must consider the readiness of the team to receive a coaching intervention. Two aspects of readiness are pertinent to consider: the degree to which the team has available resources to attend to the intervention and the degree to which the issues addressed by the intervention are naturally salient for the team.[112] In regard to the first of these issues, most teams experience cyclical variations in task intensity, complexity, and workload.[113] During low workload periods, team leaders can guide a process whereby a team reviews and reflects on its previous performance episodes and prepares to engage in future performance. When a team shifts its resources back to task performance, team leaders can monitor the team to assess whether agreed-upon strategies are being executed and whether established goals are being met. In this manner, team leaders synchronize a team's task performance and learning cycles.

In addition to concerns about cyclical variations in workload, team leaders should also take into account when particular issues are most salient for a team.[114] Research on temporal issues in teams suggests there are natural transitions that teams make as they work toward a deadline.[115] The phases teams move through are demarcated by unique focal issues. When certain issues are more salient for teams, they are more readily addressed by team coaching. Thus, a team leader provides coaching at critical junctures rather than acting as a supervisor who continuously intervenes as performance unfolds. The behaviors leaders enact to provide team coaching at the beginnings, midpoints, and endings of team performance are discussed next.

Beginnings

BEST PRACTICE #18. *Utilize prebriefings to instill shared affect, cognition, and behavior.*

Prebriefings set the stage for subsequent team performance.[116] For example, research with aviation crews suggested a team leader's communications during prebriefings created a climate of teamwork, which, in turn, had a significant impact on the frequency and effectiveness of compensatory behaviors demonstrated by the crews.[117] These findings are bolstered by the results of research with manufacturing teams, which suggested team coaching was related to the development of team psychological safety, team learning, and team performance.[118] Moreover, research also suggests leader prebriefings are a vehicle through which to impart shared mental models and thereby routine and adaptive performance.[119]

Team leader coaching interventions delivered prior to team performance target a team's collective motivation and commitment to perform as a cohesive unit.[120] For example, team leaders can engage in transformational behaviors[121] to evoke a shared mission and a shared belief in the team's capability to execute a mission successfully. This type of supportive behavior can instill a sense of competency specific team efficacy as well as generalized potency.[122] Team leaders can also use a questioning approach that encourages discussion and informal reinforcements when suggestions are raised in order to create a climate for teamwork. Similarly, team leaders who provide supportive, nondefensive responses to questions can create psychological safety or the shared belief the team is safe for interpersonal risk taking.[123] Team leaders also establish open channels of communication during prebriefings by encouraging team members to share their thoughts and concerns prior to task performance.

Midpoints

BEST PRACTICE #19. *Offer novel task performance strategies.*

Team leader coaching interventions delivered at the midpoint of task performance are undertaken to review the performance strategies that have been employed by a team during its prior performance.[124] The purpose of reviewing and reflecting on current performance strategies is to identify approaches that make better use of available resources or are a better fit to new challenges that have arisen in a team's context. Examining current performance strategies allows a team to tweak the fit of these approaches with the environmental contingencies present in a team's operational context.[125]

Team leaders initiate structure[126] at the midpoints of team task performance by identifying how current strategies can be altered or by suggesting the use of novel performance strategies that may be more appropriate for accomplishing a team's objectives. For example, team leaders can provide situation assessment updates on how the team is doing, what the team should be doing, and what can be done to adapt to a changing situation. During this process, team leaders should communicate situational contingencies that could change a team's goals or subgoals, as well as alternative strategies for responding to these contingencies.[127] Moreover, team leaders use the midpoints of task performance to encourage team members to continually scan their operational environment to identify and anticipate significant challenges on the horizon that may impact their newly revised performance strategy as the team completes its performance episode.

Endings

BEST PRACTICE #20. *Engage teams in a two-way discussion of lessons learned and how they can be utilized to address challenges on the horizon.*

Team leader coaching interventions at the end of performance are educational in nature because they target a team's knowledge, skill, and emergent states (that is, collective efficacy, shared mental models, psychological safety) for development.[128] A postaction review is a systematic process during which members, leaders, and other concerned stakeholders share their observations of a team's performance processes and outcomes.[129] Despite the favorable or unfavorable outcome(s) of a team's coordinated efforts, this time should be set aside for learning, with a focus on fostering future performance improvements.[130]

Team leaders use the endings of team task performance to develop a team's competence by questioning team members' understanding of why they engaged in particular team and task processes. A central aspect of this endeavor is to encourage a team to generate explanations for its performance. This line of questioning, which compels team members to mindfully reflect over their prior performance, facilitates the development of strategic knowledge and shared mental models that, in turn, guide future performance episodes. Leaders also use the endings of team performance to recognize and reinforce spontaneous displays of effective team processes.

Research conducted with U.S. Navy teams has identified eight team leader behaviors that characterize an effective postaction review. Specifically, team leaders conducting postbriefings should (1) provide a self-critique early in the review, (2) accept feedback and ideas from others, (3) avoid person-oriented feedback, (4) provide specific constructive suggestions, (5) encourage active team member participation in lieu of simply stating one's own observations and interpretations of team performance, (6) discuss both teamwork and taskwork processes, (7) make reference to lessons learned from prior prebriefs, and (8) vocalize satisfaction when a team or its members demonstrate improvements.[131]

EXECUTIVE SUMMARY

Organizational scholars have advanced a myriad of theories of leadership that make somewhat unique assertions about what leaders do and how they go about doing it.[132] In fact, it has been asserted that "there are almost as many definitions of leadership as those who have attempted to define the concept."[133] Although the authors believe each of these approaches offers a unique lens through which to understand team leadership, differentiation without integration ultimately results in chaos.

This chapter consolidated the burgeoning number of approaches to understanding team leadership under Hackman's five conditions for team effectiveness. Nearly 100 years of leadership theory and empirical research was applied to illuminate what team leaders do to put in place the conditions that facilitate team effectiveness. Thus, this chapter breaks from the tradition of touting a single theory as the most appropriate framework and thereby answers the call to illuminate a broader array of what leaders do in teams.[134]

From the perspective advanced herein, the science and art of fostering team effectiveness becomes an ongoing process of creating a real team, which has a compelling direction, an enabling structure, a supportive context, and access to expert coaching. The following best practices should be adhered to when establishing and sustaining effective teams:

1. *Team leaders create real teams* by defining team task interdependencies and reinforcing those linkages with congruent goals and performance feedback. Moreover, team leaders identify who is currently accountable for team outcomes and designate the decision making authority responsible parties have for their work.

2. *Team leaders articulate a compelling direction* by exercising their authority to establish common objectives that stimulate and inspire teams by challenging the status quo. Moreover, by communicating a common mission that is consequential to those who undertake it, direction serves to fully engage a team's talents.

3. *Team leaders establish an enabling structure* by designing a team's work so its members take ownership of their tasks. They set boundaries for acceptable behavior by specifying what teams must and cannot do to seize opportunities and how within-team dyadic interactions should be conducted. Moreover, they strive to create an optimal blend within the team by allocating an appropriate number and mix of personnel to a team.

4. *Team leaders help ensure a supportive organizational context* exists by institutionalizing multitiered performance-contingent reward systems. Moreover, they work with support personnel and senior stakeholders to ensure the information provided to a team is performance targeted and that there are ample opportunities for team development.

5. *Team leaders provide expert coaching* by seeking natural opportunities to create learning experiences, particularly at the beginnings, midpoints, and endings of team performance. Through the use of prebriefings and postaction reviews, team leaders distill lessons learned, instill shared affect, cognition,

and behavior, and offer novel task performance strategies that can be utilized to address upcoming challenges or adapt to current contingencies.

Although far from exhaustive, these practices can help guide team leaders along the path to achieving team effectiveness. Team leaders who spend a majority of their time establishing these five conditions rather than directly intervening in team performance will likely find that their teams are increasingly capable and willing to adaptively respond in a coordinated manner, and thus they and their teams will ultimately be deemed more effective in the wild.

PART THREE

Leading the Organization

CHAPTER NINE

Best Practices in Leading Organizational Change

Workplace Recovery Following Major Organizational Transitions

Mitchell Lee Marks

J ust about every work organization in recent years has gone through a merger, acquisition, downsizing, restructuring, or other major transition. While we live and work in an era when "the only constant is change," there comes a time when senior executives will genuinely conclude that the disruptiveness of transition is over and will prod their people to look ahead to new opportunities. The employees, however, may be neither ready nor willing to charge ahead. Their vision will be obscured by the emotional residue of anger, distrust, and depression left over from a challenging transition. Nor will they have the confidence that they can achieve the desired results—their self-esteem will be battered and their faith in their organization broken. Most significantly, the troops will not see how any personal gain will result from business success. Instead, they will fixate on memories of their fallen comrades: the casualties of layoffs and downsizings, and the "walking wounded" whose careers were sidetracked by mergers and acquisitions.

WORKPLACE RECOVERY

This chapter describes best practices in leading *workplace recovery* after major organizational transition. It is based on the observation—derived from personal involvement in more than one hundred major organizational transitions and a review of both academic and practitioner-oriented publications—that transitions such as mergers, acquisitions, restructurings, and downsizings are very difficult events to lead and, even when relatively well managed, produce unintended consequences for organizations and their members. Once the dust has settled from a transition, there is a need to help people recover from its inadvertent effects rather than assume that employees are ready to move forward. By *recovery,* I mean addressing both the emotional realities and the business imperatives associated with regrouping after a transition or series of transitions.

A formal workplace recovery effort revives organizations and their people by instilling new life and energy after the disruptiveness of transition. Recovery prepares people to contribute to new strategic and economic opportunities through positive changes in perceptions, practices, policies, and processes. When aligned, these changes resuscitate individual employee spirit, work team productivity, and organizational performance. The objective of workplace recovery is not merely to recuperate following a merger, acquisition, downsizing, or other major transition, but to rebound with a workforce that has an enhanced capacity to operate competitively.

Incremental versus Transitional Change

To appreciate the ways in which transition impacts employee well-being and organizational performance—as well as the actions required to recover from a transition—it is helpful to distinguish between incremental organizational changes and transitional organizational changes. *Incremental change* refers to the evolutionary adjustments, improvements, and product or service alternations that organizations need in order to satisfy the increasing demands of customers and keep up with current changes in technology. *Transition* refers to major disruptions in an organization's core competencies, offerings, markets, and business models.

Transition is much more debilitating to work organizations and their members and has deeper psychological impact than more rudimental occurrences of incremental change in the workplace.[1] Incremental change is a path to a known state: something discrete, with orderly steps. Moving the start of the weekly staff meeting from 9:00 AM to 8:00 AM is an example of such a change. It may cause some conflicts and require some accommodation—people have to leave home for work earlier or cancel other early morning commitments—but its discrete nature allows people to know exactly what to expect and lets them get on with their lives inside and outside the organization.

A transition, by comparison, is a path to an unknown state: something discontinuous that involves many simultaneous and interactive changes and the selection of "breakthrough" ways of thinking, organizing, and doing business. When pharmaceutical company Pfizer acquired Warner Lambert, the integration strategy called for enhancements in the process of discovering and developing new drugs. That prompted transitional changes in Pfizer's Global Research and Development organization, including a radical structural redesign, the closing of some laboratories, and a cultural transformation that emphasized collaboration rather than competition across regions. In other words, transition poses a break from the past. It involves death and rebirth; existing practices and routines must be abandoned and new ones discovered and developed. Adapting to transition is much more psychologically taxing than adapting to incremental change.

The Saturation Effect

Some scholars and practitioners suggest that in many industries, life is now discontinuous, abrupt, and distinctly nonlinear, as radically different ideas and commercial developments render established products and services outmoded.[2] Concurrently, they argue that periods of stability are a thing of the past and that classic models of leading organizational change are obsolete.

The problem with this perspective of organizational life is that recurrent discontinuous change is not a natural condition of life, and that resistance is a to-be-expected response.[3] People can handle only so much disruption in their work situations. Over time their threshold for dealing with stress, uncertainty, and disorientation is met. Their ability to cope with all the changes is impaired, resulting in detrimental attitudes, maladaptive behaviors, disappointing performances, and the many other unintended consequences of organizational transition.

Increasingly, people in organizations are being exposed to multiple waves of transition, often with one overlapping another. Take the case of MK Enterprises (a fictionalized name, but a real situation). At its peak in the mid-1990s, MK boasted revenues of $19 billion, employed 22,000 people, and had a reputation as a stable, well-managed company. It also was regarded as an excellent place to work. People took jobs there because they wanted a place of employment with stability, predictability, and growth.

In 1995, MK made an opportunistic acquisition of a competitor's operations. In announcing the acquisition to employees, chief executive officer (CEO) Michael Dingold acknowledged there would be some redundancy in positions but promised to take care of this through attrition, assuring his troops there would be no layoffs. As tough economic times set in toward the end of the decade, however, MK's debt obligation loomed larger and larger. Revenues remained flat, expenses increased, and margins eroded. Within three years, Dingold ordered two major restructurings—the first to streamline decision making in general and the second to eliminate bureaucratic hurdles slowing the introduction of new products to market.

The restructurings changed the organization's design and reporting relationships, but produced few cost savings. Still confronted by debt and flat growth, the company had to cut expenses dramatically. In 2000, Dingold announced the first reduction-in-force program in MK's history. It was voluntary, providing enhanced early retirement benefits for employees over fifty-five and severance pay incentives for all other employees. Despite its voluntary nature, the program sent shock waves through the ranks of MK managers and employees.

A few months after the reduction-in-force announcement, Dingold proclaimed a new vision for MK: it would become the "premier" company in its industry segment. Soon Dingold initiated two projects to achieve this vision. First, he engaged a prominent consulting firm to conduct a value-added work analysis. Shortly thereafter, Dingold returned from a conference on organizational learning to announce that he had commissioned a training company to deliver a "continuous improvement process" program to all MK managers.

As the economy weakened in late 2000 and into 2001, MK managed a small operating profit but could not reduce its heavy debt load. The broader economic malaise diminished long-term prospects for revenue growth, and Dingold concluded that severe cost cutting was necessary for his company's survival. In June 2001 he announced that MK would have to implement an involuntary downsizing program.

Each of these events resulted in the experience of cumulative stress for MK employees. For several months, MK employees observed and vicariously experienced disruptions in other companies in their industry and heard rumors of impending change at their own workplace. Then MK employees were subjected to the acquisition, poor economy, restructuring, voluntary reduction in force, programs like value-added work analysis and continuous improvement, and finally the involuntary reduction in force. By then, many MK employees had become numbed by the dizzying course of events. Literally and figuratively, the ability to cope and contend with disruptions to their work situation had become saturated.[4]

Sometimes the saturation effect occurs on an individual level and not necessarily companywide. Still, when a critical mass of people in an organization's workforce gets saturated with transition impact, it brings down the entire organization. In many organizations like MK, employees have suffered intellectual and emotional paralysis brought on by their saturated coping capacity. They are psychologically worn out, unable to get revved up about meeting new challenges. (We return to the case of MK Enterprises later in this chapter and see how the organization and its people recovered after this series of transitions.)

The Healthy Side of Transition

Certainly organizations need to "rightsize" by eliminating unnecessary work and "reinvent" by adopting new ways of doing things in response to economic, legal, technological, and consumer changes. If organizations did not change, they would not remain competitive. Moreover, a transition can be a beneficial impetus for workplaces and employees. A CEO, business unit leader, or department head with the right mix of visionary and charismatic leadership skills can rally employees around the notion that a merger, acquisition, or downsizing is not only a necessary response to business realities, but a proactive opportunity to improve how work is approached and conducted in the organization. Similarly, a middle manager or supervisor can use the transition as an opportunity to enhance teamwork, build better cross-functional relations, and identify and correct impediments to work group productivity.

And individuals can experience a personal form of renewal as a result of organizational transitions. Although many employees stay mired in maladaptive responses to the stress and uncertainty of a transition, others come to recognize that in crisis there is opportunity. Unfortunately, however, using transition as an opportunity for personal growth, team development, or organizational renewal is very much the exception, not the rule. Reports of mergers, acquisitions, and downsizings rarely describe productive, regenerating, or even rebalancing outcomes. In contrast, they depict transitions as painful and wrenching. As a result, there is a serious need for leadership to embrace a program for workplace recovery following mergers, acquisitions, downsizings, and other major organizational transitions.

FIVE REALITIES OF ORGANIZATIONAL TRANSITIONS

One facet of leading workplace recovery is coming to terms with the fact that the way in which transitions typically are managed results in undesirable consequences, including stifled personal motivation, hindered team performance, and damaged organizational effectiveness. To fully understand the leadership challenge here, consider five realities of organizational transitions that distinguish them from rudimentary or incremental cases of organizational change.

REALITY #1. *Transitions are difficult events to manage.*

To be fair, major organizational transitions are very difficult to manage. Eighty-three percent of all mergers fail to deliver shareholder value and 53 percent actually destroy value.[5] Most downsizings provide one-time-only cuts in the cost of doing business but fail to return organizations to financial health or leave the organization with any true enhancements in how work is accomplished.[6] To understand why there is such a dismal track record, look no further than at how mergers, acquisitions, and downsizings transpire, both in practical and emotional terms.

Mergers and Acquisitions: Wired for Mismanagement. The very manner in which mergers and acquisitions are conceived runs counter to prescriptions of effective leadership and management:[7]

• *Inadequate vision.* Many mergers are undertaken purely for cost-cutting reasons; say, when two underutilized hospitals in a community combine or when financial institutions join forces and eliminate redundant back office functions. Often, mergers and acquisitions are reactive events in which executives hop on the bandwagon in response to a combination between other firms in their industry. However, cost cutting and band-wagoning are not sufficient for giving employees a compelling rationale for why they should sacrifice in the short run for hoped-for organizational enhancements in the long run.

- *Inadequate communication.* Mergers and acquisitions are shrouded in secrecy. Executives putting a deal together have to keep a very tight lid on their intentions, for both competitive and legal reasons.

- *Inadequate coalition building.* Combining organizations requires coordination and cooperation across combining partners. Yet managers adopt highly political behaviors in hopes of exercising control over an uncertain situation. Meanwhile, ever-pervasive culture clash produces "us versus them" dynamics that pull partners apart rather than bring them together and, as a result, interferes with effective teamwork, issue identification, and decision making.

- *Inadequate planning.* Despite the high failure rate, many executives deny the difficulty of combining two previously independent firms into one entity. Lawyers and investment bankers, who stand to make millions of dollars in fees if the deal goes through, seduce the CEO with promises of potential synergies as a deal is being conceptualized. While the financial generalists predict success, there are usually no operations managers present who can realistically test the likelihood of achieving actual synergies.

Downsizing: The Detested Task. Firing people is one of the most difficult leadership tasks. It is tough enough to do when someone is let go for performance issues, and even more difficult when people are laid off for reasons other than their personal performance on the job.

The norms that predominate in most downsizing organizations run counter to effectively managing the reduction:

- *Sense of urgency.* Like gulping down bad-tasting medicine, the assumption in many organizations is that making the cuts quickly is better than carefully. People in a downsizing are not like medicine—they are not "fast acting." Surviving employees need time to mourn the loss of coworkers, come to terms with what it means to work in an organization that lets people go even if they perform well, and ponder the long-term implications on job security and career advancement.

- *Fear of violence.* When they learn they have to lay people off, managers' thoughts immediately turn to fears of violent reactions by those affected. While workplace shootings following downsizings are highly publicized, they are very rare.

- *Stigma of failure.* Even though downsizing is well engrained in the managerial repertoire, it remains a stigma. When people hear that a company is cutting jobs, the assumption is that it is in dire financial straits. This stigma prompts leaders to downplay the event, minimize communication, and act like little or nothing is happening rather than communicate openly and fully about the event, its purpose, and its implications for going forward.

REALITY #2. *Transitions are difficult events for people to cope with.*

As previously noted, adapting to transition is much more psychologically taxing than is adapting to change. And, after years of mergers, acquisitions, downsizings, and other major transitions, people's ability to cope with transition has become saturated. Even when they themselves have not gone through a difficult transition, people learn vicariously from the experiences of their friends, relatives, neighbors, and counterparts in other organizations.

William Bridges identifies three stages of individual adaptation to organizational transition:[8]

1. *Current reality.* This is the ending of the old. It starts with recognizing the ending, saying good-bye to the status quo. People experience feelings such as uncertainty, sadness, grief, loss, fear, anxiety, anger, disenchantment, and disillusionment during this phase.

2. *Neutral zone.* This is the in-between phase. Once someone is able to let go of the old, they pass through the neutral zone. The neutral zone is a kind of no man's land—the individual is no longer connected with the old reality but has not yet arrived at the new reality. It is confusing and often fraught with mixed messages, a feeling of chaos, and powerful emotions. People in the neutral

zone often feel lost, apathetic, listless, disoriented, foggy, distant, ungrounded, and unfocused.

3. *New reality.* This is the beginning of the new state for the individual. After contending with the neutral zone, the person settles into the new reality. People who arrive at this phase feel reenergized, refocused, excited about and engaged in their situation, and grounded. Importantly to business organizations, they feel clear about the work that needs to be accomplished.

Not all people make it to the new reality. Some never let go of the old reality, despite all the changes that may be going on around them. Some get stuck in the quagmire of the neutral zone—they accept that the old is gone but they never latch on to the new. While individuals move through the three phases at varying speeds, all go through the phases sequentially.

REALITY #3. *Mismanaged transitions have negative, not merely neutral, consequences on people and organizations.*

In principle, a transition should enable an organization to improve its competitiveness without impairing its ability to execute its strategy. In practice, however, a transition can exact a heavy toll on organizational effectiveness and employee well-being. The unintended consequences of mismanaged mergers, acquisitions, and downsizing have critical consequences, both human and business.

THE UNINTENDED HUMAN CONSEQUENCES. While a broad review is beyond the scope of this chapter, the unintended consequences of mismanaged transitions on workplaces and their members have been well documented.[9] These include the loss of confidence in management, heightened cynicism and distrust, decreased morale, reduced loyalty, and, in general, a dismal outlook for future life in the organization. Especially debilitating to surviving employees is the perceived loss of control over their work situation. No matter how well they do their jobs, they could be hit in the next wave of layoffs.

The unintended psychological consequences of transitions are pervasive. In a longitudinal study of 10,000 U.S. employees, those from organizations that had been engaged in a merger or acquisition reported less favorable results than those who had not in every industry group and every facet of working life measured.[10]

The unintended consequences of mismanaged transitions also are manifested behaviorally. Survivors of major organizational transitions work harder but not smarter—the workload doesn't get smaller when the work force does.[11] What about the promise of enhanced organizational effectiveness that accompanies the announcements of many organizational transitions? The reality is that no one has time to stop and think of creative ways to approach work. Compounding the sheer volume of work confronting people who survive a transition is a lack of direction in prioritizing which tasks to tackle first. Survivors want to get out of the blocks quickly and impress new leaders. But their intentions are thwarted when they do not know what the business priorities are or where to turn for the equipment, information, or support they need.

Risk taking plummets following a transition.[12] Employees are so scared that there is a self-imposed pressure not to make waves or take risks, just at the time when innovation is needed. Further cuts may be in the offing, and no one wants a blemish on their record that might be used against them when the next list of victims gets drawn up. Instead, managers and employees go with what they know, relying on what has worked for them in the past. The problem is that what may have worked in the past is not necessarily appropriate for the post-transition organization.

THE UNINTENDED BUSINESS CONSEQUENCES. The costs of mismanaged transitions have been measured in financial as well as human terms. When all the work remains but not all the staff, most companies are not prepared to handle the workload. Financial analysts do a very good job of predicting savings that result from a reduction in headcount, but underestimate the costs required to cover the tasks that had been handled by laid-off employees. Among the costs downsizing firms have to contend with are increases in retraining remaining workers, using temporary workers, outsourcing functions, and paying for overtime. Some firms also lose the wrong employees—people with critical skills or needed talents take advantage of incentives to leave the company.

Health care costs incurred by organizations rise for both victims and survivors of downsizings. It is easy to see how health care costs increase for transition casualties. The psychological trauma of losing one's position, or of unceremoniously being invited to leave through an early retirement program, triggers psychosomatic ailments. Plus, early retirees have more time to visit health care providers and ring up expenses. Not so obvious—but equally costly—are increased health care costs for survivors, who are also subjected to the psychosomatic effects of intense stress on the job. Working harder to cover the work of others also results in a higher accident rate. Especially problematic is when older employees return to jobs involving physical labor after being in less strenuous supervisory jobs.

Importantly, anticipation or concern about job loss may be as damaging as job loss itself.[13] Job insecurity has been found to be associated with increased medical consultations for psychological distress and with increased disability claims for back pain.[14]

REALITY #4. *If properly managed, transitions have the potential to unfreeze organizations and their members.*

A transition holds the potential to "unfreeze" an organization and its people,[15] and establishes an opportunity to significantly change corporate culture and reinforce new ways of doing things. A major transition disturbs the status quo: it jars people, changes relationships, redefines work team composition and goals, and disrupts accustomed ways of doing things. It also is an opportunity to think in a proactive manner about what life after the transition could be like.

What makes a transition so stressful for people—its ability to separate them from their accustomed ways of thinking and acting—concurrently provides the benefit of unfreezing people. A transition also has the potential to put organizational structures, systems, strategies, programs, processes, and cultures "into play." Hiring guidelines, reward systems, decision-making criteria, problem-solving approaches, reporting relationships, and all other aspects of the organization are temporarily pliable and ready to be set in a new mold. At the individual level, workplace recovery after transition hinges on changing perceptions and behaviors. This, in turn, requires unlearning familiar concepts or assumed mental models of cause-and-effect relationships and replacing them with new impressions and associations.

REALITY #5. *People have to let go of the old before they can accept the new.*

Many efforts at organizational change fail because the leaders who initiate them and the staffers who implement them do not accept the reality that people have to end the old before they can accept the new. In some organizations, this natural process of individual adaptation to transition is understood, but not wholeheartedly embraced. These employers dismiss allowing people to deal with their feelings as an inappropriate use of time and other resources. This reasoning ignores the fact that people will go through the phases of holding on, letting go, and accepting the new whether the organization likes it or not. Time and attention get diverted away from work activities in any event. Rather than deplete resources, a workplace recovery program accelerates the speed with which people come to terms with and move through their adaptation process.

There is another key reason why the adaptation process often is ignored in organizations engaged in transition: senior executives typically have made progress in letting go of the old before others in the organization have begun their adaptation process. Senior executives may have been involved in secret premerger discussions, deliberated the need for a downsizing, or pondered the cultural implications well before the transition was announced to the overall organization. They literally have several months' head start in the process of psychologically rejecting the old and adapting to the new.

As Figure 9.1 shows, those at the top levels in an organization begin their process of moving from holding on to letting go of the old and

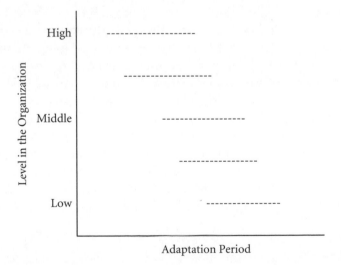

Figure 9.1.   Adaptation to Transition by Hierarchical Level.

accepting the new well before employees at other levels. Senior executives, those with the most at stake, often have the most intense reactions to a transition, and experience strong forces for maintaining the status quo. They adapt to change and mourn their losses through what typically is a private process, but one that nonetheless consumes personal attention and time. Significantly, however, their adaptation process is accelerated by the high degree of control they enjoy relative to others in the organization. Senior executives are the architects of the transition; they understand why change is needed and where it is headed. All other members of the organization have much less influence and a lot more uncertainty when it comes to adaptation.

By the time executives at the top of the organization are looking ahead to new realities, people lower in the hierarchy are only beginning or, at best, are in the middle of their adaptation process. In large organizations, transition implementation may not ripple down to the lowest levels for quite some time. Many employees do not experience their first wave of transition-related change— and thus do not *begin* their adaptation process —until senior executives have put the old behind them and are well on their way to accepting the new. Just as lower-level employees are beginning to contend with holding on and letting go, senior executives frequently repress memories of the pain and confusion of leaving the old behind. Consequently, they are unsympathetic to others' needs for holding on. Having let go of the past, they are concerned with the future. Either because they are impatient to move on or because they refuse to consciously accept the pain of their own personal transition, executives sometimes forget that beginning the new starts with ending the old.

TWO REQUIREMENTS AND TWO LEVELS OF WORKPLACE RECOVERY

Workplace recovery accepts and works with the realities of organizational transition and individual adaptation, rather than denying or futilely attempting to work around them. One of these realities is that people have to end the old before they accept the new. Thus, there are two requirements for workplace recovery after transition:

1. Weaken the forces for maintaining the old.
2. Strengthen the forces for developing the new.

Every person and organization encounters forces for maintaining the status quo and forces for change. These forces operate counter to each other, with a continually shifting balance.[16] Adaptation to transition occurs more as a fading out and in than as a quick cut. Initially, forces for maintaining the status quo are strong and are expressed through outright resistance to change or, at best, the absence of a will to act. Over time, the forces for the desired new organization can predominate and provide the necessary impetus for letting go of the old and moving on to and accepting the new.

The forces for the old and for the new are varied and cover both personal and organizational matters. To sufficiently weaken forces for the old and strengthen forces for the new, workplace recovery must address both the *emotional realities* and the *business imperatives* associated with a transition or a series of transitions. Research has shown that organizational changes and transitions are always connected with emotional experiences.[17] Leaders who manage transition effectively rely on and cope with emotions by bringing them to the surface and understanding how they affect work activities and relationships as groups face challenges and organizational changes.[18]

Business imperatives are the things that need to get done for business success to occur. These include everything from setting strategies to selecting work procedures, from patterns of communicating with people to ways of rewarding them. To facilitate ending the old, certain aspects of the business imperatives that predominated in the pre-transition organization must be abandoned or made less prominent— that is, the forces for their maintenance must be weakened. To strengthen forces for accepting the new, employees must understand not only what is changing, but also why the changes are being made and how those changes will contribute to both business and personal success. By addressing the two levels of emotional realities and business imperatives, leaders can accelerate the speed with which employees let go of the unintended pain and consequences they experience during and after transitions, while simultaneously using transitions as opportunities to build new and better workplaces. Thus, leading workplace recovery is not just about helping people feel better or become more capable in their job performance, but also about informing and enhancing management and leadership decision making on business issues.[19]

THE ELEMENTS OF WORKPLACE RECOVERY

The two requirements of workplace recovery (weakening forces for the old and strengthening forces for the new) and the two levels of workplace recovery (emotional realities and business imperatives) produce four elements of workplace recovery after transition (see Figure 9.2):

1. *Empathy:* Letting people know leadership acknowledges that things have been difficult and, for at least a while longer, will continue to be difficult

2. *Engagement:* Creating understanding of and support for the need to end the old and accept the new

3. *Energy:* Getting people excited about the desired posttransition organization and supporting them in realizing it

4. *Enforcement:* Solidifying new mental models that are congruent with the desired posttransition organization

Empathy

The first element of workplace recovery is to express empathy to employees. This means making it *clear* that leadership is cognizant of

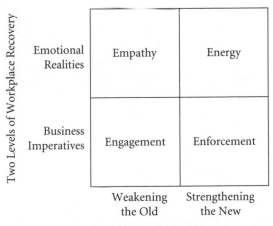

Two Levels of Workplace Recovery

	Weakening the Old	Strengthening the New
Emotional Realities	Empathy	Energy
Business Imperatives	Engagement	Enforcement

Two Tasks of Workplace Recovery

Figure 9.2.   The Elements and Actions of Workplace Recovery.

the needs, feelings, problems, and views of employees who have lived through a merger, acquisition, restructuring, or downsizing. Empathy weakens forces blocking employee adaptation to transition. Employees are not accustomed to hearing their superiors admit that times have been tough and that transition has taken a toll on people. In fact, the tendency for many leaders is to avoid admitting mistakes or responsibility and instead attribute poor business outcomes to external factors like the economy or threat of terrorism.[20]

Recall the case of MK Enterprises. Executives there conveyed empathy though a combination of activities. The starting point was acknowledging the realities and difficulties of living through multiple transitions over a several-year period. CEO Michael Dingold owned up to his role in contributing to the pain of the past, initially through a *mea culpa* delivered at a town hall meeting. Employees at MK were surprised to hear their leader admit his awareness of the difficulty people had been through. Observing their CEO talking and acting in new ways at this and other events prompted employees to think about their own responsibility in letting go of the old and accepting the new.

Next, Dingold backed up his words with actions that displayed empathy toward employees. He freed up resources—including budgets and employee time—for workshops to help employees understand the complexity and intricacies of the transition and adaptation processes. These workshops featured two important components. First, they educated employees on transition and adaptation in a manner that showed these to be normal human responses to organizational events. Second, they helped individuals understand where they did and did not have control, and guided them in letting go of what was beyond their control so they could focus on actions that were within their control.

Another leadership action that conveyed empathy at MK was to sanction events and ceremonies that accelerated the letting-go process. "Venting meetings" in which employees could express their pent-up anger and other negative feelings were particularly helpful. Most employees find it difficult to express negative feelings at the workplace.[21] However, a carefully facilitated venting meeting can get people to open up in a supportive and safe environment. Even for employees who do not speak up, simply vicariously listening to others express similar views contributed to weakening the negative emotions left over from living through a difficult transition.[22] To keep the meeting on a productive track, it helps to have a trained facilitator lead the session. And it also helps to have senior leaders clear a path for these and similar activities by getting the word out to all executives, managers, and supervisors that the recovery effort is genuine and that time and resources must be made available for employees to partici-pate in these activities.

Engagement

The second element of workplace recovery weakens forces against desired change by engaging people in understanding the business imperatives of recovery and eliminating roadblocks to achieving them. The actions leaders can take to engage employees in workplace recov-ery are consistent with the calls for breaking down resistance and enhancing involvement by organizational scholars from the classic to the contemporary.[23]

Engagement at MK began in a very practical manner, by helping people accomplish their immediate work objectives by clarifying pri-orities and providing resources to get the job done. All superiors and subordinates conducted "work expectation meetings" in which shared priorities and expectations were established. When placed in the con-text of broader organizational opportunities and constraints, these meetings also achieve the benefit of alerting employees to the princi-pal challenges facing the organization and engaging them in address-ing those challenges.[24]

Next, MK engaged people in the recovery process by stepping up communication and employee involvement. This was Organizational Behavior 101: the more people understood what was going on and felt involved in the process, the less resistant they would be to ensuing dis-ruptions to their work situation. However, leadership at MK did not shrug off this requirement of recovery as a no-brainer. Executives spent the time required to go beyond a cursory communication effort and committed to keeping people in the know through frequent and thorough communication. They made—and stuck to—this commit-ment knowing they were stretched thin between running the business and managing the transition. In addition, most of MK's corporate support staff had been let go in the waves of layoffs. Involvement also meant taking people off-line from their jobs and giving them the time to problem solve and recommend ways of truly working smarter—a difficult call given that employee ranks had been downsized and the financial community was wanting a short-term turnaround in operational results.

Increasing communication and involvement had a symbolic as well as a substantive value: it demonstrated that leadership was aware of the need to stay in touch with employees and was genuinely interested in their viewpoint. This led to a third engagement tactic at MK: identifying and eliminating barriers to adaptation. If leadership did not know—*from an employee perspective*—what the barriers to letting go were, then it could not take appropriate actions to weaken people's grips on the old. The best way to understand what was inhibiting people from ending the old at MK was to ask them. Employee attitude surveys and focus group interviews were cost-effective methods for engaging employees and identifying obstacles to the letting-go process. The findings provided leadership with specific opportunities to weaken forces against desired change.

Energy

While the first two elements weaken forces for the status quo, the next two strengthen forces for the desired posttransition organization. The third element of workplace recovery is to generate employee energy for understanding, accepting, and adapting to new realities in the posttransition organization. This occurs when employees know what is in it for them to accept the posttransition organization and feel they can succeed in it. It is this link between organizational success and personal impact that is the foundation for creating energy.

The nucleus for creating energy for recovery at MK was a clearly articulated vision of a new and better organization. In contrast to his previous vague vision of becoming a "premier" organization, CEO Michael Dingold conveyed how MK now was positioned for success in a rapidly changing business sector, provided the business case for why further change was essential, and gave details regarding the new organizational order—the changes in the MK's direction, mission, culture, and architecture that would contribute to an enhanced workplace. As a testament to how visions can take a variety of forms, Dingold worked with a small group of executives to generate a set of "guiding principles" that became criteria for adopting new practices that brought the new organizational order to life. For example, one principle was "integrate career development efforts with business goals." Thus, meetings that previously had been limited to narrow reviews of business objectives now integrated discussions of individual career objectives and developmental opportunities. A long-term strategic planning session, in turn, became a forum for examining team members' current capabilities and developmental needs.

The vision included a clear sense of strategic direction, a compelling mission for the organization, and the guiding principles. And, as Kotter suggests, every possible vehicle to communicate the vision was utilized.[25] MK's senior executives turned boring and unread company newsletters into lively articles about the vision. They reworked tedious quarterly meetings into exciting discussions of workplace recovery. They threw out much of the company's generic management education program and replaced it with courses that focused on business problems and the new vision. And, they incorporated messages about new organizational realities into their day-by-day activities— routine discussions about business problems became opportunities to confer about how proposed solutions fit (or didn't fit) into the new organizational order.

Research shows that managers and organizations tend to maintain the status quo during difficult times.[26] To sustain the energy for moving forward, Dingold stressed the need to develop a learning environment in which employees could experiment with identifying new and better methods for achieving personal and organizational success. Trial-and-error learning was embraced as a powerful way to learn, albeit a painful way— employees had never been rewarded for raising and discussing errors in the company. For recovery to occur, employees not only had to be cognitively aware that leadership understood that mistakes would occur; they also had to feel there were incentives for turning those mistakes into learning opportunities for the overall organization.

Still feeling the pain of the lingering unintended consequences of organizational transitions, employees needed positive signs and feedback to muster up the energy to find novel approaches to making a run at MK's new business opportunities. Developing this energy could not rely solely on the annual performance review. First, MK's reward systems were lagging behind in assessing and reinforcing the new organizational order. Second, waiting a full year for the annual cycle to kick in simply would have been too long to generate and sustain employee energy. The answer was to create opportunities for short-term wins. Quarterly performance feedback cycles were established that featured relatively minor payouts. The objective was to start creating links in employees' minds between experimenting with and adopting new ways of doing things and eventual recognition and reward.

Energizing people at MK also required the "human touch." To help people struggle through the neutral zone and latch onto the new, leadership continued to connect with employees on a human level and provide both practical and emotional support. As in any recovery, confusion, cynicism, and concerns arose within the MK workforce. This prompted some individuals to regress to the comfort zone of the accustomed old. So one part of leadership being supportive at MK was being patient with people and accepting that they needed time to move through the natural adaptation process. This was shown in ways such as creating realistic rather than stretch targets. While the "gut instinct" of many managers at MK was to charge ahead as aggressively as possible, they recognized that the last thing needed in the organization—especially after people's coping ability had been saturated by several years of ongoing transition—was setting the bar so high that it would only serve to demotivate employees. Another facet of leadership emerging in MK was to encourage dialogue and disagreement as new organizational dynamics settled into place. At MK, these dynamics were accepted as inevitable components of the recovery process, rather than regarded as failures or setbacks.

Enforcement

Enforcement brings the momentum for desired change to the level of consistency required for true cultural and cognitive change. Senior leadership aligns all of the obvious and subtle components of the organization—systems, procedures, actions, impressions, innuendos, and so on—to send as clear a message as humanly possible to strengthen the forces for the desired new posttransition organization. Consistency compels people to accept new organizational realities and abandon old ones. There is no way around the fact that the less consistent these messages, the less quickly the organization will recover from the unintended consequences of transition.

There were three components of enforcement at MK: alignment, involvement, and measurement. To strengthen forces for desired change, organizational systems and operating standards at MK had to be revised to fit posttransition realities. As noted, the compensation system and, in particular, the annual performance review process at

MK lagged behind and continued to measure and reinforce the old organizational order rather than the new. A major overhaul was set in place. In addition to aligning the "hardware" of systems and policies, the "software" of people and behaviors needed to be aligned at MK. For example, the next generation of top management needed to personify new organizational realities. As a result, criteria for promotion and selection changed.

With macro-level systems and standards in place, enforcement of the new organizational order continued by aligning individual on-the-job behaviors with the desired vision. Building on senior leadership's vision and strategic direction for the posttransition organization, managers and supervisors developed business unit or functional mission statements to guide employee behavior. Then, in work groups, employees translated the vision, mission, and operating guidelines into day-to-day operating procedures. This clarified how employees could align their work with the vision and provided answers to prominent questions of how people could contribute to overall organizational success. Moving back up the hierarchy, supervisors and managers reviewed proposed new ways of approaching work to ensure they supported the mission and vision and to provide coordination across work areas. Thus, while based on the core vision of senior leadership, this approach generated the consistency of direction and support from all hierarchical levels that is required for true and lasting change. It also complemented the emotional energy of the vision with practical changes in employees' day-to-day work activities.

Enforcement at MK benefited from measuring and tracking the development of the new organizational order. Various data were collected to monitor the extent to which the desired posttransition organization was truly being realized. Feedback regarding the success of workplace recovery was disseminated to every level in the hierarchy. Some measurements were objective (for example, measures of productivity, quality, and voluntary turnover); others, such as attitude surveys and focus group interviews, had the added benefits of involving people and enhancing upward and downward communication. This was especially important at MK, where the espoused posttransition culture included intentions to increase involvement and communication.

The formal and coordinated process of workforce recovery at MK truly was a turning point for the organization and its people. The most recent wave of employee research found that employees were more likely to discuss current and emerging business opportunities rather than look back at the "good old days" during pretransition or the "dark days" of the transition itself. Workplace recovery not only assisted in wringing out pent-up emotions and loosening attachments to the old ways, it generated optimism for the future and strengthened acceptance of new ways of thinking and acting in the organization. Also importantly, it provided a sense of stability in the ever more turbulent business world. As a result, MK has stabilized its financial performance and received positive endorsements from financial analysts.

TIMING WORKPLACE RECOVERY

The elements of workplace recovery are not necessarily sequential. This is because the phases of individual adaptation to transition do not have discrete boundaries—the forces for maintaining the status quo and the forces for growth continually operate counter to each other, with a constantly shifting balance. You don't abruptly stop weakening the forces for the old and then turn your attention to strengthening the forces for the new. Rather, you continue to weaken the resisting forces even as you strengthen the desired forces.

Some activities sensibly occur at specific points in the recovery process. Expressing empathy for what people have been through during a difficult transition should occur early in the recovery process, to help employees let go of their anger and be more receptive to engagement in the process. Some actions may seemingly occur "out of order." Take the articulation of the new vision. Discussing it with people is an Element 3 activity that strengthens forces for accepting the new. A well-articulated vision also is likely to weaken forces for maintaining the status quo by confronting employees' concerns that leadership is unclear about where the organization is headed. So it is not unusual to begin communicating it early in the recovery process.

Some activities may span all four elements. Communication and involvement are obvious examples, as well as diagnosing barriers to the adaptation process. Diagnosis is an excellent way to engage people in the recovery process—when guided by a skillful interviewer and confident that "heads will not roll" for being candid, employees readily talk about what is on their minds and are curious about what others are thinking. While this is an Element 2 activity, it makes good sense to conduct some form of diagnosis when designing activities throughout the process—the more accurately you know what is interfering with ending the old, the more precisely you can focus your efforts to weaken them; conversely, the more clearly you understand the opportunities to strengthen acceptance of the new, the better you can appropriate resources to those areas.

The order and timing of workplace recovery activities vary from one situation to another. You conduct a diagnosis, consider your resources, and customize your efforts accordingly. Each element contributes in its own way, however: expressing empathy helps you gain employee attention and convey to people that you are aware of the difficulty of transition, engaging people helps them understand and support why the old must be abandoned and what the new has to offer, energy helps motivate people to contribute to the creation of a more effective and competitive posttransition organization, and enforcement helps lock in desired new behaviors, perceptions, and expectations consistent with the desired posttransition organization.

EXECUTIVE SUMMARY

To help organizations and their members overcome the unintended consequences of major organizational transitions, the model of workforce recovery presented in this chapter identifies four areas of leadership action:

1. *Empathy:* Letting people know leadership acknowledges that things have been difficult and, for at least a while longer, will continue to be difficult.

2. *Engagement:* Creating understanding of and support for the need to end the old and accept the new.

3. *Energy:* Getting people excited about the desired posttransition organization and supporting them in realizing it.

4. *Enforcement:* Solidifying new mental models that are congruent with the desired posttransition organization.

CHAPTER TEN

Best Practices in Leading at Strategic Levels

A Social Responsibility Perspective

David A. Waldman

There can be little doubt that executive leaders of organizations have come under increased scrutiny in recent times. In the United States, corporate scandals that are associated with leadership failures have fueled legislative reactions, such as the Sarbanes-Oxley Act. Employees and the public as a whole largely perceive the image of corporate leaders in an unfavorable manner, including attributions of distrust and greed.[1] Similarly, organizations and leaders at strategic or the highest echelons of organizations are becoming increasingly concerned with corporate social responsibility and how it can be used for competitive advantage.[2] There is a growing recognition that characteristics and behaviors on the part of leaders at the upper echelons of organizations may be relevant to performance in the area of social responsibility.[3] In sum, the ground is fertile for academics to help strategic leaders better understand such challenges and the best practices for dealing with them.

The purposes of this chapter are threefold. First, I put forth an argument for why a social responsibility theme is so relevant to effective leadership at strategic levels. Second, I outline the leadership principles and practices that promote or support socially responsible leadership. Third, I address the challenges facing leaders and organizations wishing to put such principles and practices into place.

WHY FOCUS ON SOCIAL RESPONSIBILITY?

Corporate social responsibility (CSR) can be defined as actions on the part of the firm that further the needs or goals of an identifiable stakeholder group or a larger societal collective.[4] Identifiable stakeholders include constituents inside the firm (that is, employees), as well as those who are external to the firm (that is, shareholders, customers or consumer groups, and environmentalists). CSR can be further delineated as actions that go beyond those that are required by law. For example, CSR can involve programs designed to further the development of employees, or to partner with environmental or consumer groups to ensure actions on the part of firms designed to further the needs or desires of such groups beyond legal requirements. CSR can also involve actions that are directed toward the greater society or community, such as philanthropy or the sponsoring of community-based development projects.

In contrast, most executives are concerned with the immediate, business-specific interests of their firms. Day-to-day pressures from markets and shareholders dictate a strong concern for profits and returns on investments as priorities over social issues. Even the training grounds for future business leaders have been described as "propagating ideologically inspired amoral theories [that free] students from any sense of moral responsibility."[5] For example, the basic tenets of the framework of Harvard Business School strategy professor Michael Porter[6] suggest that companies need to compete not only with their competitors, but also with suppliers, employees, regulators—and even customers.

The upshot of such assumptions is a narrow emphasis on self-interests, or a profit and investment returns stance on the part of many executives. By following such assumptions, leaders may come to have a purely instrumental view of their constituents. For example, employees may be viewed simply as a resource to be used and manipulated rather than as partners in the pursuit of organizational goals. As a result, executives may approach constituents in a competitive or even manipulative manner to extract outcomes that are one-sided and advance the narrower interests of themselves and shareholders.

There is an alternative perspective. Specifically, I argue for the necessity of socially responsible leadership for two key reasons: greater employee and organizational effectiveness as well as fewer counterproductive regulations. First, and foremost, as outlined following, a case can be made that a socially responsible perspective benefits the organizations for which executives are stewards. Indeed, there is some empirical evidence of a linkage between corporate social performance (in terms of better relations with such primary stakeholders as employees, customers, and suppliers) and shareholder wealth.[7]

But why should there be such a linkage? There is growing evidence that when employees believe that their firms have a high level of social responsibility prestige (as compared to financial or market prestige), they identify more with, and are committed to, those firms.[8] In turn, as a result of identification and commitment, employees realize better performance. In addition, executives advocating values that stress the importance of relations with a broad set of stakeholder groups (for example, employees, customers, environmentalists, and so forth) in their decision making (as compared to values that simply stress economic or profits-based factors) are more likely to be viewed by followers as demonstrating leadership characterized by vision and integrity. Such leadership is, in turn, more likely to be associated with firm performance.[9]

Second, it is in the interests of societies and capitalistic systems that they encourage firms to pursue CSR policies that are inherently voluntary in nature. The alternative to a CSR stance is a more traditional, competitive (and even selfish) position that pits firms not only against each other, but also against various constituent groups (for example, employees, consumer groups, environmentalists, and so on). The costs of constituents who are at odds with one another could potentially affect the immediate maximization of shareholder wealth.[10] Societies that are less conducive to CSR policies often spawn costly forms of government regulation. For example, the traditional position necessitates broad governmental control and regulation in an attempt to maintain the common good of society. Unfortunately, the result can be counterproductive regulations that result from a backlash when competitive or selfish tendencies on the part of firms and their executives threaten the common good.

A clear example can be seen in the recent Sarbanes-Oxley Act of Congress in the United States, designed to ensure the proper enactment and reporting of financial activities on the part of firms.[11] This piece of legislation requires significant expenditures by firms to ensure compliance, but such expenditures do nothing to support real productivity or innovation. Indeed, a recent estimate suggested that for companies with revenues less than $1 billion, the average annual cost of compliance is approximately $3.4 million.[12] As such, Sarbanes-Oxley can be viewed as a drain on organizational performance and financial returns necessitated by a capitalistic system in which firms are remiss (or potentially remiss) in policing themselves in terms of social responsibility and ethical behavior.[13] This legislation also represents the type of backlash that can occur when people in executive roles do not practice the types of leadership philosophies and behaviors described in this chapter. This is not to say that leadership practice can ever fully substitute for, or prevent, legislative initiatives such as Sarbanes-Oxley. The restraints that these initiatives put on productivity and innovativeness, however, can be minimized by greater attention being placed on leader social responsibility, as described next.

A MODEL OF SOCIAL RESPONSIBILITY AND LEADERSHIP

Values need to form the backbone of leadership that emphasizes social responsibility (see Figure 10.1). They are particularly relevant to one form of leadership that has been shown to be highly effective: charismatic leadership. In terms of behaviors, these exceptionally effective leaders articulate visions that are based on strongly held ideological values and powerful imagery. They also stimulate thinking that fosters innovative solutions to major problems and emphasize radical change and high-performance expectations. In addition, they generate high degrees of follower confidence, intrinsic motivation, trust and admiration in the leader, and emotional appeal.[14]

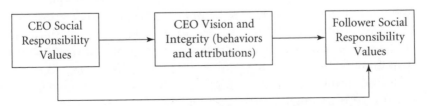

Figure 10.1. A Model of Socially Responsible Leadership.

While there are negative examples of charismatic leaders, charisma just as often represents a positive source of power that can be used for good and worthwhile purposes. This is especially true when charismatic leadership is socialized to seek positive and ethical outcomes.[15] Morality, specifically in terms of social responsibility, forms the basis of what is called *socialized* charismatic leadership. Under such leadership, followers and leaders are able to progress to the highest levels of moral development.[16] At these levels, they act in an independent and ethical manner, regardless of the expectations or norms of other individuals or groups. An example would be the executive who supports and reinforces ethical and open financial disclosure procedures, despite the norm among his or her peers of "getting away with what you can." This premise is illustrated in more detail in the discussion that follows. Here a set of foundational principles is proposed, along with best practices associated with each principle.

Principle #1

Effective and sustainable leadership at strategic levels is based on strongly held values stressing social responsibility.

Individuals with a strong disposition toward social responsibility possess beliefs and values reflecting high moral standards, a feeling of obligation to do the right thing, and a concern about others.[17] Numerous examples come to mind of executives or entrepreneurs who are known to personify such values and are charismatic leaders. They include Anita Roddick of The Body Shop, Ben Cohen of Ben & Jerry's Ice Cream, Paul Newman of Newman's Own products, and Tom's of Maine. For example, Ben Cohen and Paul Newman used a combination of high-quality ingredients, support of local businesses, and donations of after-tax profits to differentiate their products successfully and develop high-quality brands. A less-known example is David Varney, the chairman of mmO$_2$, Europe's leading provider of mobile communications services. Varney implemented a strategy to demonstrate his commitment to CSR by working with stakeholders to develop socially responsible policies with respect to adult content and its distribution on the Internet, and to explicitly restrict the use of an input that might motivate harm toward animals.[18] In one way or another, through their actions and policies, all of these charismatic leaders reflect the values of social responsibility.

BEST PRACTICES RELEVANT TO PRINCIPLE #1. How exactly might leaders at strategic levels pursue a higher moral plane and base their decision making and other actions on social responsibility values? In the following, I describe a few key practices in terms of executives: (1) examining how their behaviors and decisions align on Kohlberg's[19] morality scale, (2) questioning their decision making in terms of its effects on a broad group of constituents, and (3) showing a strong commitment to social responsibility, rather than paying lip service or only an instrumental commitment.

1. *Examine the morality of your behaviors and decisions.* First, consider the typical stage of morality for most people in society and your peer groups, including yourself. Specifically, examine how your behaviors and decisions align on Kohlberg's[33] morality scale. The aim, of course, is to move yourself up the scale. At Kohlberg's *preconventional* stage, people follow rules or act in deference to authority in order to avoid punishment. My guess is that relatively few executives operate at this lowest stage. The *conventional* stage of morality occurs when an individual fulfills duties and obligations as prescribed according to a collective's norms, essentially living up to the expectations of others. In contrast to the preconventional stage, it is likely that a large percentage, and perhaps a preponderance, of executives could be characterized at this conventional stage of morality. In contrast, the *postconventional* stage occurs when an individual follows internalized principles of justice and right versus wrong. They are acting according to ethical standards, regardless of the expectations of others. By so doing, the postconventionally moral individual is balancing concern for self with concern for others.[20] Although many executives might want to think of themselves as operating at this advanced stage of morality, I am not sure that such is actually the case.

Let's consider an example. The acquisition of Gillette by Proctor & Gamble represents a highly publicized business event in recent times. As reported by Millar,[21] as part of the buyout deal, the Gillette chief executive officer (CEO), vice chairman, and chief financial officer (CFO) pocketed $124 million, $41 million, and $22 million, respectively. It could be argued that these individuals "did the right thing." After all, the shareholder value for Gillette increased after the announcement of the takeover, and the Gillette executives simply received their market value in payoffs as part of the deal. However, it could also be argued that instead of "doing the right thing," the Gillette executives "did things right." They played by the rules of the game, and by so doing, they operated at Kohlberg's[22] conventional stage of morality. In other words, they did what any executives would be encouraged to do in the current climate of business. However, the result in this example is that the greater executive culture of our capitalistic system has implicitly, if not explicitly, reinforced greed and self-serving behavior.

Yet the question remains as to how exactly executives could personify a higher stage of morality in the Proctor & Gamble takeover of Gillette situation, thereby demonstrating the type of social responsibility leadership proposed in this chapter. One possibility is that leaders take bold, unconventional steps in the demonstration of their social responsibility values. For example, the Gillette executives could have accepted their payoffs and donated perhaps as much as 50 percent to efforts to assist the thousands of employees who are projected to be displaced as a result of the acquisition. Note that I am not suggesting some form of veiled socialism whereby executives would be *mandated* to provide donations of this sort. Instead, I am suggesting *volunteer* actions, such as those described, that would personify socially responsible leadership. If many such steps were taken and publicized, the negative image of executives of large firms might significantly improve. Imagine the implication for organizations and society if the terms *selfishness, manipulation,* and *greed* were no longer associated with business executives.

2. *Consider a full range of stakeholders in your decision making.* Executive-level decisions usually affect multiple stakeholder groups. For example, when considering acquisitions or divestitures, executives might not only examine financial figures and balance sheets or their own personal benefit. Instead, they might consider future relations with employees of a targeted takeover firm. They might also consider potential negative effects on the needs of customers of the firm, or even product safety.

3. *Show a strong personal commitment to social responsibility.* It is relatively easy to make an executive decision by allocating a certain amount of funds to charities or community-based projects. On the other hand, it shows greater commitment to become personally involved in such projects, and in turn to lead by example. For instance, Jeff Swartz, president and CEO of Timberland, Inc., gets personally involved in community-based projects sponsored by Timberland in

the New England area. The program is known as Serv-A-Palooza, and it involves employee projects to refurbish schools, build playgrounds, and so forth.

Similarly, it shows a higher degree of commitment to CSR when strategic decision making is forced to take into account and balance the long-term needs of a broad set of stakeholders rather than simply the short-term needs of shareholders. Stakeholders could include consumers, employees, and environmentalists, among others. In short, the true demonstration of CSR values requires strong *affective* commitment on the part of the leader. In contrast, weaker values may be reflected by more of a *calculative* commitment (that is, What do I or the company stand to gain by CSR?) or *normative* commitment (that is, How do our CSR actions compare to competitors or other firms in the community?). A leader with a more calculative commitment would operate on the basis of determining the monetary returns to investing in CSR. For the purpose of presenting a favorable appearance, he or she would probably attempt to portray such a commitment favorably with a more heartfelt, affective image. The leader with normative commitment would base the pursuit of CSR on others, such as competitive firms. Such a leader would want to "keep up with Company Y" by aligning the extent of CSR actions of his or her firm with those of others. In contrast to both calculative and normative commitment, the leader characterized by genuine and affective commitment would be consistent over time and base CSR actions and investments largely on moral grounds. Ben Cohen of Ben & Jerry's is representative of such leadership. However, one should not necessarily equate affective commitment to CSR with its unbridled pursuit. At Ben & Jerry's, all strategic decisions and operational plans require the simultaneous consideration of CSR, profits and economic gain, and product innovativeness and quality. The company's motto is that "we did good by doing good."

Principle #2

Socially responsible leadership at strategic levels requires (1) visionary behavior and (2) integrity and transparency.

One of the important insights from research on effective charismatic leadership is the central importance of vision.[23] Leadership vision can be defined as a future-oriented articulation or image of an organization's purpose and direction that inspires enthusiasm and is

ambitious, but is within a latitude of acceptance on the part of followers.[24] Further, as compared to strategic goals, visions tend to be
less concrete, encompass a broader time span, and contain a higher
content of idealistic values, beliefs, and purpose, as opposed to
business-oriented content. For example, the vision of Fannie Mae is
"to strengthen the social fabric by continually democratizing home
ownership"; the vision of Hewlett-Packard is "to make technical contributions for the advancement and welfare of humanity."

As is evident, a key distinguishing aspect of vision is the direct
appeal to the personal values and beliefs of followers.[25] This appeal
tends to engender intense, favorable reactions and attributions on the
part of followers.[26] In the case of vision, favorable attributions on
the part of followers may include the generation of confidence, perceptions of intelligence or foresight, instilling optimism, and strong
admiration, respect, or trust. In contrast, little enthusiasm or admiration may be generated by future-oriented articulations stressing
such things as the maximization of shareholder wealth. As noted by
Collins and Porras, "listen to people in truly great companies talk
about their achievements—you will hear little about earnings per
share."[27]

What promotes perceptions of a visionary leader, especially one
who is able to link social responsibility and vision? From research, we
know that leaders perceived to be visionary include references to a
broad range of constituencies in their communication—and as noted
previously, social responsibility involves considering the needs of a
wide range of constituencies or stakeholders. In addition, they emphasize their own values and moral justifications pertaining to those constituencies in that communication. In doing so, they are challenging
the status quo, which may emphasize more narrow or short-term concerns of the firm. Moreover, when a leader's social responsibility values become evident, followers will tend to attribute foresight and
admiration to the leader.

As an example of a vision that could generate more mixed reactions in followers in terms of social responsibility, consider the vision
of Jack Welch of General Electric. His earliest vision was to be the
number one company in market share for any given business unit. It
certainly inspired enthusiasm, was ambitious, and embodied a sense
of purpose—all of which are characteristics of vision. At the same
time, its strict emphasis on winning in the marketplace, and lack of
any social theme, may not be representative of the type of vision that

would generate widespread support and identity with the organization on the part of followers.[28] This is not to say that business content must be absent in order to classify a future-oriented articulation as a vision. Rather, to generate maximum enthusiasm among a broad range of followers, more socially responsible elements need to be present in the vision.

Integrity is a second dimension of leadership relevant to socialized charisma. A leader's integrity can be defined in terms of the following behavior: (1) being open and sharing critical information with followers, (2) keeping one's word, and (3) serving the interests of followers rather than one's own. Favorable reactions on the part of followers are likely to include perceptions of integrity and selflessness, as well as trust in the leader.[29]

The leader's values regarding the importance of others' needs and concerns need to include those of followers. The leader will be seen as serving the interests of followers in his or her decisions and actions. In addition, the leader's selflessness and sense of ethics engender follower trust in the leader. I am not by any means suggesting that leaders totally abandon their own self-interests. Nevertheless, I do propose that for a leader to demonstrate integrity, he or she must demonstrate a balance between the pursuit of self-interests versus showing deference to the needs and interests of followers and the greater organization. For example, as mentioned earlier, *voluntary* donations to employee assistance on the part of Gillette executives would represent the type of leadership suggested here.

A likely outcome of the leadership processes depicted in Figure 10.1 is the building of a social responsibility culture among followers. It is therefore important that leaders communicate or symbolize messages that contain many references to values and moral justifications. Unlike attitudes, values are likely to be relatively enduring over time[48] and not readily changed. The vision and integrity of a strategic leader, based in social responsibility values, will enhance concomitant values of followers. As such, their decision making is likely to stress a broad range of constituents and include concerns for ethics and responsibility toward others.

In summary, my characterization of leadership based in social responsibility rests upon deeply held values that help guide behaviors and decision making. The behaviors that followers will perceive with this form of leadership consist of (1) emphasizing the pursuit of a vision, (2) acting decisively, (3) displaying high standards of ethics,

(4) placing the concerns of others above their own concerns, and (5) communicating openly.

BEST PRACTICES RELEVANT TO PRINCIPLE #2. A number of practices are relevant to the effective pursuit of visionary leadership and integrity at executive levels. I describe these practices within the context of a social responsibility perspective. They include (1) building shared vision, (2) intellectually stimulating followers in the pursuit of balancing the needs of multiple stakeholders, and (3) allowing or even encouraging morality and spirituality in the workplace.

1. *Build a shared vision.* The key term here is *shared* vision. An important aspect of vision involves the extent to which it is shared by followers versus one that is appealing to, say, only senior leaders. According to Senge,[30] a leader's vision becomes shared when it builds upon a desire on the part of followers to pursue a common important undertaking, and when it connects to their personal visions. As a result, the followers are committed to carrying out the vision. To achieve such outcomes, it may be appropriate to place some emphasis on the active role of followers in vision formation.

Two key factors must come into play to help ensure shared vision. First, as described earlier, when a leader's vision is based on socially responsible values, there will tend to be a greater connection to the self-concept and values of followers. Although there may be some followers in certain organizations who may not be attracted to a socially responsible vision or values (for example, investment bankers), this connection is likely to result in the widespread sharing of, and commitment to, the vision. How should leaders go about finding the appropriate mix of CSR values for themselves and their organizations? Which stakeholder groups should be emphasized? The answers to these questions are not easy, but they can be most readily addressed through the type of shared leadership practices described here.

The second, and perhaps most important, approach is to engage in practices of shared leadership. Pearce and Conger defined *shared leadership* "as a dynamic, interactive influence process among individuals in groups for which the objective is to lead one another. . . . The influence process involves more than just downward influence on subordinates."[31] As such, shared leadership involves an influence process that is broadly distributed among a set of individuals, rather than being only concentrated in the hands of a single, hierarchical leader.

At first glance, shared leadership may seem overly difficult or even anathema to the type of visionary leadership described earlier. The problem is that many writings portray the inspirational or visionary leader in largely heroic terms.[32] But in real life, there are several relevant practices that come to mind. These practices can be seen in the case of the general manager of Goodyear-Mexico, Hugh Pace. He introduced the outline of a new vision that would take the subsidiary from being a producer devoted to the local Mexican market to being an exporter operating globally.[33] He then subsequently used a shared leadership approach that involved a series of meetings and a retreat with top management personnel. These individuals represented a number of nationalities, including those of Mexico, France, Argentina, and the United States. In essence, Pace allowed the top management team at Goodyear-Mexico to reshape his initial vision, based on agreement concerning commonly held values. The end result was a shared vision emphasizing social responsibility values pertaining to employee job security and development, as well as the continuous improvement of product quality so that the tires produced by Goodyear-Mexico could be marketed globally to satisfied customer groups.

The larger vision was, in turn, rolled out with the goal of shaping visions in lower-level subunits. The hope was that these lower-level visions would be aligned with the larger vision, and a vision shared across the organization would be realized. Two things helped to ensure this outcome. First, as noted above, senior management was in agreement in terms of the larger picture and vision of where the organization was heading and what values would be stressed along the way. Second, Hugh Pace was adept at practicing an often forgotten, but nevertheless important practice of effective leadership at strategic levels: leadership by walking around. He also recognized the importance of distant leadership, as described in more detail below, with regard to the successful implementation of vision. But he recognized its challenges in terms of being able to ensure that the vision reached throughout the organization. Accordingly, he would attempt to get out of his office and engage in dialogues with individuals or small groups of lower-level employees. Although he could not personally communicate with all 2,000 employees of Goodyear-Mexico, a substantial number could be reached, and others were likely to hear inspiring stories that at the very least would lessen resistance to the new vision.

2. *Stimulate followers to find ways to balance the needs of multiple stakeholder groups in actions and decisions.* To fully understand the power of leadership vision as applied to the pursuit of social responsibility, one must consider the complex challenges of balancing the needs of multiple stakeholder groups when deriving and implementing a vision. The key may lie in the effective practice of what we call "intellectual stimulation" on the part of the strategic leader.

An intellectually stimulating leader will attempt to scan and think broadly about the environmental context and the manner in which a wide variety of organizational stakeholders may be served.[34] These leaders suggest (and get followers to suggest) creative ways of simultaneously satisfying the demands of shareholders and the desires of groups such as environmentalists or consumers demanding a product produced in a socially responsible manner (for example, the demands of many Nike customers for shoes manufactured under humane conditions). They describe a more dynamic picture of how the various external forces interact with each other and capture the necessity of effectively taking into account the needs of multiple, relevant stakeholder groups. They portray to followers a richer perspective of firm performance and competitive advantage that goes beyond such narrower notions as cost leadership or product differentiation.[35] In short, intellectually stimulating leaders realize that, increasingly, organizational success requires strong relationships with a variety of key stakeholders, as well as a perspective that includes social responsibility.

A key goal of the intellectually stimulating leader is to enhance followers' understanding that the demands of achieving performance goals can be balanced with the desire to pursue CSR. Such thinking may be a challenge for followers who are consumed by the day-to-day pressures of pursuing short-term performance goals. Yet the intellectually stimulating leader will use his or her own ideas and questions to stimulate followers' understanding of how socially responsible outcomes can be achieved, while simultaneously generating adequate returns for shareholders. Through intellectual stimulation on the leader's part, followers will be better able to view the issue of integrating strategy with social responsibility, such that the latter will be viewed more as an opportunity than a threat.

Intellectually stimulating strategic leaders are likely to provide followers and board members with an enhanced realization that the company does not exist in isolation from the needs and pressures posed by specific stakeholders, as well as by the larger community and society. For example, intellectually stimulating leaders may attempt to show how improving the educational level of the workforce can impact the firm's competitive advantage.[36] Intellectual stimulation may actually be the most important aspect of charismatic forms of leadership in realizing a high level of social responsibility performance on the part of a firm.[37]

To illustrate how it is possible to simultaneously pursue performance goals and social responsibility, I use the case example of a CEO of a Fortune 500 company. During the previous 6 months, the CEO had been trying to energize his executive leadership team and other senior managers to focus on a totally new conceptualization of the firm's strategy. Yet because of the uniqueness and change involved in the strategy, the executive team responded with skepticism. As part of his efforts, the CEO organized a three-day retreat with his top two hundred executives to discuss the new strategy and build commitment to its implementation. During the first day, the CEO and other speakers provided details on the new strategy and engaged in a variety of discussions. But early on, it was clear that the CEO was not fully connecting to the group. In line with previous suggestions regarding the use of intellectual stimulation, he changed gears and started talking about how the new strategy would help the company contribute to the global fight against AIDS. He began by showing the word *imagine* to his top management team. Then he talked about how the war against AIDS could benefit from the new strategy, even though the company is not in the medical field at all.

The impact of the five-minute talk about AIDS was eye opening. The mood of the group showed a discernable change. Managers started showing a stronger interest in the topic. During all formal and informal discussions for the remainder of the retreat, many references were made to the battle against AIDS. Upon completion of the retreat, the participants rated the discussion about AIDS as one of the highlights of the retreat. The gathering started with a large group of skeptical executives and ended with energized and mobilized executives. The upshot is that followers may be more motivated and energized to implement visions and strategies that have strong social responsibility elements. Further, it may be imperative for leaders to intellectually stimulate followers by showing how corporate performance goals and strategies can be melded with social responsibility.

3. *Allow, and even encourage, employees to bring spirituality or moral values into the workplace.* Spirituality can be a sensitive and even politically charged issue these days in organizations—though I am not suggesting such things as prayer sessions in the workplace. However, there is an ongoing contradiction involving spirituality/morality and organizational work life. Specifically, the norm of organizations is that when employees come to work, their spirituality, or even desire to engage in moral actions, should remain at the door. Rather, the typical employment contract narrowly stresses performance-based activities and goals that will further the business objectives of the firm—and spirituality/morality is nowhere to be found in that contract.

In order to attain a higher degree of commitment, it is increasingly important for organizations to understand this disconnect that the typical employment contract implicitly or explicitly tends to stress. Many employees have a desire to connect to higher (and even spiritual) purposes, and that desire is not easily turned off when they are in their work environments. Simply put, employees have a growing desire to reconcile their daily work lives with their morality and spiritually based beliefs.[38] Furthermore, if leaders themselves are to stress integrity and morality, it would seem consistent that lower-level employees be allowed to do so as well. Nevertheless, it is understandable that strategic leaders might fear becoming entangled in a web of legal, philosophical, or even religious differences.

That said, the type of moral, socially responsible leadership described previously will allow followers to connect their self-concepts to, and identify with, a socially responsible vision for their organizations.[39] Social identity theory may help provide an additional framework for better understanding linkages among socially responsible leadership, identification processes, and employee pursuit of spirituality. Specifically, social identity theory suggests that group membership (for example, one's organization) can provide a powerful source of identification for individuals and in turn influence attitudes and behavior.[40] Socially responsible leaders may be effective at forming a collective identity based on appealing values that go beyond the self-interests of individuals and even the greater organization. Accordingly, employees would connect their organizational identity with the greater good of society and be motivated to pursue a socially responsible vision.

Yet the vision and values of the firm are likely to become more real to employees if they are allowed and even encouraged to be personally involved in socially responsible activities. As an example, Timberline, Inc., encourages projects involving its employees (largely on company time) that benefit individuals and organizations in their community. For example, groups of employees spend time working together to renovate a children's summer camp. By engaging in such activities, the firm is allowing employees to personally identify with the firm's socially responsible values.

Principle #3

Socially responsible leadership at strategic levels involves distant as well as proximal relationship building.

In the prior discussion, the word *followers* is used in a generic sense, as is the case in most theories of leadership. In other words, there is no consideration for issues such as levels of separation (organizationally or geographically) between leaders and followers. Indeed, historically, leadership theories have been framed narrowly at dyadic or small-group levels where such separation, especially organizational, is not especially relevant. However, when examining leadership phenomena at strategic levels, it is essential to consider effects on followers who are both close to the leader (proximal) and those who are distant. Proximal can imply closeness in terms of organizational or physical proximity. So, for example, the top management team will report to a CEO, and thus be organizationally proximal. They may also be physically proximal by being located at a common site.

Yet relevant "followers" may not be so proximal in either an organizational or physical sense. They could include supervisors and workers who are far removed in the organizational hierarchy, or located thousands of miles away from the CEO or even a division general manager. This is more and more the case in a truly global economy. Nevertheless, the potential influence of the leader on such followers is real and important. Therefore, strategic leaders need to be concerned not only with relationship building with regard to proximal followers, but also with regard to nonproximal followers. How can a relationship be formed with followers who are distant and not so proximal? I am reminded of a folk rock song from a number of years back that referred to John F. Kennedy. A key line in the song suggested that President Kennedy was a friend of his. One can presume that the writer of the song had never communicated, nor come into physical proximity, with John Kennedy, and yet he or she felt some sort of bond of friendship. How is this possible? As described below, the answer can be found in the types of communication and behavioral strategies used by astute strategic leaders.

Through processes that are termed *image building* and *social contagion*,[41] strategic leaders are able to have a positive influence on followers who are typically distant in either physical or organizational terms. As an example, Anita Roddick, CEO of The Body Shop, spearheaded the development of a new product category, specifically, cosmetics using ingredients that are based on non-animal testing procedures. Although Roddick was not directly in contact with many lower-level employees, her staff were inspired by a vision that was based on such socially responsible values. In addition, knowledge of such socially responsible strategic actions was spread among employees through newsletters, word of mouth, and so forth. In other words, Roddick's vision became "contagious" through various means of formal and informal social communication processes.

BEST PRACTICES RELEVANT TO PRINCIPLE #3. The management of proximal relationships with followers (for example, the top management team) may seem like a daunting enough task for a top-level executive. However, Principle #3 would suggest that nonproximal or distant relationships are of equal importance. But how can such relationships be managed and nourished, especially when the executive has multiple layers and perhaps thousands of employees in his or her organization?

Image or impression management, combined with leadership by walking around (or meeting around) represents a key practice relevant to the implementation of Principle #3. My premise is based on the assumption that to motivate and lead employees who are geographically removed, the leader will have to spend a significant percentage of time getting out and meeting with, and listening to, employees at multiple hierarchical levels and perhaps multiple geographic locations. Despite advances in technology (for example, e-mail and teleconferencing), there simply is no substitute for the "getting out" role of executive leadership.

The importance of such behavior has been discussed in various literatures. For example, in research on mergers and acquisitions, various authors have stressed that it may be important for the strategic leader not just to engage in the glamorous activities associated with negotiating a deal, but also to maintain involvement by performing the many externally and internally oriented activities required to steward such a major organizational change.[42] External activities are geared toward such constituents as stockholders and industry analysts. More forgotten are those activities involving internal constituents (that is, lower-level managers and employees). Gadiesh, Buchanan, Daniell, and Ormiston stress the need for continuous, enthusiastic "crusading" to get the vision across.[43] They also suggest that such hands-on leadership cannot simply be delegated to lower-level leaders. That is, the strategic leader himself or herself must stay engaged in the process by maintaining face-to-face contact and presenting fact-based and well-reasoned arguments to employees at various hierarchical levels.

Sam Walton and Mary Kay Ash represent specific examples of leaders known for their leadership-by-walking-around practices. In the case of Walton, he would frequently visit a Wal-Mart store in his own pickup truck for the purpose of talking to employees and listening to their concerns or problems or their success stories. Mary Kay Ash was known for her personal meetings with, and rewarding of, sales representatives. Such leaders were viewed broadly as inspirational by rank-and-file employees with minimal, or perhaps no, direct contact.

CONCLUDING THOUGHTS AND FURTHER IMPLICATIONS

I have made a case in this chapter for effective leadership principles and practices at strategic levels taking into account a social responsibility perspective. The growing complexity of the environment of organizations and, specifically, stakeholder groups in the environment necessitate such a perspective. A remaining question is how strategic leaders will come to possess social responsibility values, as well as accompanying vision and integrity.

Perhaps the answer can be found in the attraction-selection-attrition (ASA) model proposed by Schneider.[44] It suggests that followers (especially those at higher management levels) will be attracted to, selected by, and retained in an organization when their beliefs and values are in line with the organization's founder or current top executive.[45] Shamir and others described specifically how leaders are likely to recruit followers who share their values, and that followers are likely to choose a leader based on the extent to which he or she is perceived to represent their values.[46] In short, although it is possible that a top management team would possess values that diverge to some extent from the leader or organizational context, in practice it would be difficult for such a team to exist over the long term.[47] It follows from the ASA model that social responsibility values will be bred and nurtured in organizations in which prior leaders were role models of such values.

On the other hand, it may be increasingly necessary for boards of directors to actively pursue CEOs and executives who personify the leadership model presented here, especially when it is clear that their organizations have little history of social responsibility and leadership integrity. The changing and increasingly complex landscape of the business environment may necessitate a broader perspective and perhaps require a new take on leader selection at the top of organizations.

EXECUTIVE SUMMARY

There is, first, evidence that more socially responsible firms yield higher performance over time, especially in terms of employee commitment to, and identification with, those firms. Second, at a societal level, widespread executive leadership based on social responsibility values is likely to result in fewer scandals of the type witnessed in recent years (for example, Enron), as well as diminish legislative and regulatory backlash (for example, the Sarbanes-Oxley Act) that serves only to make firms more bureaucratic and less efficient.

This chapter presents a set of three principles outlining the nature of socially responsible, executive leadership. First, socially responsible values form the backbone of effective and sustainable leadership at executive levels. Second, based on such values, effective leaders will emphasize (1) visionary behavior and (2) integrity and transparency. The emphasis is on the important value of socially responsible vision as a means of connecting to and motivating followers. Integrity and transparency follow from socially responsible values, and these leadership qualities seem to be increasingly necessary and expected of leaders at strategic levels. Third, socially responsible leadership at strategic levels involves distant as well as proximal relationship building. In other words, socially responsible leaders will understand and take steps to build positive relationships with followers at multiple organizational levels and, if relevant, in multiple geographic locations. To do so requires attention to image and impression management.

Coinciding with these principles, this chapter outlines specific practices to guide leaders toward effectiveness. Examples include employing methods to build a *shared* vision, intellectually stimulating followers to derive ways to balance the needs of multiple stakeholder groups, allowing employees to bring spirituality or moral values into the workplace, and leading by walking around and meeting with individuals or groups who are removed hierarchically or geographically from the leader. In sum, such practices represent the embodiment of the principles of effective strategic-level leadership described in this chapter.

CHAPTER ELEVEN

Best Practices in Corporate Boardroom Leadership

Jay A. Conger

Historically, leadership within corporate boards has been a lopsided affair. The chief executive officer (CEO) of the company is often the de facto leader of the board. Board directors rarely assume active leadership roles. They prefer instead to play the role of advisers. When acts of director leadership do appear, they are typically late—for example, when an organization is deep into a crisis. As a result, board members relinquish their leadership role as overseers of both the CEO and the corporation.

Few boards in recent history exemplify the failure of director leadership more than did the corporate board of Enron. On the one hand, the nonexecutive directors comprised a group of sophisticated individuals who could potentially have unraveled the company's complicated and unethical financial dealings. They included a Stanford accounting professor, an economist, a global financier, a former national financial regulator, and prominent former CEOs. They could have forced an earlier and more public examination of Enron's accounting and finance practices. Instead, they suspended the company's ethics code to engage in controversial partnerships and financial arrangements at the prompting of company officials and external advisors. The directors themselves appeared not to have understood the full consequences of their decisions around the off-balance-sheet deals that inflated the company's earnings and hid its debt. On closer inspection, the directors were more passive and accepting of strong leadership on the part of founder Ken Lay and CEO Jeff Skilling. Lay did not tell directors about internal whistleblowers' warnings about misleading financial reports. The directors did not receive information about accountants' concerns about third-party transactions. Even as disparaging information began to appear publicly from whistleblowers, the directors did not initially act to learn about the real nature of the hidden money-losing assets or to interview employees who could have revealed the truth. Unfortunately, this imbalance in leadership on the Enron board is not uncommon. It is caused by a set of unique tensions in the degree of leadership that a board requires and how leadership is distributed across the group of directors.

How do we avoid boardroom leadership failures like Enron? Moreover, how can we encourage directors to assume a far greater leadership role in the boardroom? Many of today's best practices in boardroom governance are aimed specifically at ensuring a healthier balance of leadership between the CEO and the directors. In principle, this is how boards should operate. After all, a board's oversight role implies a strong leadership role.

That said, a new generation of boards is asserting greater leadership. They are experimenting with governance practices that are encouraging them to lead rather than follow. Alternative forms of leadership, such as nonexecutive chairpersons and lead directors, are appearing as a counterbalance to the CEO's authority. In addition, important shifts have begun to occur in the growing leadership role of board committees. The catalyst for these leadership initiatives has been a range of crises that have unfolded at formerly successful companies like Enron, Mitsubishi Motors, Parmalat, Skandia, Swissair, Tyco, and WorldCom. In all of these cases, the boards stood passively by while company CEOs either made poor strategic decisions or undertook unethical activities. As a result, pressure from the financial community and shareholders to adopt stronger governance practices, along with regulations such as the Sarbanes-Oxley Act of 2002 and new stock exchange listing requirements, are shifting leadership power to the independent directors in boardrooms. For example, the Sarbanes-Oxley Act requires independent audit committees and disclosure of which directors on the audit committee are financial experts. Formal explanations are required when committee members are not financial experts.

In one recent survey of corporate directors of the largest companies in the United States, nearly three-quarters of the directors who responded said that their "CEOs have less control over their boards," and 40 percent indicated that this has happened to a "great" or "very great extent."[1] This chapter examines the fundamental dilemmas of shared leadership in the boardroom and provides a set of best practices to foster a healthier balance of leadership between the CEO and board members.

THE BOARD OF DIRECTORS' HISTORIC LEADER: THE CHIEF EXECUTIVE OFFICER

In North America, chief executive officers are most often the official leaders of the boardroom.[2] This is due in large part to the natural advantages of their position. As CEOs, they have far greater access to current and comprehensive information about the state of their companies. In contrast, given their part-time roles and "outsider" status (in large corporations, the vast majority of directors are not employees of the board's organization), the typical director's knowledge about company affairs is extremely limited. Most directors are all too aware of this gap in their own understanding and therefore concede authority to the CEO. In addition, most directors see their first role as serving the CEO and their secondary role as providing oversight. Many directors are CEOs themselves, and they share in an etiquette that suggests restraint from aggressively challenging a fellow CEO or from probing too deeply into the details of someone else's business. All of these factors encourage directors under most circumstances to defer to the CEO when it comes to leading the boardroom. As a result, the CEO usually determines the agenda for meetings and controls what information directors receive. The CEO plays a highly influential role in selecting who sits on the board and who is a member of some of the board's committees. If not the "official leader," the CEO is usually the de facto leader of the board. The rare times when a board feels that it must assume a leadership role typically occur during the selection of a new CEO, when a change of company ownership is underway, or when a deep crisis grips the company and the CEO's leadership is in question.

The CEO's authority is further strengthened by the fact that many CEOs hold the board's chair as well. From a CEO's vantage point, there are clear advantages to serving in this role of chairperson.[3] First of all, it centralizes board leadership into a single individual. There is no ambiguity about who leads the board. Accountability can be pinned on one person. Second, it eliminates any possibility of a dysfunctional conflict between the CEO and a board chair. Rivalries that might produce ineffectual compromises or result in drawn-out decisions simply do not occur. Third, it avoids the possibility of having two public spokespersons addressing the organization's stakeholders. Fourth, certain efficiencies are achieved by having the most informed individual be the board chair. Otherwise, the CEO might have to expend significantly greater time and energy updating the chair on issues before every meeting. In addition, it may be far easier to recruit CEO talent given the strong preference of most CEOs to hold both roles. Many CEOs strongly believe that the CEO should be the board's chair.

Brewing for more than a decade, however, is a growing debate over whether this unity of command on the board best serves the company's stakeholders or principally the CEO. It essentially lacks an effective system of checks and balances. An early catalyst for the debate was a highly publicized decision in November 1992 by General Motors to end the CEO's role as the board chair. The impetus for the change was a crisis during which General Motors had losses approaching some $7.5 billion. Company officer John Smith was appointed CEO with a mandate of running the company's day-to-day operations, while board member John G. Smale (former chairman and CEO of Procter & Gamble Co.) was chosen as board chair. At the time, there was an enthusiastic reception for the idea among shareholder activists and a great deal of favorable publicity from the media. Some three years later, CEO Smith, however, assumed the board chair position as the crisis subsided. The model of the nonexecutive chair was discarded. In recent years, the idea has returned following the highly visible corporate debacles of companies like Enron and WorldCom. In addition, other models of boardroom leadership are gaining in popularity.

In the discussion that follows, we examine the three principal alternatives to the CEO model of boardroom leadership: the nonexecutive chairperson, the lead director, and leadership in board committees. We discuss their individual advantages, implementation challenges, and the best practices that enhance their viability.

THE NONEXECUTIVE CHAIRMAN: ARE TWO LEADERS MORE EFFECTIVE THAN ONE?

Though the idea of a separate or nonexecutive chair has been circulating for at least a decade, only recently has it gained momentum as a practice. For example, it is estimated that only approximately 16 percent of the United States' largest 500 firms have separate chairpersons and CEOs.[4] That said, this statistic is an increase from approximately 6.5 percent in 1998. The slow inroads made by the practice suggest strong resistance to the idea. This, however, has not stopped governance commissions and activist pension funds from promoting the idea. In its study of board best practices, the Blue Ribbon Commission on Director Professionalism, a prestigious twenty-eight-member group created by the National Association of Corporate Directors and headed by noted governance specialist Ira Millstein, concluded that boards should consider formally designating a nonexecutive chairman or other independent board leader. In the United Kingdom, all but a handful of the largest 100 firms have a separate CEO and chairperson. Approximately three-quarters have chairpersons who are nonexecutives or who serve part time. The CEO runs the company, while the chairperson runs the board.

The main arguments in favor of a separate or nonexecutive chair have to do with enhancing the ability of the board to monitor the CEO's performance. It is assumed that directors will feel more at ease to raise challenges to the CEO if the board is led by a fellow nonexecutive director. In addition, mutual fund managers often assume that CEOs seek first to serve themselves and secondarily the shareholders. A nonexecutive chair whose mandate is to enhance shareholder value is less likely to be compromised, or so the belief goes. Moreover, to some extent, it frees the CEO to focus on leadership of the company rather than on the time-consuming demands of leading the board.

Two professors at Indiana University's School of Business, Catherine Daily and Dan Dalton, have looked at the research to date on whether separate CEO and board chair roles do indeed produce better performance outcomes. Examining sixty-nine studies over a 40-year period, they discovered that organizations that separate the CEO and boardroom chairperson role do not perform at a higher level than those where the roles are combined.[5] So it is clear from this research that the presence of a nonexecutive chairperson is not sufficient in itself to affect performance.

One of the core dilemmas the researchers have argued is that in many cases the separate board chair is *a former CEO* of the firm, which may explain why performance in many cases does not improve. In one case with which we are familiar, the son of the company's founder sits as nonexecutive chairman and is described under the company's governance information as a "nonemployee" chairman. In any case, there is no independent and objective counterbalance to the CEO given that the chairperson is likely to have been the one who chose the CEO and sometimes vice versa. A CEO whose board chair is the company's former CEO describes the dilemma:

> If he [the board chair] has been involved in selecting the new guy to be CEO, the chair is in a kind of funny position of not being able to be critical of the new guy for some time. He's got to preserve the honeymoon aspect. If a new guy comes in and wants to change anything, there is also the unavoidable explicit criticism of the old guy insofar as how he did things. If the new guy comes in and wants to dramatically change direction, he has the old guy who is lurking there either biting his tongue or, heaven forbid, arguing with him about it. If the new guy wants to kill some of the pet projects of the old guy, it is an awkward situation.[6]

Interestingly, the rationale for keeping former CEOs on as board chairpersons is often not based on concerns of leadership. The closest argument made vis-à-vis leadership is that the arrangement will assist the incoming CEO in transition to the new role. The thinking goes that the new CEO's predecessor is more available as a coach who can easily share wisdom and insight into company issues by virtue of holding the seniormost board role. Oftentimes, the role is bestowed out of a desire to reward or placate the former CEO. For example, many directors see the chairperson's role as a "reward" for years of service, especially in the case of long tenured or highly successful CEOs or company founders. It is an honorarium for their years of contribution to the organization. Just as commonly, retiring CEOs simply do not want to let go. Reflecting on his own experiences, Denys Henderson, the former chairman and CEO of Imperial Chemical Industries (ICI), captured the dilemma: "In my own case [as a former

CEO who becomes the board chair], it was difficult at first to give up day-to-day control because I was still very energetic, and it was clear that further change in the organization was required. I found it a considerable challenge to move from 'energy mode' to 'wisdom mode.'"[7] In summary, when boards find themselves creating separate chair positions for former CEOs either to reward or to placate them, they will have compromised the board's leadership.

On the other hand, a nonexecutive chair who is not the former CEO is a preferred form of board leadership. That said, it must be an individual who is highly admired by the directors themselves and who has the self-confidence and industry knowledge to take a leadership role, especially during times of trouble. The chair must also be someone who can be dedicated to following both the company and the industry closely. In addition, the nonexecutive chairperson should not hold board directorships elsewhere, given the role's potentially high demands. Some estimate that in large, diversified companies operating under normal conditions, a nonexecutive chairperson may need to spend up to 100 days a year keeping abreast of the company.[8] In a crisis situation, however, this could easily be the minimum number of days required. As a result, standing CEOs of other companies are not appropriate board chairs given the demands on their time. On the other hand, a recently retired outsider CEO may make an ideal chairperson.

Since the board chair works closely with the CEO, the selection process itself should involve the CEO. At the heart of this model of dual board leadership is a balancing act between a chairperson and a CEO. There needs to be strong positive chemistry between the CEO and chairperson, but at the same time the chairperson must be unafraid to challenge the CEO. In the selection process, the chemistry issue is best determined by the two individuals themselves. On the other hand, the chairperson's ability to challenge is best determined by the directors. The best selection model is to have the board nominating committee choose from a roster of candidates after having received input from the CEO.

Another critical factor determining the success of this leadership model of the nonexecutive chairperson is to develop clear and negotiated expectations about each other's roles from the start. Denys Henderson of ICI outlines what must happen at the very beginning of the relationship: "It's important that the chairman and the CEO agree from the beginning what each person's role will be. The last thing you want is a fight over turf. The agreement should be put down in writing and eventually approved by the board. But the process of understanding each other's viewpoint is more important than the final text."[9]

Some of these roles of the nonexecutive chair might include the following:

1. Setting board meeting agendas in collaboration with the CEO, board committee chairs, and the corporate secretary, along with a yearly calendar of all scheduled meetings

2. Governing the board's activities and assigning tasks to the appropriate committees

3. Presiding at the annual shareholders' meeting and at all board meetings

4. Facilitating a candid and full deliberation of all key matters that come before the board

5. Ensuring that information flows openly among the committees, management, and the overall board

6. Organizing and presiding at no less than two executive sessions composed only of outside directors on an annual basis to review the performance of the CEO, top management, and the company

7. Reviewing annually the governance practices of the board

8. Reviewing annually the committee charters

9. Serving as an ex-officio member of all board committees

Despite growing support for nonexecutive chairpersons, they are likely to continue to be a rarity. There are a number of important hurdles to be faced in adopting this form of board leadership—all of which are significant. One is the potential for heightened legal liability for the nonexecutive chair. Beyond the legal risks is, of course, the issue of time, as noted earlier. The time investment on the part of a nonemployee chair is likely to be much higher than for the average board member. At a certain point, these investments become impractical for most directors. "You cannot be active in any other company or have any other activity because this [chair position] becomes a full time job. It almost has to be someone who is retired or unemployed," explained one director very familiar with the nonexecutive chair model. Directly related to the time challenge is the issue of information. The chairperson who is or has been the company's CEO has a much richer database to draw upon when contemplating the firm's issues. In contrast, a nonemployee chair's knowledge is often similar to that of any outsider director. A former CEO who has served in the chair's role captures the dilemma: "A nonemployee chairman is a very stressful position. You have many of the responsibilities and account-abilities [of an employee chairperson]. But you are not in the net-work . . . not in the day-to-day things that happen. You read about them in the newspaper because you don't expect the CEO to call you every five minutes. Things that happen that you didn't know about you probably would have challenged if they had been brought to your attention before they happened."

In addition, research by Jay Lorsch at the Harvard Business School and Andy Zelleke at the Wharton School compared U.S. boards with British boards, where it is standard practice to separate the chairper-son and CEO roles. In the United Kingdom, most of these nonexecu-tive chair positions are filled by former CEOs from different companies. They devote up to a 100 days a year to their boards. They typically have an office at the company's headquarters and are there 2 to 3 days a week. In terms of responsibilities, they help determine the board's agenda and supply information for board meetings. They chair the nominations committee and serve on the compensation and audit committees. They see themselves as the representative of the nonexec-utive directors and as the principal representatives of the shareholders. What Lorsch and Zelleke discovered in their research was that the nonexecutive chair was not a panacea to solving leadership imbalances in the boardroom. For example, they found that the lines of responsi-bility among the chairs and the CEOs and the board are not always clear. Sometimes the chair and CEO found themselves tussling over territorial issues and in the worst cases falling into power struggles. When the nonexecutive chairpersons have strong points of view, they may find themselves directly intervening in their CEOs' decisions. What the research showed is that a nonexecutive chair must exercise a degree of self-restraint. The chair must not fall into management of the com-pany but rather focus attention on only leading the board. As noted earlier, the boardroom roles and responsibilities of the chair and the CEO must be very well defined beforehand. Both individuals must be able to immediately address conflicting expectations.

The final hurdle to the nonexecutive chair role is the CEO. Most CEOs consider the idea of sharing leadership on the board cumbersome and inefficient. Their bias is toward a single leader—themselves. This view is perhaps the greatest single reason why it is unlikely that many boards will adopt the leadership model of a nonexecutive chair. One recent survey confirms that even directors on large U.S. corporate boards feel similarly—that a nonexecutive chairman would make it more difficult to attract good CEO candidates. Nonetheless, for boards who find themselves in a position where a nonexecutive chair seems impractical, there are other forms of board leadership. A lead director position and/or strong committee leadership vested in outside directors can be reasonable substitutions. Next we explore these two forms of board leadership.

THE LEAD DIRECTOR: ONE STEP TOWARD AN INDEPENDENT BOARD

A more acceptable form of board leadership to many CEOs is the concept of the lead director. The popularity of this alternative form of leadership has grown dramatically. In a 2004 survey of the boards of large U.S. firms, 84 percent of the directors responding said that their board had a lead director. This compares to 36 percent in 2003.[10] Companies such as Intel, Merrill Lynch, Microsoft, Office Depot, and Raytheon have adopted lead directors.

While the lead director does not assume the role of chairperson, he or she is in essence the directors' representative to the CEO. The lead director is both an ombudsman and a facilitator of the governance process. The role can include preparing the agenda for board meetings to chairing meetings of the independent directors to raising controversial issues one on one with the CEO. In the case of a management crisis, the lead director is likely to take over as the board's formal chair. The more restricted role for the lead director recognizes two realities. One, the CEO is the boardroom leader, and two, all of the directors are responsible for the governance of the corporation.

In the ideal case, the lead director is a highly respected member of the board who also serves in another leadership capacity such as chair of a board committee. The lead director should naturally be an outside director whose strength of personality and background experiences can effectively challenge those of the CEO. Similar to the nonexecutive chairperson model, however, the lead director should also have significant executive experience but should not be chosen merely on the basis of seniority. For example, sometimes boards wish to honor a longstanding member or an "elder statesperson" with a lead director position, but this criterion determines little about the individual's ability to lead. Moreover, longstanding members may have lost a measure of their objectivity given their long-term relationships with the CEO.

It is important to draw a clear distinction that the lead director "leads" in terms of boardroom *process* rather than in taking a stand on various issues. An effective lead director's role in most cases is not to be a sparring partner. The role is to ensure that the board approaches its responsibilities in a manner that guarantees the board's independence and provides a complementary source of leadership to the CEO's. A number of the functions that a lead director might play in this regard include:[11]

1. Setting the board's agenda in collaboration with the CEO, board committees, major shareholders, and other major stakeholders to ensure that multiple and independent perspectives are represented

2. Acting as an intermediary between the outside directors and the CEO such that sensitive issues or concerns might be raised in a manner that provides voice for directors who might not otherwise raise an issue or who might wish not to have a subject discussed publicly

3. Organizing sessions of the independent members of the board to privately review company performance, management's effectiveness, and the CEO's performance

4. Conducting exit interviews of executives who resign from the corporation to determine whether such resignations reflect problems within the organization or with the CEO's style and approach

5. Occasionally meeting with major shareholders to ascertain their concerns and expectations (Such smaller meetings where company management is not present unless requested might encourage more open discussion than public annual meetings.)

BOARD COMMITTEE LEADERSHIP: WHERE THE REAL LEADERSHIP CAN OCCUR

Some of the greatest emergence of boardroom leadership in recent years has come from boardroom committees—in other words, individual committees making decisions with a high degree of independence from company executives. This has been, in part, driven by the presence of a far greater number of outside directors who sit on board committees and act in the capacity of committee chairpersons. This is reinforced by one important by-product of governance reform: board committees now choose their chairpersons, whereas in the past CEOs often hand-selected the committee chairs.

In some ways, this shift in power is not entirely surprising. CEOs rarely have the time to be active members of all of their board committees. As a result, this is one of the boardroom activities in which CEOs feel comfortable playing more of a consultative or advisory role, allowing the committees to lead themselves. Reinforcing this is the fact that the board governance movement has discouraged CEOs from playing a directive role in committees and has placed a strong emphasis on outside directors assuming key leadership roles. This is also a by-product of the corporate scandals at Enron, Tyco, and WorldCom, where senior company leaders strongly shaped the agendas and decisions of board committees.

There are, however, a number of steps that board committees should proactively undertake to ensure they not only retain their leadership but enhance it. For example, in order for outsiders to take advantage of their majority positions in committees, they often need to develop action plans and positions of their own rather than be guided by those of the CEO. Since the outside directors may not have a reason to get together independently of their board activities, it is important that their board committee activities provide them with this opportunity. Meetings held without company executives, where directors can discuss sensitive issues concerning executive succession and corporate performance, need to become a norm. These may also be the only opportunity a committee has to develop strong positions that are contrary to the stated preferences of senior management. In addition, it is critical for committees to have the ability to meet when they feel that events call for it. They must be able to call these meetings on short notice when they feel that a crisis or rapidly developing change requires it. It is also critical that board committees have a vehicle for placing issues that they identify on the board's agenda without significant advance notice. As well, board committees must be in a position to seek outside specialists who can make objective assessments about the company's operations, and they must be able to do this without management's prior permission.

One clear way that committees can hold a CEO accountable is through an annual review of performance. In essence, an effective evaluation process is an act of leadership on the board's part. Such assessments should include goals for the annual performance of the CEO as well as the systematic evaluation of how well these goals have been accomplished. Goals need to include both the personal development goals for the CEO and the organizational performance targets that the board deems as critical for the year. They need to be clear and specific as well as challenging but realistic. Timelines, wherever possible, are important. The results of this annual review should be tied to determining the CEO's total compensation level. It is very important that the evaluation include constructive and detailed feedback to the CEO concerning the outcomes of their objectives. The evaluation process itself is best controlled by the compensation committee.

The membership of committees is critical in determining the degree of leadership that independent directors can have over the operation of the corporation. One committee that should be completely made up of outside directors is the compensation committee. Beyond the compensation committee, the committee of the board (usually a nominating or corporate governance committee) responsible for selecting new directors should also be predominantly, if not exclusively, made up of outside directors. The historical norm has been for the CEO to be a very active participant in the selection of preferred directors. The concern here is that while the CEO may not be a member of the nominating committee, the CEO may essentially select the new directors with the committee then "rubber stamping" this choice. From the standpoint of best practices in corporate governance, the nominating committee should establish specific criteria for filling any board vacancies. These criteria are then submitted to the full board for approval before a search is undertaken. While the CEO is consulted during the process, the committee makes the final judgment on nominations, which are voted upon by the full board.

There is, however, one potential problem associated with a nominating committee composed of outsiders. By placing selection in the hands of a few, these directors can profoundly shape the makeup of the board itself. This might result in problems if this group had very strong biases about "appropriate" directors. One relatively easy way to overcome this problem is to set term limits on committee memberships and to rotate all the outside directors in and out of the committee.

In conclusion, strong committee leadership is where some of the greatest progress has been made to date in terms of corporate governance practices that balance out the CEO's leadership and authority. This is also where we can expect the progress to continue given the many hurdles facing the alternative of instituting nonexecutive chairs. By relying solely on committee leadership, however, certain important trade-offs are made. For example, leadership is splintered across a number of individuals. No single director has overall responsibility for the board and for ensuring that its range of activities is both well coordinated and meets high standards of corporate governance. Given their more narrow focus, committees can at best only shape portions of the overall agenda. Under a system reliant upon committee leadership, there may be no central ombudsman to give the full board a collective voice. All of these factors suggest that committee leadership is only a partial solution to building truly effective board leadership.

SUPPORTIVE GOVERNANCE PRACTICES

In addition to the leadership roles described in this chapter, there are several additional governance practices that may facilitate a better balance of leadership in the boardroom. The most common practice is to ensure that the majority of directors are true outsiders—in other words, they hold no positions within the company nor possess any financial ties or consulting relationships with the company. Formal governance guidelines can also play an important role. In one study by researchers Edward Lawler and David Finegold, only the adoption of formal governance guidelines proved to be significantly related to board effectiveness and leadership.[12] Guidelines essentially provide a structure for boards to make them more effective in their decision-making and leadership dynamics.

Several other practices can help in the leadership equation. For example, there should be two or more sessions of the board held annually with only outside directors present. The CEO would not attend these meetings. These sessions can encourage directors to speak candidly among themselves without the direct influence of the CEO.

Regular channels of information to the board that are independent of management need to be in place—for example, direct communication links with employees, customers, suppliers, and investors. As mentioned earlier, the CEO typically controls the quality and quantity of the information that the board receives. Board directors need to be able to access information independently should the need arise. It is also important that the board has staff and an independent budget so that it can conduct its own analysis of issues where and when it feels the need. Finally, it is critical that boards promote an environment at meetings where discussion and debate are the norm, versus formal presentations by management and rigid and packed meeting agendas.

EXECUTIVE SUMMARY

The foundation for a balance of leadership in boardrooms is a set of governance practices that provide the basis for a strong and independent board—one that provides a healthy counterbalance to the power and influence of the CEO. From this platform of independence, directors can exercise far greater leadership. The following will be the characteristics of well-led boards of directors as we move into the twenty-first century:

- Independent directors (with no formal business or family ties to the firm prior to joining the board) constitute a clear majority (at least two-thirds) of all board members.

- The knowledge and abilities of these directors are assessed regularly against the firm's changing market and technological demands to ensure that they have the skills necessary to effectively oversee the firm's actions and provide leadership.

- Independent directors chair and control all key committees— compensation, audit, and nominating/corporate governance. The compensation committee consists solely of outside directors.

- The board has clear leadership—by separating the chairman and CEO roles, or appointing a lead director and/or having regular executive sessions where no inside directors are present.

- Candidates for either the nonexecutive chairperson or the lead director role are chosen carefully with the following criteria in mind: they are company outsiders and are not holding a full-time executive role in another organization nor serving as directors on other boards; they are highly admired by fellow directors and the CEO, and they have significant company and industry knowledge; they are capable of challenging the CEO when required.

- Several sessions of the board are held annually with only outside directors present. The CEO does not attend these meetings.

- Regular channels of information to the board that are independent of management are in place—for example, direct communication links with employees, customers, suppliers, and investors.

- The board has staff and/or resources so that it can conduct its own analysis of issues when it feels the need (for example, in benchmarking executive compensation).

- A regular CEO and executive succession planning process is conducted on an annual basis at a very minimum. It is a rigorous review of talent that reaches down several levels. It also exposes directors to company executives on both a formal and informal basis.

By following these types of boardroom governance practices, boards can ensure that they will possess the capability for greater leadership.

PART FOUR

Leading in Today's World

CHAPTER TWELVE

Best Practices in Leading under Crisis

Bottom-Up Leadership, or How to Be a Crisis Champion

Ian I. Mitroff

N ot a day goes by without the occurrence of a new crisis or the painful unfolding and continuation of one that has already occurred. It is literally *Crisis du Jour!* The September 11, 2001, attack on the World Trade Center, the Enron/Andersen debacle, the Catholic Church scandals, Martha Stewart's indictment, NASA's *Challenger* travails, the London transit bombings are not only prominent examples of major crises, but they demonstrate clearly that crises have become an integral part of the landscape. Their names are so well

---

The names of the people and the organizations in this chapter have been intentionally changed in order to conceal and to protect their identities. Nonetheless, all of the cases are based on real situations. However, in order to protect even further the identities of the parties involved, some of the cases are composites.

This chapter is abstracted from Ian I. Mitroff, *Why Some Companies Emerge Stronger and Better from a Crisis: Seven Essential Lessons for Avoiding Disaster,* New York: AMACOM, 2005.

known that they have become synonymous with crises themselves. Clearly something fundamental has changed about the world. Crises are now the norm, not the rare exception. The sooner and the quicker that we learn the leadership lessons that crises have to teach us, then the sooner and the better we will be able to cope.

Crises test a person's and an organization's character like nothing else. Crises bring out the best and the worst in all of us. They raise us up. They bring us down. They inspire us to perform great acts of bravery and heroism—far beyond anything we would have thought possible. And then, in the very next moment, they bring us to our knees. Nothing focuses the mind so much as a crisis. Nothing more wounds the soul. They are an ultimate test of leadership capability.

Everyone who has ever lived through a major crisis has wished that he or she had had more, not less, training and preparation. If one has mastered the lessons that leading successfully in a crisis has to teach, then one can not only survive a major crisis but emerge even stronger and more effective than before. The lessons are for everyone who wishes to live a fuller and more meaningful life.

The following (actual) case illustrates painfully what happens when an individual in a leadership role has not had the proper preparation and training for crises, and as a result, has not learned the critical lessons for crisis leadership.

A MAJOR CRISIS AT RURAL BOOKS

Long before she got to the door of her office, Mary Douglas, the chief executive officer (CEO) of Rural Books, could hear that her phone was ringing off the hook. It had a nasty sound. As soon as Mary opened the door to her office, she saw that her answering machine was blinking furiously. She had already missed sixteen calls, and it wasn't even 6:30 AM. It was not a good omen. It was, in fact, the beginning of a long nightmare.

Headquartered in Montana, Mary had established Rural Books about 10 years earlier. RB, as its loyal fans called it, produced a highly successful line of field books for identifying, preparing, and cooking wild fruit, nuts, berries, and so on. The books were extremely popular with rural and city folks alike.

On any weekend, hundreds, if not thousands, of people could be seen walking in the woods with their trusted RBs at their sides. The books were not only lightweight, but extremely easy to carry. In fact, they were organized around simple pullout guides. The guides were extremely popular because they not only showed which things were edible and tasty, but where they could be found as well. One of Mary's earliest and most clever ideas was a simple cord that readers could hang around their necks and from which they could suspend the guides.

RBs were especially known for their clear and simple pictures of the wild foods that were safe to eat versus those that were unsafe. The safe foods were clearly labeled and located on one page while those that were unsafe were located on a completely separate page. The pages even had different colors, green for safe and red for dangerous or unsafe. In this way, RBs helped to ensure that there would not be confusion as to what was dangerous and not. In the 10 years of the books' existence, no one had ever suffered any illness whatsoever from following its recommendations.

Mary picked up the phone. Robert Turnbull, senior executive vice president and the head of RB's east coast division, was on the line. He was half shouting and mumbling at the same time. There were unmistakable signs of both stress and panic in his voice. Typically calm and easygoing, it was a significant departure from his usual behavior. Mary had, in fact, never heard him sound more distressed in the 5 years that they had worked together.

"Mary, have you seen CNN this morning? They are running a story linking us to the deaths of a family of four. The parents were in their early thirties; the kids were just two and three.

"CNN is also reporting that we are responsible for the serious illness of scores of others. At this time, no one knows the full extent of the injuries. It could be in the hundreds.

"All I can tell you is that CNN is saying that people became seriously ill after eating poisonous berries. CNN is claiming that we mislabeled some of the pages in our books.

"They are also saying something that makes no sense at all. They are claiming that it's a case of product tampering. Hell, we don't make food or pharmaceutical products. What is there to tamper with?

"That is all I can tell you at this time. I don't know anything more myself. I have our production and security people checking into it, but what do we say and do in the meantime? I'm getting calls from CNN, the *Wall Street Journal*, the *New York Times*, our investment brokers, everyone. It's complete pandemonium here. They are asking tough questions that I don't have the answers to like, 'Was it a terrorist group, a group of disgruntled employees? Can you in fact rule out any of these possibilities at this time? Was it an intentional act of sabotage? Are the reports of labor troubles at RB true?' What do we say and do? I need help fast!"

Mary's mind was reeling. All she could do was mumble, "I'll get back to you ASAP."

RB was prepared for fires and explosions that could burn down its offices and its production facilities, but not for anything like this. The possibility of product tampering, let alone terrorism and disgruntled employees, had never crossed Mary's mind. And yet, she recalled that radical environmental groups had recently been making claims that RB was endangering the environment because of all the people that were trampling—or as they put it, "loving to death"—pristine areas. A few had even sent threatening letters to RB, but she had quickly dismissed them as cranks. She also recollected that local militia groups were making threats as well because too many people were wandering too close to their compounds.

"Oh my God," Mary exclaimed, "what am I going to do? I don't have the foggiest clue where to begin."

THE LACK OF APPROPRIATE TRAINING IN CRISIS LEADERSHIP

Mary's case is unfortunately not only typical but representative of the vast majority of organizations. At best, many organizations are prepared for a few isolated crises such as fires and natural disasters. A few are even prepared for direct threats to their core businesses, for instance, food contamination and product tampering. However, the companies that are prepared for these are mainly in the food and pharmaceutical industries. In these industries, the links between their products and product tampering are direct and obvious.

Because Mary and her top team had never received the proper training in crisis leadership, they were unable to think outside the box of their expectations. As a result, they were unable to imagine and to anticipate the particular type of product tampering that was directly applicable to their business. For instance, were the labels of the foods that were safe to eat versus those that were unsafe intentionally or accidentally reversed when the pages were typeset? Either case, either intentionally or accidentally reversing the labels of the pages, is a form of product tampering that applies directly to the book business. Altering key information in a product when this information is crucial to the safety and the well-being of people is a major form of product tampering. Product tampering is not confined to the alteration of food or pharmaceuticals.

In addition, if Mary and her top team had also received proper training, then they would have prepared for the strong and often overwhelming emotions that are a fundamental part of every major crisis. September 11, Enron/Andersen, the Catholic Church, Martha Stewart, NASA, and a seemingly endless series of crises in recent years demonstrate clearly that crises exact a severe emotional toll on those who experience or are part of them. Without a strong leadership response, the damage to the organization can be irreparable.

The costs of crises are not only severe in terms of dollars, but also in terms of emotional distress. Those who have been through major crises often use the same words to describe their experiences that soldiers who have been in battle and have suffered severe trauma use to describe what they have gone through.

If Mary and her team had learned the lessons that successful crisis leaders have to teach, then they would have been able to respond faster and more effectively and thereby have lowered substantially both the economic and the emotional costs of the crisis they were facing. Notice carefully that this does *not* mean that RB would never experience a major crisis at all. In today's world, there are no such guarantees. On the contrary, *every* organization is virtually guaranteed to experience at least one major crisis in its history. It merely means that Mary and her top team would have recovered sooner and with far fewer costs.

SHATTERED ASSUMPTIONS: A FUNDAMENTAL CHALLENGE OF CRISES

Every crisis, no matter how different it is on its immediate surface, violates a common set of assumptions that we have been making about the world, others, and ourselves. When these assumptions are shown to be false, our basic social contract with the world is torn apart and ripped out from under us. The end result is a deep existential crisis that is experienced as a fundamental loss of meaning and purpose. We feel betrayed to our very core.

If there is *a* major theme that underlies this chapter, it is the central role that assumptions play in the construction and the management of reality. Assumptions are the bedrock upon which we both construct and manage our world. If our fundamental assumptions are wrong, then everything that is built on them is also wrong. This is why it is so important to surface, to analyze, and to debate our assumptions, especially the more critical that they are. This is one of the most important tasks of crisis leadership.

Deep feelings of betrayal are a significant part of every major crisis that I have studied or with which I have consulted. The reason is that the collapse or the invalidation of assumptions is experienced as betrayal. Since one of the worst consequences of betrayal is the felt loss of meaning in our lives, a renewed sense of purpose—in its broadest terms, spirituality—becomes essential in restoring our belief, confidence, and faith in the goodness of the world. For this reason, spirituality is an integral component of crisis leadership as well.

One thing is clear. Crises big and small increasingly define who and what we are. Major acts of betrayal and major crises are the common threads that tie us together. It is the Age of Crises and Betrayal.

Oklahoma City Bombing: An Example of Shattered Assumptions

April 19, 1995, began like any other typical morning. As usual, Sarah Conway (not her real name) left her house at 7:15 AM. At 7:30 AM, she deposited her two children, ages three and five, at the day care center on the second floor of the Alfred P. Murrah Federal office building in Oklahoma City, where Sarah worked on the fifth floor.

It was a perfect arrangement. Sarah could pop in and check on her children whenever she wanted. And the children were constantly comforted and reassured by the fact that their mother was always nearby and available.

At precisely 9:03 AM, Sarah and her two children were killed almost instantly as the result of a horrendous explosion. One hundred and sixty-eight innocent men, women, and children (19 of the 168 were children) were murdered when a car bomb planted by Timothy McVeigh, an American terrorist, literally tore the Alfred P. Murrah Federal office building apart. The lives of the surviving families, relatives, and friends were forever shattered as well.

By now, these facts are of course well known. However, in the long run, one of the least emphasized aspects of the bombing I believe will prove in time to be just as important as the physical havoc and destruction. This is the fact—one that I cannot emphasize too much—that the bombing demolished some of our most basic assumptions about the safety and the security of our nation. As a result, the general mood of the citizens of Oklahoma and the American public as a whole was altered dramatically. Our lives were changed forever.

What I illustrate in the following are the assumptions nested within assumptions—like the Russian dolls with dolls within—that crisis fundamentally tests and overturns. These assumptions are rarely challenged before the crisis. In hindsight, leaders and their organizations should have challenged these beforehand.

THE THREE MAJOR ASSUMPTIONS OF OKLAHOMA CITY UNDERMINED BY THE BOMBING. Prior to the bombing, three major assumptions were taken for granted. They were regarded as "basic truths." Just to raise them to the surface for discussion and debate would have been extremely difficult, if not impossible. And yet, in a few short seconds, they were completely obliterated.

The first major assumption made by those traumatized by the Oklahoma City bombing was that by virtue of the city's location, deep inside the heartland of America, terrorism would not happen there. Many people believed that terrorism could only occur in certain dangerous locations such as Europe and the Middle East. Oklahoma City is protected from the "outside world." The rest of the world may be dangerous, but Oklahoma is not.

Many people also made the assumption that an American would not kill other Americans. An American would not commit an act of terrorism against other Americans. Terrorists may be "home grown" in other cultures, but not in ours.

Finally, the third major assumption that was shattered by the events in Oklahoma City was that taking the lives of innocent men and women, and especially that of young children, is unthinkable. What "crime" could these innocents have possibly committed to justify such a heinous act?

Every major crisis exposes and invalidates similar assumptions. The end result is invariably the same: the overwhelming feeling that we have been fundamentally misled, in effect, betrayed by our own convictions. Suddenly and without warning, the world and our lives no longer make sense. Little wonder then why, in the case of Oklahoma City, President Clinton and the Reverend Billy Graham had no choice but to come to the site of the bombing to preside over a day of "spiritual healing" for the entire nation. When something so senseless and unprecedented happens on so large a scale, unusual steps must be taken to restore our sense of well-being. This is one of the primary roles of leaders in the aftermath of a crisis.

THE MORE GENERIC ASSUMPTIONS. Behind these three assumptions that were shattered by the Oklahoma City bombing are more generic ones that were also shattered:

• The world is basically safe and secure; certainly America is safe and protected from attack.

- Americans are just and ethical; they can be trusted not to kill other Americans.

- Americans share a common set of values such that the killing of innocent people is literally unthinkable; in other words, when it comes to basic values, all Americans are essentially alike.

Most people are of course neither fully aware nor conscious of these underlying assumptions. They certainly do not voice them directly or in the same words that I have used. Nonetheless, from the interviews that I have conducted over the years, it is clear that people "feel them deeply in their bones." They feel a deep sense of betrayal when the assumptions, the basic premises that they have depended upon to function and to make sense of the world, no longer work.

THE MOST GENERAL SET OF ASSUMPTIONS. When the tragedy of 9/11 occurred in New York, new as well as similar sets of assumptions were invalidated. As a result, the existential crisis penetrated even deeper into the American psyche. In turn, 9/11 was exacerbated further by the scandals that rocked American corporations and the Catholic Church. Indeed, all of these crises exposed the full and deeper set of basic assumptions that we were making about the world.

We assume that the world (one's person, organizations, basic institutions, society) is safe, secure, stable, and predictable. The way things are today is what they will be tomorrow. Continuity prevails. We want to believe that what is true today will necessarily be true tomorrow. Crises are rare aberrations, and they are the not the normal state of affairs. After a crisis event, we assume that the world will return to what it was before. Things can be fixed, mended, and repaired. We rely on the basic human cognition of hope through our beliefs in the continuity, safety, and stability of the world.

We also assume that the world is good and just. The unjust will receive appropriate and swift punishment, and the guilty will not go free and unpunished. This belief that the world is a just one buffers us from the anxiety we would experience from a lack of control when terrible events such as terrorism occur. We don't want to believe that life is not fair, because then it does not matter what we do or how good of a person we are, something bad could happen to us. So, instead, we rely on the assumption of a just world.

Even if a crisis does occur, we believe that it (the damage in general) is limited in scope and magnitude. Crises are confined to certain persons, organizations, and so on. In other words, crises will *not* cut across all levels of society. We believe that not only are there clear boundaries, but also that these boundaries will be respected and maintained. In contrast, 9/11 clearly violated this assumption through its impact on the entire airline industry and the tourist industry, in particular.

We are also hampered by the assumption that people are inherently good. We believe people can be trusted to keep their word, promises, and so on. Most people do *not* have a defective character. This assumption allows us to view evil as limited. A particularly important variant of this principle is the notion that the world can be divided into us and them, the "good guys" and the "bad guys." We assume that there is a clear differentiation between us and the Axes of Evil.

Americans assume that because "I am good, competent, and loyal, I am blameless and undeserving of what happened to me." We think that we can trust our instincts not to betray us. We make the assumption that the crisis was *un*intentional and *not* deliberate. It was accidental and unplanned. We force ourselves to assume that the perpetrators feel guilt and remorse for their acts, and therefore, the perpetrators deserve to be forgiven. We believe they are worthy of forgiveness.

Finally, one assumes that there were no serious advance warnings that I, my organization, my society was about to experience a major crisis. In other words, there was no way that I could have known about the crisis in advance.

No wonder major crises are so traumatic. One's entire belief system—one's entire set of assumptions—is completely destroyed.

Sadly, virtually all crises follow the same pattern. For instance, the crisis in the Catholic Church invalidated a set of assumptions uncomfortably close to those that were involved in Oklahoma City. This is the special sense in which all crises—however much they differ on their surface—are essentially the same. And this is the point for going back and reexamining Oklahoma City, plus many of the other crises that have happened subsequently. Unless we learn from past crises— history in general—then we are doomed to experience them over and over again. If every crisis invalidates the same kinds of assumptions over and over again, then if we can speed up the recognition of these assumptions, it will be possible to recover better, sooner, and faster from the growing number of crises that beset and overwhelm us on a daily basis. This is one of the most essential roles that leaders can play for their organizations.

SEVEN LESSONS FOR EFFECTIVE CRISIS LEADERSHIP

Seven major lessons emerge from those leaders and their companies that have successfully managed, and survived, major crises. Mastering these lessons allows *everyone* to become a "crisis leader" in his or her organization, and more important, in his or her life. They are precisely the lessons that crisis leaders have mastered.

Lesson 1: Deny Denial; Grieve before a Crisis Occurs

Emotional preparation for crises is the most difficult and the most important preparation of all. As the leaders of organizations, you must get beyond your own denial. You must confront it straight on by accepting the fact that the worst not only can, but will, happen to you and to your family, organization, society. Do not waste your time and energy asking why it happened to me and to us. Crises are unfortunately equal opportunity events. They happen to everyone. You can and will survive—even prosper—*but if and only if* you are prepared emotionally, physically, intellectually, and spiritually.

To prepare for crises, hire grief counselors before they occur to work through the powerful emotions associated with all crises. Get the grieving over so that you can get back to living sooner and more fully. Accept the painful fact that the abnormal (that is, intentionally evil acts such as 9/11) has become the new normal state of affairs. You must also accept the fact that in today's unrelenting 24/7/365 media-saturated world, there are no secrets any more. The media can find out anything they want to about anyone, any corporation, and so on. Secret documents and private conversations are exposed regularly on the 6:00 PM news and the front pages of major newspapers. Therefore, you must abide by the principle, "If you deny and lie, then you will be tried in the court of public opinion; you will be hung out to dry."

Lesson 2: Be a Responsible "Troublemaker"

Crises do not give a damn for the ways in which we have organized the world. Respect no organizational chart by asking impertinent questions regardless of your position in the organization. It's up to you to raise thorny and troublesome issues.

Every type of crisis can happen to every organization. For instance, you don't have to be in the food or drug business to experience product tampering. Every business is subject to a *form* of tampering that is particular to it—only the form varies, not the fundamental threat itself.

Crises cut across all corporate departments, functions, and silos at will. They do not respect human and natural boundaries. Therefore, "out of the box" and "beyond the silos" thinking is an absolute necessity. Rely on big picture thinking by challenging yourself to think the unthinkable and expect the unexpected.

Lesson 3: Embrace Fuzziness

Get beyond harmful "black and white" and "us versus them" dichotomies. Give up the notion of "good" versus "bad" guys. Abandon the myths and the fantasies of perfect and complete control and knowledge. We never had them anyway. Teach yourself to accept and embrace uncertainty. Everything is connected and interconnected in weird and wonderful ways. Expect to be constantly shocked and surprised. Embrace wonder and surprise.

Lesson 4: Be Patiently Impatient

You can effectively prepare for and deal with crises through a combination of advancing and retreating. Go slow steadily. Gently confront by not confronting. Accept and respect people's fears and anxieties, but do not become enmeshed in them. The fact that you are beyond denial does not mean that everyone else in the organization is. Do not become paralyzed by your fears and those of others. Instead, give people time and space to vent and to work through their fears and anxieties. Never dismiss them. This only makes them worse.

Lesson 5: Think Like a Sociopath; Act Like a Saint

Effective crisis preparation requires you to imagine the worst that can happen by thinking like a controlled paranoid. You must scrutinize your organization from the vantage point of a terrorist, but don't become one. One strategy to help you understand the criminal mind is to hire ex-cons and reformed terrorists. Probe constantly for "ticking time bombs" throughout your entire organization. Bring people together to share ticking time bombs and conduct exercises in which people are rewarded to think like "internal assassins." You know more about your organization than any outsider ever could, so you should use your insider's knowledge responsibly to protect your organization against those who want to bring it down. Finally, heed Nietzsche's famous warning: "Take care that when you do battle with monsters that you do not become a monster."

Lesson 6: Down with the Old; Design and Implement New Organizations

Today's current organizations are the problem. They are not the solution. Crises create the demand for new organizations and new corporate functions. One approach is to appoint a chief crisis officer. No organization can afford *not* to spend *at least* 2 percent of its after-tax profits on crisis leadership. Design and implement a world-class crisis command center (CCC). One of the key functions of the CCC is to integrate information from around the globe with regard to potential crises. Another key function is to pick up the early warning signals that accompany and precede *all* crises. *Crisis leadership is one of the new key competitive advantages of all organizations.* Crisis leadership cannot be done on a part-time or piecemeal basis. Being constantly aware, vigilant, and prepared are full-time jobs.

Lesson 7: Spirituality Is *the* Ultimate Competitive Advantage

Crises exact an enormous toll on the psyche, soul, and spirit of individuals and organizations. Therefore, cultivate and practice spirituality in your organization and in your personal life. The best organizations develop an ethical and spiritual culture. Above all others, this is the one thing that gets them through crises. *They emerge even stronger and better than before.* On every dimension—financial and otherwise—ethically based and spiritually attuned organizations substantially outperform those organizations that do not value ethics and do not practice spirituality at work. In spite of this, ethically based and spiritually attuned organizations do good and are good for their own sake, not for profits. If you do good for its own sake, then profits will follow. *A spiritual approach to leadership is the ultimate competitive advantage.*

EXECUTIVE SUMMARY

Crises are commonplace in today's turbulent environment. Examples abound from the terrorist attacks on September 11 to the many corporate scandals such as Enron/Andersen and natural disasters such as the tsunami in Southeast Asia and Hurricane Katrina in Louisiana. I have no doubt that by the time this chapter is printed another organization will be suffering a public and damaging crisis. Senior leaders of organizations must expect to experience at least one major crisis during their tenure at the top.

Due to a lack of foresight and rigorous preparation, many leaders and their organizations fall victims to crises. Rural Books was clearly not prepared for the product-tampering crisis that occurred, and as a result they faltered in their response. Even when you know a crisis is looming and the potential devastation has been demonstrated through computer modeling or other analyses, such as in the scenario planning that occurred before Hurricane Katrina, organizational leaders without a solid response plan will fail. The end result will be both financial and emotional suffering and possibly the demise of the organization. A lack of preparation for crises is essentially a recipe for disaster. Leaders must proactively and rigorously prepare their organizations for a broad range of potential crises.

Some of the greatest barriers to effective preparation are the basic assumptions we hold about our lives and our organizations. While they allow us to manage our reality and give us a sense of control, they also create an illusion of invulnerability. We assume that crises are rare occurrences and that our normal, everyday world is safe, secure, and just. We also mistakenly assume that only bad things happen to bad people and that most people are good and well intended. We make a clear distinction between good and evil—in reality, the lines may be more blurred. We also believe that on the rare chance that a crisis did happen, it would be very limited in scope and not affect many people or many facets of our lives. We assume that crises are random, uncontrollable events and there is no way for us to predict or avoid them. These assumptions make us vulnerable and unprepared for crisis. These are the assumptions that leaders must continually challenge.

When crises do occur, they violate one of these basic assumptions and leave us with feelings of betrayal, lack of control, and confusion. A prime example was the shattered assumptions of safety and security after the bombing of the Oklahoma City federal building. As a result, many realized how vulnerable life really is. If such a crisis can occur in America's heartland, it can happen anywhere. In addition to the pain over the loss of loved ones, many people felt betrayed and confused by the upsetting of these basic assumptions that made up their reality and gave them a sense of control. Leaders must quickly and effectively address these feelings of betrayal. They must offer hope and pragmatic optimism as well as empower their organizations to find constructive solutions.

If leaders do not work hard to challenge these misguided assumptions, tragic consequences will occur at some point. Successful crisis leaders must speed up the recognition and awareness of these assumptions across their organization. It is critical therefore to build an organizational culture in which analyzing and questioning assumptions is practiced throughout all levels of the organization. Lower-level or front-line leaders are often the ones who are most attuned to the areas where the organization is vulnerable. So it is critical to engage all levels of leadership to challenge basic assumptions and anticipate a range of possible crises.

Successful crisis leaders expect the worst and prepare for it—physically, intellectually, and spiritually. One approach is to hire grief counselors prior to the crisis to work with employees to overcome their denial so they are emotionally prepared for disaster. You as a leader must embrace the uncertainty and ambiguity that exists in the environment. In working with employees, you must balance their fear with your expression of understanding. Be sensitive to the fact that they will experience fear, confusion, and betrayal as you delicately displace their old assumptions. By recognizing and overcoming these assumptions before a crisis, the successful crisis leader is able to soften the emotional blow when a crisis does occur. This type of careful emotional preparation will lead to a resilient organization.

Finally, to prepare for crises, you should implement the organizational strategies of anticipation and innovation. Crisis leaders anticipate crises by thinking like a terrorist without becoming one. Hire ex-convicts or ex-terrorists to help you understand the criminal mind. For example, casinos will often hire ex-card sharks or ex-cheaters to help them discover where they are most vulnerable. You must be prepared to implement new and innovative organizational systems and structures to prepare for crisis. Create a position for a chief crisis officer who is responsible for crisis preparation. Another option is to establish a crisis command center. With emotional preparation, anticipation, innovation, and a spiritual climate, you can develop a resilient and crisis-prepared organization.

CHAPTER THIRTEEN

Best Practices in Leading Diverse Organizations

Lynn R. Offermann
Kenneth Matos

A quick look around most large organizations today is enough to illustrate how diversity in cultural, racial, educational, and other backgrounds is increasing in organizations across the country. Not only is the diversity of the American workforce better reflected at all levels in U.S. organizations, but as globalization and technology advance, the ability and need to act frequently on an international stage increases as well. For leaders, this diversity presents a new challenge to their capabilities, in that they are now charged with developing effective work relationships with people from different backgrounds, many of whom bring orientations and expectations toward leadership that may be quite different from those of their leaders.

Unfortunately, leaders have generally not been trained to deal with this kind of broad diversity. Many U.S. organizations still put more emphasis on acquiring a diverse staff than they do on assisting leaders in working with these diverse followers once on board. Yet we maintain that it is the leadership of diversity that most promises net business rewards as well as the sought-after retention of diverse staff. Current business needs call for the development of *culturally intelligent leadership*—leaders who are able to transcend their own cultural programming to function effectively in interactions with staff who differ from them in terms of gender, race, culture, sexual orientation, and a myriad of other possible characteristics and temperaments.[1]

This chapter addresses the needs of leaders who wish to further develop their capabilities in working with diverse staff. We begin by examining the value that leaders gain from addressing organizational diversity and the costs of ignoring it. We then examine some of the key concepts and approaches to understanding diversity in organizations that can provide a foundation for understanding and developing specific practices and initiatives. A summary of best practices for leaders of diverse organizations based on the experiences of successfully diverse organizations follows, along with a discussion of some of the most significant challenges in the implementation of diversity leadership. The chapter concludes by presenting two examples of how leaders can put these best practices to work: (1) by developing a comprehensive organizational approach to embracing diversity, and (2) by developing the capabilities of diverse staff through mentoring.

THE VALUE OF DIVERSITY

Researchers initially responded to the increase in diversity in the workforce by examining organizational demography—that is, the distributions of different demographic groups within and across organizations. From there, interest developed not in just who was in the workforce, but rather in what the implications were of having members of different subgroups working together. Based largely on work in social psychology, an approach called *relational demography* emerged. Relational demography theory proposes that it is the comparison of oneself with others in their work unit that can influence attitudes and behavior. In comparing self and coworkers, demographic characteristics such as gender, race, and culture are highly visible bases for categorization and for constructing social identities. Indeed, Bargh concludes that gender and race-based stereotypes are almost always activated when people form impressions of one another.[2] On the basis of these impressions, in-groups and out-groups are determined, and those perceived as being like oneself are viewed more favorably, while unfavorable attitudes and behavior may be displayed toward those perceived to be in an out-group. Thus, leaders may unconsciously respond to out-group members in a more negative fashion than to similarly performing in-group members, expecting less from them and perhaps judging their behavior more harshly. Leaders who expect little from their out-group members are likely to provide lower amounts of encouragement and support than they do to in-group members, and in turn receive lower-quality work. This further reinforces the belief that out-group members deserve less favorable treatment. Leaders who are unable to recognize and adjust their own subtle reactions early on may find themselves creating self-fulfilling prophecies whereby employees originally perceived as likely to be low performers solely on the basis of demographic differences in fact become low performers because they are treated differently.

As this example shows, the effects of these demographically based impressions and actions on the day-to-day performance of leaders and organizational groups are subtle and complex. It is therefore not surprising that the literature on workplace diversity and performance has yielded mixed results, suggesting that group diversity is a double edged sword with the potential to increase creativity by offering different perspectives and voices at the potential expense of higher member dissatisfaction and a lack of identification with the group. A recent review of 40 years of empirical research in organizational demography and diversity concludes that unless steps are taken to counteract the negative effects, diversity is likely to impair group functioning.[3] The most commonly cited example of this impairment is increased turnover rates. Racial/ethnic dissimilarity compared to others in the group has been found to predict low commitment and intention to stay in the organization, as well as greater absenteeism.[4] Such dissimilarity has also been associated with less favorable attitudes toward the group and the perception of poorer promotion opportunities. For a diverse staff, perceived discrimination has been found to be a significant organizational stressor, affecting levels of organizational commitment and job satisfaction.[5] Dissatisfaction and stress can then lead talented staff to look elsewhere for employment.

On the other hand, the potential benefits of diversity appear at many levels. Reviews of the major benefits of attending to employee diversity have noted a reduction of costs due to decreased turnover rates among members of minority groups and broadening creativity from people with various perspectives. For example, research has shown that top management teams in multinational corporations benefit from cultural heterogeneity and can achieve better performance without a loss of cohesion.[6]

Evidence also suggests that companies that implement good diversity programs are more likely to attract and retain employees as well as create a good reputation in the market. For example, one study found that individuals examining alleged organizational recruiting materials that either did or did not feature a managing diversity program evaluated the organization with the diversity program as significantly more attractive to them.[7] This suggests that providing support for a diverse workforce may be a potent recruiting tool. As the workforce continues to diversify, maintaining a positive environment for diverse staff may differentiate those organizations able to attract and keep the best talent from those that cannot.

Successfully attending to diversity issues also appears to be good for organizational profit, with evidence that investors bid up the stock price of organizations that were recognized by the U.S. Department of Labor for their high-quality affirmative action programs, and found that announcements of discrimination settlements were associated with small but significant negative changes in stock prices.[8] Thus, the evidence strongly suggests that superior diversity management provides competitive benefits to an organization in a variety of ways.

In thinking about how organizations may best capitalize on their organizational diversity, managers and other organizational leaders are key in making diversity work for the organization's interests. They can help staff identify with an inclusive organizational culture rather than with potentially divisive demographic in-groups such as race or gender. It falls on group and organizational leaders to bring out the best from diverse perspectives in a way that maintains positive interpersonal relations and capitalizes on the potential of staff diversity. Their position as decision and policy makers, as well as organizational role models, places leaders in an unparalleled position to guide the diversity management efforts of their organizations. For leaders, the benefits of success and the risks of failure should create potent motivation to see it in the best interests of both themselves and their organizations to develop leadership strategies for successfully using the skills of their diverse personnel. The creation of inclusive work climates is now a key concern of U.S. organizations, and will continue to be a responsibility of organizational leaders for years to come.

UNDERSTANDING THE NATURE AND MECHANISMS OF DIVERSITY IN ORGANIZATIONS

The starting point in most diversity research is an examination of the characteristics of people in relation to those of others around them. As mentioned earlier, demographic characteristics such as gender, race, and culture are highly visible bases for categorization and for constructing social identities. As a result, organizational interest as well as research has tended to focus on these characteristics. While by no means the only organizational diversity variables, they are the most heavily researched, generally accessible, and illustrative examples of the underlying processes of individual and organizational responses to diversity. Therefore, while much of what follows may be applicable to understanding the effects of differences in age, sexual orientation, education, socioeconomic class, and other characteristics, our discussion centers on the three characteristics of gender, race, and culture—especially focusing on culture, which we believe is understudied in U.S. organizational contexts and offers the most varied and generalizable range of examples.

Gender and Racial Diversity

Within a purely American context, gender and racial diversity have received the lion's share of attention. Proportions of members of different groups become important in priming salient categories of group membership, making people more aware of the differences among them. For example, the literature on gender diversity in organizations suggests that the proportion of women and men in a group can have significant impact. As Kanter noted in her landmark work, individuals working where demographic distributions are highly skewed such that they are in an obvious minority tend to be more visible, are often perceived in stereotypical ways by majority group members, and become more aware of their social identity.[9] Thus, a lone White in a group of Blacks will become more aware of her racial identity, as will others in the group, than she would if she worked in a group predominantly composed of other Whites. In addition, being in a numerical minority heightens that group's visibility in a way that may result in greater stereotyping by the majority group. Such reactions can have direct and indirect effects on the ways in which subordinates work with one another, with those in the numerical minority seen as "tokens" and treated differently than those in the majority. Hence, it is important for leaders to consider the extent of numerical dominance of specific demographic groups within their units and the likely impact of those proportions for work behavior of both majority and minority staff.

There is little doubt that people are affected by the demographic compositions of their work groups, but the literature is less clear about how and when minority status leads to specific negative outcomes. For example, in the area of gender diversity, men appear to display more negative reactions to minority status than do women, possibly because the influx of women as potential competitors for organizational opportunities is perceived as undermining the more advantageous positions men enjoyed in the past.[10] Men in the minority display lower levels of satisfaction and commitment, while women in the minority are less likely to have as great a negative reaction. This is particularly noteworthy because men in predominantly female jobs report almost no hostility from female colleagues and are socially integrated, whereas women in predominantly male organizations have reported hostility and less integration.[11] Research on the impact of race and ethnic diversity on intergroup relations shows a consistent finding that individuals who differ from the majority race are more likely to leave, have lower job satisfaction and commitment, and receive lower performance evaluations.[12] As with gender diversity, these effects have sometimes been more pronounced for whites than for minorities.

These findings are not encouraging to organizations that have no other moral, legal, or practical alternative to embracing the diversity of the workforce. However, the psychological literature offers some hope, in that the same cognitive categorization processes that can highlight differences can also generate more inclusive categories that can accommodate diverse characteristics. Organizations in which the social networks and events emphasize common goals and identities may be able to enhance group processes and performance. Other research has shown that when attempts are made to promote identification with a larger group and minimize subgroup identity, intergroup bias can be reduced. Similarly, where social categories overlap and people from different groups share membership in a common group, bias can be reduced.[13] Furthermore, research suggests that membership in multiple in-groups creates a more complex and inclusive social identity that may be associated with individuals displaying a greater tolerance of out-group members.[14] So for leaders, encouraging identification with the company rather than one's demographic group might help people from different backgrounds become more aware of their common interests.

In addition to creating an inclusive culture promoting a common identity, leaders can be careful to see that competition for organizational resources does not escalate hostility and tension between groups. Instead, research suggests that common goals requiring intergroup cooperation can lessen tension and allow cross-group friendships to emerge. For example, members of a project team may differ in gender and race, but to the extent that they see their fates interlinked in terms of project success and resulting rewards, they may be more open to working with dissimilar others.

Cultural Influences on Leadership Behaviors and Expectations

In addition to concerns about race and gender in the workforce, it is important to extend consideration to the integration of staff from a variety of cultural backgrounds. With the increase of globalization and multinational businesses and markets, the influence of cultural diversity increases in importance. To many non-Americans, the differences of male and female Americans of various races is often less striking or influential than the differences they note between American cultural expectations and their own. In the eyes of much of the world, Americans, Black or White, male or female, are *American* before they are anything else. Leaders must therefore be able to move beyond a de facto definition of diversity as a predominantly race- and gender-based construct and attend to the emerging definitions that address variance in cultural, experiential, and behavioral characteristics.

Based on his classic study of approximately 88,000 IBM employees in more than sixty countries, Hofstede proposed the following four dimensions of organizationally relevant cultural value differences: power distance, uncertainty avoidance, individualism-collectivism, and masculinity-femininity.[15] These cultural values can be extremely helpful in understanding both leader and follower behavior worldwide. The best-known and most heavily investigated of the four dimensions is individualism-collectivism, a value that differentiates between cultures in which individual identity, goals, and personal choice are revered and those cultures in which a strong collective identity links individuals to cohesive in-groups. The United States is among the most individualistic of cultures, where leaders may allow for and expect greater individual initiative from their staff, and where culturally similar staff may expect and relish opportunities and rewards for initiative. However, in collectivistic cultures, there may be a greater emphasis on teams and discomfort with individual freedom of action. Individualists, on the other hand, may demonstrate a resistance to teamwork. Based on these differences, leaders from a collectivistic culture might find an individualist's preference for solo projects as self-promoting and uncooperative, whereas leaders from individualistic cultures might underestimate the importance of teamwork to unit success.

Likewise, Hofstede's concept of power distance has relevance to the study of leadership in that it deals directly with expectations of and relationships to authority. *Power distance* is defined as the extent to which there is an acceptance of unequal distribution of power within a culture. In low power distance cultures like the United States, leader-subordinate relations can be close and less formal in nature; in high power distance cultures these relationships are expected to be more distant and formal, based on one's position in the hierarchy. High power distance cultures are consistent with autocratic and paternalistic management, whereas low power distance should be more compatible with managerial approachability and employee participation. Leaders from lower power distance cultures need to be aware that what they perceive as a lack of initiative from some staff may be merely the respectful waiting for instruction from the leader that would be expected in high power distance societies. Again, incompatibility between leaders and their staff may produce strain in their relationships, ranging from employee discomfort with leader expectations to leader dissatisfaction with employee performance.

Uncertainty avoidance reflects the extent to which members of a culture value predictability and find ambiguity stressful. Members of high uncertainty avoidance cultures prefer rules and stable jobs with long-term employers; members of low uncertainty cultures may be more willing to take risks, change employers, and tolerate organizational ambiguity and change. U.S. culture has traditionally been more tolerant of ambiguity, and U.S.-born leaders may expect their staff to be as well. Staff from high uncertainty avoidance cultures may expect their leaders to exert and keep control (certainty) in their work units, thereby avoiding change, whereas staff from low uncertainty avoidance cultures may be more comfortable with change, and expect their leaders to give them more latitude in behavior. Thus, a one-style-fits-all leadership approach is not going to be welcomed by all.

Finally, the masculinity-femininity dimension distinguishes between "masculine" cultures in which ambition, assertiveness, and challenge are highly valued and "feminine" cultures in which greater emphasis is placed on harmony, cooperation, and good working relationships. Masculine cultures tend to emphasize work over family and leisure, and can be associated with higher work stress compared to feminine cultures. As a result, leader demands for overtime or weekend work that might be seen as acceptable (if undesirable) to staff accustomed to masculine cultures might be viewed far more negatively by staff from more feminine cultures.

Culturally Intelligent Leadership

Demographic differences between leaders and their staffs have organizational consequences. Tsui and O'Reilly found that increasing differences between superior-subordinate demographic characteristics was associated with lower superior ratings of subordinate effectiveness, less attraction toward subordinates, and the experience of greater role ambiguity by subordinates.[16] In New Zealand, Chong and Thomas found higher levels of follower satisfaction when leaders and followers were ethnically similar.[17] Clearly, leaders need to make greater efforts to work more effectively with demographically dissimilar staff if organizations want to capitalize on the resources brought in by a diverse workforce. The ability to engage in the mental processes and adaptive behaviors needed to function effectively as a leader in diverse organizations is what we call *culturally intelligent leadership*. Culturally intelligent leadership requires a commitment to creatively combining the strengths and weaknesses of diverse staff in the service of superior organizational performance.

Regrettably, discussions of leadership in diverse contexts have often focused on the need to understand others without a comparable consideration of understanding oneself. Yet, as Hall states, "Culture hides much more than it reveals, and, strangely, it hides itself most effectively from its own participants. The real job is *not* to understand foreign cultures, but to understand one's own."[18] Although leaders may be unaware of the impact of their own culture on their behavior, followers can see it. Research by Offermann and Hellmann found that the cultural values of power distance and uncertainty avoidance held by managers related to subordinate perceptions of their manager's leadership style.[19] As predicted, power distance was significantly and negatively associated with leader communication, delegation, approachability, and team building. These findings are consistent with the view that high power distance is associated with a greater tendency for leaders to retain power themselves rather than empower others through sharing information, building teams, and delegating. Uncertainty avoidance was significantly associated with leadership behaviors displaying control, and significantly negatively associated with delegation and approachability. Leaders valuing certainty may act on this value by exerting more control over staff and sharing less power with them.

Many people dislike the thought of being "programmed" by culture and prefer to deny the impact of the collective on individual thought and behavior. Consistent with the United States ranking as one of the most highly individualistic nations in the world, many Americans do not like being grouped into any cultural category, sometimes even denying that there is a U.S. "culture" and preferring to see their behavior as freely and individually chosen. Yet non-Americans are able to see patterns of U.S. cultural values just as Americans see those of others: primarily through differences with one's own values. To use Hofstede's terms, the United States is individualistic, low in power distance, low in uncertainty avoidance, and fairly masculine in orientation. This manifests itself as a culture that values individual happiness, equality, practicality, is comfortable with change, achievement oriented, and data driven.[20] This cultural heritage underlies much of U.S. management philosophy, including an emphasis on individual responsibility, individual rewards, action orientation, valuing tasks over relationships, a measurement-driven approach, and a focus on short-term gains and "quick wins," just to name a few. It is also a cultural heritage that needs to be acknowledged and understood before trying to lead others who hold different values.

Nonetheless, leaders must be careful in interpreting such cultural effects: not all Americans share these values, nor are citizens of other nations any more universally consistent. In any culture, there will be individual variation within a country around the values of the society in general. Thus, culture should be viewed at the group level: it should not be assumed that a particular person will behave in a certain way, but rather that when a group of people from countries with a specific value orientation are averaged, that average may differ in predictable ways from averages of groups from cultures with different values. Furthermore, the pattern produced by examining multiple values simultaneously and in interaction may be more instructive than any single cultural value. Together these values yield useful information about the potential inclinations of many leaders as well as followers.

Unfortunately, many leaders are unaware of the cultural lenses they use to view the world, or how their own cultural background affects the way in which they view others. The ethnocentric tendency to use one's own group as the standard of correctness against which all others are judged sets the stage for in-group bias. For example, as observers of staff behavior, leaders, like all of us, presumably make attributions for the causes of the behaviors observed. Psychological research on attribution theory suggests that people often make errors in attributions, the most basic of which is overestimating the importance of personal and dispositional factors as the causes of behavior and underestimating the influence of situational factors. Although these types of errors are well documented with European American samples, there is evidence that Asians may focus more on social roles, obligations, and situational constraints in making attributions and so may make fewer dispositional attribution errors than their Western counterparts.[21] If leaders make erroneous attributions for the performance of diverse followers, their behavior may also be inappropriate. Work by Offermann, Schroyer, and Green found that leader attributions about the causes of subordinate performance can affect the way in which a leader subsequently interacts with them, with leaders more behaviorally active when working with groups who they believed performed poorly due to effort (an unstable cause) rather than ability (a stable cause).[22] Based on this work, if a leader misattributes unsatisfactory performance of culturally different staff to lack of ability (rather than, say, lack of clarity about what they were supposed to do or lack of resources to get the job done), it would be predicted that the leader may give up on them and miss the opportunity to develop people who could perform well. Without the leader's assistance, failure becomes more likely, creating a self-fulfilling prophecy. Bias is not, however, inevitable. Effectively understanding diverse others rests on being open to a number of very different but equally effective methods of achieving organizational goals.

Many leaders begin with the view that people are people, and one style of leadership should fit all. That is, a leadership style, successful with one set of followers, should work with others, even if those others are demographically different. Many leadership approaches have historically countered by advocating tailoring style to situation, with the core aspects of the situation defined differently by different models. Unfortunately, many "tailored" theories progress to categorize followers into groups based on some commonality (such as in-group versus out-group, or level of maturity) rather than truly consider people as individuals. The temptation to try to categorize staff by culture is strong as well. Unfortunately, some diversity programs in the United States have succeeded only in teaching leaders new categorical "boxes" into which they can place staff based on culture of origin. Though probably well meaning, this may be ineffective or offensive. For example, despite cultural traditions, not all Japanese dislike being singled out for praise, while some Americans find individualized recognition uncomfortable. Leader errors can be very costly in terms of employee motivation.

Errors like these may become even more common as time goes on. Hybridization of culture is increasingly common, where even radically different cultures can be part of a person's background, all contributing to a unique and "multivoiced self."[23] To categorize a complex human being on the basis of membership in a single group limits understanding of what makes that person willing and able to give his or her full effort to their leader and organization. Given this complexity, successful leaders in diverse environments must be willing to forego the boxes, and to treat people as unique combinations of values, preferences, and needs. In this respect, leadership models such as Leader-Member Exchange Theory (LMX), which suggest that leaders concentrate on developing significant, high-quality, one-on-one relationships with staff members interested in such relationships, may present the most useful perspectives on leadership in diverse environments. Understanding each individual in all his or her complexity holds the best promise of developing meaningful and positive leader-follower relations.

RESPONDING TO DIVERSITY: BEST PRACTICES IN LEADING DIVERSE FOLLOWERS

Many U.S. organizations claiming interest in leading diverse groups and organizations devote the majority of their resources and energy to affirmative action programs, reflecting a narrow perspective whereby diversity concerns are limited to differences in gender and race. Success is often measured in terms of whether recruiters achieve quantitative requirements or goals. This focus is in itself a reflection of the American value on objective quantification—if we have the right numbers in each demographic category, everything is fine. Although insufficient, actively recruiting a representative work-force is a necessary first step in creating an effective yet diverse workforce. You cannot lead those who aren't present. But numerical representation is an insufficient measure of successful diversity man-agement, as it fails to determine whether the diversity recruited is stay-ing around and adding value to the organization's mission. The first and perhaps most important "best practice" is to get beyond the num-bers. Once diversity has been brought into an organization, working successfully with the resulting diverse workforce requires additional thought and action.

Although the belief that effective leadership can be developed or learned is not universally shared, we do think leaders can learn skills and techniques that can help them function more effectively in diverse organizations. It is possible for people to value their own heritage without denigrating that of others. It is, however, foolhardy to think that development techniques created in one country will necessarily prove universally applicable. For example, 360-degree feedback processes are widely popular in the United States but have sometimes run into problems when used cross-culturally.[24] In the individualis-tic United States, leadership development tends to emphasize practi-cal experience and the development of the individual, whereas other parts of the world might choose to emphasize theoretical aspects, power dynamics, and the development of shared collective leadership.

To meet these different training needs, there are many intercultural training and education opportunities available for leaders hoping to develop greater competency in this area, and evidence suggests that even short-term training is usually beneficial. Development goals often focus on three areas: changing people's thinking (increasing knowledge of cultural differences and issues), affective reactions (how to manage challenges and enjoy diversity rather than merely tolerate it), and changing behaviors. Leaders must be prepared to make mistakes and learn from them. Cultures that are more tolerant of risk and com-fortable with ambiguity may have an easier time in such intercultural training. But the leader's approach to dealing with the inevitable hiccups and missteps that come with dealing with diversity can make an enormous difference. As Dalton notes, "An attitude of deep-seated courtesy and respect often buys forgiveness of behavior based on cultural misunderstanding."[25] Skills like being insightful and open to criticism, seeking opportunities to learn, being flexible, seeking and using feedback, being sensitive to cultural differences, and being able to bring out the best in people are best-practice characteristics that bode well for any leader in diverse environments, at home or abroad.

At the organizational level, there are many strategies that have been implemented by leaders and organizations hoping to reap the benefits of diversity. Looking at a broad range of organizations that are successfully leading diverse workforces shows a wide variation in the scope and intensity of programs offered, requirements for participation, and opportunities for cross-cultural exchange. However, there are some general commonalities that offer suggestions to leaders for developing competencies in managing in diverse environments. Our "Top Ten" most prominent similarities in best practices include:

1. *Leaders view managing diversity as a business imperative.* First and foremost, successful leaders in diverse organizations see managing diversity as critical to the success of their enterprises. It is not just the right or nice thing to do, but it is something that must be done if they are to meet their organizational mission. It is fully accepted as a core leadership responsibility.

2. *Leaders at all levels must be out front and visible as champions of diversity.* Leader statements in support of diversity can send a powerful message to leaders and staff about the organization's expectations. Leaders should use every means possible to integrate diversity into their daily business and to communicate their commitment both verbally and through their behaviors in hiring, promoting, and giving plum assignments to capable people of all different backgrounds.

3. *Take a broad view of high-potential employees.* Leaders may unduly limit the domain of acceptable job behavior to that with which they are culturally familiar and attempt to force others into that mold, experiencing predictable difficulties. The true benefit of a diverse workforce is to capitalize on the varied skills and capabilities brought by diverse staff rather than attempt to homogenize them.

4. *Share the unwritten rules.* Often leaders inaccurately assume everyone shares their expectations without the need to specify them. For example, cultures differ widely in their views of time, with Westerners tending to view time as a limited commodity and non-Westerners seeing time as more expansive. These different views may affect expectations about deadlines and the promptness of meeting start times, with some non-Westerners being more relaxed about promptness. Clearly explaining expectations on issues like these can yield far better compliance from those whose cultural expectations may differ from one's own.

5. *Try different approaches.* As noted earlier, follower expectations of their leaders may differ significantly based on cultural differences. For example, Schmidt and Yeh identified common leader influence strategies across Australian, English, Japanese, and Taiwanese managers, but noted that both their relative importance and tactical definition differed by nationality.[26] For example, although Taiwanese and Japanese leaders combined both hard (assertiveness) and soft (reasoning) tactics, they differed in that Taiwanese endorsed greater use of sanctions while Japanese emphasized sanctions less and bureaucratic channels more than the Taiwanese. Even cultures that appear similar, like the United States and United Kingdom, can show differences. This study showed that U.K. leaders emphasized assertiveness and appealing to higher authorities more than U.S. leaders, who emphasized reasoning more. The culturally intelligent leader must be prepared and able to adapt his or her ways of interacting with diverse staff to accommodate cultural differences and to help their multicultural staffs to better adapt to the demands of their organizations.

6. *Set high expectations for all staff.* Organizational research on goal setting clearly suggests that challenging goals promote superior performance. Leaders who do not expect as much from dissimilar staff are likely to get less, perpetuating a self-fulfilling prophecy. Goals should be set at the upper end of the follower's capability; this will provide challenge while ensuring that the individual can actually do what is required.

7. *Provide training as an ongoing education process.* Many organizations have found incorporating diversity into ongoing leadership development activities to be more successful than stand-alone

programs in conveying the message that attending to diversity is an integral part of day-to-day leadership. This does not mean that diversity-focused programs cannot be useful, but rather that their value is enhanced by being part of a larger effort to promote inclusiveness throughout the organization.

8. *Consider "best practices" from other organizations, but tailor to your own organization's needs.* Every organization is unique in terms of demands, resources, and staff demographics; strategies for managing diversity will need to consider the particular organization's history, needs, and employees. Know your own organization and choose best practices that will best address local needs.

9. *Be inclusive.* Diversity includes everyone in the mix, and no one should be excluded or blamed for past societal discrimination. AT&T found this out the hard way by putting about 100,000 employees through diversity programs that left some of their White male employees feeling left out and attacked.[27] Xerox had a similar experience with White men feeling excluded, and learned that successful initiatives make it clear that diversity includes White men along with everyone else.[28] These and other negative experiences with diversity programs underscore the need to carefully evaluate programs and remove any that increase intergroup tensions in favor of those that increase openness and curiosity.

10. *Learn from your diverse staff.* Successful leadership requires taking the time to actively listen and to carefully watch for potential cultural factors that may be interfering with a staff member's ability to function successfully. Listening to employees was a key theme for success articulated a by recent meeting of four hundred executives dealing with workplace diversity issues.[29] Leaders should structure time for discussions with staff, both individually and collectively, to discern any problems or concerns they may have.

IMPLEMENTATION CHALLENGES FOR LEADING DIVERSITY

Incorporating these best practices involves a commitment to significant cultural change by embracing and using diversity as an organizational strength. One of the practical difficulties with implementing the more individualized leadership styles that we have suggested are concerns regarding potential fairness issues. Although fairness is one of the more universal ethical premises, it may mean different things in different places. Responsibility for maintaining fairness typically falls to leaders, challenging their wisdom in balancing issues of fairness and equality. Some leaders interpret fairness as exactly equal treatment, without consideration of individual needs or capabilities. In this manner of thinking, then, everyone in a given position should have the same training, the same conditions, and the same opportunities. Clearly, such "equality" will hamper the ability of leaders to give each staff member what she or he needs to thrive and will doom those requiring different treatment to failure. If you applied this logic to your home garden, you would quickly find that many of your hoped-for flowers would die, as some need more sun, some more shade, some more acidic soil, some more alkaline. Success comes from matching treatment with optimal conditions for growth, without viewing different needs as inherent inadequacies.

Yet leaders often resist giving certain staff members "special treatment." For example, Grimsley reports a situation in which Moslem staff asked their manager for permission to work through lunch and leave earlier during the daytime-fasting month of Ramadan rather than take a "lunch" break when they could not eat.[30] Interestingly, it was the manager's peers—not other staff—who objected to her accommodating the wishes of these staff members, apparently fearing that a precedent of accommodation would be set that might later be difficult to break. Thus, individualizing may require not only discerning appropriate adaptations but also the courage to defend one's judgments to peers and management. For example, managers at Celanese Chemical had to forcefully push against their own senior management to delay the opening of a new $125 million plant in Singapore for more than a month in order to open on the next "lucky day," as prescribed by local tradition.[31] Yet to do otherwise might have proven far more expensive in the long run, with locals potentially reluctant to work at an "unlucky" plant or purchase its products.

People do not need to think, feel, or act in similar ways in order to reach agreement on practical issues and work together cooperatively. Leaders have always played key roles in developing and communicating shared norms and practices, and diversity may make these roles ever more important. Leaders can help their organizations forge a broader and more inclusive perspective on "how we do things around here" that represents a combination of different approaches that diverse people can endorse as their own even if it differs in significant respects from some of their culturally formed values. To the extent that different perspectives are integrated into organizational practices, leaders can expect greater acceptance of them as opposed to a more autocratic approach that emphasizes the traditions of a single national culture, gender, or race, and places that tradition in opposition to the others represented in the organization. This suggests that leaders adopt a more synergistic approach, one that allows for a combination of styles or methods without a presumption of inherent superiority of any single way.[32] By listening to staff and incorporating their traditions, leaders can help move organizations away from a parochial "Our way is the only way" position or an ethnocentric "Our way is the best way" approach to a position that represents the best combination of options for maximum effectiveness.

BEST PRACTICE EXAMPLES

There are many ways leaders and organizations can implement the best practices described previously. Each method has its own advantages and challenges; describing each one or even several in a useful amount of detail would be the province of a book unto itself. Here, we outline two approaches that we believe effectively address most of our best practice suggestions. First is a broad organizational approach to incorporating diversity into all aspects of the business, and is exemplified by the efforts of Marriott International. Marriott has been highly cited as a leader in successfully responding to diversity issues, and their experience, detailed below, can be instructive to other organizations. Second, we outline an approach that can help leaders learn about their organization's specific diversity issues and possible solutions, and that can be initiated by individual leaders themselves as well as more broadly by organizations: mentoring.

Diversity at Marriott

With more than 133,000 employees worldwide, comprising a wide range of backgrounds and nationalities, Marriott is succeeding by consciously embracing the diversity of its workforce. Recent accolades for their efforts in leading a diverse staff include the Lifetime Achievement Award from the National Society of Minorities in Hospitality in 2005, being named by *DiversityInc* magazine as one the "Top 50 Companies for Diversity," and "Best Company" ratings by *Hispanic*

Business, Black Enterprise, Latina Style, and *Working Mother* magazines. Their efforts at leading a diverse workforce certainly contributed to their overall ranking by *Fortune* magazine as one of the most admired companies in America.

Table 13.1 briefly summarizes some of Marriott's successful leadership initiatives, focusing on those that help managers to work with a diverse workforce. As can be seen, these initiatives form a comprehensive package that stresses the value of diversity throughout the

---

Finding Diverse Leaders and Followers

Recruitment Programs
- Partnerships with external organizations increase exposure of their diverse memberships to Marriott.
- Marketing campaigns, research, and advertising include explicit diversity objectives and orientations.
- Staffing objectives explicitly reference management accountabilities.

Developing Leaders to Manage Diversity
- Career acceleration programs maintain explicit focus on including minorities and women.
- Women and Minority Training and Development Day consists of workshops targeting the career development needs of women and minorities.
- Executive coaching programs provide a network of effective and inexpensive coaching programs to interested high-potential managers.
- Leadership Education Series: Leading and Growing in Today's Environment aids managers in identifying and capitalizing on their individual leadership development needs and opportunities.
- Women's Leadership Development Initiative provides a multifaceted approach that includes leadership development opportunities, networking, support systems, and programs to enable women leaders to excel in their careers and personal lives.
- Diversity awareness training is tailored for both new hires and managers.
- Diversity Web site provides individual access to diversity training tools and resources.

Managing a Diverse Business
- Executive Education Program enables executives to build leadership capacity and business acumen and develop and maintain strong relationships with external business partners.
- Supplier diversity programs maintain explicit goals for developing and maintaining relations with diverse suppliers.
- Diverse marketing strategies maintain a multicultural approach to advertising and marketing to clients.
- Minority owner and franchisee initiatives support the development of minority- and women-owned and operated Marriott franchises.

Table 13.1. Marriott's Diversity Programs.

organization, from strong efforts to recruit diverse individuals, to training staff, and developing leadership that appreciates differences and the benefits that those differences can provide. Marriott initiatives even encompass supporting diversity in how they choose their suppliers and how they appeal to various clienteles.

Unlike many less successful organizations, a key feature of Marriott's approach is that diversity issues are not addressed solely by a stand-alone program that implies separation of diversity issues from the basic aspects of the business. Thus, diversity is not just an issue of bringing in demographically different staff, but in finding ways to integrate and use that diversity throughout their organization. The value of diversity is integrated throughout the organization as a key aspect of meeting their organizational mission, fostering the kind of common purpose that should help people transcend their demographic identities and work together cooperatively to serve Marriott's clients. Marriott views their success as not due solely to any particular program or set of programs. Rather, it is through the combination of initiatives and leadership actions that the broad message goes out to every corner of the organization that diversity matters to the success of their enterprise.

Although these programs work well for Marriott, no program or set of programs can guarantee success in all places, and what works for Marriott may not work elsewhere. Each organization needs to tailor its approach to diversity to fit its own staff, based on the organization's history, staffing patterns, and business strategy. However, in any organization, success in leading a diverse staff comes as much through leadership commitment and careful implementation as through particular programs or initiatives. In that regard, the words of Marriott chairman and chief executive officer J. W. Marriott, Jr., are instructive: "Our commitment to diversity is absolute. It is the only way for us to attract and retain the very best talent available. It is the only way to forge the business relationships necessary to continue our dynamic growth. And it is the only way to meet our responsibilities to our associates, customers, partners and stakeholders."[33]

Mentoring Diverse Staff

Another way to implement many of our best practice suggestions is through focusing on developing diverse staff through mentoring. *Mentors* are traditionally defined as individuals possessing advanced knowledge and experience who make an active effort to support the development and upward mobility of a more junior individual's (protégé's) career. Mentoring may be formal or informal; instituted by the organization or naturally evolving from a preexisting relationship between mentor and protégé. Thanks to advanced communication technologies, mentors and protégés no longer need to work in the same organizations, hierarchies, or even locations, though long distance mentoring has some limitations. Both formal and informal individual mentoring relationships can be expanded into mentoring networks, collections of individual mentors that offer advice and support to the same protégé(s). Even the definition of mentor has expanded to recognize the advantages of receiving mentoring from a variety of organizational members, not just higher-ranking leaders. Peers or junior staff members with new information to share can serve as valuable mentors to leaders as well as leaders serving as mentors to more junior staff.

BENEFITS OF MENTORING IN A DIVERSITY CONTEXT. Compared to other interventions, mentoring offers a unique combination of advantages that make it a particularly good diversity leadership technique. Its flexibility makes it highly responsive to diversity and allows for the development of programs tailored to specific organizational needs. Mentoring can be sustained for as long as the participants feel necessary to provide an ongoing source of ideas and skills development, or it may start and stop as the situation demands.

Face-to-face conversations offer many options for learning from diverse staff, and provide a better environment for discussing sensitive issues and an organization's unwritten rules than an all-staff meeting. Such conversations also help leaders to better gauge their protégés' capabilities, allowing leaders to develop insight into how high-potential employees can come in a variety of guises and set appropriately high standards that inspire better performance. Leaders can try different approaches with each protégé to find the methods that work best for each one. Because mentoring and mentoring networks can be opened to all employees, majority and minority, they can provide a high level of inclusiveness and avoid excluding any group.

In addition, mentoring can help produce more tangible outcomes for employees and organizations. Several studies have shown that those who are mentored enjoy higher salaries along with increased promotion rates and career mobility. Mentoring has also been found to have a positive impact on career and job satisfaction while decreasing the turnover intentions of protégés.[34] Some companies have used mentoring relationships to provide updated skills training to senior employees through "reverse mentoring" relationships. Employees with more recent and advanced training in technology or industry techniques, such as recent graduates, have provided valuable computer skills training to senior executives who may not feel comfortable or have the time to attend generalized classes.

Another valuable aspect is the opportunity to use mentoring as a clear signal of a leader's commitment to diversity. Leaders in most organizations do not have the time or emotional resources to have a personal relationship with every individual organizational member. By focusing their own mentoring efforts on those who are or will be in a position to mentor others, leaders can set the tone for inclusiveness throughout the company, creating networks of diversity champions throughout the organization. Mentoring diverse protégés can serve as an example to organizational minorities that their demographic characteristics are not an obstacle to advancing in the organization even if they are not personally mentored. Mentored managers will have a better sense of their leaders' support of diversity and be better empowered to apply the same perspectives in their own decision making.

When leaders are aware of the effects of diversity in organizations and follow conscious and open-minded approaches, mentoring can be a strong force for developing diverse staff as well as developing leaders themselves. In diverse contexts, culturally intelligent leadership requires the ability to discern problems and openly seek new solutions in sometimes creative ways, and mentoring can help open channels of communication between leaders and diverse followers. Although mentoring is only one option that leaders can use to develop their diverse staff members, it is a very visible way to demonstrate commitment to a diverse workplace at all levels and to lead by example.

EXECUTIVE SUMMARY

Leaders need to remember that most traditional leadership theories were developed and tested on White males from the United States or other Anglo-Saxon cultures, cultures that are characterized by low power distance, low uncertainty avoidance, fairly high masculinity, and very high individualism. The generalizability of these leadership approaches to other races, genders, and cultures must be determined, with the hope of developing a more globally relevant understanding of leadership behavior. Scholars of leadership have not devoted sufficient time to carefully rethinking our traditional theories and models to accommodate this far more diverse followership. As organizations become more global, it is critical that leadership theory and practice be increasingly reexamined through the lens of culture. Leaders in our global society will increasingly need to extend their skills in developing positive leader-follower relationships with diverse followers.

In this chapter, we have emphasized the need for leaders to embrace the creation of an inclusive work climate that supports diverse staff as a vital requirement for effective leadership. We have presented a number of strategies found to be effective in successfully diverse organizations, and we encourage leaders to consider how they might fit into their own organizations. We have also suggested mentoring as a process that combines many of the best practice strategies, a key way that leaders can help their diverse followers succeed, both by mentoring diverse staff themselves and by seeing that diverse staff members have access to a variety of other mentors as well.

There are many lessons to be learned from the experiences of successful organizations. The most basic lesson is that success is certainly possible: many multinational and international organizations have thrived despite significant value differences among their diverse employees. They have done it not by denying differences in values or perspectives, or by forcing diverse staff into a single corporate mold, but rather by coalescing around shared organizational expectations and practices and making those expectations and practices known and understood by all. Bringing in diverse staff is the easier part of embracing diversity in organizations: the more difficult part for today's leaders is changing the tacit assumptions and everyday behaviors that often unintentionally limit the contributions and prospects of a diverse workforce.

CHAPTER FOURTEEN

Best Practices in Cross-Cultural Leadership

Mary B. Teagarden

> *The Jack Welch of the Future cannot be like me. I spent my entire career in the United States. The next head of General Electric will be somebody who spent time in Bombay, in Hong Kong, in Buenos Aires. We have to send our best and brightest overseas and make sure they have training that will allow them to be the global leaders who will make GE flourish in the future.*
>
> —*Jack Welch*, Global Explorers *(1999)*[1]

The need for effective cross-cultural leadership is not a recent business challenge. As the nature and scope of international business has evolved in recent decades, so has the way we consider the skills required of leaders in the international, or more recently global, business environment. In the late 1980s and 1990s the need for effective cross-cultural leadership was highlighted by business expansion into Asia, especially China, just as it had been highlighted in the 1970s and 1980s by expansion into Europe. More important, during the 1990s the emphasis shifted from a European, Latin American, or Asian "regional specialist" focus that complemented the international perspective of earlier times to a global or pan-regional focus. The days of the "old China hand" or the Mexico specialist with deep local cross-cultural knowledge and competency are fading and giving way to "globalists" with sophisticated, portable transcultural competency. The importance of this shift cannot be overlooked: cross-cultural leadership for a regional specialist is relatively straightforward; transcultural leadership for a global leader is much more complex and tightly intertwined with many other skills, behaviors, and competencies, and it takes much, much longer to develop.

Of equal importance, the focus of cross-cultural leadership has shifted from *selecting* and *training* the "right" executive for an international assignment—frequently an underperformer, in the 1970s and 1980s—to selecting the best and the brightest today, either an executive needed to execute critical strategic initiatives or a high-potential employee for an international stretch assignment to develop their global leadership skills and build the company's leadership pipeline. In the 1970s and early 1980s, most markets were domestic and therefore were the domain of an organization's top performers, high potentials, and stars. The underperformer was often assigned to international markets that were considered of minor importance—consequently, a "problem" was geographically out of sight, out of mind, and out of the line of real business activity. To make matters more challenging, global leadership skills are no longer bounded within the organization: they are extended to global alliances, mergers and acquisitions, and supply chain partners. Likewise, an organization's global leaders are no longer "over there" somewhere; they are now everywhere—here *and* there at all levels of the organization. The field of cross-cultural leadership has gotten very complex and much more strategically important in the past decade. It comprises the competencies that differentiate both highly successful international organizations and highly successful global leaders.

Doug Ivestor, former chief executive officer (CEO) of Coca-Cola, observed, "As economic borders come down, cultural barriers go up, presenting new challenges and opportunities in business."[2] And economic borders are coming down faster than ever. Javidan and House observed, "When cultures come into contact, they may converge on some aspects, but their idiosyncrasies will likely amplify."[3] One key to being an effective cross-cultural leader is understanding this convergence—what unites us—and divergence—what makes us different. Two significant themes parallel the dynamic evolution of globalization. One theme is the importance of cross-cultural leadership, the ability to lead and make sense across cultures and contexts that are different from the leader's own. A second, and by far the most alarming, theme is that there is a dramatic shortage of leaders with these competencies.[4] John Quelch, former dean of the London Business School, observes, "The lack of world-wide multicultural managerial talent is now biting into companies' bottom lines through high staff turnover, high training costs, stagnant market shares, failed joint ventures and mergers and the high opportunity costs that inevitably follow bad management selections round the globe."[5] Fewer than one in five CEOs of Fortune 500 organizations is satisfied with the current supply of global management talent capable of effective cross-cultural leadership.

Cross-culture leadership is an umbrella concept that comprises many issues. In this chapter, we address five questions that are fundamental to understanding the topic. The first is, Does cross-cultural leadership really matter? In other words, how critical is it to the future success of today's corporations? A second issue is, How do we best understand and define the cross-cultural leadership concept? Third, what does it take to lead cross-culturally? Specifically, what are the behaviors, competencies, and skills that distinguish leaders who are adept cross-culturally? Fourth, how do we develop cross-cultural leaders? Finally, we must consider knowledge: What specifically does a cross-cultural leader need to know? This chapter answers these questions with a focus on cross-cultural leadership best practices. It can serve as a guide to the leader who wants to become more cross-culturally adept and for the human resource professional who is guiding the development of these leaders.

DOES CROSS-CULTURAL LEADERSHIP MATTER?

In the past the ability of an executive leader to think, understand, and work within the global environment was not nearly as important as it is today.

—*Marshall Goldsmith (2003)*[6]

Global business activity has grown exponentially. By 2005, the growth in employment in the foreign operations of Fortune 500 companies was seven times higher than the growth in their domestic operations.

Increasingly, employees are "there," not "here," and these employees and the multinationals in which they work must be led by cross-culturally competent leaders. In the 1990s alone, international flows of investment increased by more than 300 percent, and the international flows into developing countries—which are cross-culturally more challenging—increased by more than 600 percent. There is no hiding place: U.S. corporations face foreign competition even if they remain in their home country, since 70 percent to 90 percent of all U.S. corporations face some form of foreign competition in the United States, their home market. This highlights the importance of cross-cultural leadership for even the most "domestic" of leaders. And this globalization tsunami shows no signs of abating.

When the boom in information technology is superimposed on the globalization tsunami, we see the emergence of networked, integrated workspaces that extend the need for cross-cultural leadership skills into global, virtual, and even asynchronous contexts. To make matters more complex, cross-border mergers grew in number by four times between 1997 and 2000—from 2,100 to more than 9,200. That pace continues. By 2000, more than 40 percent of all mergers and acquisitions were cross-border, a statistic that highlights the importance of cross-cultural leadership in leading across organizational boundaries. U.S. companies purchased $20 billion worth of Asian companies and $43 billion worth of Latin American companies in 2000.[7] Almost overnight, the world has gotten smaller *and* bigger for cross-cultural leaders. It has gotten smaller because businesses are so extensively networked and integrated with partners around the world. It has gotten bigger because there are significant business opportunities beyond the domestic corporation's organizational and national boundaries.

The unprecedented global search for goods and services coupled with intense pressure on costs has propelled businesses toward internationalization to compete or even survive. In the borderless world economy, resources—goods, services, technology, people, and capital—flow and move freely across national boundaries. Despite this flux, the fundamental resource necessary to formulate and implement global strategies and coordinate resource flows in global business activities is people—the human talent of any organization. There is a consensus that globally competitive organizations sustain their edge through the unique talent of their human resources and their systems for managing a supply of cross-culturally competent global leaders and workers who are capable of coordinating global strategic efforts of the organization and simultaneously integrating individual local host-country strategies.[8] Specifically, the single critical success factor in globalizing business lies with the pool of highly competent global leaders and skilled global workers who possess the global knowledge of production and service capabilities and consumer demands for products and services around the world.[9] Cross-cultural leadership competency is the lynchpin for this success.

In this context, management guru Peter Drucker cautioned, "Tomorrow's business challenges are less technical than they are cultural. Culture must be managed just like any other business phenomenon."[10] Cross-cultural competencies elevate a good business leader to the highly competent global leader status needed to meet globalization challenges. Understanding and appreciating cultural values, practices, and subtleties in those places where the organization operates or aspires to operate is the starting point. The leader's flexibility to respond "positively and effectively" to different cultural values and practices is fundamental.[11] This requires the willingness to be open to others' ideas and opinions and the motivation to do so. As we will see, cross-cultural leadership is a complex, multidimensional concept. Excelling at cross-cultural leadership best practices—selecting, developing, and deploying them— is a critical success factor for companies aspiring to outperform competitors in the globalized business environment.[12] Cross-cultural leadership matters. It matters now more than ever before. There is no hiding place for companies or their leaders in the new, complex, integrated, dynamic, global business environment.

HOW DO WE BEST UNDERSTAND CROSS-CULTURAL LEADERSHIP?

The Buddha asked his disciples to get a large magnificent elephant and four blind men. He then brought the four blind men to the elephant and told them to find out what the elephant would "look" like. The first blind men touched the elephant leg and reported that it "looked" like a pillar. The second blind man touched the elephant tummy and said that the elephant was a wall. The third blind man touched the elephant's ear and said that it was a piece of cloth. The fourth blind man held on to the tail and described the elephant as a piece of rope. And all of them ran into a hot argument about the "appearance" of an elephant.

—*Buddhist Sutra*

The answer to the question, "How do we best understand cross-cultural leadership?" depends on whom one asks. The cross-cultural leadership literature mimics the fable of the grasp of the blind men and the elephant. Not unlike the elephant, the cross-cultural leader is sometimes defined by the role he or she fills, sometimes by the competitive environment in which the leader operates, often through a lens of the skill sets needed for cross-border assignments, and, although much less common, sometimes by the mindset that underpins the leader's effectiveness. What unifies these perspectives is the reality of the global business environment, and the fact that regardless of the descriptions these leaders cross and bridge cultures in their work context. Nevertheless, Stewart Black, Allen Morrison, and Hal Gregerson remind us that "every global leader requires a certain set of unique skills and abilities that arise from country affiliation, industry, company, and functional dynamics."[13]

We begin our journey through the field of cross-cultural leadership with an examination of four main perspectives that are often complementary and mutually reinforcing. We focus on these four because they flesh out the dimensions of the topic and highlight some of the basic tensions in the field. Leadership is contextually bound and cross-cultural leadership even more so. The *role perspective* offered by Bartlett and Ghoshal helps us understand the power that context has on leaders from a variety of functional roles needed in international contexts. A *context-driven perspective* is described by the Corporate Leadership Council's identification of the "new global general manager" who must transcend the traditional roles described by Bartlett and Ghoshal and function with fluidity among and between these. Although cross-cultural leadership is contextually bound, it is carried out by individuals—thus we also consider the leader him- or herself through an examination of an *interactive perspective* represented in the "Mobility Pyramid," a framework that bridges context, roles, and the individual leader's motivations and abilities. Finally, we consider a *behavioral perspective* developed by the GLOBE (Global Leadership and Organization Behavior Effectiveness) research consortium that identifies specific leadership behavior sets that are appropriate under different cultural contexts.

The Role Perspective

The *role perspective*, exemplified by Bartlett and Ghoshal, considers the leader's role as the key determinant, and they suggest that today's international business climate creates an organizational need for three groups of "highly specialized yet closely linked" global leaders to manage the "transnational" organization.[14] One group includes the *business manager,* who is needed to further the company's global-scale efficiency and competitiveness. This requires perspective to recognize opportunities and risks *across* national and functional boundaries. The business manager's primary goal is to capture the full benefit of *integrated* worldwide operations. This first group has evolved as business has shifted from an international to a global orientation where business activity in multiple countries has to be coordinated and controlled, for example, by a global supply chain manager.

The second group is the *country manager,* who plays a crucial role in meeting local customer needs, satisfying a host government's requirements, and defending their company's market position against local and external competition. The country manager's primary responsibility is to be *sensitive and responsive to the local market.* Historically, the country manager—for example, Intel's country manager for China or Danone's Eastern European regional manager—was the most common cross-border assignment and the one we know the most about.

The third is the *functional manager,* whose primary responsibility is to build an organization that uses learning to create and spread innovations. This requires transferring specialized knowledge while also *connecting* scarce resources and capabilities *across* national borders. The emergence of this third group is a reflection of one of the key drivers of globalization, the complexity of technology with which organizations now grapple—global product management or global technology management are functions representative of this role.

Bartlett and Ghoshal found that the greatest constraint in creating a transnational organization is a severe shortage of executives with the skills, knowledge, and sophistication to operate in a more tightly linked and less classically hierarchical network. From this role perspective, organizational forces, both *structure and strategy,* contextualize cross-cultural leadership and determine the skills, abilities, competencies, and roles that lead to the global organization's effectiveness. Regardless of the leader's role, crossing cultures and contexts and the need for competencies to do so are the commonalities for each of these three global leader groups.

The Context-Driven Perspective

The Corporate Leadership Council's "new" global general manager exemplifies the *context-driven perspective* on cross-cultural leadership, one that emphasizes the strength of the contemporary global reality. The council identifies a "new" global general manager—one with the skills and abilities needed in the global competitive environment. They found that the "role of the 'new' global general manager is vastly more complex than that of the traditional country manager."[15] The council's study identifies specific responsibilities for new general managers that include entering new markets, launching operations in new geographies, making acquisitions and alliances, managing joint ventures, and stewarding new business initiatives. This research indicates that new general managers are responsible for driving operations along both product and geographical lines within an organizational matrix. These new global leaders' responsibilities can be for all corporate operations within a particular country or for a particular product line within a region that includes several countries. This study also highlights a shortage of new global leaders. "Exacerbating this shortage is the fact that the sought-after global leader requires management skills that go well beyond traditional managerial competencies; the 'new' general manager must steward an enterprise with fully *integrated* operations *across multiple geographies.*"[16] From this perspective, we see that the *nature of the job* itself—integration across multiple geographies—partially determines cross-cultural leadership skills, abilities, and competencies that are the building blocks of organizational effectiveness. Once again, crossing cultures and contexts and the need for competencies to do so is the commonality for new global leaders.

The Interactive Perspective

A third view, the *interactive perspective,* is based on a hierarchical notion of cross-cultural leadership captured in the "Mobility

Pyramid"—a perspective pioneered by Price Waterhouse Coopers' London staff. The Mobility Pyramid is built around the confluence of the leader's ability or willingness to relocate and the organization's need for a leader in the foreign location. From this perspective, multinationals are encouraged to manage their international human resource requirements, giving consideration to employees' mobility preferences and realities and the company's needs. The Mobility Pyramid identifies five different kinds of mobility-based assignments: Glopats, Globals, Regionals, Mobile Local Nationals, and Rooted Nationals, each with distinct geographic, cross-cultural, and task considerations.[17]

Glopats are leaders with a world perspective, who can "fit in" and contribute wherever the organization operates, and are frequently on the move tackling short- and medium-term assignments. Glopats need the most sophisticated, expert cross-cultural leadership competencies, skills, and abilities, which might best be referred to as *transcultural.* They rarely have time or need to master the local culture. The transcultural demands mean that Glopats must learn how to learn culture quickly.

Globals are leaders who move around the world on medium-term assignments. Globals need advanced cross-cultural leadership proficiency, but enjoy a longer time frame than Glopats to develop proficiency in the specific local culture.

Regionals accept short-, medium-, or long-term assignments within a geographic region and/or at a regional headquarters. Regionals need cross-cultural competence and have a long time frame to master regional cultures, one of which is usually the Regional's home culture. If they are not local, they may be mistaken for local because of their depth of localized cross-cultural knowledge and effectiveness. Regionals are capable of assuming the "cultural mentor" role for Globals and Glopats.

Mobile Local Nationals are functional experts and regional managers prepared for cross-border task force memberships, short-term projects, and training assignments abroad. This includes commuter assignments—one of the fastest growing forms of expatriate mobility in Europe. Mobile Local Nationals need both cross-cultural awareness and communication skills and virtual teaming skills, at least at the "advanced beginner" level. Mobile Local Nationals may be capable of assuming the "cultural mentor" role for Glopats, Globals, and Regionals.

Rooted Local Nationals are functional experts and general managers tied to their home base. Rooted Local Nationals need an awareness level of cross-cultural skills that would be characterized as a novice skill level.

The Behavioral Perspective

Finally, a *behavioral perspective* on cross-cultural leaders comes from the Global Leadership and Organizational Behavior Effectiveness study and fills a substantial knowledge gap concerning the cross-cultural forces relevant to effective leadership in many societies around the world. This empirical research clearly shows that cultural forces influence many aspects of leadership. Most of the leadership research during the past 50 years was conducted in the West—the United States, Canada, or Western Europe. The GLOBE study overcomes this limitation by studying leadership and behavior in sixty-two societies.[18] Specifically, they looked at leadership by examining "prototypical requisites for leadership positions; privileges, power and influence granted to leaders; degree to which leadership roles are filled by ascription or achievement; model leader behavior patterns; preferences for and expectations of leaders; and follower and subordinate reaction to different kinds of leader behavior."[19] The research identifies ten culture clusters of "culturally endorsed implicit leadership theory" leadership profiles that help delineate culture-specific boundaries of acceptable, effective leader behaviors and practices.

From the GLOBE study we see that followers' expectations also influence an individual's cross-cultural leadership effectiveness. If we consider the all-important leadership communication function, we can see how this plays out. The GLOBE researchers found that the typical American manager communicates using direct and explicit language anchored in facts, figures, and rational thinking. Contrast this with the GLOBE finding that Russian and Greek managers communicate using indirect and vague language. Facts and figures are suspect and are not taken seriously when available because they are hard to come by. Additionally, Greek managers believe effective communication is discussion and exploration of issues without any commitment or explicit results. For the Swedish manager, effective communication is in-depth dialogue that focuses on the content of the communication. Managers in the Philippines and Malaysia avoid conflict and communicate in a caring and paternalistic manner with followers. If gender is added to the mix, South Korean male managers believe that one-way, paternalistic communication that they initiate is appropriate. The expectations of Russian, Greek, Swedish, South Korean, Filipino, or Malaysian followers of effective communications are worlds apart from the typical American communication style. Unless the American leader is sensitive to these realities and adjusts his or her style, miscommunication will be the most likely outcome.

There is not one kind of cross-cultural leader; they vary by the scope of their responsibilities, the content of their work, the complexity of their work, the location of their work, their willingness and ability to travel globally, the expectations of their followers, their emotional maturity, their career stage, and their own developmental needs. What cross-cultural leaders do have in common is the fact that they cross cultures and contexts regularly in their work; they must be able to maneuver across these multiple boundaries fraught with multiple local expectations; and that reflective capacity enhances the ability to do this well. As we will see, investment in the development of cross-cultural competencies is a key driver of the organization's and global leader's success.

WHAT DOES IT TAKES TO LEAD CROSS-CULTURALLY? A JUNGLE OF COMPETENCIES

The question is no longer whether everyone will have to be globalized; the question is how much, and in what ways.

—McCall and Hollenbeck,
Developing Global Executives *(2002)*[20]

The identification of global leadership competencies is a complex, daunting task. In this section of the chapter we trek through the cross-cultural competency jungle and conclude with a synthesis to guide the leader who wants to become more cross-culturally adept and the human resource professional who is guiding the development of these leaders. To begin with, cross-cultural competencies are difficult to differentiate from general leadership competencies. And recognition must be given to the ongoing dialogue about whether the truth lies in a global or a local response—a debate that has raged among academics for the past two decades. As we can see in the GLOBE example given earlier, relative to cross-cultural leaders the answer to this ongoing dialogue is not one perspective or the other but a resounding "Yes!" Yes, there are ten distinct clusters of culturally appropriate leadership profiles that help delineate culture-specific boundaries of acceptable, effective leader behaviors and practices around the world. And, yes, there are also a few universal best practices like integrity and honesty, more regionally specific best practices like vague and indirect communication instead of direct and explicit communication, and many local best practices, such as top-down, paternalistic communication between men and women in South Korea. Adept cross-cultural leaders know these differences and can behave appropriately given this knowledge.

In a study focusing specifically on *global leadership competencies*, Gaelen Kroec, Mary Ann Von Glinow, and colleagues assert that while multinationals need to identify competencies now more than ever, the ability to do so has remained elusive "not because of disagreement about them, but because they often reflect generic management skills rather than a particular [multinational's] strengths and unique culture."[21] If we reflect back on the GLOBE study communication example, we see what this means. There is agreement that effective communication skills are a hallmark of effective domestic *and* cross cultural leadership, but the GLOBE example makes it clear that effective communication is defined in the eye of the beholder—and beholders' eyes change as we move between cultures.

When discussing competencies, definitional imprecision runs rampant because competencies are sometimes equated with skills and abilities, and are sometimes defined as capabilities for doing something by using a range of skills and abilities. Even culture itself exacerbates this problem. Some competencies vary fundamentally across different countries and cultures, to the point where they would be contraindicated.[22] For example, the American direct and explicit communication style would be contraindicated were the communicator an American woman manager and the audience South Korean male subordinates. Accordingly, McCall and Hollenbeck caution, "Moving into a different culture creates more, and more dramatic, opportunities for a particular pattern of strengths and weaknesses to shift from effective in one setting to disastrous in another. Because of differences in norms and values and misunderstandings due to language, behavior that is acceptable in one culture can become a derailer in another."[23] The Swedish manager who engages in problem-solving dialogue with Japanese or Indian subordinates would be seen as a weak, technically unqualified leader since he or she did not have specific answers to their questions. Findings such as these highlight the high stakes associated with cross-cultural leadership competencies for both leaders and their organizations and the importance of understanding which competencies matter and when they matter.

There are as many lists of cross-cultural competencies as there are researchers who study them, and an organizing framework can help us make sense of this cross-cultural competency jungle. Alan Bird and Joyce Osland organize this panoply of competencies into a comprehensive framework they call the "Building Blocks of Global Competencies."[24] It rests on a base of cross-cultural and business knowledge and categorizes competencies as (1) threshold or foundation competencies that begin with traits or natural abilities; (2) attitudes and orientations; (3) interpersonal skills; and (4) systems skills. This framework suggests a progressive, cumulative, developmental path for building global leadership competencies and provides a useful bridge between the what—What are necessary cross-cultural leadership competencies?—and the how—How are they developed? We look at this framework in more detail next.

Bird and Osland suggest that *natural abilities or traits* include integrity, humility, flexibility, inquisitiveness, and hardiness. Among these traits, inquisitiveness or curiosity and hardiness or persistence in the face of obstacles are the most commonly cited in the field. *Attitudes and orientations* include cognitive complexity and cosmopolitanism, often called savvy, open-mindedness, and flexibility by other researchers. *Interpersonal skills* include mindful communication and creating and building trust. *Systems skills* include spanning boundaries, building community through change, and making ethical decisions. Table 14.1 adapts and extends the Bird and Osland framework by incorporating competencies identified by many of the experts discussed in this section including Bird and Osland; Rosen, Digh, and Singer; McCall and Hollenbeck; and the author of the Corporate Leadership Council report. Once the multiple perspectives on cross-cultural leadership competencies are mapped we see that, in fact, there is considerable agreement about competencies needed in the global competitive environment.

Skills	Bird and Osland	Rosen, Digh, Singer, and Phillips	McCall and Hollenbeck	Corporate Leadership Council
Systems Skills	Span boundaries, build community through change, make ethical decisions	Social literacy	Honesty and integrity	Start up businesses in new markets Ability to develop individuals across diverse cultures Global team building Ability to interact with local political interests
Interpersonal Skills	Mindful communication Creating and building trust	Cultural literacy	Stable personal life Cultural interest and sensitivity	Intercultural adaptability
Attitudes and Orientations	Global mindset Cognitive complexity Cosmopolitanism	Personal literacy	Able to deal with complexity Open-minded and flexible in thoughts and tactics Honesty and integrity	Ability to cope with uncertainties and conflicts Willingness and ability to embrace and integrate multiple perspectives
Threshold Traits	Integrity, humility, inquisitiveness, hardiness	Personal literacy	Resilient, resourceful, optimistic, energetic	
Knowledge	Global knowledge	Business literacy	Value-added technical or business skills	In-depth business and technical knowledge and managerial competency

Table 14.1. The Building Blocks of Global Competencies.

Rosen and colleagues categorize the multidimensionality of global leadership competencies under an umbrella concept they call *global literacy*. They identify four *competency sets* that enable a leader to see, think, act, and mobilize in *culturally mindful ways*; these include personal literacy, social literacy, business literacy, and cultural literacy, which taken together create global literacy. *Personal literacy* includes self-awareness, self-development, and self-esteem. Rosen and colleagues contend that personally literate leaders must master key behaviors that include insight, humility, flexibility, decisiveness, and optimism. *Social literacy* is the ability to unleash the power of collective intelligence through the assembly, focusing, linking, and motivating of people, and through building strong teams. The behaviors associated with *social literacy* that make this happen include trust, listening, constructive impatience, teaching, and collaborative individualism. *Business literacy* is the ability to focus and mobilize the organization by embracing multiple roles—including chaos navigator, business geographer, historical futurist, leadership liberator, and economic integrator. Finally, *cultural literacy* is valuing and leveraging cultural differences and is associated with leadership roles including proud ancestor, inquisitive internationalist, respectful modernizer, culture bridger, and global capitalist.

Rosen and colleagues comment:

When you become proficient in the four global literacies, you begin to

- *See* the world's challenges and opportunities—which expands your horizons, illuminating your perceptions of the world.
- *Think* with an international mindset—which helps you develop a global mindset with beliefs and attitudes that enable you to think internationally.
- *Act* with fresh global-centric leadership behaviors—which teaches new relationship skills that help you navigate through the global marketplace.
- *Mobilize* a world-class company—which helps you inspire and mobilize people across national cultures.[25]

In their report on the "new" global assignment, the Corporate Leadership Council found that "to meet the rising bar of global skills, leaders must possess specific, rare global skills including *intercultural adaptability*, ability to *develop individuals* across diverse cultures, global strategic thinking, *global team building*, ability to *start up* businesses in *new markets* and ability to *interact with local* political interests."[26] While this study reinforces the competencies identified by Rosen and colleagues, it also extends that study in some important ways. The council study highlights the importance of boundary-spanning skill sets for global executives.

McCall and Hollenbeck take a more focused, traditional approach and identify seven global executive competencies that they believe can be developed.[27] First, the global leader is *open-minded and flexible in thought and tactics*—able to live and work in a variety of settings with different types of people and is willing and able to listen to other people, approaches, and ideas. Second, he or she has *cultural interest and sensitivity* and is able to live and work in a variety of settings with different types of people and is willing and able to listen to other people, approaches, and ideas. Third, the global leader has the *ability to deal with complexity* and considers many variables in solving a problem; is comfortable with ambiguity and patient in evolving issues; can make decisions in the face of uncertainty; can see patterns and connections; and is willing to take risks. Fourth, the global leader is *resilient, resourceful, optimistic, and energetic*—he or she responds to a challenge; is not discouraged by adversity; is self-reliant and creative; sees the positive side of things; has a high level of physical and emotional energy; and is able to deal with stress. Fifth, the global leader demonstrates *honesty and integrity* and is authentic, consistent; the person engenders trust. Sixth, he or she has a *stable personal life* and has developed and maintains stress-resistant personal arrangements, usually family, that support a commitment to work. And seventh, the global leader has *value-added business and technical skills* including technical, managerial, and other expertise sufficient to provide his or her credibility. This study extends the previous discussions by highlighting the importance of resilience, resourcefulness, honesty, and integrity—dimensions not emphasized in the other studies.

Chris Earley and Elaine Mosakowski approach the competency issue from another angle: they identify a concept that they call *cultural intelligence*, or CQ. CQ is an extension of earlier work on emotional intelligence and comprises a blend of knowledge, behavior, and motivation. Earley and Mosakowski contend that "a person with high cultural intelligence can somehow tease out a person's or group's behavior those features that would be true of all people and all groups, those peculiar to this person or group, and those that are neither universal or idiosyncratic." They found that some aspects of cultural intelligence are innate yet "anyone reasonably alert, motivated, and poised can attain an acceptable level of cultural intelligence. . . ."[28]

Cultural intelligence comprises knowledge—rote learning about cultural aspects of foreign cultures; physicality or body language—adapting people's habits and mannerisms as evidence that you have entered their world; and, "heart," often called *resilience* by others, which is the persistence to overcome obstacles and setbacks. Unlike other aspects of personality, cultural intelligence can be developed. Earley and Mosakowski identify six profiles that describe the range of this form of intelligence in most leaders. The *provincial* is effective working with people similar to him- or herself. The *analyst* "methodically deciphers a foreign culture's rules and expectations by resorting to a variety of elaborate learning strategies. . . ."[29] The *natural* relies on intuition rather than on a systematic learning style. However, he or she "is rarely steered wrong by first impressions."[30] The *ambassador* "may not know much about the culture he has just entered, but he convincingly communicates his certainty that he belongs there."[31] Among the multinationals they studied, Earley and Mosakowski found that the ambassador was the most common type and exhibited extraordinary confidence and humility simultaneously. The *mimic* has a great degree of control over his actions and behavior, "if not a great deal of insight into the significance of the cultural cues he picks up."[32] The *chameleon* possesses high levels of all three cultural intelligence components and may be mistaken for a native of the country. They found this style is very rare—fewer than 5 percent of the cross-cultural leaders they studied—and many leaders have hybrid styles that combine two or more of these styles. Most important, Earley and Mosakowski demonstrated that cultural intelligence can be developed; more detail is provided on this process in the next section.

How does the leader who wants to become more cross-culturally adept or the human resource professional guiding the development of these leaders make sense of this cross-cultural competency jungle? Begin by understanding the "Building Blocks of Global Competencies" framework and how the different perspectives we have discussed map onto it. First, successful cross-cultural leadership rests on a base of cross-cultural and business knowledge—technical expertise plus the "facts and figures" of the countries and regions in which the leader will work. Business knowledge or technical expertise is taken as a given and is often the primary criterion used when selecting a leader for an international assignment. Alas, it is a big world, and cross-cultural knowledge is another issue. How can a leader possibly master the cross-cultural knowledge dimension? The GLOBE study is a good starting point, since it distills the world into ten distinct clusters of culturally appropriate leadership profiles that can provide the base of cross-cultural knowledge needed for cross-cultural leadership development.

Then assess yourself for threshold or foundation competencies and traits or natural abilities. You might ask which of these are the most important for your situation. Key foundation competencies begin with the all-important inquisitiveness, followed by willingness to learn from experience; integrity, humility, and resilience are almost as important. If inquisitiveness and a willingness to learn from experience are missing, efforts to develop cross-cultural leader effectiveness are not likely to be successful. Next, focus on attitudes and orientations that include the ability to deal with complexity, open-mindedness, and the ability to cope with uncertainty and conflict. Stretch assignments in international contexts that require the future leader to be uncomfortable and reframe are useful for the development of the attitudes and experiences needed. Foreign language acquisition is also a useful approach to developing the ability to reframe. The competency journey continues with the development of interpersonal skills that include mindful communication, creating and building trust, and intercultural adaptability. Here the recommendations of Earley and Mosakowski for developing cultural intelligence should be embraced. The journey concludes with the development of systems skills. In the following section we look at the development of cross-cultural leadership skills in more depth.

HOW DO WE DEVELOP CROSS-CULTURAL LEADERS?

Two things seemed pretty apparent to me. One was that in order to be a [Mississippi River] pilot a man had got to learn more than any one man ought to be allowed to know; and the other was, that he must learn it all over again in a different way every 24 hours.

—Mark Twain, Life on the Mississippi *(1883)*

I took a good deal o' pains with his education, sir; let him run the streets when he was very young, and shift for his-self. It's the only way to make a boy sharp, sir.

—*Charles Dickens,* The Pickwick Papers *(1837)*[33]

What kinds of human resources practices might facilitate the development of savvy cross-cultural leaders? Mary Ann Von Glinow, Mary Teagarden, and colleagues conducted a longitudinal, multicountry, multi-researcher study to identify such best practices. They found that indeed there were a very few universal best practices, such as the use of training and development to close technical skill gaps; more regional best practices, such as a training and development focus on "softer management practices" in Anglo countries; and many more country-specific best practices relating to compensation, selection, appraisal, training and development, and strategic orientation, for example, an emphasis on the preparation of leaders for future assignments in the United States and South Korea.[34]

We know that cross-cultural leadership effectiveness develops over time. This journey might best be characterized as one moving from awareness and knowledge—knowing about other cultures—to wisdom or cultural intelligence, the profound understanding and appreciation of different others. Leaders and future leaders come with a range of global leadership skills that comprise the leader's cross-cultural skills and abilities, and determine idiosyncratic development needs. Alan Bird and Joyce Osland provide a stage-based, developmental approach to global leadership mastery that makes an important distinction among novice and expert global managers, and levels in between. These levels closely parallel career stages. The level of mastery for the *novice stage* is "rules are learned as absolutes." For the *advanced beginner stage*, "experience produces understanding that exceeds stated facts and rules." The *competence stage* is where there is a "greater appreciation for task complexity and recognition of a larger set of cues and the ability to focus on most important cues. Reliance on absolute rules begins to disappear; risk taking and complex trade-offs occur." At the *proficiency stage*, "calculation and rational analysis seem to disappear, and unconscious, fluid, effortless performance begins to emerge." Finally, at the *expert stage*, "holistic recognition and intuition rather than rules dominates. Framing and reframing strategies as they read changing cues that others do not perceive or read is natural."[35]

The implication of this perspective is that sophisticated cross-cultural leaders with world-class expertise achieve that level of competence in a cumulative way, and each level of expertise requires different types of experience and learning upon which the subsequent level stands. For example, the novice may require cross-cultural knowledge training and career pathing that builds cross-cultural expertise, while the expert may only need networking, feedback, or reflection opportunities to enhance cross-cultural effectiveness. The "Evolution of Mastery" framework, presented in Table 14.2,[36] is adapted and extended with examples of developmental activities.

Stage	Level of Mastery	Developmental Examples
Novice	Rules are learned as absolutes	Cross-cultural knowledge training Career pathing to build cross-cultural expertise Diverse team membership
Advanced Beginner	Experience produces understanding that exceeds stated facts and rules	International posting in a moderately different culture within existing technical expertise Remote virtual team membership
Competence	Greater appreciation for task complexity Recognition of a larger set of cues and the ability to focus on most important cues Reliance on absolute rules begins to disappear; risk taking and complex trade-offs occur	Stretch assignments that include a larger technical scope and more cultural difference than prior posting Global team membership
Proficiency	Calculation and rational analysis seem to disappear, and unconscious, fluid, effortless performance begins to emerge	A second or third international posting with increasingly enlarged scope of responsibility Global team leadership
Expert	Holistic recognition and intuition rather than rules Framing and reframing strategies as they read changing cues that others do not perceive or read	Networking Developmental feedback Reflection opportunity

Table 14.2.   The Evolution of Mastery.

While there are various ways to develop cross-cultural leaders—business travel, multicultural teams, training, temporary international assignments, and expatriate assignments, for example—international experience is by far the most highly emphasized, common theme. Stewart Black and his colleagues found that foreign travel, participating in international teams and training programs with an international emphasis, and international transfers all contribute to the development of cross-culture leadership skills.[37] In fact, when Hal Gregerson and his colleagues asked executives to name the most powerful experience in their lives for developing global leadership capabilities, 80 percent of the leaders surveyed responded that living and working abroad was the single most influential experience in their lives.[38]

Additionally, McCall and Hollenbeck found that, focusing on the business side of a leader's development, "the lessons of domestic and international experience weren't all that different." Indeed, there is a common core of learning about leading and doing business. However, they continue, "Learning to work across cultures is an essential competency of the global executive, and it is for most people an emotional education as well as an intellectual one." They continue, "An executive cannot learn cultural adaptability and the competencies associated with it without actually living and working in another culture and successfully coping with the accompanying discontinuities."[39]

The Corporate Leadership Council maintains that "the cross-regional management skills needed . . . are so complex that managers must acquire hands-on experience of global business through international assignments." Secondhand experience from working on virtual teams or training programs is insufficient for the development of global leaders who can be effective crossing cultures and contexts.[40] Bird and Osland contend that "executives working 24–7–365 in an international context have more frequent, novel, significant, and emotionally intense international and intercultural experiences. These experiences often crystallize into forms of expertise that are hard for novices to replicate."[41]

While crossing cultures bootstraps the leader's development process, adequate resources and time for reflection are very important to successful global leader development.[42] These resources include what McCall and Hollenbeck call "significant other people," such as the opportunity to work in parallel with a predecessor, on-site learning from a local national, and exposure to others with global careers, and knowledge resources, such as advice from mentors or advice from others in an organizational network who have had similar task or cross-cultural experiences. Resources also include developmental training programs and related learning opportunities, such as work on a short-term assignment, for example, a special international project or an internal consulting role. Time for reflection is commonly provided in the form of an off-site development program, and less often in the form of a sabbatical or block of time away from work.

Osland observes, "Just as immersion is the most efficient and effective way to learn a foreign language, an expatriate assignment is the best way to develop global leaders."[43] McCall and Hollenbeck extend this perspective by stating that "providing the appropriate level of feedback, resources, and support to help people learn from the [international] experiences they have . . . and providing international perspectives and exposure starting early in people's careers."[44] It should be no surprise that multinationals around the world use international exposure as a vehicle for developing global leaders and their cross-cultural leadership competencies.

Earley and Mosakowski offer a process for the effective development of cultural intelligence that begins with the *assessment* or *self-assessment* of the leader's cultural intelligence strengths and weaknesses to establish a starting point for subsequent development efforts. This can be a self-assessment using the Earley and Mosakowski instrument, the results of an assessment center, or 360-degree performance appraisal. The researchers cite an example where Hughes Electronics staged a cocktail party to evaluate an expatriate manager's grasp of South Korean social etiquette. The second step is the *selection of training protocol* that focuses on his or her weaknesses. The third step is the *implementation* of the training in a way that sequentially adds capabilities. In the fourth step, the leader *organizes resources to support the approach* he or she has taken. It is important that "a realistic assessment of her workload and the time available for CQ enhancement is important." The fifth step *takes the leader into the cultural setting* he needs to master and apply the learning. The sixth step requires the leader to *reevaluate* "her newly developed skills and how effective they have been in the new setting, perhaps after collecting 360-degree feedback from colleagues individually or eavesdropping on a casual focus group that was formed to discuss her progress."[45]

Additionally, strategic repatriation policies cannot be overlooked as the final step in the development of cross-cultural leaders. Paula Caligiuri and Mila Lazarova found that multinationals agree that they enjoy an increase in global competence through the development of the cross-cultural leadership competencies of their business leaders.[46] However, these same multinationals also cite the low retention rate of global assignees upon repatriation as one of their greatest concerns. Development of talent is prohibitively expensive, and perhaps absurd, if the multinational is not able to retain that talent upon return. With repatriate turnover, the multinational loses a critical source of competitiveness—human talent—or worse, they provide potential global competitors with this talent. Caligiuri and Lazarova identify four reasons why this occurs. First, multinationals often do not integrate selection, performance management, and repatriation systems into one strategic process when it is necessary. Second, some turnover upon repatriation is functional, and possibly even strategic. Third, multinationals tend to treat all global assignments as if they had the same strategic objective when they do not. And, finally, multinationals believe that all global assignees tend to have long-term careers with the multinational when they do not.

To resolve this dilemma, Caligiuri and Lazarova suggest four classifications of global assignments, including technical assignments, developmental/high-potential assignments, strategic/executive assignments, and functional/tactical assignments, each with specific performance expectations and repatriation policies. Expatriates on a *technical assignment* have relatively little interaction with host country locals and describe their work as "quite similar" to what they do at home. "These assignments include technicians at an oil refinery, systems engineers on continuation at a client site, systems analysts interfacing with a computer system, and the like."[47] Repatriation of the technical assignee is a function of where those skills are needed within the organization, and retention from a cross-cultural leadership perspective is relatively unimportant. They may return to their home country, be assigned to a third country, or their temporary assignment might be terminated. The *functional/tactical* assignment is similar to the technical assignment with one key difference: "Significant interactions with host nationals are necessary in order for the assignment to be deemed successful."[48] The person selected for a functional/tactical assignment will fill a technical or managerial gap in the host country; this is the most common expatriate assignment.

While these expatriates are sent to fill technical gaps, they come to realize that cross-cultural skills are needed for success.

Developmental and high-potential assignments should be part of the multinational's strategic human resource development plan to build global competencies for sustainable competitive advantage. These programs are often rotational, and the goal is the individual cross-cultural leader's development. Repatriation is often a move to the next assignment in the rotation, and retention of these employees is of high strategic significance. *Strategic and executive assignments* are usually filled by individuals who are being developed for high-level management positions in the future. These assignments are hybrids, both strategic and developmental in nature. These employees are the core "critical" group of assignees who may have the task of entering a new market, developing a county base in a new area, being the general manager of a joint venture, or the like. For these individuals, repatriation is often well thought out and a part of the overall succession planning initiative of the multinational. "An important aspect of the repatriation process will be to ensure that the position for which these individuals are being groomed will actually utilize their developed global skills."[49] Best practice includes an integrated selection, performance management, and repatriation system that is aligned with the strategic planning process in which turnover is proactively managed. Global assignments should be differentiated based on strategic importance, with great care being taken to retain global assignees who have long-term career potential within the multinational.

WHAT DOES THE CROSS-CULTURAL LEADER NEED TO KNOW?

Today, companies increasingly need softer people skills . . . and perhaps most important, working across cultures with Chinese, Germans, Indians, Italians, Russians, and a world full of suppliers and partners.

—Business Week (2005)[50]

What does the leader who wants to become more cross-culturally adept or the human resource professional guiding the development of these leaders need to know? First, does this leader or future leader have a willingness to learn from experience and the motivation to do so? Identification of this motivation is critical, since this willingness is the first step of what can be a very long, iterative journey. The next question that needs to be answered is one regarding the strategic rationale for the international assignment: Is the leader developing these skills for a long-term global career or for a short-term, more tactical assignment? This is important because it takes us to the center of one of the most fundamental debates in cross-cultural leader development: Does the global leader need country-specific cross-cultural knowledge or does she need to have well-developed cross-cultural acumen at the proficient or expert level—in other words, cultural intelligence? At a minimum, cross-cultural leaders—the Glopats and Globals or the developmental/high-potential expatriates and strategic/executive expatriates discussed earlier—must have a comprehensive view of different countries' cultural practices. The GLOBE study found that it is imperative to understand the "culturally endorsed implicit leadership theory" leadership profile of the culture cluster in which they will be working. These *globally literate* leaders must be able to answer questions such as:

- What leadership qualities and business practices are fundamental to my own national culture?
- How can I create business cultures that mobilize diverse people in a multicultural world?
- How do businesses in different countries operate in culturally unique ways?
- What are the lessons and innovations to be learned around the world?[51]

Development of cross-cultural leaders with the ability to answer sophisticated questions such as these requires that the company make a major investment in human capital, an investment that is well planned and integrated throughout the leader's career path. At the same time, it also requires willingness on the future leader's part to make the personal investment needed to reach the expert or proficient cross-cultural leadership level. The company and the leader are truly partners in this development journey. Development of cross-cultural leadership skills at this expert or proficient mastery level takes time.

There are no shortcuts. The development journey requires that the leader be assigned to real work in cross-cultural settings in a progressively sequenced stretch assignment career path, one that takes the leader from novice to expert proficiency levels. The future leader must know and accept that he or she will feel awkward at many points throughout this process.

First, second, and even third international postings with increasingly enlarged scopes of responsibility provide opportunities for the development of expert cross-cultural leadership proficiency. Taking the leader to the expert cross-cultural leadership level also requires providing a resource-rich environment for the leader that should include networking opportunities with other global leaders at world summits like the World Economic Forum at Davos, Switzerland, or international forums at the Aspen Institute. Other helpful experiences would include rich developmental feedback from multiple sources (ideally in cross-cultural settings) on multiple dimensions—such as 360-degree performance feedback and executive coaching, and opportunities for reflection through developmental training programs, sabbaticals, and time away from day-to-day work pressures. The leader must be willing to actively listen, actively reflect, and actively learn!

On the other hand, those expatriates on more tactical assignments— the Regionals or Mobile or Rooted Nationals or the technical or functional/tactical expatriates discussed earlier—must have many of the interpersonal skills identified in Table 14.1, including cross-cultural communication effectiveness, intercultural adaptability, and competence in developing and maintaining good interpersonal relationships. These competencies also take time to develop and should be part of a strategic human resource planning system. However, there are techniques—classroom training, role playing, and simulations, for example—that bootstrap the expatriate's skills and accelerate the time needed for cross-cultural success for those going on more tactical assignments. Best practices for leader development for these more tactical assignments include predeparture and postdeparture cross-cultural knowledge and skill training and, once in the new role, the use of cultural mentors, a function often filled by Rooted or Mobile Local Nationals.

The journey to cross-cultural leadership at the proficient- or expert-level mastery is a long one. Taking stock of personal progress on a regular basis can keep the journey on the right track. Asking the following questions on an annual basis can help the leader aspiring to grow cross-cultural competency with this process:

- How have I contributed to my organization's global competitiveness?
- What have I added to my international experience track record?
- What have I learned that will add to my cross-cultural competencies?
- How many new people have I gotten to know? How diverse are these people?
- Have I strengthened my international and diverse domestic relationships?
- Have I been choosing stretch assignments that make me interact with different others?
- What experiences have I had that push me out of my comfort zone?
- What have I learned about myself from these experiences?
- If my cross-cultural leadership competencies are not growing, have I made the wrong job or organization choice?
- If so, is it best for me and the organization that I move on?

EXECUTIVE SUMMARY

The most common reason that organizations do not have exceptional global leadership is a lack of commitment to the process of developing it. The problem is not lack of know-how. . . . The problem is that with the complexity and risk, few organizations have adopted a model robust enough to fit the challenge and then committed the time and resources necessary to implement it.

—Morgan McCall and George Hollenbeck, Developing Global Executives *(2002)*[52]

In this chapter we have seen many dimensions of this complexity and many of the obstacles that inhibit implementation of a robust cross-cultural leader development process or model. Organizations can increase the probability of successfully developing cross-cultural leaders by implementing the following four practices.

First, *organizations must have clarity on what kind of global executives with what kinds of skills are needed from a strategic perspective.* Consider Komatsu: United States-based Caterpillar is Komatsu's toughest competitor the world over. "*Maru-C*" or "Encircle Caterpillar" is Komatsu's vision and rallying cry. All Komatsu managers on a senior-position career path are therefore required to serve at least one assignment in the United States.

Second, *organizations should use experience as a teacher by providing relevant developmental opportunities for those capabilities the organization is trying to develop.* For example, in the 1980s Colgate-Palmolive had a difficult time finding high-quality employees for top international assignments. In response, they implemented a program of systematically providing opportunities for high-potential managers to work in a variety of global markets to develop those critical cross-cultural leadership skills for top executives. They no longer have difficulty finding high-quality employees for top international assignments.

Third, *organizations must provide appropriate levels of feedback, resources, and support to help people learn from the experiences they have.* The Conference Board's recent study on global talent development found that 47 percent of the survey respondents believe that providing targeted feedback on performance and potential is the most effective tactic in accelerating and nurturing global talent.[53]

Finally, *by providing international perspectives and exposure starting early in people's careers, organizations maximize the quality of their cross-culturally expert pipeline.*

Cross-cultural leadership best practice begins with a deep understanding of the contributions that human capital makes in today's dynamic, competitive global business environment. Does the organization's ability to compete require international assignments? Increasingly the response is a resounding yes, even for "domestic" companies that cannot escape the globalization tsunami. The single critical success factor in globalizing business lies with the pool of highly competent global leaders who possess the global knowledge of production and service capabilities and consumer demand for products and services around the world. Cross-cultural leadership competency is the lynchpin for this success, and cross-cultural competencies elevate a business leader to highly competent global leader status. Best practice mandates the development of a pool of leaders with cross-cultural competencies to meet the organization's strategic imperatives and competitive demands.

Who are cross-cultural leaders? There is not one kind of cross-cultural leader; they vary by the scope of their responsibilities, the content of their work, the complexity of their work, the location of their work, their willingness and ability to travel globally, the expectations of their followers, their career stages, and their own development needs. What cross-cultural leaders do have in common is the fact that they cross cultures and contexts regularly in their work; they must be able to maneuver across these multiple boundaries fraught with multiple local expectations; and that reflective capacity enhances the ability to do this well. Best practice is moving beyond a focus simply on the development of cross-cultural competencies to providing the leader with the resources—often knowledge, networks, and time— needed for reflection and learning from international experiences and the key drivers of the organization's and the global leader's own success.

Approaches to the identification of cross-cultural leadership competencies are numerous and fraught with definitional imprecision: whether we call them global competencies, global literacies, or cross-cultural leadership skills, the panoply of global leadership and cross-cultural competencies can be categorized as (1) threshold or foundation competencies that begin with traits or natural abilities and rest on cross-cultural knowledge and a base of business or technical skills; (2) attitudes and orientations; (3) interpersonal skills; and (4) systems skills. There is consensus that these competencies can be developed through a combination of international and local stretch assignments orchestrated through the strategic succession planning, and that traits like open-mindedness, resilience, cognitive complexity, curiosity, and willingness to learn are very important to a cross-cultural leader's effectiveness. Best practice requires the organization to link the identification of competencies needed and the timing and location of these needs to the organization's strategy.

Mastery of cross-cultural leadership competencies is progressive and cumulative. Global leaders identify the international assignment as the single most influential experience in their lives. The development of cross-cultural leadership competencies requires the reinforcement of international experience with an appropriate level of feedback, resources, and support to enable reflective learning. Multinationals around the world use a combination of expatriation and extensive international business travel to develop cross-cultural competencies. Given the relatively high turnover rate among repatriated assignees, strategic repatriation policies must be considered as the final step in the development of cross-cultural leaders. Attention must be given to the strategic alignment of the multinational's need for talent and the competencies that the repatriated assignees bring upon their return. Best practices in cross-cultural leadership competency development require the use of international assignments that include feedback, resources, and support that enable reflective learning, with care being given to the management of turnover among repatriated assignees.

Cross-cultural leaders who are filling Glopat and Global positions must have a comprehensive view of different countries' cultural practices. They must understand cultural differences and cultural similarities and be able to lead effectively across different cultures by reading changing cues that others do not read. These globally literate leaders must be able to answer questions such as:

- What leadership qualities and business practices are fundamental to my own national culture?
- How can I create business cultures that mobilize diverse people in a multicultural world?
- How do businesses in different countries operate in culturally unique ways?
- What are the lessons and innovations to be learned around the world?[54]

Expatriates on more tactical assignments also need cross-cultural interpersonal skills, including cross-cultural communication effectiveness, intercultural adaptability, and competence in developing and maintaining good interpersonal relationships. Best practice mandates that the multinational clarify its reasons for using the expatriate and then manage the development of cross-cultural leadership skills accordingly. The best way to accelerate global leadership development is to identify talent early and nurture cross-cultural competency development step by step. Globalization is a powerful force. Cross-cultural leadership development is a critical success factor for corporations aspiring to excel in the globalized business environment. Cross-cultural leadership matters, and it matters now more than ever before. There is no hiding place for companies or their leaders in the new, complex, integrated, dynamic, global business environment.

CHAPTER FIFTEEN

Getting It Right

The Practice of Leadership

Ronald E. Riggio
Jay A. Conger

Effective leadership is not easy, and there is no easy path to becoming an effective leader. Leadership is in and of itself one of the most complex of human endeavors. Moreover, leading in today's increasingly complicated and fast-paced world is becoming more and more difficult. Add into that mix the greater complexity of organizations and a more empowered (and demanding) group of followers, and the challenge of being an effective leader seems almost insurmountable.

The theme of this book, and of the conference that preceded it, was to gather together scholars, each an expert in a particular area of leadership, and ask them to extract from a vast and rich body of research the insights that could truly inform the practice of leadership. The ultimate goal was to inform practicing leaders about what works and what does not.

A topic as complex as leadership can be studied from multiple angles and broken down into a number of foundational or key elements; each of these elements can in turn be analyzed in great detail. The chapters in this book represent those elements that we felt were the most important factors in determining effective leadership for today's world. Together, they represent a solid core for understanding how organizations and individuals can maximize their leadership potential and effectiveness.

So what do we know about the practice of leadership? One thing is certain: from decades of research we know more about getting it wrong than about getting it right. From leader selection to assessment, from leading diverse groups to leading in times of crisis, from leading individuals to leading international groups, from leading strategically to leading ethically, we can say with some certainty what leadership approaches will not succeed. For example, the research evidence in leader selection suggests that unstructured interviews are not as effective as other selection methods, and handwriting analysis (graphology) is particularly ineffective (see Chapter One). Yet it is perplexing to see how often these ineffective strategies are used in practice. Similarly, it is not surprising to see the attention directed toward studying bad leadership,[1] and to understanding the reasons why leaders fail.[2] Popular books chronicle the ethical failures of leaders and explore how leaders get derailed.[3] On the other hand, it is harder to say authoritatively what will succeed.

But this is often the path of the human and social sciences. We learn about good health practices by studying how poor diet, hygiene, and inactivity cause disease. We learn how the human brain functions by studying localized damage to brain centers. We have greater understanding of how the mind functions by studying common errors, such as optical illusions and fundamental biases.[4] And we can learn more about good leadership practices by learning why and how leaders fail.

Understanding how to get the practice of leadership right is typically more complicated because so often the answer is "It depends." Good leadership involves the leader doing the right thing for the particular circumstances—taking into account the task, the followers, the situation, the timing, and the process. For this very reason, formulaic approaches and techniques are likely to have very mixed results when it comes to leadership. Each situation presents a unique combination of opportunities and challenges that no simple framework can fully answer for the leader facing that situation. That said, in recent years, the field of leadership research has matured greatly. Researchers today recognize the complexity of the leadership task. Models and frameworks are no longer simple and universal. We no longer just study airplane crews and basketball teams to extrapolate leadership lessons for the manager. The field has also matured in its understanding of leadership practices. Today we are able to provide more useful and sophisticated advice than we could have 10 or 15 years ago, thanks to rich studies of practicing leaders and their successes and failures. With that in mind, let's turn now to the lessons learned from the expert authors we assembled for the task of informing our ability to practice leadership.

From Part One of this book, on leader selection and development, we can conclude that we know the most about assessing leaders, we can determine some of the better (if not the best) practices for selecting leaders, and we probably know the least about sure-fire ways to develop leaders. Yet there is still much in each area that informs the successful practice of leadership.

Ann Howard (Chapter One) makes a very compelling case that getting leader selection right has huge financial and performance impact on the organization. As she reviews the "technology" of leader selection (for example, screening tests, biodata, interviews, assessment centers), it becomes clear that the use of the more sophisticated selection tools, such as assessment centers that feature simulations of multiple leader functions, is superior to relying primarily on inferences gained from interviews and a review of candidates' résumés and career achievements. Howard also advocates using multiple screening and selection methods and sticking to a process that fits the organization's specific needs and its abilities to support the selection system, including the costs and benefits of the various selection methods.

The "takeaways" from Howard's chapter include:

- When possible, use sophisticated selection tools that simulate leader behaviors (for example, assessment centers) when hiring.

- Use multiple selection methods. Don't rely on (or give too much weight to) one method (for example, a single interview performance) or piece of information.

- Tailor your selection methods to your particular needs, with an emphasis on the leadership outcomes you need and want.

- Make sure that the selection system becomes embedded in the organization and aligned with other organizational systems and values.

In their comprehensive chapter, London, Smither, and Diamante (Chapter Two) are also interested in assessing leaders for selection purposes, but focus greater attention on evaluating leader performance for development purposes and for better understanding of how leaders impact group and organizational performance. These authors emphasize the use of multiple assessment methods to most effectively measure different aspects of leader performance. For instance, the means for measuring a leader's financial impact may be quite different from assessments made for evaluating a leader for developmental purposes. Important practice points include:

- Assessment of leader performance and accompanying feedback needs to be an ongoing practice of continuous improvement rather than a once-a-year event.

- Assessment of leader performance needs to pay attention to the *outcomes* of a leader's efforts and also help to understand the *process* by which leaders do their jobs.

- Use a balanced scorecard of measures that aligns organizational, team, and individual goals with associated performance indicators to adequately assess high-level leader performance.

- Ensure that the performance assessment methods are sound and are appropriate for the particular needs of the organization, the team, and the individual leader.

In Chapter Three, Patricia O'Connor and David Day argue strongly that the focus on developing individual leaders who are expected to deal with the multiple challenges of today's increasingly complex world is wrongheaded. Instead, these authors assert that we need to develop collective forms of leadership that involve people participating throughout the organization sharing in the creation of a unified leadership.

Several of the most important takeaway messages from this chapter include:

- Build collective leadership identities such that individuals in the organization see themselves as part of the shared leadership effort.

- Look for problem or project areas in the organization that require shared leadership, are open to an action learning approach, and would benefit from it.

- Invest the time and resources so that the action learning can become well integrated into the organization; give the program the time and support needed so that it can succeed.

- Realize that although action learning can lead to significant outcomes, it should be compatible with the organization's current needs and structure.

McCall and Hollenbeck (Chapter Four) provide a critique of many of the existing leadership development programs for top-level executives. These programs' failure, according to these authors, is that they try to develop a general "laundry list" of leader competencies. Instead, what is needed are more customized notions of competent performance on the job as a framework for leadership development efforts. Despite their criticism of traditional competency approaches, the authors echo some of the best practices (for example, experience-based learning; development programs that are tailored to specific leadership situations) promoted in earlier chapters. The chapter also offers important guidelines for using executive coaches for leadership development.

Important takeaway messages from the McCall and Hollenbeck chapter include:

- View leadership development as an ongoing, on-the-job process of providing challenging learning experiences for leaders.

- Concentrate greater development efforts on the individuals identified as high-potential leaders.

- Benefit from the leader's own superior, who can play a significant role in helping him or her learn important leadership lessons from key experiences.

- Use properly deployed executive coaches to help leaders learn and develop from their experiences.

Part Two of this book focuses on some of the critical tasks leaders perform. Specifically, leaders use influence to help groups and organizations achieve goals. In addition, in this increasingly complex world, leaders are expected to lead not just for productivity but also for creativity. Even the most productive and creative organizations and groups can fall prey to ethical violations that can wreak havoc and ultimately destroy the unit, so ethical leading is a critical task. Finally, leading teams is discussed in depth.

Gary Yukl (Chapter Five) discusses the various sorts of influence tactics leaders use to build follower commitment or to gain their compliance in an effort to achieve work outcomes. To effectively wield tactics of influence, a leader needs to consider elements of the situation, including the characteristics of the followers, the leader's personal history with them, and other factors. By fully understanding how and why different types of influence may or may not work, the leader can be much more successful.

Specific takeaway messages from Chapter Five include:

- Elicit follower commitment to a request or proposal by using the most effective proactive influence tactics: rational persuasion, inspirational appeals, consultation, and collaboration.

- Link inspirational appeals to an appealing vision and ensure that they are consistent with the followers' ideals and values.

- Increase followers' involvement and commitment level by using consultation and collaboration.

- Using logical combinations of influence tactics may be more effective than relying on one type of influence alone.

Mumford and colleagues' chapter on leading for innovation (Chapter Six) is a rich analysis of the complexities of leading creative groups and work teams. It is often believed that creative groups of knowledge workers are self-led teams using "shared leadership." Although this is true to some extent, the authors argue that there are many important functions performed by leaders of creative teams. For example, the leader should provide a safe, collaborative environment in which idea generation and some element of risk taking are promoted. As the authors state, the leader needs to "manage people just as they manage ideas."

Some of the important lessons learned include:

- Stay actively involved in the development of new ideas and help bring the ideas to fruition.

- Use a sense of mission or common purpose to encourage team member innovation and commitment.

- Lead creative groups effectively by having high levels of relevant knowledge and expertise as well as the ability to lead the process.
- Promote sophisticated creativity training for leaders of innovative groups and organizations who need to recognize and respond to novel ideas.

Craig Johnson's chapter (Chapter Seven) states that ethical leadership is one of the most important challenges for leaders. He argues that leaders have an obligation to shoulder the ethical *burdens* of leadership. These include being acutely sensitive to issues of ethics and considering ethics to be a key part of "doing business." In addition, effective and ethical leaders are proactive—taking steps to avoid creating a climate that either encourages or condones unethical behavior. Moreover, leaders must be ethical role models for followers. Considering the visibility and status given to high-level organizational leaders (and the near-celebrity standing of Fortune 500 chief executive officers [CEOs]), it is imperative that top leaders be exemplars of ethicality both in the organization and in their personal lives.

According to Johnson, ethical leaders need to:

- Be aware of and not fall prey to unhealthy motivations (for example, insecurity, greed, ego) and destructive behaviors.
- Proactively work to create a positive ethical climate.
- Develop methods to critically evaluate situations from an ethical perspective.
- Work to develop one's own personal virtues and patterns of ethical actions, and encourage ethical behaviors in others.

The chapter on team leadership by Stagl, Salas, and Burke (Chapter Eight) suggests that although many of today's high-level teams of skilled professional workers may engage in self-management and shared leadership, team leaders still play a vital role in the performance and effectiveness of work teams. Team leaders play a critical role in the creation of work teams and in guiding and supporting their efforts. Best practices for effectively leading teams include:

- Define team members' respective roles and foster successful interdependencies among team members (as opposed to simply letting it happen on its own).

- Define clearly the responsibilities, outcomes, and goals of individuals and of the collective team; reward and celebrate accomplishments.
- Provide inspiration and motivation by providing compelling vision and direction for the team and emphasizing the common mission.
- Use coaching teams to help team members coordinate activities, facilitate team performance, and help them develop into high-performing teams.

Part Three of the book explores leadership at the organizational level, examining how leaders play a part in organizational transitions, effective leadership at strategic levels, and how corporate boards play a crucial part in organizational leadership.

An expert on how organizations handle major transitions such as mergers, takeovers, and whole-scale downsizing efforts, Mitchell Marks (Chapter Nine) uses these significant transitions as a framework for understanding leadership in particularly stressful times. Marks emphasizes that leading during a major organizational transition is best approached in a step-by-step process with distinct phases and tasks for the leader.

Some of the best practices in leading organizational transitions include:

- Recognize the natural "human" reactions to stressful transitions—fear, anger and resentment, resistance to changes—and take proactive steps to recognize these while helping employees resolve them.
- Get people involved in the transition process by providing honest information and empowering them to participate in the positive transition from the old to the new organization.
- Demonstrate commitment to the organizational transition through a compelling vision of the future, through commitment to the process, and by providing the resources needed to successfully accomplish the transition.
- Pay attention to enforcing the posttransition organization through alignment of vision, enforcing appropriate on-the-job behaviors, and measuring and tracking the new structure and organizational culture.

David Waldman discusses the practice of leadership at strategic levels (Chapter Ten). He advocates taking a social responsibility orientation and provides justification for why a strategy driven by social responsibility is a better way to lead an organization. Specifically, Waldman provides evidence that over time socially responsible firms outperform those that are less socially responsible, and they avoid the devastating scandals that have plagued many once-great organizations (for example Adelphia, Enron, WorldCom).

Waldman argues that socially responsible leaders have a broader view of the organization's impact, focusing beyond short-term profits and emphasizing the quality of relationships with multiple stakeholders— customers, stockholders, the organization's employees, and the local and larger communities. In order to lead effectively at the strategic level, best practices include:

- Articulate a shared vision that will energize followers and also appeal to the organization's multiple stakeholders.

- Promote shared leadership that involves followers in the strategic process in order to develop a truly compelling vision.

- Foster an environment that encourages organizational members to engage and live their moral values at work.

- Demonstrate integrity, and be straightforward and "transparent" in sharing information that has direct effects on the organization's stakeholders.

In his chapter on board leadership, Jay Conger (Chapter Eleven) begins with the premise that leadership by corporate boards is oftentimes lacking. Conger argues that some high-profile corporate disasters might have been avoided had their boards exercised appropriate oversight and good leadership.

Conger points out what's wrong with the historic tradition of allowing the chief executive officer to perform as the board's head. He makes the "Two heads are better than one" argument, noting that an independent board chair or even a lead director can help foster independent oversight of the company and the CEO and provide diverse perspectives on issues and problems. An alternative—and one that is becoming more popular—is having strong committee leadership, although this solution has the drawback of providing no centralized board "authority."

For improving board leadership it is important that:

- Board members view themselves as playing a leadership role, as opposed to being mere advisors to the CEO. Regardless of the leadership structure of the organization, boards that take their leadership role to heart are more likely to avoid the bad decisions and ethical debacles that have destroyed many once-mighty corporations.

- Independent directors should constitute a majority and control key board committees.

- The board should be able to conduct independent analyses of issues and outcomes without having to rely solely on information provided by the CEO.

- The board should conduct serious and regular evaluations of the CEO's performance and engage in proactive succession planning.

Part Four, the final part of the book, focuses primarily on leading in today's complex world. It begins with a discussion of leading during crisis situations—a critical capability in this era of national and international disasters—continues with a discussion of leading diverse organizations, and ends with a focus on global leadership.

In his chapter on leading during crisis situations, Ian Mitroff (Chapter Twelve) argues that leading in times of crisis requires proactive thinking and planning. He suggests that the forms of leadership needed during crises are fundamentally different from leadership that is successful in "normal" times.

To lead successfully in a crisis-ridden world:

- Be proactive; play the "devil's advocate" and imagine worst-case scenarios; question your personal assumptions and those of your organization about "normality."

- Prepare emotionally and spiritually for the shock and loss a crisis will inevitably cause.

- Create an organizational mechanism to deal with crises; train key individuals in the organization in crisis management and run practice scenarios.

- Learn the leadership requirements necessary for uncertain circumstances.

In their chapter on leading diverse organizations, Offermann and Matos (Chapter Thirteen) emphasize that leading today's increasingly diverse groups represents a significant leadership challenge. Diverse work groups and organizations have both benefits and significant costs. For example, greater diversity is associated with critically thinking groups with members holding multiple viewpoints and perspectives that can be beneficial to a unit's ability to be creative. Diverse organizations are also more attractive places to work—better able to attract and retain employees. On the other hand, diversity can lead to divisiveness and dissatisfaction, particularly if not managed well. The key element for managing diversity to maximize benefits and minimize costs is effective leadership.

Important conclusions from this chapter include:

- Look broadly at diversity, beyond simply gender and racial diversity, considering also cultural and subcultural differences and issues. The leader needs to provide a unifying vision and a culture committed to common goals and acceptance of diverse members.
- Be sensitive to others' cultural differences, but also be aware of how one's own culture can impact others.
- Champion diversity, be flexible and adaptable, be insightful and inclusive, and set and communicate challenging goals and positive expectations for all followers.
- Use mentoring programs as one of the best ways to manage diverse work groups and help mentor-leaders and protégés better understand persons from diverse backgrounds.

In her chapter on cross-cultural leadership (Chapter Fourteen), Mary Teagarden asserts that corporate success in today's world requires competent global leaders. In this chapter, Teagarden describes the characteristics, skills, and qualities needed for effective global leadership, as well as providing guidelines for the development of these cross-cultural attributes. For leaders, the takeaway messages from this very detailed discussion of the topic include:

- Become "culturally intelligent"—able to cross cultures and contexts and function effectively in a variety of settings.

- Develop cross-cultural competency through a step-by-step process of building a knowledge base and strengthening key competencies (for example, dealing with complexity, inquisitiveness, adaptability) that combine for success.

- Develop cross-cultural leadership by requiring executives to gain significant experience living and working in international assignments.

- Develop cross-cultural leaders through an integrated system of selecting the best prospects, cross-cultural training, strategic international assignments, and ongoing performance feedback.

An important question is whether there are common themes that can be distilled from this wide array of chapters. The answer is "Yes." There are several important themes about leadership effectiveness and success that appear in many of the book's chapters.

Leaders need to engage and involve followers. It is quite clear from decades of research that an essential task of leaders is to motivate followers. While motivation can be encouraged in a transactional way, such as by offering rewards for desired behaviors or outcomes, it takes much more to build long-term commitment to the leader and to the group or organization. To get this sort of deep commitment, leaders need to inspire followers through a compelling vision or mission. They must make all members of the group or their organization feel as if they are part of the process. Moreover, in today's cutting-edge organizations, where team members are likely to be highly knowledgeable and talented, it is critical for the leader to allow his or her followers to take an active role in setting course and in making decisions. This engagement builds more than affective commitment on the part of followers. It often leads simply to better outcomes. The concept of "shared leadership" is one that is mentioned in many of this book's chapters, and it seems increasingly important in leading modern organizations.

Effective leaders monitor, measure, and adapt. Good leaders must be constantly vigilant. They keep their finger on the pulse of followers and of the organization. Many of our authors mention the importance of staying "tuned in" to followers and employees at all levels, whether through "management by walking around," formal or informal mentoring programs, formal feedback mechanisms, or shared strategic planning and decision making.

Many chapters also emphasize the importance of measuring the outcomes of leadership efforts—the impact on performance measures, the effect on followers, and the impact on the bottom line. Effective leadership requires that leaders have ongoing streams of critical data at their fingertips to help them better understand what is going on in their organizations.

Several chapter authors highlight the fact that the best leaders adapt to the ever-changing circumstances that are commonplace in today's world. In actuality, these three elements—monitoring, measuring, and adapting—go hand in hand. Effective leadership is about knowing and understanding your followers, being aware of how the organization is performing, and making the necessary adjustments to keep everything and everyone moving forward in a positive direction.

Leaders need to model the way. Leaders need to be true to their visions, missions, and values. It is very hard to get others to buy into a vision, to be true to the organization's mission, or to adhere to shared values if the leader is not out in front setting the pace and serving as a positive role model. This is particularly true in regard to ethical practices, but it involves other areas as well.

Several of the authors suggest that leaders need to "get their hands dirty"—getting intimately involved with teams and developing relevant expertise. For example, Mumford and associates suggest that when leading highly creative groups the best leaders are those with relevant expertise, but also those who understand the creative process.

Leaders need to be proactive. Effective leaders, like masters of chess, think several moves ahead, considering possibilities and "What if?" scenarios. Moreover, by anticipating future needs and courses of action, the leader can prevent problems before they happen. In his chapter on leading during crises, Ian Mitroff goes so far as to suggest that leaders should work through the emotional aspects of a worst-case-scenario crisis even in the absence of any impending threat.

There are no shortcuts; effective leadership is a long-term, developmental process. All too often, leaders search for the seemingly elusive key to success—the one best means or method of leading successfully. Unfortunately, there are no easy answers to leading effectively.

Leading well in today's world often strains leaders to their limits. It requires a great deal of knowledge and skill. Leaders need to be able to initiate and maintain high-quality relationships with followers and others. Leaders must analyze, strategize, prioritize, mobilize, empathize, and economize—and do all of this well, consistent with the organization's mission, in an ethical manner, and in an increasingly uncertain environment. Is it really any wonder that truly great leaders are scarce? Is it any wonder that our approaches to leadership development need to be more long term, rigorous, and sophisticated?

Bearing in mind that there are no easy solutions, it is clear that developing oneself as an effective leader requires a great deal of time and effort. It takes a lot of personal commitment and motivation. Like medicine and many other professions, leadership is partly science and partly practice. The science of leadership involves scholars' ongoing search for what works and what doesn't. The term *practice* suggests that leaders can always learn how to do it better. Our intent has been to take what has been learned from scholarship and use it to inform leadership practice. Our aim has been to help good leaders become even better and to help the very best leaders become truly exceptional. The world needs them.

~~~ Notes

Chapter One: Best Practices in Leader Selection

1. Hogan, R., and Kaiser, R. B. "What We Know about Leadership." *Review of General Psychology,* 2005, *9*(2), 169–180.
2. Fernandez-Araoz, C. "Hiring without Firing." *Harvard Business Review,* 1999 (July–August), 109–120.
3. Lucier, C., Schuyt, R., and Tse, E. "CEO Succession 2004: The World's Most Prominent Temp Workers." *strategy+business,* 2005 (39), 29–43.
4. Pittinsky, T. L., Rosenthal, S. A., Welle, B., and Montoya, R. M. *National Leadership Index 2005: A National Study of Confidence in Leadership.* Cambridge, Mass.: Harvard University, John F. Kennedy School of Government, Center for Public Leadership, 2005.
5. Bernthal, P. R., and Erker, S. *Selection Forecast: Recruiting and Hiring Talent.* Pittsburgh: Development Dimensions International, 2005.
6. Lucier and others, "CEO Succession 2004."
7. "Insider CEOs Believed to Outperform Outsider CEOs According to Business Influencers." [http://www.burson-marsteller.com/pages/news/releases/2004/press-03-03-2004].
8. Campbell, J. P., McCloy, R. A., Oppler, S. H., and Sager, C. E. "A Theory of Performance." In N. Schmitt, W. Borman, and Associates (eds.), *Personnel Selection in Organizations* (pp. 35–70). San Francisco: Jossey-Bass, 1993.
9. Ibid.
10. Bernthal and Erker, *Selection Forecast.*
11. Harter, J. K., Schmidt, F. L., and Hayes, T. L. "Business-Unit-Level Relationship between Employee Satisfaction, Employee Engagement, and Business Outcomes: A Meta-Analysis." *Journal of Applied Psychology,* 2002, *87*, 268–279.
12. Robertson, I. T., and Smith, M. "Personnel Selection." *Journal of Occupational and Organizational Psychology,* 2001, *74*(4), 441ff.
13. Bernthal and Erker, *Selection Forecast.*
14. Hausknecht, J. P., Day, D. V., and Thomas, S. C. "Applicant Reactions to Selection Procedures: An Updated Model and Meta-Analysis." *Personnel Psychology,* 2004, *57*, 639–683.

15. Russell, C. "A Longitudinal Study of Top-Level Executive Performance." *Journal of Applied Psychology,* 2001, *86*(4), 560–573.

16. Howard, A. "Identifying, Assessing, and Selecting Senior Leaders." In S. J. Zaccaro and R. Klimoski (eds.), *The Nature and Context of Organizational Leadership* (pp. 305–346). San Francisco: Jossey-Bass, 2001.

17. Lucier and others, "CEO Succession 2004."

18. Bernthal and Erker, *Selection Forecast.*

19. Ibid.

20. Crenshaw, J. "The Use of Video and Audio Technology in the Structured Interview Process: A Meta-Analytic Review of Reliability and Race-Based Group Differences." Paper presented at the 20th Annual Conference of the Society for Industrial/Organizational Psychology, Los Angeles, 2005.

21. Robertson and Smith, "Personnel Selection."

22. Chan, D. "Current Directions in Personnel Selection Research." *Current Directions in Psychological Science,* 2005, *14*(4), 220–223.

23. Campbell and others, "A Theory of Performance."

24. Jansen, P.G.W., and Stoop, B.A.M. "The Dynamics of Assessment Center Validity: Results of a 7-Year Study." *Journal of Applied Psychology,* 2001, *86*(4), 741–753; Russell, C. "A Longitudinal Study of Top-Level Executive Performance." *Journal of Applied Psychology,* 2001, *86*(4), 560–573.

25. Russell, "Longitudinal Study of Top-Level Executive Performance."

26. Howard, A., and Bray, D. W. *Managerial Lives in Transition: Advancing Age and Changing Times.* New York: Guilford, 1988.

27. Bartram, D. "Assessment in Organisations." *Applied Psychology: An International Review,* 2004, *53*(2), 237ff.

28. Garman, A. N. "Assessing Candidates for Leadership Positions." In R. L. Lowman (ed.), *California School of Organizational Studies: Handbook of Organizational Consulting Psychology: A Comprehensive Guide to Theory, Skills, and Techniques* (pp. 185–211). San Francisco: Jossey Bass, 2002; Howard, "Identifying, Assessing, and Selecting Senior Leaders."

29. Bartram, "Assessment in Organisations."

30. Ibid.

31. Cejka, Search & Solucient, LLC. *Hospital CEO Leadership Survey.* St. Louis, Mo., and Evanston, Ill.: Authors, 2005.

32. Hausknecht and others, "Applicant Reactions to Selection Procedures."

33. McDaniel, M. A., and others. "Use of Situational Judgment Tests to Predict Job Performance: A Clarification of the Literature. *Journal of Applied Psychology,* 2001, *86*(4), 730–740.

34. Hogan and Kaiser, "What We Know about Leadership."

35. Robertson and Smith, "Personnel Selection."

36. Fernandez-Araoz, "Hiring without Firing."

37. Hogan and Kaiser, "What We Know about Leadership."

38. Arthur, W. Jr., Woehr, D. J., and Graziano, W. G. "Personality Testing in Employment Settings: Problems and Issues in the Application of Typical Selection Processes." *Personnel Review,* 2001, *30*(6), 657–676.

39. Day, D. V., and Silverman, S. B. "Personality and Job Performance: Evidence of Incremental Validity." *Personnel Psychology,* 1989, *42,* 25–36.

40. McCall, W. M., and Lombardo, M. M. *Off the Track: Why and How Successful Executives Get Derailed.* Greensboro, N.C.: Center for Creative Leadership, 1983.

41. Arthur and others, "Personality Testing in Employment Settings."

42. Hogan, R., Hogan, J., and Roberts, B. W. "Personality Measurement and Employment Decisions: Questions and Answers." *American Psychologist,* 1996, *51*(5), 469–477.

43. Bartram, "Assessment in Organisations."

44. Hausknecht and others, "Applicant Reactions to Selection Procedures."

45. Robertson and Smith, "Personnel Selection."

46. Hogan and others, "Personality Measurement and Employment Decisions."

47. Hough, L. M., and others. "Criterion-Related Validities of Personality Constructs and the Effect of Response Distortion on Those Validities." *Journal of Applied Psychology Monograph,* 1990, *75*(5), 581–595.

48. Bernthal and Erker, *Selection Forecast.*

49. Cascio, W. *Applied Psychology in Human Resource Management* (5th ed.). New York: Prentice Hall, 1997.

50. Judge, T. A., and Piccolo, R. F. "Transformational and Transactional Leadership: A Meta-Analytic Test of Their Relative Validity." *Journal of Applied Psychology,* 2004, *89*(5) 755–768.

51. Russell, "Longitudinal Study of Top-Level Executive Performance."

52. Reilly, R. R., and Chao, G. T. "Validity and Fairness of Some Alternative Employee Selection Procedures." *Personnel Psychology,* 1982, *35,* 1–62.

53. Howard and Bray, *Managerial Lives in Transition.*

54. Schmidt, F. L., and Hunter, J. E. "The Validity and Utility of Selection Methods in Personnel Psychology: Practical and Theoretical Implications of 85 Years of Research Findings." *Psychological Bulletin,* 1998, *124,* 262–274.

55. Shackleton, V., and Newell, S. "Management Selection: A Comparative Survey of Methods Used in Top British and French Companies." *Journal of Occupational Psychology,* 1991, *64,* 23–36.

56. Conway, J. M., Jako, R. A., and Goodman, D. F. "A Meta-Analysis of Interrater and Internal Consistency Reliability of Selection Interviews." *Journal of Applied Psychology,* 1995, *80*(5), 565–579.

57. Hough, L. M., and Oswald, F. L. "Personnel Selection: Looking toward the Future—Remembering the Past." *Annual Review of Psychology,* 2000, *51,* 631–664.

58. Crenshaw, "Use of Video and Audio Technology in the Structured Interview Process."

59. Huffcutt, A. I., and others. "Comparison of Situational and Behavior Description Interview Questions for Higher-Level Positions." *Personnel Psychology,* 2001, *54,* 619–644; Pulakos, E. D., and Schmitt, N. "Experience-Based and Situational Interview Questions: Studies of Validity." *Personnel Psychology,* 1995, *48,* 289–308.

60. Taylor, P. J., and Small, B. "Asking Applicants What They Would Do versus What They Did Do: A Meta-Analytic Comparison of Situational and Behaviour Employment Interview Questions." *Journal of Occupational and Organizational Psychology,* 2002, *75,* 277–294.

61. Huffcutt and others. "Comparison of Situational and Behavior Description Interview Questions."

62. Robertson and Smith, "Personnel Selection."

63. Hunter, J. E., and Hunter, R. F. "Validity and Utility of Alternative Predictors of Job Performance." *Psychological Bulletin,* 1984, *96,* 72–98.

64. Howard, A. "A Reassessment of Assessment Centers: Challenges for the 21st Century." *Journal of Social Behavior and Personality, Assessment Centers: Research and Applications* [Special issue], 1997, *12*(5), 13–52; Thornton, G. C. III, and Rupp, D. E. *Assessment Centers in Human Resource Management: Strategies for Prediction, Diagnosis, and Development.* Mahwah, N.J.: Erlbaum, 2005.

65. Cascio, *Applied Psychology in Human Resource Management;* Thornton, G. C. III, and Byham, W. C. *Assessment Centers and Managerial Performance.* New York: Academic Press, 1982.

66. Howard and Bray, *Managerial Lives in Transition.*

67. Toegel, G., and Conger, J. A. "360-Degree Feedback: Time for Reinvention." *Academy of Management Learning and Education Journal,* 2003, 297–311.

68. Howard and Bray, *Managerial Lives in Transition.*

69. Sackett, P., and Ellington, J. E. "The Effects of Forming Multi-Predictor Composites on Group Differences and Adverse Impact." *Personnel Psychology,* 1997, *50,* 707–721.

70. Conway and others, "Meta-Analysis of Interrater and Internal Consistency Reliability of Selection Interviews."

71. Ibid.

72. Chan, D., and Schmitt, N. "Video-Based versus Paper-and-Pencil Method of Assessment in Situational Judgment Tests: Subgroup Differences in

Performance and Face Validity Perceptions." *Journal of Applied Psychology,* 1997, *82,* 143–159.

73. Young, B. S., Arthur, W. Jr., and Finch, J. "Predictors of Managerial Performance: More Than Cognitive Ability." *Journal of Business and Psychology,* 2000, *15*(1), 53–72.

74. Goffin, R. D., Rothstein, M. G., and Johnston, N. G. "Personality Testing and the Assessment Center: Incremental Validity for Managerial Selection." *Journal of Applied Psychology,* 1996, *81*(6), 746–756.

75. Huffcutt, A. I., Roth, P. L., and McDaniel, M. A. "A Meta-Analytic Investigation of Cognitive Ability in Employment Interview Evaluations: Moderating Characteristics and Implications for Incremental Validity." *Journal of Applied Psychology,* 1996, *81*(5), 459–473.

76. Sawyer, J. "Measurement *and* Prediction, Clinical *and* Statistical." *Psychological Bulletin,* 1966, *66,* 178–200.

77. Bernthal and Erker, *Selection Forecast.*

78. Ryan, A. M., and Sackett, P. R. "Relationships between Graduate Training, Professional Affiliation, and Individual Psychological Assessment Practices for Personnel Decisions." *Personnel Psychology,* 1992, *45,* 363–387.

79. Kwaske, I. H. "Individual Assessments for Personnel Selection: An Update on a Rarely Researched but Avidly Practiced Practice." *Consulting Psychology Journal: Practice and Research,* 2004, *56*(3), 186–195.

80. Ryan and Sackett, "Relationships between Graduate Training, Professional Affiliation, and Individual Psychological Assessment Practices for Personnel Decisions."

81. International Task Force on Assessment Center Guidelines. *Guidelines and Ethical Considerations for Assessment Center Operations.* Pittsburgh: Development Dimensions International, 2000.

82. Howard, "Reassessment of Assessment Centers."

83. Howard and Bray, *Managerial Lives in Transition.*

84. Thornton and Rupp, *Assessment Centers in Human Resource Management.*

85. Gaugler, B. B., Rosenthal, D. B., Thornton, G. C. III, and Bentson, C. "Meta-Analysis of Assessment Center Validity." *Journal of Applied Psychology,* 1987, *72,* 493–511.

86. Conway and others, "Meta-Analysis of Interrater and Internal Consistency Reliability of Selection Interviews."

87. Bernthal and Erker, *Selection Forecast.*

88. Schmidt and Hunter, "Validity and Utility of Selection Methods in Personnel Psychology."

89. Cropanzano, R. "The Justice Dilemma in Employee Selection: Some Reflections on the Trade-Offs between Fairness and Validity." *The Industrial-Organizational Psychologist,* 1994, *31*(3), 90–93.

90. Anderson, N., Lievens, F., van Dam, K., and Ryan, A. M. "Future Perspectives on Employee Selection: Key Directions for Future Research and Practice." *Applied Psychology: An Internal Review,* 2004, *53*(4), 487–501.

91. Schmidt and Hunter, "Validity and Utility of Selection Methods in Personnel Psychology."

92. Bernthal and Erker, *Selection Forecast.*

93. Schmidt and Hunter, "Validity and Utility of Selection Methods in Personnel Psychology."

94. Cropanzano, "Justice Dilemma in Employee Selection."

95. Cronshaw, S. F. "Lo! The Stimulus Speaks: The Insider's View on Whyte and Latham's 'The Futility of Utility Analysis.'" *Personnel Psychology,* 1997, *50,* 611–615.

96. Rogers, R. W., Wellins, R. S., and Conner, D. R. *The Power of Realization: Building Competitive Advantage by Maximizing Human Resource Initiatives.* Pittsburgh: Development Dimensions International, 2002.

Chapter Two: Best Practices in Leadership Assessment

1. Maynard, M. "Lower Your Window Shades: Today's Film in 'The Rookie.'" *New York Times,* October 27, 2004, p. BU5.

2. Ibid.

3. Lucier, C., Schuyt, R., and Handa, J. "CEO Succession 2003: The Perils of Good Governance." Booz Allen Hamilton. [http://www.boozallen. de/ content/downloads/5h_ceo_2004.pdf]. October 19, 2004.

4. Sala, F. "Executive Blind Spots: Discrepancies between Self- and Other-Ratings." *Consulting Psychology Journal: Practice and Research,* 2003, *55*(4), 222–229.

5. Garman, A. N. "Assessing Candidates for Leadership Positions." In R. Lowman (ed.), *California School of Organizational Studies: Handbook of Organizational Consulting Psychology: A Comprehensive Guide to Theory, Skills, and* Techniques (pp. 185–211). San Francisco: Jossey-Bass, 2002.

6. Bartram, D. "Assessment in Organizations." *Applied Psychology: An International Review,* 2004, *53*(2), 237–259.

7. McCall, M. "Identifying Leadership Potential in Future International Executives: Developing a Concept." *Consulting Psychology Journal,* 1994, *46*(1), 49–63.

8. Freedman, A. M. "Pathways and Crossroads to Institutional Leadership." *Consulting Psychology Journal: Practice and Research,* 1998, *50*(3), 131–151.

9. Riggio, R. E., Riggio, H. R., Salinas, C., and Cole, E. J. "The Role of Social and Emotional Communication Skills in Leader Emergence

Effectiveness." *Group Dynamics: Theory, Research, and Practice*, 2003, *7*(2), 83–103.

10. Fletcher, C. "Impression Management in the Selection Interview." In R. A. Giacalone and P. Rosenfeld (eds.), *Impression Management in the Organization*. Hillsdale, N.J.: Erlbaum, 1989.

11. Levinson, H. "Organizational Character." *Consulting Psychology Journal: Practice and Research*, 1997, *49*, 246–255.

12. Sperry, L. "Character Assessment in the Executive Selection Process." *Consulting Psychology Journal: Practice and Research*, 1999, *51*(4), 211–217.

13. Thomas, J. L., Dickson, M. W., and Bliese, P. D. "Using Personal Values and Motives to Predict Success as a Leader in the U.S. Army Reserve Training Corps." *The Leadership Quarterly*, *12*, 181–196.

14. Coyne, I., and Bartram, D. "Personnel Managers' Perceptions of Dishonesty in the Workplace." *Human Resource Management Journal*, 2000, *10*(3), 38–45.

15. Jenkins, A. *Companies' Use of Psychometric Testing and the Changing Demand for Skills: A Review of the Literature*. London, England: London School of Economics and Political Science, Center for the Economics of Education, 2001.

16. Sperry, "Character Assessment in the Executive Selection Process."

17. Ibid.

18. Thomas and others, "Using Personal Values and Motives to Predict Success."

19. Schein, E. H. *Organizational Culture and Leadership: A Dynamic View* (2nd ed.). San Francisco: Jossey-Bass, 1992.

20. Baum, J. R., and Locke, E. A. "The Relationship of Entrepreneurial Traits, Skills, and Motivation to Subsequent Venture Growth." *Journal of Applied Psychology*, 2004, *89*(4), 587–598.

21. Ryan, A. M., and Sackett, P. R. "Relationships between Graduate Training, Professional Affiliation, and Individual Psychological Assessment Practices for Personnel Decisions." *Personnel Psychology*, 1992, *45*, 363–387.

22. Sessa, V. I., and Taylor, J. J. *Executive Selection: Strategies for Success*. San Francisco: Jossey-Bass, 2000.

23. Huffcutt, A. I., Conway, J. M., Roth, P. L., and Stone, N. J. "Identification and Meta-Analytic Assessment of Psychological Constructs Measured in Employment Interviews." *Journal of Applied Psychology*, 2001, *86*(5), 897–913.

24. Garman, "Assessing Candidates for Leadership Positions."

25. Task Force on Assessment Center Guidelines. "Guidelines and Ethical Considerations for Assessment Center Operations." *Public Personnel Management*, 1998, *18*, 457–470.

26. Ritchie, R. J. "Using the Assessment Center Method to Predict Senior Management Potential." *Consulting Psychology Journal*, 1994, *46*(1), 16–23.

27. Schmidt, F. L., and Hunter, J. E. "The Validity and Utility of Selection Methods in Personnel Psychology: Practical and Theoretical Implications of 85 Years of Research Findings." *Psychological Bulletin,* 1998, *124,* 262–274. Also see Ryan and Sackett, "Relationships between Graduate Training, Professional Affiliation, and Individual Psychological Assessment Practices for Personnel Decisions."

28. Young, B. S., Arthur, W. Jr., and Finch, J. "Predictors of Managerial Performance: More Than Cognitive Ability." *Journal of Business and Psychology,* 2000, *15,* 53–72.

29. Miner, J. B., Smith, N. R., and Bracker, J. S. "Role of Entrepreneurial Task Motivation in the Growth of Technologically Innovative Firms: Interpretations from Follow-up Data." *Journal of Applied Psychology,* 1994, *79,* 627–630.

30. Hogan, J., and Holland, B. "Using Theory to Evaluate Personality and Job-Performance Relations: A Socioanalytic Perspective." *Journal of Applied Psychology,* 2003, *88,* 100–112.

31. Hurtz, G. M., and Donovan, J. J. "Personality and Job Performance: The Big Five Revisited." *Journal of Applied Psychology,* 2000, *85,* 869–879.

32. Kaplan, R. S., and Atkinson, A. A. *Advanced Management Accounting.* Upper Saddle River, N.J.: Prentice Hall, 1998.

33. Ibid.

34. Ibid.

35. Ibid.

36. Kaplan, R. S., and Norton, D. P. "Using the Balanced Scorecard as a Strategic Management System." *Harvard Business Review,* 1996, *74,* 75–85; Kaplan, R. S., and Norton, D. P. "Strategy Maps." *Strategic Finance,* 2004, *85,* 26–35.

37. Simons, R. *Performance Measurement and Control Systems for Implementing Strategy.* Upper Saddle River, N.J.: Prentice Hall, 2000.

38. Sloan, E. B. "Assessing and Developing Versatility: Executive Survival Skill for the Brave New World." *Consulting Psychology Journal,* 1994, *46*(1), 1061–1087.

39. Stogdill, R. M., and Coons, A. E. (eds.). *Leader Behavior: Its Description and Measurement.* Columbus: Ohio State University, Bureau of Business Research, 1957.

40. Bass, B. M., and Avolio, B. J. *Multifactor Leadership Questionnaire.* Palo Alto, Calif.: Consulting Psychologists Press, 1990.

41. Smither, J. W., London, M., Flautt, R., Vargas, Y., and Kucine, I. "Can Executive Coaches Enhance the Impact of Multisource Feedback on Behavior Change? A Quasi-Experimental Field Study." *Personnel Psychology,* 2003, *56*(1), 23–44.

42. Waldman, D. A., Atwater, L. E., and Antonioni, D. "Has Multisource Feedback Gone Amok?" *Academy of Management Executive,* 1998, *12*(2), 86–94.

43. Greguras, G. J., Robie, C., Schleicher, D. J., and Goff, M. III. "A Field Study of the Effects of Rating Purpose on the Quality of Multisource Ratings." *Personnel Psychology,* 2003, *56,* 1–21.

44. McCauley, C. D., Ruderman, M. S., Ohlott, P. J., and Morrow, J. E. "Assessing the Developmental Components of Managerial Jobs." *Journal of Applied Psychology,* 1994, *79*(4), 544–560.

45. Kincaid, S. B., and Gordick, D. "The Return on Investment of Leadership Development: Differentiating Our Discipline." *Consulting Psychology Journal: Practice and Research,* 2003, *55*(1), 47–57.

46. Spencer, L. "The Economic Value of Emotional Intelligence Competencies and EIC-Based HR Programs." In C. Cherniss and D. Goleman (eds.), *The Emotionally Intelligent Workplace: How to Select for, Measure, and Improve Emotional Intelligence in Individuals, Groups, and Organizations.* San Francisco: Jossey-Bass, 2001.

47. Cascio, W. F. "Executive and Managerial Assessment: Value for the Money?" *Consulting Psychology Journal,* 1994, *46*(1), 42–48.

48. Spencer, "Economic Value of Emotional Intelligence Competencies and EIC-Based HR Programs."

49. Garman, "Assessing Candidates for Leadership Positions."

Chapter Three: Shifting the Emphasis of Leadership Development

1. Albert, S., Ashforth, B., and Dutton, J. "Organizational Identity and Identification: Charting New Waters and Building New Bridges." *Academy of Management Review,* 2000, *25,* 13–17.

2. Day, D. V., Gronn, P., and Salas, E. "Leadership Capacity in Teams." *Leadership Quarterly,* 2004, *15,* 857–880; O'Connor, P.M.G., and Quinn, L. "Organizational Capacity for Leadership." In C. D. McCauley and E. Van Velsor (eds.), *The Center for Creative Leadership Handbook of Leadership Development* (pp. 417–437). San Francisco: Jossey-Bass, 2004.

3. Sedikides, C., and Brewer, M. B. (eds.). *Individual Self, Relational Self, Collective Self.* Philadelphia: Psychology Press, 2001.

4. Lord, R. G., and Brown, D. J. *Leadership Processes and Follower Self-Identity.* Mahwah, N.J.: Erlbaum, 2004, 6.

5. Weick, K. E. "The Collapse of Sensemaking in Organizations: The Mann Gulch Disaster." *Administrative Science Quarterly,* 1993, *38,* 628–652.

6. Kahane, A. *Solving Tough Problems: An Open Way of Talking, Listening, and Creating New Realities.* San Francisco: Berrett-Koehler, 2004.

7. Ibid., 32–33.
8. Day, D. V. "Leadership Development: A Review in Context." *Leadership Quarterly*, 2000, *11*, 581–613.
9. O'Connor and Quinn, "Organizational Capacity for Leadership."
10. Palus, C., McCauley, C., and Drath, W. *Connected Leadership Practice.* Unpublished manuscript, Greensboro, N.C., Center for Creative Leadership, 2005.

Chapter Four: Getting Leader Development Right

1. Kotter, J. P. *The General Managers.* New York: Free Press, 1982.
2. McCall, M. W. Jr., Lombardo, M., and Morrison, A. *The Lessons of Experience.* New York: Free Press, 1988.
3. Ghosn, C., and Ries, P. *Shift: Inside Nissan's Historic Revival.* New York: Currency/Doubleday, 2003.
4. Yost, P. R., Mannion-Plunkett, M., McKenna, R. B., and Homer, L. "Lessons of Experience: Personal and Situational Factors That Drive Growth." In R. B. McKenna (Chair), *Leadership Development: The Strategic Use of On-the-Job Assignments.* Symposium conducted at the Society for Industrial/Organizational Psychology, San Diego, 2001.
5. Mahler, W. R., and Wrightnour, W. F. *Executive Continuity: How to Build and Retain an Effective Management Team.* Homewood, Ill.: Dow Jones-Irwin, 1973.
6. Sorcher, M. "Are You Picking the Right Leaders?" *Harvard Business Review,* 2002 (February), 78–85.
7. Charan, R., Drotter, S., and Noel, J. *The Leadership Pipeline.* San Francisco: Jossey-Bass, 2001.
8. Spreitzer, G. M., McCall, M. W. Jr., and Mahoney, J. "Early Identification of International Executives." *Journal of Applied Psychology,* 1997, *82*(1), 6–29.
9. Gabarro, J. J. *The Dynamics of Taking Charge.* Boston: Harvard Business School Press, 1987.
10. Welch, J., and Byrne, J. A. *Jack: Straight from the Gut.* New York: Warner Books, Inc., 2001, 168.
11. Kidder, T. *The Soul of a New Machine.* New York: Random House, 1997.
12. Peters, T. J., and Austin, N. *A Passion for Excellence: The Leadership Difference.* New York: Warner Books, 1986.
13. Hollenbeck, G. P. "Coaching Executives: Individual Leader Development." In R. Silzer (ed.), *The 21st Century Executive* (pp. 137–167). San Francisco: Jossey-Bass, 2001.

Chapter Five: Best Practices in the Use of Proactive Influence Tactics by Leaders

1. Research programs that identified distinct types of influence tactics are described in Yukl, G. *Leadership in Organizations* (6th ed.). Upper Saddle River, N.J.: Prentice Hall, 2006.

2. Examples of the way leaders use inspirational talks to motivate commitment by followers is described in books such as the following: Bass, B. M. *Leadership and Performance beyond Expectations.* New York: Free Press, 1985; Conger, J. A. *The Charismatic Leader: Behind the Mystique of Exceptional Leadership.* San Francisco: Jossey-Bass, 1989.

3. Studies on situational determinants of tactic use include Yukl, G., Guinan, P. J., and Sottolano, D. "Influence Tactics Used for Different Objectives with Subordinates, Peers, and Superiors." *Group and Organization Management,* 1995, *20,* 272–296.

4. Studies on cross-cultural determinants of tactic use include Kennedy, J., Fu, P. P., and Yukl, G. "Influence Tactics across Twelve Cultures." In W. Mobley and P. Dorfman (eds.), *Advances in Global Leadership,* Vol. 3 (pp. 127–148). Oxford, England: JAI Press, 2003; Yukl, G., Fu, P. P., and McDonald, R. "Cross-Cultural Differences in Perceived Effectiveness of Influence Tactics for Initiating or Resisting Change." *Applied Psychology: An International Review,* 2003, *52,* 68–82.

5. Studies on effectiveness of different tactics include Yukl, G., and Tracey, B. "Consequences of Influence Tactics Used with Subordinates, Peers, and the Boss." *Journal of Applied Psychology,* 1992, *77,* 525–535; Yukl, G., Chavez, C., and Seifert, C. F. "Assessing the Construct Validity and Utility of Two New Influence Tactics." *Journal of Organizational Behavior,* 2005, *26*(6), 705–725.

6. An example of research on tactic combinations is the following: Falbe, C. M., and Yukl, G. "Consequences for Managers of Using Single Influence Tactics and Combinations of Tactics." *Academy of Management Journal,* 1992, *35,* 638–653.

7. An example of research on sequencing of tactics is the following: Yukl, G., Falbe, C. M., and Youn, J. Y. "Patterns of Influence Behavior for Managers." *Group and Organization Management,* 1993, *18,* 5–28.

8. This example comes from the research by Fu, P. P., and Yukl, G. "Perceived Effectiveness of Influence Tactics in the United States and China." *Leadership Quarterly,* 2000, *11,* 251–266.

9. See Yukl, *Leadership in Organizations.*

10. Examples of research on resistance tactics include the following: Yukl and others, "Cross-Cultural Differences in Perceived Effectiveness of Influence Tactics for Initiating or Resisting Change."

11. See Yukl, G., and Lepsinger, R. *Flexible Leadership: Creating Value by Balancing Multiple Challenges and Choices.* San Francisco: Jossey-Bass, 2004.

12. Seifert, C., Yukl, G., and McDonald, R. "Effects of Multisource Feedback and a Feedback Facilitator on the Influence Behavior of Managers towards Subordinates." *Journal of Applied Psychology,* 2003, *88,* 561–569.

Chapter Six: Creating the Conditions for Success

1. Mumford, M. D., and Gustafson, S. B. "Creativity Syndrome: Integration, Application, and Innovation." *Psychological Bulletin,* 1988, *103,* 27–43.

2. Damanpour, F. "Organizational Innovation: A Meta-Analysis of Effects of Determinants and Moderators." *Academy of Management Journal,* 1991, *34,* 555–590; Cardinal, L. B. "Technological Innovation in the Pharmaceutical Industry: The Use of Organizational Control on Managing Research and Development." *Organization Science,* 2001, *12,* 19–37; Feurer, R., Chaharbaghi, K., and Wargin, J. "Creative Teams at Hewlett-Packard." *Human Resource Management International Digest,* 1996, *4,* 17–21; Rich, J. D., and Weisberg, R. W. "Creating All in the Family: A Case Study in Creative Thinking." *Creativity Research Journal,* 2004, *16,* 247–259.

3. Florida, R. *The Rise of the Creative Class.* New York: Basic Books, 2002.

4. Dess, G. G., and Pickens, J. C. "Changing Roles: Leadership in the 21st Century." *Organizational Dynamics,* 2000, *28,* 18–34.

5. Abra, J. "Collaboration in Creative Work: An Initiative for Investigation." *Creativity Research Journal,* 1994, *7,* 1–20.

6. Finke, R. A., Ward, T. B., and Smith, S. M. *Creative Cognition: Theory, Research, and Applications.* Cambridge, Mass.: MIT Press, 1992.

7. Weisberg, R. W. "Creativity and Knowledge: A Challenge to Theories." In R. J. Sternberg (ed.), *Handbook of Creativity* (pp. 226–259). Cambridge, England: Cambridge University Press, 1999; Mumford, M. D. "Blind Variation or Selective Variation? Evaluating Elements in Creative Thought." *Psychological Inquiry,* 1999, *10,* 343–348.

8. Brophy, D. R. "Understanding, Measuring, and Enhancing Individual Creative Problem-Solving Efforts." *Creativity Research Journal,* 1998, *11,* 123–150; Mumford, M. D., Mobley, M. I., Uhlman, C. E., Reiter-Palmon, R., and Doares, L. "Process Analytic Models of Creative Capacities." *Creativity Research Journal,* 1991, *4,* 91–122.

9. Mumford, M. D., Baughman, W. A., and Sager, C. E. "Picking the Right Material: Cognitive Processing Skills and Their Role in Creative

Thought." In M. A. Runco (ed.), *Critical Creative Processes* (pp. 19–68). Cresskill, N.J.: Hampton, 2003; Ward, T. B., Patterson, M. J., and Sifonis, C. M. "The Role of Specificity and Abstraction in Creative Idea Generation." *Creativity Research Journal*, 2004, *16*, 1–9.

10. Huber, J. C. "Invention and Inventivity as a Special Kind of Creativity with Implications for General Creativity." *Journal of Creative Behavior*, 1998, *32*, 58–72.

11. Hall, R., and Andriani, P. "Managing Knowledge for Innovation." *Long Range Planning*, 2002, *35*, 29–48.

12. Chandy, R. K., and Tellis, G. J. "The Incumbent's Curse? Incumbency, Size and Radical Innovation." *Journal of Marketing*, 2000, *64*, 1–17.

13. Danneels, E., and Kleinschmidt, E. J. "Product Innovativeness from the Firm's Perspective: Its Dimensions and Their Relation with Project Selection and Performance." *Journal of Product Innovation Management*, 2001, *18*, 357–363.

14. Keller, R. T. "Cross-Functional Project Groups in Research and New Product Development: Diversity, Communications, Job Stress, and Outcomes." *Academy of Management Journal*, 2001, *44*, 547–559.

15. Halberstam, D. *The Reckoning.* New York: Morrow, 1986.

16. Capon, N., Farley, J. U., Lehmann, D. R., and Hulbert, J. M. "Profiles of Product Innovators among Large U.S. Manufacturers." *Management Science*, 1992, *38*, 157–169.

17. Ettlie, J. E. "Organizational Policy and Innovation among Suppliers to the Food-Processing Sector." *Academy of Management Journal*, 1983, *26*, 27–44.

18. Souitaris, V. "External Communication Determinants of Innovation in the Context of a Newly Industrialized Country: A Comparison of Objective and Perceptual Results from Greece." *Technovation*, 2001, *21*, 25–34.

19. Ford, C. M., and Gioia, D. A. "Factors Influencing Creativity in the Domain of Managerial Decision Making." *Journal of Management*, 2000, *26*, 705–732.

20. O'Connor, G. C. "Market Learning and Radical Innovation: A Cross-Case Comparison of Eight Radical Innovation Projects." *Journal of Product Innovation Management*, 1998, *15*, 151–166.

21. Koberg, C. S., Uhlenbruck, N., and Sarason, Y. "Facilitators of Organizational Innovation: The Role of Life-Cycle Stage." *Journal of Business Venturing*, 1996, *11*, 133–149.

22. Kickul, J., and Gundry, L. K. "Breaking through Boundaries for Organizational Innovation: New Managerial Roles and Practices in E-commerce Firms." *Journal of Management*, 2001, *27*, 347–361.

23. O'Connor, "Market Learning and Radical Innovation."

24. Basadur, M., and Hausdorf, P. A. "Measuring Divergent Thinking Atti-tudes Related to Creative Problem Solving and Innovation Management." *Creativity Research Journal,* 1996, *9,* 21–32.

25. Rodan, S. "Innovation and Heterogeneous Knowledge in Managerial Contact Networks." *Journal of Knowledge Management,* 2002, *6,* 152–163.

26. Bonnardel, N., and Marméche, E. "Evocation Processes by Novice and Expert Designers: Towards Stimulating Analogical Thinking." *Creativity and Innovation Management,* 2003, *13,* 176–186.

27. Mumford, M. D., and Van Doorn, J. R. "The Leadership of Pragmatism: Reconsidering Franklin in the Age of Charisma." *Leadership Quarterly,* 2001, *12,* 274–309.

28. Ericsson, K. A., and Charness, W. "Expert Performance: Its Structure and Acquisition." *American Psychologist,* 1994, *49,* 725–747; Tushman, M. L., and O'Reilly, C. A. *Winning through Innovation.* Cambridge, Mass.: Harvard Business School Press, 1997; West, M. A. "Sparkling Fountains or Stagnant Ponds: An Integrative Model of Creativity and Innovation Implementation in Work Groups." *Applied Psychology: An International Review,* 2002, *51,* 355–387.

29. Anacona, D., and Caldwell, D. "Demography and Design: Predictors of New Product Team Performance." *Organization Science,* 1992, *3,* 321–341.

30. Georgsdottir, A. S., and Getz, I. "How Flexibility Facilitates Innovation and Ways to Manage It in Organizations." *Creativity and Innovation Management,* 2004, *13,* 166–175.

31. Howell, J. M., and Boies, K. "Champions of Technological Innovation: The Influences of Contextual Knowledge, Role Orientation, Idea Genera-tion, and Idea Promotion on Champion Emergence." *Leadership Quarterly,* 2004, *15,* 130–149.

32. Hauschildt, J., and Kirchmann, E. "Teamwork for Innovation—The 'Troika' of Promoters." *R&D Management,* 2001, *31,* 41–49.

33. Gronn, P. "Distributed Leadership as a Unit of Analysis." *Leadership Quarterly,* 2002, *13,* 423–451.

34. Zaccaro, S. J., Rittman, A. L., and Marks, M. A. "Team Leadership." *Leadership Quarterly,* 2001, *12,* 451–483.

35. Hurst, D. K., Rush, J. C., and White, R. E. "Top Management Teams and Organizational Renewal." *Strategic Management Journal,* 1989, *10,* 87–105.

36. Hitt, M. A., Hoskisson, R. E., Johnson, R. A., and Moesel, D. D. "The Market for Corporate Control and Firm Innovation." *Academy of Management Journal,* 1996, *39,* 1084–1196.

37. Danneels and Kleinschmidt, "Product Innovativeness"; Dougherty, D., and Hardy, B. F. "Sustained Innovation Production in Large Mature

Organizations: Overcoming Organization Problems." *Academy of Management Journal,* 1996, *39,* 826–851.

38. Mumford, M. D., Strange, J. M., Scott, G. M., and Gaddis, B. "Creative Problem-Solving in Leadership: Directions, Actions and Reactions." In J. C. Kaufman and J Baer (eds.), *Creativity across Domains: Faces of the Muse* (pp. 205–223). Mahwah, N.J.: Erlbaum, 2004.

39. Jelinek, M., and Schoonhoven, C. B. *The Innovation Marathon: Lessons Learned from High Technology Firms.* Oxford, England: Blackwell, 1990; Debruyne, M., Moenaert, R., Griffin, A., Hart, S., Hultink, E. J., and Robben, H. "The Impact of New Product Launch Strategies on Competitive Reaction to Industrial Markets." *Journal of Product Innovation Management,* 2002, *19,* 159–170; Dougherty, D., and Heller, T. "The Illegitimacy of Successful Product Innovation in Established Firms." *Organization Science,* 1994, *5,* 200–281; Cohen, W. M., and Levinthal, D. A. "Absorptive Capacity: A New Perspective on Learning and Innovation." *Administrative Science Quarterly,* 1990, *35,* 128–152.

40. Cardinal, L. B., and Hatfield, D. E. "Internal Knowledge Generation: The Research Laboratory and Innovative Productivity in the Pharmaceutical Industry." *Journal of Engineering and Technology Management,* 2000, *17,* 247–272.

41. Mumford, M. D., Scott, G. M., Gaddis, B., and Strange, J. M. "Leading Creative People: Orchestrating Expertise and Relationships." *Leadership Quarterly,* 2002, *13,* 705–750.

42. Rickards, T., Chen, M. H., and Moger, S. "Development of a Self-Report Instrument for Exploring Team Factor, Leadership, and Performance Relationships." *British Journal of Management,* 2001, *12,* 243–250; Pinto, J. K., and Prescott, J. E. "Variations in Critical Success Factors over Stages in the Project Life Cycle." *Journal of Management,* 1988, *14,* 5–18.

43. West, "Sparkling Fountains or Stagnant Ponds."

44. Hoffman, L. R., Hamburg, E., and Maier, N. "Differences and Disagreement as Factors in Creative Group Problem Solving." *Journal of Abnormal and Social Psychology,* 1962, *64,* 206–214.

45. Mumford and others, "Leading Creative People."

46. Ford, C. M. "A Theory of Individual Creative Action in Multiple Social Domains." *Academy of Management Review,* 1996, *21,* 1112–1142.

47. Drazin, R., Glynn, M. A., and Kazanjian, R. K. "Multilevel Theorizing about Creativity in Organizations: A Sense Making Perspective." *Academy of Management Review,* 1999, *24,* 286–329.

48. Kidder, T. *The Soul of a New Machine.* New York: Avon, 1981.

49. Ford, "Individual Creative Action"; Jaussi, K. S., and Dionne, S. D. "Leading for Creativity: The Role of Unconventional Behavior." *Leadership Quarterly,* 2003, *14,* 351–368.

50. Andrews, F. M., and Farris, G. F. "Supervisory Practices and Innovation in Scientific Teams." *Personnel Psychology,* 1967, *20,* 497–515.

51. Barnowe, J. T. "Leadership and Performance Outcomes in Research Organizations." *Organizational Behavior and Human Performance,* 1975, *14,* 264–280.

52. Farris, G. F. "The Effect of Individual Roles on Performance in Innovative Groups." *R&D Management,* 1972, *3,* 23–28.

53. Baughman, W. A., and Mumford, M. D. "Process Analytic Models of Creative Capacities: Operations Involved in the Combination and Reorganization Process." *Creativity Research Journal,* 1995, *8,* 37–62; Finke and others, *Creative Cognition.*

54. Weber, R. N., and Perkins, D. J. *Inventive Minds: Creativity in Technology.* New York: Oxford University Press, 1992.

55. Andriopoulos, C., and Lowe, A. "Enhancing Organisational Creativity: The Process of Perpetual Challenging." *Management Decision,* 2000, *38,* 734–742.

56. Arvey, R. D., Dewhirst, H. D., and Boling, J. C. "Relationships between Goal Clarity, Participation in Goal Setting, and Personality Characteristics on Job Satisfaction in a Scientific Organization." *Journal of Applied Psychology,* 1976, *61,* 103–105.

57. Mumford, M. D., Marks, M. A., Connelly, M. S., Zaccaro, S. T., and Reiter-Palmon, R. "Development of Leadership Skills: Experiences and Timing." *Leadership Quarterly,* 2000, *11,* 87–114; Mumford and others, "Leading Creative People."

58. Mumford, M. D., Connelly, M. S., and Gaddis, B. "How Creative Leaders Think: Experimental Findings and Cases." *Leadership Quarterly,* 2003, *14,* 411–432.

59. Ibid.

60. Lonergan, D. C., Scott, G. M., and Mumford, M. D. "Evaluative Aspects of Creative Thought: Effects of Idea Appraisal and Revision Standards." *Creativity Research Journal,* 2004, *16,* 231–246; Redmond, M. R., Mumford, M. D., and Reach, R. J. "Putting Creativity to Work: Leader Influences on Subordinate Creativity." *Organizational Behavior and Human Decision Processes,* 1993, *55,* 120–151.

61. Csikszentmihalyi, M. "Implications of a Systems Perspective for the Study of Creativity." In R. J. Sternberg (ed.), *Handbook of Creativity* (pp. 312–338). Cambridge, England: Cambridge University Press, 1999.

62. Mumford, M. D., Blair, C., Dailey, L. R., Leritz, L. E., and Osburn, H. K. "Errors in Creative Thought? Cognitive Biases in a Computer Processing Activity." *Journal of Creative Behavior,* in press.

63. Blair, C. *Criteria Used in Appraising Ideas.* Unpublished master's thesis, Norman: University of Oklahoma, 2005.

64. Licuanan, B., Dailey, L. R., and Mumford, M. D. *Idea Evaluation: Error in Evaluating Highly Original Ideas.* Unpublished manuscript, Norman: University of Oklahoma, 2004.

65. Dailey, L. R., and Mumford, M. D. *Evaluative Aspects of Creative Thought: Errors in Appraising the Implications of New Ideas.* Unpublished manuscript, Norman: University of Oklahoma, 2004.

66. James, L. R., James, L. A., and Ashe, D. K. "The Meaning of Organizations: The Role of Cognition and Values." In B. Schneider (ed.), *Organizational Climate and Culture* (pp. 40–84). San Francisco: Jossey-Bass, 1990.

67. Ekvall, G., and Ryhammer, L. "The Creative Climate: Its Determinants and Effects at a Swedish University." *Creativity Research Journal,* 1999, *12,* 303–310; McGourty, J., Tarshis, L. A., and Dominick, P. "Managing Innovation: Lessons from World Class Organizations." *International Journal of Technology Management,* 1996, *11,* 354–368.

68. Oldham, G. R., and Cummings, A. "Employee Creativity: Personal and Contextual Factors at Work." *Academy of Management Journal,* 1996, *39,* 607–634.

69. Mumford, M. D., and Hunter, S. T. "Innovation in Organizations: A Multi-Level Perspective on Creativity." In F. Dansereau and F. J. Yammarino (eds.), *Research in Multi-Level Issues,* Vol. IV (pp. 11–74). Oxford, England: Elsevier, 2005.

70. Jaussi and Dionne, "Leading for Creativity."

71. Taggar, S. "Group Composition, Creative Synergy, and Group Performance." *Journal of Creative Behavior,* 2001, *35,* 261–286.

72. Nyström, H. *Creativity and Innovation.* New York: Wiley, 1979.

73. Curral, L. A., Forrester, R. H., and Dawson, J. F. "It's What You Do and the Way You Do It: Team Task, Team Size, and Innovation-Related Group Processes." *European Journal of Work and Organizational Psychology,* 2001, *10,* 187–204.

74. Gassman, O., and van Zedwitz, M. "Trends and Determinants of Managing Virtual R&D Teams." *R&D Management,* 2003, *33,* 243–263.

75. Drazin and others, "Multilevel Theorizing about Creativity."

76. Abra, "Collaboration in Creative Work"; Mumford, M. D., Feldman, J. M., Hein, M. B., and Nago, D. J. "Tradeoffs between Ideas and Structure: Individual versus Group Performance in Creative Problem-Solving." *Journal of Creative Behavior,* 2001, *35,* 1–23.

77. Allen, T. J., and Cohen, S. I. "Information Flow in Research and Development Laboratories." *Administrative Science Quarterly,* 1969, *14,* 12–19.

78. Keller, "Cross-Functional Project Groups"; Thamhain, H. J. "Managing Innovative R&D Teams." *R&D Management,* 2003, *44,* 297–322.

79. Mumford, M. D., Schultz, R. A., and Van Dorn, J. R. "Performance in Planning: Processes, Requirements, and Errors." *Review of General Psychology,* 2001, *5,* 213–240.

80. Maidique, M., and Zirger, B. J. "A Study of Success and Failure in Product Innovation: The Case of the U.S. Electronics Industry." *IEEE Transactions in Engineering Management,* 1984, *31*(4), 192–203.

81. Mumford and others, "Performance in Planning."

82. Mumford, M. D., Schultz, R. A., and Osburn, H. K. "Planning in Organizations: Performance as a Multi-Level Phenomenon." In F. J. Yammario and F. Dansereau (eds.), *Research in Multi-Level Issues: The Many Faces of Multi-Level Issues* (pp. 3–35). Oxford, England: Elsevier, 2002.

83. Hammond, K. J. "Case-Based Planning: A Framework for Planning from Experience." *Cognitive Science,* 1990, *14,* 385–443.

84. Dörner, D., and Schaub, H. "Errors in Planning and Decision-Making and the Nature of Human Information Processing." *Applied Psychology: An International Review,* 1994, *43,* 433–453.

85. Gollwitzer, P. M. "Implementation Intentions: Strong Effects of Simple Plans." *American Psychologist,* 1999, *54,* 493–503.

86. Lovelace, K., Shapiro, D. L, and Weingart, L. R. "Maximizing Cross-Functional New Product Teams' Innovativeness and Constraint Adherence: A Conflict Communications Perspective." *Academy of Management Journal,* 2001, *44,* 779–793; Keller, "Cross-Functional Project Groups."

87. Lovelace and others, "Maximizing Product Teams' Innovativeness and Constraint Adherence."

88. Anacona and Caldwell, "Demography and Design."

89. Keller, "Cross-Functional Project Groups."

90. Damanpour, "Organizational Innovation"; Mumford and others, "Leading Creative People."

91. Amabile, T. M., Schatzer, E. A., Moneta, G. B., and Kramer, S. J. "Leader Behaviors and Work Environment for Creativity: Perceived Leader Support." *Leadership Quarterly,* 2004, *15,* 5–32; Ekvall and Ryhammer, "The Creative Climate."

92. Dougherty and Hardy, "Sustained Innovation Production."

93. Jelinek and Schoonhoven, *Innovation Marathon.*

94. Howell and Boies, "Champions of Technological Innovation."

95. Mumford and others, "Leading Creative People."

96. Lemann, N. *The Big Test: The Secret History of the American Meritocracy.* New York: Farrar, Straus, and Giroux, 2000.

97. Csikszentmihalyi, "Systems Perspective for the Study of Creativity."

98. Nyström, *Creativity and Innovation.*

99. Basadur and Hausdorf, "Measuring Divergent Thinking Attitudes"; Scott, G. M., Leritz, L. E., and Mumford, M. D. "The Effectiveness of Creativity Training: A Meta-Analysis." *Creativity Research Journal,* 2004, *16,* 361–388.

100. West, "Sparkling Fountains or Stagnant Ponds."

101. Mumford, M. D., Zaccaro, S. J., Harding, F. D., Jacobs, T. O., and Fleishman, E. A. "Leadership Skills for a Changing World: Solving Complex Social Problems." *Leadership Quarterly,* 2000, *11,* 11–35.

102. Mumford, M. D., and Manley, G. G. "Putting the Development in Leadership Development: Implications for Theory and Practice." In S. Murphy and R. Riggio (eds.), *The Future of Leadership Development* (pp. 237–261). Mahwah, N.J.: Erlbaum, 2003.

103. London, M. "Best Practices in Leadership Assessment." Paper presented at the 15th Annual Kravis-de Roulet Development Leadership Conference, Claremont, California, 2005.

104. Marks, M. C. "Best Practices in Leading for Organizational Change." Paper presented at the 15th Annual Kravis-de Roulet Development Leadership Conference, Claremont, California, 2005; Salas, E., and Pearce, C. "Best Practices in Team Leadership." Paper presented at the 15th Annual Kravis-de Roulet Development Leadership Conference, Claremont, California, 2005.

Chapter Seven: Best Practices in Ethical Leadership

1. Yukl, G. *Leadership in Organizations* (5th ed.). Upper Saddle River, N.J.: Prentice-Hall, 2002, 410.

2. Weaver, G. R., Trevino, L. K., and Cochran, P. L. "Corporate Ethics Practices in the Mid-1990s: An Empirical Study of the *Fortune 1000*." *Journal of Business Ethics,* 1999, *18,* 283–294.

3. Weaver, G. R., Trevino, L. K., and Cochran, P. L. "Integrated and Decoupled Corporate Social Performance: Management Commitments, External Pressures, and Corporate Ethics Practices." *Academy of Management Journal,* 1999, *42,* 539–552.

4. Badaracco, J. L. "Business Ethics: Four Spheres of Executive Responsibility." *California Management Review,* 2001, *34,* 64–79.

5. Johnson, C. E. *Meeting the Ethical Challenges of Leadership: Casting Light or Shadow* (2nd ed.). Thousand Oaks, Calif.: Sage, 2005.

6. Palmer, P. "Leading from Within." In L. C. Spears (ed.), *Insights on Leadership: Service, Stewardship, Spirit, and Servant-Leadership* (pp. 197–208). New York: Wiley, 1996, 200.

7. Lipman-Blumen, J. *The Allure of Toxic Leaders.* Oxford, England: Oxford University Press, 2005.

8. Kellerman, B. *Bad Leadership: What It Is, How It Happens, Why It Matters.* Boston: Harvard Business School Press, 2004, 34.

9. Palmer, P. *Let Your Life Speak: Listening for the Voice of Vocation.* San Francisco: Jossey-Bass, 2000.

10. Peters, T. J., and Waterman, R. H. Jr. *In Search of Excellence.* New York: Harper & Row, 1992.

11. Moxley, R. S. "Hardships." In C. D. McCauley, R. S. Moxley, and E. Van Velsor (eds.), *The Center for Creative Leadership Handbook of Leadership Development* (2nd ed.) (pp. 183–203). San Francisco: Jossey-Bass, 2004.

12. Huffington, A. *Pigs at the Trough: How Corporate Greed and Political Corruption Are Undermining America.* New York: Crown, 2003.

13. Block, P. *Stewardship: Serving Service over Self-Interest.* San Francisco: Berrett-Koehler, 1996.

14. Sternberg, R. J. "Smart People Are Not Stupid, But They Sure Can Be Foolish." In R. J. Sternberg (ed.), *Why Smart People Can Be So Stupid* (pp. 232–242). New Haven, Conn.: Yale University Press, 2002.

15. Nash, L. *Good Intentions Aside: A Manager's Guide to Resolving Ethical Problems.* Boston: Harvard Business School Press, 1990, 212.

16. "Cleaning Up the Mess." *Economist.* [Retrieved July 25, 2005, from The Newspaper Source]; Creswell, J. "Scandal Hits—Now What?" *Fortune,* July 7, 2003, 127–129.

17. Griffin, R. W., and O'Leary-Kelly, A. M. (eds.). *The Dark Side of Organizational Behavior.* San Francisco: Jossey Bass, 2004.

18. Pearson, C. M., and Porath, C. L. "On Incivility, Its Impact and Directions for Future Research." In Griffin and O'Leary-Kelly (eds.), *Dark Side of Organizational Behavior* (pp. 404–425).

19. Buss, A. H. *The Psychology of Aggression.* New York: Wiley, 1961.

20. Levy, A. C., and Paludi, M. A. *Workplace Sexual Harassment* (2nd ed.). Upper Saddle River, N.J.: Prentice Hall, 2002.

21. Diboye, R. L., and Halverson, S. K. "Subtle (and Not So Subtle) Discrimination in Organizations." In Griffin and O'Leary-Kelly (eds.), *Dark Side of Organizational Behavior* (pp. 131–158).

22. Baron, R. A. "Workplace Aggression and Violence: Insights from Basic Research." In Griffin and O'Leary-Kelly (eds.), *Dark Side of Organizational Behavior* (pp. 23–61).

23. Offerman, L. R., and Malamut, A. B. "When Leaders Harass: The Impact of Target Perceptions of Organizational Leadership and Climate on Harassment Reporting and Outcomes." *Journal of Applied Psychology,* 2002, *87,* 885–893.

24. Gudykunst, B., and Kim, Y. Y. *Communicating with Strangers: An Approach to Intercultural Communication* (3rd ed.). New York: McGraw-Hill, 1997.

25. Pearson, C. M., Andersson, L. M., and Porath, C. L. "Assessing and Attacking Workplace Incivility." *Organizational Dynamics,* 2000, *29,* 123–137.

26. Barling, J. "The Prediction, Experience, and Consequences of Workplace Violence." In G. G. VandenBos and E. Q. Bulato (eds.), *Violence on the Job: Identifying Risks and Developing Solutions* (pp. 29–49). Washington, D.C.: American Psychological Association, 1996.

27. Useem, M. *The Leadership Moment.* New York: Times Business, 1998, chap. 7.

28. Victor, B., and Cullen, J. B. "The Organizational Bases of Ethical Work Climates." *Administrative Science Quarterly,* 1988, *33,* 101–125.

29. Gellerman, S. W. "Managing Ethics from the Top Down." *Sloan Management Review,* 1989 (Winter), 77–79.

30. Holt, S. "Personal Lives of Executives Under Scrutiny." *Seattle Times,* March 8, 2005, p. C1.

31. Collins, J. C., and Porras, J. I. "Building Your Company's Vision." *Harvard Business Review,* 1996 (September–October), 65–77.

32. Starbucks. *Mission Statement.* 2005. [http://www.starbucks.com].

33. Paine, L. S. "Managing for Organizational Integrity." In *Harvard Business Review on Corporate Ethics* (pp. 85–112). Boston: Harvard Business School Press, 2003, 96.

34. Johnson, C. E. *Transforming Organizational Ethics.* Thousand Oaks, Calif.: Sage, 2007, chap. 9.

35. Pearson, C. M., and Porath, C. L. "On the Nature, Consequences and Remedies of Workplace Incivility: No Time for 'Nice'? Think Again." *Academy of Management Executive,* 2005, *19,* 7–18.

36. Paine, L. S. *Value Shift: Why Companies Must Merge Social and Financial Imperatives to Achieve Superior Performance.* New York: McGraw-Hill, 2003.

37. Cohen, D. V. "Creating and Maintaining Ethical Work Climates: Anomie in the Workplace and Implications for Managing Change." *Business Ethics Quarterly,* 1993, *3,* 343–348.

38. Aguilar, J. "Recruiters 'Stand Down.'" *Rocky Mountain News,* May 20, 2005, p. 24A. [Lexis Nexis Academic]; Rogers, R. "Army Stand Down to Reaffirm

Rules of Recruiting." *San Diego Union-Tribune,* May 19, 2005, p. B3. [Lexis Nexis Academic].

39. Palmer, *Let Your Life Speak.*
40. Lipman-Blumen, *Allure of Toxic Leaders.*
41. Kellerman, *Bad Leadership.*
42. Kupperman, J. "Character and Ethical Theory." *Midwest Studies in Philosophy,* 1988, *XIII,* 115–125.
43. Johannsen, R. L. *Ethics in Human Communication* (5th ed.). Prospect Heights, Ill.: Waveland Press, 2002.
44. Freiberg, K., and Freiberg, J. *Nuts! Southwest Airlines Crazy Recipe for Business and Personal Success.* New York: Broadway Books, 1996.
45. Etzioni, A. *The Spirit of Community: The Reinvention of American Society.* New York: Touchstone, 1993.
46. Kirkpatrick, W. K. "Moral Character: Story-Telling and Virtue." In R. T. Knowles and G. F. McLean (eds.), *Psychological Foundations of Moral Education and Character Development: An Integrated Theory of Moral Development* (pp. 169–184). Washington, D.C.: Council for Research in Values and Philosophy, 1992.
47. O'Connor, E. S. "Compelling Stories: Narrative and the Production of the Organizational Self." In O. F. Williams (ed.), *The Moral Imagination: How Literature and Films Can Stimulate Ethical Reflection in the Business World* (pp. 185–202). Notre Dame, Ind.: University of Notre Dame Press, 1997.
48. MacIntyre, A. *After Virtue: A Study in Moral Theory* (2nd ed.). Notre Dame, Ind.: University of Notre Dame Press, 1984, 216.
49. Dotlich, D. L., Noel, J. L., and Walker, N. *Leadership Passages: The Personal and Professional Transitions That Make or Break a Leader.* San Francisco: Jossey-Bass, 2004.
50. Moxley, "Hardships."
51. Bennis, W. G., and Thomas, R. J. *Geeks and Geezers: How Era, Values and Defining Moments Shape Leaders.* Boston: Harvard Business School Press, 2002.
52. Rest, J. R. *Moral Development: Advances in Research and Theory.* New York: Praeger, 1986.
53. Werhane, P. H. *Moral Imagination and Management Decision-Making.* New York: Oxford University Press, 1999.
54. Bird, F. B. *The Muted Conscience: Moral Silence and the Practice of Ethics in Business.* Westport, Conn.: Quorum Books, 1996.
55. Werhane, *Moral Imagination and Management Decision-Making.*
56. Paine, *Value Shift.*
57. "Nike on the Offensive." *Oregonian,* April 14, 2005, p. B8.

58. Paine, *Value Shift.*

59. Kohlberg, L. *The Psychology of Moral Development: The Nature and Validity of Moral Stages,* Vol. 2. San Francisco: Harper & Row, 1984.

60. Rest, J. R., Narvaez, D., Bebeau, J. J., and Thoma, S. J. *Postconventional Moral Thinking: A Neo-Kohlbergian Approach.* Mahwah, N.J.: Lawrence Erlbaum, 1999.

61. Dukerich, J. M., Nichols, M. L., Elm, D. R., and Vollrath, D. A. "Moral Reasoning in Groups: Leaders Make a Difference." *Human Relations,* 1990, *43,* 473–493.

62. James, H. S. "Reinforcing Ethical Decision Making through Organizational Structure." *Journal of Business Ethics,* 2000, *28,* 43–58.

63. Werhane, *Moral Imagination and Management Decision-Making.*

64. Paine, "Managing for Organizational Integrity."

65. Eisenberg, M. "Emotion, Regulation, and Moral Development." *Annual Review of Psychology,* 2000, *51,* 665–697.

66. Salovey, P., Hsee, C. K., and Mayer, J. D. "Emotional Intelligence and the Self-Regulation of Affect." In D. M. Wegner and J. W. Pennebaker (eds.), *Handbook of Mental Control* (pp. 258–277). Englewood Cliffs, N.J.: Prentice Hall, 1993.

67. Trevino, L. K., and Weaver, G. R. *Managing Ethics in Business Organizations: Social Scientific Perspectives.* Stanford, Calif.: Stanford University Press, 2003.

68. Adams, J. S., Taschcian, A., and Shore T. H. "Codes of Ethics as Signals for Ethical Behavior." *Journal of Business Ethics,* 2001, *29,* 199–211.

69. Gross-Schaefer, A., Trigilio, J., Negus, J., and Ro, C. "Ethics Education in the Workplace: An Effective Tool to Combat Employee Theft." *Journal of Business Ethics,* 2000, *26,* 89–100.

70. Northwestern Mutual Life. "Fear and Violence in the Workplace: A Survey Documenting the Experience of American Workers." In G. VandenBos and E. Z. Bulatao (eds.), *Violence on the Job: Identifying Risks and Developing Solutions* (pp. 385–397). Washington, D.C.: American Psychological Association, 1996.

71. Valentine, S., and Barnett, T. "Ethics Code Awareness, Perceived Ethical Values, and Organizational Commitment." *Journal of Personal Sales and Management,* 2003, *23,* 359–367.

72. Van Velsor, C. D., and McCauley, C. D. "Introduction: Our View of Leadership Development." In C. D. McCauley and E. Van Velsor (eds.), *The Center for Creative Leadership Handbook of Leadership Development* (pp. 1–22). San Francisco: Jossey-Bass, 2004.

73. Hosmer, L. T. "Trust: The Connecting Link between Organizational Theory and Philosophical Ethics." *Academy of Management Review,* 1995, *20,* 379–403.

74. Dirks, K. T., and Ferrin, D. "Trust in Leadership: Meta-Analytic Findings and Implications for Research." *Journal of Applied Psychology*, 2002, *87*, 611–628.

75. Kottler, P., and Lee, N. *Corporate Social Responsibility: Doing the Most Good for Your Company and Your Cause.* New York: Wiley, 2005.

76. Waddock, S. A., and Graves, S. B. "The Corporate Social Performance-Financial Performance Link." *Strategic Management Journal*, 1997, *18*, 303–319.

77. Reidenbach, R. E., and Robin, D. P. "A Conceptual Model of Corporate Moral Development." *Journal of Business Ethics*, 1991, *10*, 273–284.

78. Ciulla, J. (ed.). *Ethics: The Heart of Leadership* (2nd ed). Westport, Conn.: Praeger, 2004.

Chapter Eight: Best Practices in Team Leadership

1. Zaccaro, S. J., Rittman, A. L., and Marks, M. A. "Team Leadership." *Leadership Quarterly*, 2001, *12*, 451–483.

2. Foels, R., Driskell, J. E., Mullen, B., and Salas, E. "The Effects of Demographic Leadership on Group Member Satisfaction: An Integration." *Small Group Research*, 2000, *31*, 676–701.

3. Burke, C. S., Stagl, K. C., Klein, C., Goodwin, G. F., Salas, E., and Halpin, S. "What Types of Leader Behaviors Are Functional in Teams?: A Meta-analysis." *Leadership Quarterly*, 2006, 288–307.

4. Day, D. V., Gronn, P., and Salas, E. "Leadership Capacity in Teams." *Leadership Quarterly*, 2004, *15*, 857–880.

5. Hackman, J. R. *Leading Teams: Setting the Stage for Great Performances.* Boston: Harvard Business School Press, 2002.

6. Yukl, G., and Van Fleet, D. "Theory and Research on Leadership in Organizations." In M. D. Dunnette and L. M. Hough (eds.), *Handbook of Industrial and Organizational Psychology* (pp. 147–197). Palo Alto, Calif.: Consulting Psychologists Press, 1992; Ziegert, J. C. *A Unified Theory of Team Leadership: Towards a Comprehensive Understanding of Leading Teams.* Paper presented at the 19th annual conference of the Society for Industrial and Organizational Psychology, Chicago, April 2004.

7. Burke and others, "Leader Behaviors in Teams."

8. Ibid.

9. Hackman, *Leading Teams*.

10. Ibid.

11. Wageman, R. "How Leaders Foster Self-Managing Team Effectiveness: Design Choices versus Hands-On Coaching." *Organization Science*, 2001, *12*, 559–577.

12. Salas, E., Stagl, K. C., Burke, C. S., and Goodwin, G. F. "Fostering Team Effectiveness in Organizations: Toward an Integrative Theoretical Framework of Team Performance." In J. W. Shuart, W. Spaulding, and J. Poland (eds.), *Modeling Complex Systems: Motivation, Cognition and Social Processes.* Nebraska Symposium on Motivation, 51. Lincoln: University of Nebraska Press, in press.

13. Cannon-Bowers, J. A., Tannenbaum, S. I., Salas, E., and Volpe, C. E. "Defining Team Competencies and Establishing Team Training Requirements." In R. Guzzo, E. Salas, and Associates (eds.), *Team Effectiveness and Decision Making in Organizations* (pp. 333–380). San Francisco: Jossey-Bass, 1995; Marks, M. A., Mathieu, J. E., and Zaccaro, S. J. "A Temporally Based Framework and Taxonomy of Team Process." *Academy of Management Review,* 2001, *26,* 356–376.

14. Kozlowski, S.W.J., and Klein, K. "A Multilevel Approach to Theory and Research in Organizations: Contextual, Temporal, and Emergent Processes." In *Multilevel Theory, Research, and Methods in Organizations: Foundations, Extensions, and New Directions* (pp. 3–90). San Francisco: Jossey-Bass, 2000; Kozlowski, S.W.J., Gully, S. M., Nason, E. R., and Smith, E. M. "Developing Adaptive Teams: A Theory of Compilation and Performance across Levels and Time." In D. R. Ilgen and E. D. Pulakos (eds.), *The Changing Nature of Work and Performance: Implications for Staffing, Personnel Actions, and Development* (pp. 240–292). San Francisco: Jossey-Bass, 1999.

15. Hackman, J. R. "The Design of Work Teams." In J. Lorsch (ed.), *Handbook of Organizational Behavior* (pp. 315–342). Englewood Cliffs, N.J.: Prentice-Hall, 1987.

16. Hackman, J. R., and Oldham, G. R. *Work Redesign.* Reading, Mass.: Addison-Wesley, 1980.

17. Hackman, *Leading Teams.*

18. Ibid.

19. Saavedra, R., Earley, P. C., and Van Dyne, L. "Complex Interdependence in Task-Performing Groups." *Journal of Applied Psychology,* 1993, *1,* 61–72.

20. Janz, B. D., Colquitt, J. A., and Noe, R. A. "Knowledge Worker Team Effectiveness: The Role of Autonomy, Interdependence, Team Development, and Contextual Support Variables." *Personnel Psychology,* 1997, *50,* 877–903.

21. Campion, M. A., Medsker, G. J., and Higgs, A. C. "Relations between Work Group Characteristics and Effectiveness: Implications for Designing Effective Work Groups." *Personnel Psychology,* 1993, *46,* 823–850; Campion, M. A., Papper, E. M., and Medsker, G. J. "Relations between Work Team

Characteristics and Effectiveness: A Replication and Extension." *Personnel Psychology*, 1996, *49*, 429–452.

22. Mathieu, J. E., and Ruddy, T. M. "External Leadership and Statistical Process Control Influences on Team Processes and Performance: A Quasi-Experiment." In J. R. Rentsch (Chair), *Keys to High Team Performance on Complex Tasks*. Symposium presented at the 20th annual conference of the Society for Industrial and Organizational Psychology, Los Angeles, April 2005.

23. Shea, G. P., and Guzzo, R. A. "Groups as Human Resources." In G. R. Ferris and K. M. Rowland (eds.), *Research in Personnel and Human Resource Management*, Vol. 5 (pp. 323–356). Greenwich, Conn.: JAI Press, 1987; Thomas, E. J. "Effects of Facilitative Role Interdependence on Group Functioning." *Human Relations*, 1957, *10*, 347–366.

24. Fleishman, E. A. "Twenty Years of Consideration and Structure." In E. A. Fleishman and J. G. Hunt (eds.), *Current Developments in the Study of Leadership* (pp. 1–40). Carbondale: Southern Illinois University Press, 1973.

25. DeShon, R. P., Kozlowski, S.W.J., Schmidt, A. M., Milner, K. R., and Wiechmann, D. "A Multiple Goal, Multilevel Model of Feedback Effects on the Regulation of Individual and Team Performance in Training." *Journal of Applied Psychology*, in press.

26. Rutkowski, K. A., and Steelman, L. A. "Testing a Path Model for Antecedents of Accountability." *Journal of Management Development*, 2005, *24*, 473–486.

27. Weldon, E., and Weingart, L. R. "Group Goals and Group Performance." *British Journal of Social Psychology*, 1993, *32*, 307–334.

28. Hackman, *Leading Teams*.

29. Fleishman, "Twenty Years."

30. Hass, M. *Organizing Knowledge Work: A Study of Project Teams at an International Development Agency*. Unpublished doctoral dissertation, Cambridge, Mass.: Harvard University, 2002.

31. Fleishman, "Twenty Years."

32. Hackman, *Leading Teams*.

33. Murphy, K. R., and Cleveland, J. N. *Understanding Performance Appraisal: Social, Organizational, and Goal-Based Perspectives*. Thousand Oaks, Calif.: Sage, 1995.

34. Hackman, *Leading Teams*.

35. Eisenhardt, K. M., and Schoonhoven, C. B. "Organizational Growth: Linking Founding Team Strategy, Environment, and Growth among U.S. Semi-Conductor Ventures, 1978–1988." *Administrative Science Quarterly*, 1990, *35*, 484–503.

36. Hackman, *Leading Teams*.

37. Eaton, N. K., and Neff, J. F. "The Effects of Tank Crew Turbulence on Tank Gunner Performance." ARI Technical Paper 350. Alexandria, Va.: U.S. Army Research Institute for the Behavioral and Social Sciences, September 1978.

38. Katz, R. "The Effects of Group Longevity on Project Communication and Performance." *Administrative Science Quarterly,* 1982, *27,* 81–104.

39. Burke, C. S., Stagl, K. C., Salas, E., Pierce, L., and Kendall, D. L. "Understanding Team Adaptation: A Conceptual Analysis and Model." *Journal of Applied Psychology,* in press.

40. Fleishman, "Twenty Years."

41. Korsgaard, M. A., Schweiger, D. M., and Sapienza, H. J. "Building Commitment, Attachment, and Trust in Strategic Decision-Making Teams: The Role of Procedural Justice." *Academy of Management Journal,* 1993, *38,* 60–84.

42. Graen, G. B., and Uhl-Bien, M. "Relationship-Based Approach to Leadership: Development of Leader-Member Exchange (LMX) Theory of Leadership over 25 Years: Applying a Multi-Level Multi-Domain Perspective." *Special Issue: Leadership: The Multiple-Level Approaches,* Part 1. *Leadership Quarterly,* 1995, *6,* 219–247.

43. Hackman, *Leading Teams*.

44. Ibid.

45. Mohrman, S. A., Cohen, S. G., and Mohrman, A. M. *Designing Team-Based Organizations.* San Francisco. Jossey-Bass, 1995.

46. Fleishman, E. A., Mumford, M. D., Zaccaro, S. J., Levin, K. Y., Korotkin, A. L., and Hein, M. B. "Taxonomic Efforts in the Description of Leader Behavior: A Synthesis and Functional Interpretation." *Leadership Quarterly,* 1991, *4,* 245–287.

47. Hackman, *Leading Teams*.

48. Welch, J., and Welch, S. *Winning.* New York: HarperCollins, 2005.

49. Bass, B. M. *Leadership and Performance beyond Expectations.* New York: Free Press, 1985; House, R. J. "A 1976 Theory of Charismatic Leadership." In J. G. Hunt and L. L. Larsen (eds.), *Leadership: The Cutting Edge.* Carbondale: Southern Illinois University Press, 1977.

50. Hershock, R. J., Cowman, C. D., and Peters, D. "From Experience: Action Teams That Work." *Journal of Product Innovation Management,* 1994, *11,* 95–104.

51. Klein, C., Stagl, K. C., Salas, E., Van Eynde, D. F., and Parker, C. "Leading from Within: Transformational Leadership in NASA's Space Shuttle Mission Management Team." Under review.

52. Hackman, *Leading Teams*.

53. House, R. J., and Shamir, B. "Toward the Integration of Transformational, Charismatic, and Visionary Theories." In M. M. Chemers and R. Ayman (eds.), *Leadership Theory and Research: Perspective and Directions* (pp. 245–270). New York: Academic Press, 1993.

54. Bass, B. M. *Bass and Stogdill's Handbook of Leadership.* New York: Free Press, 1990; Bass, B. M. *Transformational Leadership: Individual, Military and Educational Impact.* Mahwah, N.J.: Erlbaum, 1998.

55. Hackman, *Leading Teams.*

56. Ibid.

57. Fleishman and others, "Taxonomic Efforts."

58. Kozlowski, S.W.J., Gully, S. M., Salas, E., and Cannon-Bowers, J. A. "Team Leadership and Development: Theory, Principles, and Guidelines for Training Leaders and Teams." In M. Beyerlein, S. Beyerlein, and D. Johnson (eds.), *Advances in Interdisciplinary Studies of Work Teams: Team Leadership,* Vol. 3 (pp. 253–292). Greenwich, Conn.: JAI Press, 1996.

59. Hackman, *Leading Teams.*

60. Hackman and Oldham, *Work Redesign.*

61. Cummings, T. G. "Self-Regulating Work Groups: A Socio-Technical Synthesis." *Academy of Management Review,* 1978, *3,* 625–634.

62. Deci, E. L. *Intrinsic Motivation.* New York: Plenum, 1975.

63. Manz, C. C., and Sims, H. P. *SuperLeadership.* New York: Berkley Books, 1990.

64. Hackman, "Design of Work Teams."

65. Ibid.

66. Hackman, J. R. "Group Influences on Individuals in Organizations." In. M. D. Dunnette and L. M. Hough (eds.), *Handbook of Industrial and Organizational Psychology,* Vol. 3. (pp. 143–193). Palo Alto, Calif.: Consulting Psychologists Press, 1992.

67. Hyatt, D. E., and Ruddy, T. R. "An Examination of the Relationship between Work Group Characteristics and Performance: Once More into the Breech." *Personnel Psychology,* 1997, *50,* 553–585.

68. Ibid.

69. Sundstrom, E., McIntyre, M., Halfhill, T., and Richards, H. "Work Groups: From the Hawthorne Studies to Work Teams of the 1990s and Beyond." *Group Dynamics,* 2000, *4,* 44–67.

70. Fleishman, "Twenty Years."

71. Hackman, *Leading Teams.*

72. Kozlowski and others, "Team Leadership and Development."

73. Kets de Vries, M.F.R. "Leadership Group Coaching in Action: The Zen of Creating High Performance Teams." *Academy of Management Executive,* 2005, *19,* 61–76.

74. Fleishman and others, "Taxonomic Efforts."

75. Bell, S. T. *Team Composition Variables and Team Performance: A Comprehensive Meta-Analysis.* Poster session presented at the 20th annual conference of the Society for Industrial and Organizational Psychology Conference, Los Angeles, April 2005; Kozlowski, S.W.J., and Bell, B. S. "Work Groups and Teams in Organizations." In W. C. Borman, D. R. Ilgen, and R. J. Klimoski (eds.), *Handbook of Psychology: Industrial and Organizational Psychology,* Vol. 12 (pp. 333–375). London, England: Wiley, 2003.

76. Kameda, T., Stasson, M. F., Davis, J. H., Parks, C. D., and Zimmerman, S. K. "Social Dilemmas, Subgroups, and Motivation Loss in Task-Oriented Groups: In Search of an 'Optimal' Team Size in Division of Work." *Social Psychology Quarterly,* 1992, *55,* 47–56.

77. Steiner, I. D. *Group Process and Productivity.* New York: Academic Press, 1972.

78. Kidd, J. S. "A Comparison of One-, Two-, and Three-Man Work Units under Various Conditions of Workload." *Journal of Applied Psychology,* 1961, *45,* 195–200; O'Connell, M. S., Doverspike, D., and Cober, A. B. "Leadership and Semiautonomous Work Team Performance." *Group and Organization Management,* 2002, *27,* 50–65.

79. Kameda and others, "Social Dilemmas, Subgroups, and Motivation Loss"; Wageman, R. "Interdependence and Group Effectiveness." *Administrative Science Quarterly,* 1995, *40,* 145–180.

80. Driskell, J. E., Hogan, R., and Salas, E. "Personality and Group Performance." In *Group Processes and Intergroup Relations: Review of Personality and Social Psychology* (pp. 91–112). Beverly Hills, Calif.: Sage, 1987; Jackson, S. E., and Joshi, A. "Research on Domestic and International Diversity in Organizations: A Merger That Works?" In N. Anderson, D. Ones, H. Sinangil, and C. Viswesvaran (eds.), *Handbook of Industrial, Work and Organizational Psychology* (pp. 206–231). London: Sage, 2001.

81. Kozlowski and Bell, "Work Groups and Teams."

82. Barry, B., and Stewart, G. L. "Composition, Process, and Performance in Self-Managed Groups: The Role of Personality." *Journal of Applied Psychology,* 1997, *82,* 62–78.

83. Hackman, *Leading Teams.*

84. Ibid.

85. Wageman, "How Leaders Foster Self-Managing Team Effectiveness"; Mohrman and others, *Designing Team-Based Organizations;* Wageman, "Interdependence and Group Effectiveness"; Pritchard, R. D., Jones, S., Roth, P., Stuebing, K., and Ekeberg, S. "Effects of Group Feedback, Goal Setting, and Incentives on Organizational Productivity." *Journal of Applied Psychology,* 1988, *73,* 337–358.

86. Bass, *Leadership and Performance.*

87. Druskat, V. U., and Kayes, D. C. "The Antecedents of Team Competence: Toward a Fine-Grained Model of Self-Managing Team Effectiveness." *Research on Managing Groups and Teams,* 1999, *2,* 201–231.

88. Gladstein, D. L. "Groups in Context: A Model of Task Group Effectiveness." *Administrative Science Quarterly,* 1984, *29,* 499–517.

89. Vroom, V. H. *Work and Motivation.* New York: Wiley, 1964.

90. Fleishman and others, "Taxonomic Efforts."

91. Gibson, C. B., and Kirkman, B. L. "Our Past, Present, and Future in Teams: The Role of Human Resource Professionals in Managing Team Performance." In A. I. Kraut and A. K. Korman (eds.), *Evolving Practices in Human Resource Management: Responses to a Changing World of Work* (pp. 90–117). San Francisco: Jossey-Bass, 1999.

92. Whitsett, D. A., and Yorks, L. "Looking Back at Topeka: General Foods and the Quality-of-Work-Life Experiment." *California Management Review,* 1983, *25,* 93–109.

93. Bennis, W. *The Leadership Advantage: Leader to Leader.* Hoboken, N.J.: Jossey-Bass, 1999; Stagl, K. C., Salas, E., Rosen, M. A., Priest, H. A., Burke, C. S., Goodwin, G. F., and Johnston, J. H. "Distributed Team Performance: A Multilevel Review of Distribution, Demography, and Decision-Making." In F. Yammarino and F. Dansereau (eds.), *Multi-Level Issues in Organizations,* Elsevier, in press.

94. Hyatt and Ruddy, "Relationship between Work Group Characteristics and Performance."

95. Janz and others, "Knowledge Worker Team Effectiveness."

96. Lanzetta, J. T., and Roby, T. B. "Effects of Work Group Structure and Certain Task Variables on Group Performance." *Journal of Abnormal and Social Psychology,* 1956, *53,* 307–314.

97. Ancona, D. G., and Caldwell, D. F. "Bridging the Boundary: External Activity Performance in Organizational Teams." *Administrative Science Quarterly,* 1992, *37,* 634–655.

98. Griffin, A., and Hauser, J. R. "Integrating R&D and Marketing: A Review and Analysis of the Literature." *Journal of Product Innovation Management,* 1996, *13,* 191–215.

99. Hackman, *Leading Teams.*

100. Ancona and Caldwell, "Bridging the Boundary."

101. Campbell, J. P., and Kuncel, N. R. "Individual and Team Training." In Anderson and others, *Handbook of Industrial, Work and Organizational Psychology* (pp. 272–312).

102. Campbell, J. P., McCloy, R. A., Oppler, S. H., and Sager, C. E. "A Theory of Performance." In N. Schmitt and W. C. Borman (eds.), *Personnel Selection in Organizations* (pp. 35–70). San Francisco: Jossey-Bass, 1993.

103. Freeman, C., and Simmon, D. A. *Taxonomy of Crew Resource Management: Information Processing Domain.* In R. S. Jensen (ed.), *Proceedings of the 6th Annual International Symposium on Aviation Psychology* (pp. 391–397). Columbus: Ohio State University, 1991.

104. Salas, E., Fowlkes, J. E., Stout, R. J., Milanovich, D. M., and Prince, C. "Does CRM Training Improve Teamwork Skills in the Cockpit?: Two Evaluation Studies." *Human Factors,* 1999, *41,* 326–343.

105. Hackman, *Leading Teams.*

106. Wageman, "Interdependence and Group Effectiveness."

107. Ibid.

108. Hackman, J. R., and Wageman, R. "A Theory of Team Coaching." *Academy of Management Review,* 2005, *30,* 269–287, at 269.

109. Salas, E., Rozell, D., Mullen, B., and Driskell, J. E. "The Effect of Team Building on Performance: An Integration." *Small Group Research,* 1999, *30,* 309–329.

110. Burns, G. "The Secrets of Team Facilitation." *Training and Development,* 1995, *49,* 46–52; Tannenbaum, S. I., Smith-Jentsch, K. A., and Behson, S. J. "Training Team Leaders to Facilitate Team Learning and Performance." In J. A. Cannon-Bowers and E. Salas (eds.), *Making Decisions under Stress: Implications for Individual and Team Training* (pp. 247–270). Washington, D.C.: APA, 1998.

111. Hackman, *Leading Teams.*

112. Hackman and Wageman, "A Theory of Team Coaching."

113. Yammarino, F. J. "Group Leadership: A Levels of Analysis Perspective." In M. A. West (Ed.), *Handbook of Work Group Psychology.* London, England: Wiley, 1996.

114. Hackman and Wageman, "A Theory of Team Coaching."

115. Gersick, C.J.G. "Time and Transition in Work Teams: Toward a New Model of Group Development." *Academy of Management Journal,* 1988, *31,* 9–41; Gersick, C.J.G. "Marking Time: Predictable Transitions in Task Groups." *Academy of Management Journal,* 1989, *31,* 12–37.

116. Tannenbaum and others, "Training Team Leaders."

117. Smith-Jentsch, K. A., Salas, E., and Brannick, M. T. "Leadership Style as a Predictor of Teamwork Behavior: Setting the Stage by Managing Team Climate." In K. Nilan (Chair), *Understanding Teams and the Nature of Teamwork.* Symposium presented at the 9th annual conference of the Society for Industrial and Organizational Psychology, Nashville, April 1994.

118. Edmondson, A. "Psychological Safety and Learning Behavior in Work Teams." *Administrative Science Quarterly,* 1999, *44,* 350–383.

119. Marks, M. A., Zaccaro, S. J., and Mathieu, J. E. "Performance Implications of Leader Briefings and Team-Interaction Training for Team Adaptation to Novel Environments." *Journal of Applied Psychology,* 2000, *85,* 971–986.

120. Hackman, *Leading Teams.*
121. Bass, *Transformational Leadership.*
122. Gully, S. M, Incalcaterra, K. A., Joshi A., and Beaubien, J. M. "A Meta-Analysis of Team Efficacy, Potency, and Performance: Interdependence and Level of Analysis as Moderators of Observed Relationships." *Journal of Applied Psychology,* 2002, *87,* 819–832.
123. Edmondson, A. C. "Speaking Up in the Operating Room: How Team Leaders Promote Learning in Interdisciplinary Action Teams." *Journal of Management Studies,* 2003, *40,* 1419–1452.
124. Hackman, *Leading Teams.*
125. Hackman and Wageman, "Theory of Team Coaching."
126. Fleishman, "Twenty Years."
127. Kozlowski and others, "Team Leadership and Development."
128. Hackman, *Leading Teams.*
129. Tannenbaum and others, "Training Team Leaders."
130. Kozlowski and others, "Team Leadership and Development"; Smith-Jentsch, K. A., Blickensderfer, E., Salas, E., and Cannon-Bowers, J. A. "Helping Team Members Help Themselves: Propositions for Facilitating Guided Team Self-Correction." *Advances in Interdisciplinary Studies of Work Teams,* 2000, *6,* 55–72.
131. Tannenbaum and others, "Training Team Leaders."
132. Salas, E., Burke, C. S., and Stagl, K. C. "Developing Teams and Team Leaders: Strategies and Principles." In D. Day, S. J. Zaccaro, and S. M. Halpin (eds.), *Leader Development for Transforming Organizations* (pp. 325–357). Mahwah, N.J.: Erlbaum, 2004.
133. Stogdill, R. M. *Handbook of Leadership: A Survey of Theory and Research.* New York: Free Press, 1974, 7.
134. Bass, B. M., and Avolio, B. J. "Transformational Leadership: A Response to Critiques." In J. G. Hunt, B. R. Baliga, H. P. Dachler, and C. A. Schriesheim (eds.), *Emerging Leadership Vistas* (pp. 49–80). Lexington, Mass.: D. C. Heath, 1993; Salas, E., Stagl, K. C., and Burke, C. S. "25 Years of Team Effectiveness in Organizations: Research Themes and Emerging Needs." In C. L. Cooper and I. T. Robertson (eds.), *International Review of Industrial and Organizational Psychology* (pp. 47–91). New York: Wiley, 2004.

Chapter Nine: Best Practices in Leading Organizational Change

1. Bridges, W. *Managing Transitions: Making the Most of Change.* Reading, Mass.: Wesley, 1991.

2. See, for example, Hamel, G. *Leading the Revolution.* Boston: Harvard Business School Press, 2000.

3. O'Toole, J. *Leading Change.* San Francisco: Jossey-Bass, 1995.

4. Marks, M. L. *Charging Back Up the Hill: Workplace Recovery after Mergers, Acquisitions, and Downsizings.* San Francisco: Jossey-Bass, 2003.

5. Cartwright, S., and McCarthy, S. "Developing a Framework for Cultural Due Diligence in Mergers and Acquisitions." In G. K. Stahl and M. E. Mendenhall (eds.), *Mergers and Acquisitions: Managing Culture and Human Resources* (pp. 253–267). Stanford, Calif.: Stanford Business Books, 2005; Ashkenas, R. N., and Francis, S. C. "Integration Managers: Special Leaders for Special Times." *Harvard Business* Review, 2000, *78*(6), 130–145.

6. DeMeuse, K., and Marks, M. L. *Resizing the Organization—Managing Layoffs, Divestitures, and Closings: Maximizing Gain While Minimizing Pain.* San Francisco: Jossey-Bass, 2003; Cascio, W. F., Young, C. E., and Morris, J. R. "Financial Consequences of Employment-Change Decisions in Major U.S. Corporations." *Academy of Management Journal,* 1997, *40*(5), 1175–1189.

7. Marks, M. L., and Mirvis, P. H. *Joining Forces: Making One Plus One Equal Three in Mergers, Acquisitions, and Alliances.* San Francisco: Jossey-Bass, 1998.

8. Bridges, *Managing Transitions.*

9. Marks, M. L., and DeMeuse, K. "Resizing the Organization: Maximizing the Gain While Minimizing the Pain of Layoffs, Divestitures, and Closings." *Organizational Dynamics,* 2005, *34*(4), 19–35.

10. Wiley, J. W., and Moechnig, K. R. "The Effects of Mergers and Acquisitions on Organizational Climate." Paper presented at the Society of Industrial/Organizational Psychologists, Los Angeles, April 2005.

11. Greenberg, J. R. "The Latest AMA Survey on Downsizing." *Compensation and Benefits Review,* 1990, *22,* 66–71.

12. Cameron, K. S., Sutton, R. I., and Whetten, D. A. *Readings in Organizational Decline: Frameworks, Research, and Prescriptions.* Cambridge, Mass.: Ballinger, 1987.

13. Latack, J. C., and Dozier, J. B. "After the Axe Falls: Job Loss as a Career Transition." *Academy of Management Review,* 1986, *11,* 375–392.

14. Catalino, R., Rook, K., and Dooley, D. "Labor Markets and Help Seeking: A Test of the Employment Security Hypothesis." *Journal of Health and Social Behavior,* 1986, *27,* 227–237; Volinn, E., Lai, D., McKinney, S., and Loesser, J. D. "When Back Pain Becomes Disabling: A Regional Analysis." *Pain,* 1998, *33,* 33–39.

15. Lewin, K. "Frontiers in Group Dynamics." *Human Relations,* 1947, *1,* 5–41.
16. Ibid.
17. Carr, Adrian. "Understanding Emotion and Emotionality in a Process of Change." *Journal of Organizational Change Management,* 2001, *14*(5), 421–434; Huy, Q. N. "Emotional Capability, Emotional Intelligence, and Radical Change." *Academy of Management Review,* 1999, *24*(2), 325–345; Kusstatscher, V., and Cooper, C. *Managing Emotions in Mergers and Acquisitions.* London: Edward Elgar Publishing, 2005; Marks, M. L., and Mirvis, P. H. "Making Mergers and Acquisitions Work: Strategic and Psychological Preparation." *Academy of Management Executive,* 2001, *15*(2), 35–47.
18. Urch Druskat, V., and Wol, S. B. "Building the Emotional Intelligence of Groups." *Harvard Business Review,* 2001, *79*(3), 80–90.
19. Greiner, L. E., and Cummings, T. G. "Wanted: OD More Alive Than Dead!" *Journal of Applied Behavioral Science,* 2004, *40,* 374–391.
21. Ross, J., and Staw, B. M. "Organizational Escalation and Exit: Lessons from the Shoreham Nuclear Power Plant." *Academy of Management Journal,* 1993, *36*(4), 701–732.
21. Ciulla, J. B. *The Working Life.* New York: Times Books, 2000.
22. Marks, *Charging Back Up the Hill.*
23. Coch, L., and French, J.R.P. Jr. "Overcoming Resistance to Change." *Human Relations,* August 1948, 512–532; Kotter, J. P. "Leading Change: Why Transformation Efforts Fail." *Harvard Business Review,* 1995 (March–April), 61–73.
24. Pascale, R., Millemann, M., and Gioja, L. "Changing the Way We Change." *Harvard Business Review,* 1997, *75*(6), 126–139.
25. Kotter, "Leading Change."
26. Chattopadyhah, P., Glick, W. H., and Huber, G. P. "Organizational Actions in Response to Threats and Opportunities." *Academy of Management Journal,* 2001, *44*(5), 937–955.

Chapter Ten: Best Practices in Leading at Strategic Levels

1. Kochan, T. A. "Addressing the Crisis in Confidence in Corporations: Root Causes, Victims and Strategies for Reform." *Academy of Management Executive,* 2002, *16,* 139–141.
2. McWilliams, A., and Siegel, D. "Corporate Social Responsibility: A Theory of the Firm Perspective." *Academy of Management Review,* 2001, *26,* 117–227.

3. Thomas, T., Schermerhorn, J. R. Jr., and Dienhart, J. W. "Strategic Leadership of Ethical Behavior in Business." *Academy of Management Executive,* 2004, *18*(2), 56–66.

4. Donaldson, T., and Preston, L. "The Stakeholder Theory of the Corporation: Concepts, Evidence, and Implications." *Academy of Management Review,* 1995, *20,* 65–91; McWilliam, A., Siegel, D., and Wright, P. M. "Corporate Social Responsibility: Strategic Implications." *Journal of Management Studies,* 2006, *43,* 1–18; Waldman, D. A., Sully, M., Washburn, N., and House, R. J. "Cultural and Leadership Predictors of Corporate Social Responsibility Values of Top Management: A GLOBE Study of 15 Countries." *Journal of International Business Studies,* in press.

5. Ghoshal, S. "Bad Management Theories Are Destroying Good Management Practices." *Academy of Management Learning and Education,* 2005, *4,* 75–91, at 76.

6. Porter, M. E. *Competitive Strategy: Techniques for Analyzing Industries and Firms.* New York: Free Press, 1980.

7. Hillman, A. J., and Keim, G. D. "Shareholder Value, Stakeholder Management, and Social Issues: What's the Bottom Line?" *Strategic Management Journal,* 2001, *22,* 125–139.

8. Carmeli, A., Gilat, A., and Waldman, D. A. "The Role of Perceived Organizational Performance in Member Identification, Behavioral Integration, and Job Performance." Under revision for the *Journal of Management Studies,* 2006.

9. Thomas and others, "Strategic Leadership of Ethical Behavior"; Waldman, D. A., Ramirez, G. G., House, R. J., and Puranam, P. "Does Leadership Matter?: CEO Leadership Attributes under Conditions of Perceived Environmental Uncertainty." *Academy of Management Journal,* 2001, *44,* 134–143.

10. Porter, *Competitive Strategy.*

11. Geiger, M. A., and Taylor, P. L. III. "CEO and CFO Certifications of Financial Information." *Accounting Horizons,* 2003, *17,* 357–368.

12. Solomon, D. "Corporate Governance (A Special Report): At What Price? Critics Say the Cost of Complying with Sarbanes-Oxley Is a Lot Higher Than It Should Be." *Wall Street Journal,* October 17, 2005, p. R3.

13. Henry, D., and Borrus, A. "Honesty Is a Pricey Policy: Execs Are Grumbling about the Steep Costs of Complying with New Financial Controls." *Business Week,* October 27, 2003, p. 100.

14. Bass, B. M. *Leadership and Performance beyond Expectations.* New York: Free Press, 1985; Bass, B. M. "Does the Transactional-Transformational Leadership Paradigm Transcend Organizational and National Boundaries?" *American*

Psychologist, 1997, *52*, 130–139; Pawar, B. S., and Eastman, K. K. "The Nature and Implications of Contextual Influences on Transformational Leadership: A Conceptual Examination." *Academy of Management Review*, 1997, *22*, 80–109; Conger, J. A., and Kanungo, R. N. *Charismatic Leadership in Organizations.* Thousand Oaks, Calif.: Sage, 1998; Shamir, B., House, R. J., and Arthur, M. B. "The Motivational Effects of Charismatic Leadership: A Self-Concept Based Theory." *Organization Science*, 1993, *4*, 577–594.

15. House, R. J., and Howell, J. M. "Personality and Charismatic Leadership." *Leadership Quarterly*, 1992, *3*, 81–108.

16. Kohlberg, L. "Moral Stages and Moralization: The Cognitive-Developmental Approach." In T. Likona (ed.), *Moral Development and Behavior: Theory, Research, and Social Issues* (pp. 31–53). Austin, TX: Holt, Rinehart and Winston, 1976.

17. Winter, D. G. "A Motivational Model of Leadership: Predicting Long-Term Management Success from TAT Measures of Power Motivation and Responsibility." *Leadership Quarterly*, 1991, *2*, 67–80.

18. Olsen, L. *Making Corporate Responsibility Work: Lessons from Real Business.* Report issued by the Ashridge Centre for Business and Society and the British Quality Foundation, 2004. [http://www.qualityfoundation.co.uk/pub_reports.htm].

19. Kohlberg, "Moral Stages and Moralization."

20. Daft, R. L. *The Leadership Experience* (3rd ed.). Cincinnati, OH: South-Western, 2005.

21. Millar, M. "Gillette Executives Expect Takeover Windfall." 2005. [http://www.personneltoday.com/Articles/Article.aspx?liArticleID=27721 andPrinterFriendly=true].

22. Kohlberg, "Moral Stages and Moralization."

23. Conger and Kanungo, *Charismatic Leadership in Organizations*; Kouzes, J. M., and Posner, B. Z. *The Leadership Challenge: How to Get Extraordinary Things Done in Organizations.* San Francisco: Jossey-Bass, 1987; Nanus, B. *Visionary Leadership.* San Francisco: Jossey-Bass, 1992; Sashkin, "Visionary Leader."

24. Berson, Y., Shamir, B., Avolio, B. J., and Popper, M. "The Relationship between Vision Strength, Leadership Style, and Context." *Leadership Quarterly*, 2001, *12*, 53–73; Conger and Kanungo, *Charismatic Leadership in Organizations;* House, R. J. "Value Based Leadership." *Personalführung*, June 1995, 476–479; Nanus, *Visionary Leadership.*

25. Nanus, *Visionary Leadership;* Sashkin, "Visionary Leader."

26. Shamir, B. "The Charismatic Relationship: Alternative Explanations and Predictions." *Leadership Quarterly*, 1991, *2*, 81–104.

27. Collins, J. C., and Porras, J. I. "Building Your Company's Vision." *Harvard Business Review*, 1996 (September–October), 65–77, at 70.

28. Carmeli and others, "The Role of Perceived Organizational Performance."
29. Gottlieb, J. Z., and Sanzgiri, J. "Towards an Ethical Dimension of Decision Making in Organizations." *Journal of Business Ethics,* 1996, *15,* 1275–1285.
30. Senge, P. M. *The Fifth Discipline: The Art and Practice of the Learning Organization.* New York: Doubleday, 1990.
31. Pearce, C. L., and Conger, J. A. "All Those Years Ago: The Historical Underpinnings of Shared Leadership." In C. L. Pearce and J. A. Conger (eds.), *Shared Leadership: Reframing the Hows and Whys of Leadership* (pp. 1–18). Thousand Oaks, Calif.: Sage, 2003, 1.
32. Bass, *Leadership and Performance beyond Expectations;* Manz, C. C., and Sims, H. P. Jr. "Superleadership: Beyond the Myth of Heroic Leadership." *Organizational Dynamics,* 1991, *19,* 18–35; Manz, C. C., and Sims, H. P. Jr. *The New SuperLeadership: Leading Others to Lead Themselves.* San Francisco: Berrett-Koehler, 2001; Tichy, N. M., and Devanna, M. A. *The Transformational Leader.* New York: Wiley, 1986.
33. Youngdahl, W., Waldman, D. A., and Anders, G. "Leading the Total Quality Transformation at Goodyear-Oxo, Mexico: An Interview with Hugh Pace." *Journal of Management Inquiry,* 1998, *7,* 59–65.
34. Conger and Kanungo, *Charismatic Leadership in Organizations.*
35. Porter, M. E., and Kramer, M. R. "The Competitive Advantage of Corporate Philanthropy." *Harvard Business Review,* 2002, *80,* 56–69.
36. Ibid.
37. Waldman, D. A., Siegel, D., and Javidan, M. "Components of CEO Transformational Leadership and Corporate Social Responsibility." *Journal of Management Studies,* in press.
38. Herman, S. W., and Schaefer, A. G. *Spiritual Goods: Faith Traditions and the Practice of Business.* Charlottesville, Va.: Philosophy Documentation Center, 2001; Neal, J. A. "Work as a Service to the Divine: Giving Our Gifts Selflessly and with Joy." *Applied Behavioral Scientist,* 2000, *43*(8), 116–133.
39. Carmeli and others, "Perceived Organizational Performance"; Shamir, B., House, R. J., and Arthur, M. B. "The Motivational Effects of Charismatic Leadership: A Self-Concept Based Theory." *Organization Science,* 1993, *4,* 577–594.
40. Van Knippenberg, D., and Hogg, M. "A Social Identity Model of Leadership Effectiveness in Organizations." *Research in Organizational Behavior,* 2003, *25,* 243–295.
41. Gardner, W. L., and Avolio, B. J. "The Charismatic Relationship: A Dramaturgical Perspective." *Academy of Management Review,* 1998, *23,* 32–58.
42. Marks, M. L., and Mirvis, P. H. *Joining Forces: Making One Plus One Equal Three in Mergers, Acquisitions, and Alliances.* San Francisco: Jossey-Bass, 1998.

43. Gadiesh, O., Buchanan, R., Daniell, M., and Ormiston, C. "The Leadership Testing Ground." *Journal of Business Strategy,* 2002, *23*(2), 12–17, at 13.

44. Schneider, B. "The People Make the Place." *Personnel Psychology,* 1987, *40,* 437–454.

45. Ibid.; Schneider, B., Smith, D. B., Taylor, S., and Fleenor, J. "Personality and Organizations: A Test of the Homogeneity of Personality Hypothesis." *Journal of Applied Psychology,* 1998, *83,* 462–470.

46. Shamir and others, "Motivational Effects of Charismatic Leadership."

47. Lachman, R., Nedd, A., and Hinings, C. R. "Analyzing Cross-National Management and Organizations: A Theoretical Framework." *Management Science,* 1994, *40,* 40–55; Pant, P. N., and Lachman, R. "Value Incongruity and Strategic Choice." *Journal of Management Studies,* 1998, *35,* 195–212.

Chapter Eleven: Best Practices in Corporate Boardroom Leadership

1. Finegold, D., and Lawler, E. *USC/Mercer Corporate Board Survey.* Los Angeles: University of Southern California, Center for Effective Organizations, 2004.

2. Conger, J. A., Lawler, E. E., and Finegold, D. L. *Corporate Boards: New Strategies for Adding Value at the Top.* San Francisco: Jossey-Bass, 2001.

3. Daily, C. M., and Dalton, D. R. "CEO and Board Chair Roles Held Jointly or Separately: Much Ado about Nothing." *Academy of Management Executive,* 1997, *11*(3), 11-20.

4. Miller, W. "Make It Chairman and CEO." *Industry Week,* January 6, 1997, p. 50.

5. Dalton, D. R., Daily, C. M., Ellstrand, A. E., and Johnson, J. L. "Meta-Analytic Reviews of Board Composition, Leadership Structure, and Financial Performance." *Strategic Management Journal,* 1998, *19,* 269–290.

6. Conger and others, *Corporate Boards,* 61.

7. Henderson, D. "Redraw the Line between the Board and the CEO." *Harvard Business Review,* 1995 (March–April), 160.

8. Ibid., 162.

9. Ibid.

10. Spencer Stuart Board Index. New York: Spencer Stuart, 2004.

11. These responsibilities are derived from ones identified in Paul Firstenberg and Burton Malkiel's article in the *Sloan Management Review,* "The Twenty-First Century Boardroom: Who Will Be in Charge?" (Fall 1994), 31–32.

12. Lawler, E. E., and Finegold, D. L. "The Changing Face of Corporate Boards." *Sloan Management Review,* 2005, *46*(2), 67–70.

Chapter Thirteen: Best Practices in Leading Diverse Organizations

1. Offermann, L. R., and Phan, L. U. "Culturally Intelligent Leadership for a Diverse World." In R. Riggio, S. E. Murphy, and F. Pirozzolo (eds.), *Multiple Intelligences and Leadership* (pp. 187–214). Mahwah, N.J.: Erlbaum, 2002.
2. Bargh, J. A. "The Cognitive Monster: The Case against the Controllability of Automatic Stereotype Effects." In S. Chaiken and Y. Trope (eds.), *Dual-Process Theories in Social Psychology* (pp. 361–382). New York: Guilford, 1999.
3. Williams, K. Y., and O'Reilly, C. A. "Demography and Diversity in Organizations: A Review of 40 Years of Research." *Research in Organizational Behavior,* 1998, *20,* 77–140.
4. Tsui, A. S., Egan, T. D., and O'Reilly, C. A. III. "Being Different: Relational Demography and Organizational Attachment." *Administrative Science Quarterly,* 1992, *37,* 549–579.
5. Sanchez, J. I., and Brock, P. "Outcomes of Perceived Discrimination among Hispanic Employees: Is Diversity Management a Luxury or a Necessity?" *Academy of Management Journal,* 1996, *39,* 704–718.
6. Elron, E. "Top Management Teams within Multinational Corporations: Effects of Cultural Heterogeneity." *Leadership Quarterly,* 1997, *8,* 393–412.
7. Williams, M. L., and Bauer, T. N. "The Effect of a Managing Diversity Policy on Organizational Attractiveness." *Group and Organizational Management,* 1994, *19,* 295–308.
8. Wright, P., Ferris, S. P., Hiller, J. S., and Krull, M. "Competitiveness through Management of Diversity: Effects on Stock Price Valuation." *Academy of Management Journal,* 1995, *38,* 272–287.
9. Kanter, R. M. *Men and Women of the Corporation.* New York: Basic Books, 1977.
10. Bobo, L. D. "Prejudice as Group Position: Microfoundations of a Sociological Approach to Racism and Race Relations." *Journal of Social Issues,* 1999, *55,* 445–472.
11. Schreiber, C. "Changing Places: Men and Women in Transitional Occupations." Cambridge, Mass.: MIT Press, 1979; Fairhurst, G., and Snavely, B. "A Test of the Social Isolation of Male Tokens." *Academy of Management Journal,* 1983, *26,* 353–361; O'Farrell, B., and Harlan, S. "Craftworkers and Clerks: The Effect of Male Coworker Hostility on Women's Satisfaction with Nontraditional Jobs." *Social Problems,* 1982, *29,* 252–264.

12. Reskin, B. F., McBrier, D. B., and Kmec, J. A. "The Determinants and Consequences of Workplace Sex and Race Composition." *Annual Review of Sociology,* 1999, *25,* 335–361.

13. Hewstone, M., Martin, R., Hammer-Hewstone, C., Crisp, R. J., and Voci, A. "Majority-Minority Relations in Organizations: Challenges and Opportunities." In M. A. Hogg and D. J. Terry (eds.), *Social Identity Processes in Organizational Contexts:* Philadelphia. Psychology Press, 2001.

14. Roccas, S., and Brewer, M. "Social Identity Complexity." *Personality and Social Psychology Review,* 2002, *6,* 88–106.

15. Hofstede, G. *Cultures and Organizations: Software of the Mind.* London, England: McGraw-Hill, 1991.

16. Tsui, A. S., and O'Reilly, C. A., III. "Beyond Simple Demographic Effects: The Importance of Relational Demography in Superior-Subordinate Dyads." *Academy of Management Journal,* 1989, *32,* 402–423.

17. Chong, L.M.A., and Thomas, D. C. "Leadership Perceptions in Cross-Cultural Context." *Leadership Quarterly,* 1997, *8,* 275–293.

18. Hall, E. T. *The Silent Language.* Greenwich, Conn.: Fawcett Premier Book, 1959, 39.

19. Offermann, L. R., and Hellmann, P. S. "Culture's Consequences for Leadership Behavior: National Values in Action." *Journal of Cross-Cultural Psychology,* 1997, *28,* 342–351.

20. Hoppe, M. "Cross-Cultural Issues in Leadership Development." In C. D. McCauley, R. S. Moxley, and E. Van Velsor (eds.), *Handbook of Leadership Development* (pp. 336–378). San Francisco: Jossey-Bass, 1998.

21. Markus, H. R., Kitayama, S., and Heiman, R. "Culture and 'Basic' Psychological Principles." In E. T. Higgins and A. W. Kruglanski (eds.), *Social Psychology: Handbook of Basic Principles* (pp. 857–914). New York: Guilford, 1996.

22. Offermann, L. R., Schroyer, C. J., and Green, S. K. "Leader Attributions for Subordinate Performance Consequences for Subsequent Leader Interactive Behaviors and Ratings." *Journal of Applied Social Psychology,* 1998, *28,* 1125–1139.

23. Hermans, H.J.M., and Kempen, H.J.G. "Moving Cultures: The Perilous Problems of Cultural Dichotomies in a Globalizing Society." *American Psychologist,* 1998, *53,* 1111–1120.

24. Leslie, J. B., Gryskiewicz, N. D., and Dalton, M. A. "Understanding Cultural Influences on the 360-Degree Feedback Process." In W. W. Tornow and M. London (eds.), *Maximizing the Value of 360-Degree Feedback: A Process for Successful Individual and Organizational Development.* (pp. 196–216). San Francisco: Jossey-Bass, 1998.

25. Dalton, M. "Developing Leaders for Global Roles." In McCauley and others, *Handbook of Leadership Development* (pp. 379–402), at 386.

26. Schmidt, S. M., and Yeh, R. "The Structure of Leader Influence: A Cross-National Comparison." *Journal of Cross-Cultural Psychology*, 1992, *23*, 251–264.

27. Swisher, K. "Diversity's Learning Curve: Multicultural Training's Challenges Include Undoing Its Own Mistakes. *Washington Post*, February 5, 1995, pp. H1, H4.

28. Sessa, V. "Managing Diversity at the Xerox Corporation: Balanced Workforce Goals and Caucus Groups." In S. E. Jackson (ed.), *Diversity in the Workplace: Human Resources Initiatives* (pp. 37–64). New York: Guilford, 1992.

29. Conference Board. *Managing Diversity for Sustained Competitiveness: A Conference Report.* Report No. 1195–97-CH. New York: Author, 1997.

30. Grimsley, K. D. "The World Comes to the American Workplace." *Washington Post*, March 20, 1999, pp. A1–A12.

31. Harvey, M., and Buckley, M. R. "Assessing the 'Conventional Wisdoms' of Management for the 21st Century Organization." *Organizational Dynamics*, 2002, *30*, 368–378.

32. Miroshnik, V. "Culture and International Management: A Review." *Journal of Management Development*, 2002, *21*, 521–544.

33. Anonymous. *Black Enterprise*, 2005 (December), 141–144, at 144.

34. McGuire, G. M. "Do Race and Gender Affect Employee's Access to Help From Mentors? Insights From the Study of a Large Corporation." In A. J. Murrell, F. J. Crosby, and R. J. Ely (eds.), *Mentoring Dilemmas: Developmental Relationships within Multicultural Organizations*, 1999 (pp. 105–120). Mahwah, NJ: Lawrence Erlbaum.

Chapter Fourteen: Best Practices in Cross-Cultural Leadership

1. Black, J. S., Morrison, A. J., and Gregerson, H. B. *Global Explorers: The Next Generation of Leaders.* New York: Rutledge, 1999, 20.

2. Javidan, M., and House, R. J. "Cultural Acumen for the Global Manager: Lessons from Project GLOBE." *Organizational Dynamics*, 2001, *29*(4), 289–305, 291. Note that Ivestor was later removed by his board, in part because of cultural insensitivity.

3. Ibid., 291.

4. See Black and others, *Global Explorers*, 6; and *The New Global Assignment: Developing and Retaining Future Leaders of the Global Enterprise.* Washington, D.C.: Corporate Executive Board Global Leadership Council, 2000, viii.

5. Quelch, J. A., and Bloom, H. "Ten Steps to a Global Human Resources Strategy." *Strategy and Business*, 1999, *14*(1), 2–13, 3.

6. Goldsmith, M., Greenberg, C. L., Robertson, A., and Hu-Chin, M. *Global Leadership: The Next Generation.* Upper Saddle River, N.J.: Prentice Hall/Financial Times, 2003, 7.

7. Javidan and House, "Cultural Acumen for the Global Manager," 290.

8. For more detailed information on this perspective see Ghoshal, S., and Bartlett, C. A. *The Individualized Corporation.* New York: HarperCollins, 1997; Bartlett, C., and Ghoshal, S. *Managing across Borders: The Transnational Solution.* Boston: Harvard Business School Press, 1989; Pfeiffer, J. *Competitive Advantages through People.* Boston: Harvard Business School Press, 1994; Michaels, E., Handfield-Jones, H., and Axelrod, B. *The War for Talent.* Boston: Harvard Business School Press, 2001.

9. Harvey, M. G., Buckley, M. R., and Novicevic, M. M. "Strategic Global Human Resource Management: A Necessity When Entering Emerging Markets." In G. R. Ferris (ed.), *Research in Personnel and Human Resource Management, 19* (pp. 1–52). Amsterdam: JAI Press, 2000.

10. As quoted in Rosen, R., Digh, P., Singer, M., and Phillips, C. *Global Literacies.* New York: Simon & Schuster, 2000, 32.

11. Javidan and House, "Cultural Acumen for the Global Manager."

12. Harvey, M., and Novicevic, M. M. "The Hypercompetitive Global Marketplace: The Importance of Intuition and Creativity in Expatriate Managers." *Journal of World Business,* 2002, *37*(2), 127–138.

13. Black and others, *Global Explorers,* xiii.

14. Bartlett, C. A., and Ghoshal, S. "What Is a Global Manager?" *Harvard Business Review,* 1992, *70*(5), 124–132. *Note:* Transnationals integrate assets, resources, and diverse people in operating units around the world. They are integrated networks of specialized yet independent units. For a full discussion of this concept, see Bartlett and Ghoshal, *Managing across Borders.*

15. *The New Global Assignment.*

16. Ibid., 2.

17. *Managing Mobility Matters—A European Perspective.* London, England: Landwell/PriceWaterhouse Coopers, internal publication 2002.

18. House, R. J., Hanges, P. H., Javidan, M., Dorfman, P. W., and Gupta, V. *Culture, Leadership and Organizations.* Thousand Oaks, Calif.: Sage, 2004.

19. Ibid., 56.

20. McCall, M. W., and Hollenbeck, G. P. *Developing Global Executives.* Boston: Harvard Business School Press, 2002, 11.

21. Kroek, G., Von Glinow, M. A., and Wellinghoff, A. "Revealing Competencies for Global Managers: Using Decision Room Technology to Identify and Align Management Competence with Corporate Strategy." Working Paper, Florida International University, 1999, 4.

22. Von Glinow, M. A. "Diagnosing Best Practice in Human Resource Management Practices." In B. Shaw and others (eds.), *Research in Personnel and Human Resources,* Suppl. 3 (pp. 612–637). Greenwich, Conn.: JAI Press, 1993; Teagarden, M. B., and others, "Toward a Theory of Comparative Management Research: An Idiographic Case Study of the Best International Human Resources Management Project." *Academy of Management Journal,* 1995, *38,* 1261–1287; House and others, *Culture, Leadership and Organizations.*

23. McCall and Hollenbeck, *Developing Global Executives,* 127.

24. Bird, A., and Osland, J. "Global Competencies: An Introduction." In H. W. Lane, M. L. Maznevski, M. Mendenhall, and J. McNett (eds.), *Handbook of Global Management: A Guide to Managing Complexity* (pp. 57–80). Oxford, England: Blackwell Publishing, 2004.

25. Rosen and others, *Global Literacies,* 58.

26. *The New Global Assignment,* ix.

27. McCall and Hollenbeck, *Developing Global Executives.*

28. Earley, P. C., and Mosakowski, E. "Cultural Intelligence." *Harvard Business Review,* 2004 (October), 139–146, at 140.

29. Ibid., 143.

30. Ibid.

31. Ibid., 144.

32. Ibid., 145.

33. These quotations are taken from Warren Bennis's *On Becoming a Leader* (Reading, MA: Addison-Wesley, 1989), to whom I am indebted for my appreciation of leadership development.

34. Von Glinow, M. A., Teagarden, M. B., and Drost, E. "Converging on IHRM Best Practices: Lessons Learned from a Globally-Distributed Consortium on Theory and Practice." *Human Resource Management,* 2002 (Special Issue), 123–141.

35. Bird and Osland, "Global Competencies."

36. Adapted from Ibid., 59.

37. Black and others, *Global Explorers.*

38. Gregerson, H. B., Morrison, A. J., and Black, J. S. "Developing Leaders at the Global Frontier." *Sloan Management Review,* 1998, *40,* 21–32.

39. McCall and Hollenbeck, *Developing Global Executives,* 113.

40. *The New Global Assignment.*

41. Bird and Osland, "Global Competencies," 72.

42. McCall and Hollenbeck, *Developing Global Executives.*

43. Osland, J. "The Quest for Transformation: The Process of Global Leadership Development." In M. E. Mendenhall, T. M. Kuhlmann, and G. K. Stahl

(eds.), *Developing Global Business Leaders* (pp. 137–156). Westport, Conn.: Quorum Books, 2001, 142.

44. McCall and Hollenbeck, *Developing Global Executives,* 180.
45. Earley and Mosakowski, "Cultural Intelligence," 146.
46. Caligiuri, P. M., and Lazarova. M. (2001) "Strategic Repatriation Policies to Enhance Global Leadership Development." In Mendenhall and others, *Developing Global Business Leaders* (pp. 244–256).
47. Ibid., 244.
48. Ibid., 251.
49. Black and others, *Global Explorers,* 219.
50. Editorial, *Business Week,* April 18, 2005.
51. Javidan and House, "Cultural Acumen for the Global Manager."
52. McCall and Hollenbeck, *Developing Global Executives,* 172.
53. Kramer, Robert. *Global Talent Development, The Conference Board,* 2005. [robert.kramer@conference-board.org].
54. Rosen and others, *Global Literacies.*

Chapter Fifteen: Getting It Right

1. Kellerman, B. *Bad Leadership: What It Is, How It Happens, Why It Matters.* Boston: Harvard Business School Press, 2005; Lipman-Blumen, J. *The Allure of Toxic Leaders: Why We Follow Destructive Bosses and Corrupt Politicians and How We Can Survive Them.* Oxford, England: Oxford University Press, 2005.
2. Kets de Vries, M.F.R. *Leaders, Fools, and Impostors: Essays on the Psychology of Leadership.* San Francisco: Jossey-Bass, 1993.
3. Price, T. L. *Understanding Ethical Failures in Leadership.* Cambridge, England: Cambridge University Press, 2006; Clarke, F., Dean, G., and Oliver, K. *Corporate Collapse: Accounting, Regulatory, and Ethical Failure* (rev. ed.). Cambridge, England: Cambridge University Press, 2003; Lombardo, M. M., and McCauley, C. D. *The Dynamics of Management Derailment.* Technical Report no. 34. Greensboro, N.C.: Center for Creative Leadership, 1988.
4. Coren, S., and Girgus, J. S. *Seeing Is Deceiving: The Psychology of Perceptual Illusions.* Hillsdale, N.J.: Lawrence Erlbaum Associates, 1978; Jones, E. E. *Interpersonal Perception.* New York: W. H. Freeman, 1990.

——— Index